SOCIAL DIVISIONS

Social Divisions

SECOND EDITION

Edited by

GEOFF PAYNE

First edition 2000
Second edition 2006
Published by
PALGRAVE MACMILLAN
Houndmills, Basingstoke, Hampshire RG21 6XS and
175 Fifth Avenue, New York, N.Y. 10010
Companies and representatives throughout the world

PALGRAVE MACMILLAN is the global academic imprint of the Palgrave Macmillan division of St. Martin's Press, LLC and of Palgrave Macmillan Ltd. Macmillan® is a registered trademark in the United States, United Kingdom and other countries. Palgrave is a registered trademark in the European Union and other countries.

ISBN-13: 978–1–4039–4439–9
ISBN-10: 1–4039–4439–3

This book is printed on paper suitable for recycling and made from fully managed and sustained forest sources. Logging, pulping and manufacturing processes are expected to conform to the environmental regulations of the country of origin.

A catalogue record for this book is available from the British Library.

A catalog record for this book is available from the Library of Congress.

10   9   8   7   6   5
15 14 13 12 11 10

Printed in Great Britain by the MPG Books Group, Bodmin and King's Lynn

With thanks to
Max Gluckman, Frank Jones and John Rex
for first interesting me in social divisions and
social cohesion

Contents

List of Figures

List of Tables

Notes on Contributors

Pamela Abbott is Professor of Social Policy at Glasgow Caledonian University and formerly Director of Social Sciences at the University of Teesside. She has published extensively on women and social class, health inequalities and research methods, while her current research is concerned with living conditions, lifestyles and health in Eastern Europe. Her publications include *Women and Social Class* (with Roger Sapsford, Tavistock 1987) and *An Introduction to Sociology: Feminist Perspectives* (with Claire Wallace, Routledge 2005).

Alan Aldridge is Reader in the Sociology of Culture at the University of Nottingham. He is the author of *Religion in the Contemporary World* (Polity Press 2000), a second edition of which is due to be published in 2006/07. Other recent works include *Surveying the Social World* (co-authored with Ken Levine, Open University Press 2001), *Consumption* (Polity Press 2003) and *The Market* (Polity Press 2005).

Matthew Bond is a Lecturer in Sociology in the Department of Sociology at the University of Oxford. His current research interests are in the sociology of modern corporations, and health policy.

Graham Crow is Professor of Sociology at the University of Southampton where he has worked since 1983. His research interests include the sociology of households and communities, sociological theory and comparative sociology. His most recent books are *Social Solidarities* (Open University Press 2002) and *The Art of Sociological Argument* (Palgrave Macmillan 2005).

Mark Hyde is a Principal Lecturer in Social Policy at the University of Plymouth. His research on disabled people in the labour market has been published in several journals, notably *Work, Employment & Society, Disability & Society* and *Sociology Review*. Currently a member of the Executive Committee of the Social Policy Association, his more recent work on the reform of pensions includes *The Marketisation of Social Security* (with John Dixon, Greenwood 2001) and *The Privatisation of Mandatory Pensions: International Perspectives* (with John Dixon and Glenn Drover, Edwin Mellon 2005).

Stevi Jackson is Professor of Women's Studies and Director of the Centre for Women's Studies at the University of York. Her main research interests are feminist theory and sexuality, with a particular emphasis on heterosexuality. She is the author of *Childhood and Sexuality* (Blackwell 1982), *Christine Delphy* (Sage 1996) and *Heterosexuality in Question* (Sage 1999). She is currently working on a series of articles on the gendered self and, with Sue Scott, a book on theorising sexuality.

David McCrone is Professor of Sociology and Director of the University of Edinburgh's Institute of Governance. A Fellow of the Royal Society of Edinburgh, he is coordinator of the research programme funded by the Leverhulme Trust on Constitutional Change and National Identity (1999–2004), and vice-chair of ESRC's Research Priorities Board (2000–04). He has written extensively on the sociology and politics of Scotland, and the comparative study of nationalism. His recent books include *The Sociology of Nationalism: Tomorrow's Ancestors* (Routledge 1998), *Has Devolution Delivered?* (Edinburgh University Press 2005), *New Scotland, New Society?* (Polygon 2001), *Understanding Scotland: the Sociology of a Stateless Nation* (Routledge 2001), and *Living in Scotland: Social and Economic Change since 1980* (Edinburgh University Press 2004).

Catherine Maclean is a Lecturer in Sociology at the University of Edinburgh. Her PhD examined social change and migration in remote rural areas through the study of a community in northwest Scotland. Her research interests include social and economic change in Scotland, the work–family interface and rural life.

David Mason is Dean of the School of Social Sciences at Nottingham Trent University. He has worked on labour markets and equal opportunity issues, the recruitment of minority ethnic nurses and diversity in the armed forces. His publications include *Race and Ethnicity in Modern Britain* (2nd edn), (Open University Press 2000) and *Explaining Ethnic Differences: Changing Patterns of Disadvantage in Britain* (Policy Press 2003).

Geoff Payne is Emeritus Professor of Sociology at the University of Plymouth and Visiting Professor of Sociology at Glasgow Caledonian University. At the time of writing, he is President of the British Sociological Association. He has published on social mobility, employment, health, community and, most recently, research methods, for example *Key Concepts in Research Methods* (with Judy Payne, Sage 2004).

Judy Payne is a Research Consultant whose work on housing, social class, health and deprivation has been published in a number of journals, including *Sociology*, *British Journal of Sociology*, *Sociological Research Online* and the *Journal of Social Policy*. Her books include *Researching Health Needs* (Sage 1999) and *Key Concepts in Social Research* (with Geoff Payne, Sage 2004).

Lucinda Platt is a Lecturer in Sociology at the University of Essex. Her research focuses on child poverty and ethnic minorities. She is the author of *Parallel Lives? Poverty among Minority Ethnic Groups in Britain* (CPAG 2002) and *Discovering Child Poverty: The Creation of an Agenda for Action 1800 to the Present* (Policy Press 2005). She is currently researching inter-generational social mobility among minority ethnic groups.

John Scott is Professor of Sociology at the University of Essex and Adjunct Professor of Sociology at the University of Bergen. He is the author of numerous books and articles on stratification, theories and methods, and business organisation, most recently *Sociology* (with James Fulcher, Open University Press 2003) and *Power* (Polity Press 2001). A former President of the British Sociological Association, he has previously taught at Strathclyde and Leicester Universities, and was co-editor of *Sociology Review*.

Sue Scott is Dean of Humanities and Social Science at the University of Keele and formerly Professor of Sociology and Postgraduate Dean at the University of Durham. Her research on gender, sexuality and the body included membership of the Women, Risk and AIDS Project: she currently holds MRC and ESRC grants for work on sex education, and children, risk and parental risk anxiety. Her publications include *Body Matters* (with David Morgan, Falmer Press 1993), *Feminism and Sexuality* (with Stevi Jackson, Edinburgh University Press 1996) and *Gender: A Sociological Reader* (with Stevi Jackson, Routledge 2001).

Phil Stanworth is a Lecturer in Sociology at the University of York. His teaching and research interests focus on the analysis of power, globalisation and place. His chapter on elites marks a return to the topic after a long absence, having published 'Elites and privilege' in P. Abrams and R. K. Brown (eds) *UK Society* (Weidenfeld & Nicolson) in 1984.

John A. Vincent is a Senior Lecturer at the University of Exeter. After gaining his doctorate in Social Anthropology from the University of Sussex for a study of an alpine community in Italy, he has conducted research in India, Uganda and Bosnia. In the UK, he has studied old people's homes in Devon and the politics of old age. His publications include *Old Age* (Routledge 1993), *Inequality and Old Age* (UCL Press 1995) and *Power, Politics and Old Age* (Open University Press 1999).

Preface

It was Catherine Gray, publisher for Palgrave Macmillan's College Division, who first suggested that an interesting book could be put together about social divisions. That sounded an intriguing idea and when I began to talk to other sociologists, they seemed to think so, too. The level of sales of the first edition (2000) suggests they were right.

There are three main changes to this new edition. In rewriting their original chapters, the contributors have been able to update their statistical information, so retaining the emphasis on timely data which was a welcomed feature of the first edition. The contributors have also incorporated the latest ideas and findings from studies in their field appearing during the last few years, which enhances the reputation of this volume for the depth of its coverage of current research. Third, three major new chapters on religion, elites and poverty have been added, so giving greater breadth and providing further development of the social divisions approach.

I originally invited chapters from a team of contributors (now expanded) who would combine academic credibility with an active concern for explaining and communicating sociology. I also knew that they all could write in a clear and engaging way. This certainly helped me over the inevitable difficulties that are part of editing a set of newly commissioned and now substantially updated pieces.

Apart, perhaps, from its first chapter, *Social Divisions* has not been primarily written as an introductory book per se, although it has been written to be engaging and accessible to a wide student readership in higher education and beyond. What we have in mind is the level of work typically found not at the start of a sociology course, but which could equally well be used in an introductory or 'intermediate' stage of most university degree programmes. We have tried to deal with some challenging ideas in a systematic, clear and rigorous way and this, combined with a breadth of topics and extensive bibliography, should mean that students (and even our fellow professional sociologists) will find some new insights in its pages. Many of its examples are taken from Britain, but the ideas and arguments are equally relevant in other 'industrial societies': our intention is that readers in other countries should be able to use and enjoy this book.

The contents have been organised so that, while seeking to develop a coherence of its own, parts of the book can be taken out and used in other contexts. Even in British universities, there is no uniformity in which parts of sociology are taught at each stage. There may perhaps be more overall consensus than most sociologists like to admit (as the QAA national benchmarking exercise, the data collected for the British Sociological Association's Working Party on the Undergraduate Curriculum by Jon Gubbay and David Jary's review of the documentation for the 1996 Teaching Quality Assurance have shown). However, that does not translate into universal accord about where to place the emphasis in early modules of sociology, whether this is in 'straight' sociology courses, or health studies, social policy or social work. What should be the balance between sociological theory, social research methods, the 'social structure of modern Britain' (or, increasingly, 'Europe': see Spybey 1997), or the 'Cook's tour' of major concepts and perspectives? The apparent similarities of current introductory texts hides a degree of variation in teaching (Bailey 1998).

Thus our choice of particular topics is not an attempt to prescribe the content of particular stages of sociology, but to assist those involved with making choices. Although there is a coherent perspective running through the book, each of the topic chapters (Chapters 2–14) is intended to be free-standing. They follow a common format, but readers who wish to do so should be able to select those chapters that most interest them: the book is not primarily designed to be read from cover to cover.

The three chapters on class, gender and ethnicity are deliberately longer than the others, because these three social divisions are centrally important in their own right, have been more extensively researched and help to gain a purchase on the other divisions. Indeed, these three topics are what most sociologists would initially think of as 'social divisions'; as such they already have an established place in the curriculum. While recognising the centrality of 'the big three', one of the key purposes of this book is to advocate that the notion of social divisions should be extended and explore the significance of other social divisions.

There is nothing revolutionary about such a view: new topics are always emerging from narrow specialisms to take a more substantial place in the sociological sun. Feminism, post-modernism and cultural and social identity, for example, initially had to struggle for space alongside more traditional topics like classic sociological theory or social stratification. Whereas most courses at one time focused on the single social division of social class, now room has been found for gender and ethnicity, if not other social divisions. Our expansion of social divisions covers areas that are of increasing consequence, in addition to class, gender and ethnicity. I hope that not too many readers' 'favourite' topics will prove to have been left out.

Social division, in whatever set of examples chosen, is something more than just a useful principle around which to assemble a number of reports about major facets of contemporary society. The cumulative effect of reading each chapter is to produce a sense of a strong, coherent perspective, a way of thinking about social conditions and the social order. The contributors did not necessarily start with this in mind nor would they all equally subscribe to the theoretical implications of this distinctive approach, now that it is being more explicitly articulated, particularly as in Chapter 15. The idea that social division represents a distinct sociological standpoint of some significance certainly became clearer during the process of developing the book. As editor, I take full responsibility for any shortcomings in representing the overview that resulted.

Social Divisions can thus be seen as working on three levels. At its most basic, it is a collection of individual chapters, each dealing with a topic of major concern in sociology, but not totally dependent on the concluding overview. Second, it has been designed as a source book to support individual interests or a variety of teaching programmes. In addition, it also offers a particular perspective for making sense of society.

To the extent that we achieve these three goals – and, of course, the reader must be the final judge of that – the outcomes owe much to the publishers and reviewers for their support and advice. The contributors to the book are due my thanks for their good-natured cooperation and willingness to write to specification.

I would also like to thank other colleagues who offered comments on ideas and drafts of the first edition, in particular Sue Hemmings. I am grateful to the University of Plymouth for my period of sabbatical leave, and the staff of the Department of Sociology, University of Edinburgh, for giving me a temporary home when I was originally preparing the first edition. My special thanks go to Judy Payne, whose assistance with the technical aspects of the production was invaluable, and whose intellectual collaboration and personal support continue to be a major source of inspiration.

GEOFF PAYNE

SECTION I

Introduction

CHAPTER 1

An Introduction to 'Social Divisions'

GEOFF PAYNE

This chapter will provide you with an introduction to the following aspects of social divisions:

- Social divisions as sociological, not biological, categories
- A provisional definition: a social division is a substantial social difference between two or more categories of people
- Social divisions consist of material and cultural differences, where one category of people is better placed than another: major examples are class, gender and ethnicity
- Social divisions and related ideas: social inequality, social stratification and social differentiation
- 'Memberships' of social divisions overlap in many different combinations
- Individuals, groups and social identity
- How we experience divisions: 'us' and 'others'
- Lesser social differences and major social divisions
- Rules of social interaction and behaviour in division
- Contemporary forms of division in post-modern/post-industrial society
- New forms of division under globalisation and social fragmentation
- Social exclusion and social division
- The plan and content of the chapters of the book

It is impossible even to begin to think about people without immediately encountering 'social divisions'. We automatically perceive other human beings as being male or female, black or white, older or younger, richer or poorer, sick or well, or friend or foe. In forming a perception of them, we place them in pigeonholes, adapting our behaviour and attitude to them in terms of the slots into which we have placed them.

The categories we use, even those like 'older', 'female', 'healthy' or 'white', which might at first sight seem to have a purely biological basis, are actually sociological labels. The meaning we bring to these labels depends on the cultural significance we have learned to attach to them during our lives up to this moment. The origins of the definitions we use, the ways in which separations between one category and another have been created and are maintained, the extent of inequalities that exist between groups, how people come to think about their own identity and the consequences of this for future action are all sociological issues. 'Age', 'gender', 'health', 'ethnicity', 'class' and so on are the 'social divisions' that shape society. If we are to make coherent sense of our own lives, let alone understand what is going on in our society and why society as a whole operates as it does, the idea of 'social divisions' is one of the most useful and powerful tools available.

This chapter goes back to basics, deliberately setting out to explain the idea of social divisions in simple terms. This means reflecting on the nature of social life as sociologists see it and our assumptions about contemporary society. The later chapters develop this simple introduction into a more detailed and advanced treatment. The full meaning and implications of a 'social divisions approach' are then brought out in the final chapter of the book.

What are 'social divisions'?

In one sense, social divisions are so self-evident as hardly to need a formal definition. You do not have to be a professional sociologist to see that society is not only made up of many separate individuals, but that some individuals are very similar to one another and so can be differentiated from other types of people. In some cases, the differences between sets of people are sharply marked, with major contrasts of social conditions and 'life chances' (the chances during a person's lifetime of sharing in society's material and cultural rewards – income, employment, education, health and so on).

However, if we need to explain why some things are *social divisions* whereas other *social differences* are not, the picture is suddenly less clear (for alternative distinctions between divisions and differences, see Carling 1991; Anthias 1998, 2001; Braham and Janes 2002; Payne 2004; Best 2005). For instance, a division does not necessarily separate people into two parts: sometimes we need to think of several distinct categories, as for example when noting differences between minority ethnic groups. Social divisions also often overlap, so that an explanation of people's employment positions may mean exploring how far class, gender, ethnicity, age or disability, for example, are contributing factors, in different combinations, to what we can observe happening. Some divisions are sharper than others. Some of them will seem more important than others, although such evaluations will change with time and also vary from reader to reader.

Thus it follows that rather than starting with a full-scale complex definition, it is probably more helpful to explore the dimensions of 'social division' in more detail. This will be done mainly by using concrete examples, like class, gender and so on, to indicate what we mean by social divisions. At this stage, a preliminary sketch of the main features of a definition of social divisions will suffice. (Alternatively, readers who would feel happier starting with an abstract definition might first like to look at the opening pages of the concluding chapter of the book.)

When we talk about social divisions, we mean those substantial differences between people that run throughout our society. A social division has at least two categories, each of which has distinctive material and cultural features. In other words, one category is better positioned than the other and has a better share of resources because it has greater power over the way our society is organised. Membership of a category is closely associated with a social identity that arises from a sense of being similar to other members and different from other categories. This affects how people conduct their social interactions. Movement from one category to another is not easy.

However, social divisions are not 'natural': they are the outcome of previous social interactions, events, decisions and struggles. Although the distinctions between categories are strong and tend to be longlasting, they are not fixed for all time. They are 'socially constructed', so that while there are always social divisions, their precise form varies from society to society.

It may help to distinguish between social divisions and several similar terms used in sociology. *Social inequalities* refer to the differences in people's share of resources (not just money, but chances of health, education and so on). Such differences are often graduated over a wide range, rather than clearly defining two or more categories. Thus, while we saw in our earlier definition that social inequality is part of the idea of social division, it is only one part. Social divisions are similarly related to *social stratification*, but stratification is a term better reserved for specialist discussions of class, status and power. In this case, we can regard social stratification as a subset of social divisions, the latter, wider term placing more emphasis on the many types of divisions and their capacity to structure identity and interactions. On the other hand, social division is a more focused and restricted idea than *social differentiation*, a general term used to describe the increasing complexity of specialised roles and relationships that are evident as societies grow in size, develop more elaborate social institutions and utilise new technologies in production.

Social division is therefore a 'middle-range' concept that offers a way of thinking about society as consisting of intelligible components, based on a set of principles. In the past it was often said that sociologists were only interested in 'social class', to the exclusion of all other divisions. Over the last quarter of a century, gender and ethnicity became more central to sociological research. Even more recently other divisions, such as sexuality and national identity, have become prominent in the sociological repertoire. This growth of new sociological interests – and its associated tendency for increased competition between sociologists to define 'what sociology is really about' – reflects the way most people's senses of personal identity had begun to draw more strongly on a range of social factors (Isin and Wood 1999). This in turn is a product of new ways of life replacing older, more traditional ones associated with former class structures.

In dealing with identity, the emphasis in this book is placed on what is shared by people as a social identity – in the sense of what identifies them and brings them together as a group – rather than on personal identity or individual differentiation. The idea of identity is important but secondary to that of division. It would be possible to develop the discussion of identity much further, but that would go beyond the scope of the present book (for a thoughtful discussion, particularly in the context of ethnicity, see Jenkins 2004).

A common feature of all these older and newly prominent social divisions is that everyone in society is involved: we all have a class, an age, an ethnic identity and so on. Each social division is 'universally inclusive': we all sit on one side or the other of each division, in this category or that, whether it seems to matter much to us or not. A person may not at this precise moment be, say, 'ill', but that is only because that person currently occupies the associated mirror image category that goes with it: in this case, 'healthy'. When or if this person becomes adult or ill, her or his currently passive awareness of the social divisions of age or health is likely to be increased.

It is also true that a reconsideration of the other examples given so far will show that social divisions tend to divide people into 'better' or 'worse' categories. Social divisions result in social inequalities. Those in the 'better' categories have more control over their own lives, usually more money and can generally be seen to lead happier lives. Those occupying the better positions often take their advantages for granted but, nonetheless, social divisions are still all about advantage and disadvantage. They are therefore also about who has the power to create and maintain this situation in which inequalities persist.

It follows from this that the various social divisions often connect and overlap, re-enforcing inequalities (although for ease of presentation we shall need to discuss each of the social divisions in its own right and normally one at a time). In any one situation, a particular social division may assume greater importance, but people do not exist in a social world where only class, or only gender or only ethnicity matters. It is not that there is a single category which is distinctive. All of us have multiple membership in a number of such groups, so that, depending on one's standpoint, people may be different in one context but similar in another. Personal links with people in one category may sometimes be at odds with one's differences from them owing to membership of some category on another social division.

The particular combination and balance of memberships also matter. For example, to be white, middle class, male and healthy is not only different from being black, working class, female and sick, but also different from being black, middle class, male and healthy. In other words, as well as looking at each division separately, we need to consider how the various divisions seem able to work in specific combinations and, in a somewhat less coherent way, also work together as a whole to make up what we know as 'society'.

One purpose of studying sociology is to discover the nature of these unequal divisions and categories of people that together add up to a society. How have they come about, how do they relate to one another in a structured way and what are the consequences of such social divisions? The idea of social divisions addresses the distinctions between sets of people and also the question that lurks behind such variation: if there are all these differences, why do they continue to operate as they do and what prevents a society (in most cases) from splitting up into warring factions?

Social divisions as a way of thinking about society

Although this book is mainly about the social inequalities and systems of social divisions that make up contemporary society, a useful starting point for that discussion is the 'individual' and 'social groups'. On the face of it, the most obvious division is between you, the reader, as an individual and the rest of humankind. One of the great perceptual paradoxes of life is that humans are simultaneously individual entities and 'social animals'. Each of us is a physically separate being, with an independent consciousness, experiencing in her or his own particular way a physical world populated with other humans, all different from us but largely behaving in ways that are intelligible to us. Each of us feels unique: one's emotions about, understanding of and reactions to new encounters are the outcome of a discrete set of previous experiences that each person, and that person alone, has accumulated.

Yet at the same time, our day-to-day life is a social one. Our very survival depends on a complex, largely invisible, taken-for-granted web of group activities that produce, deliver and regulate the production and consumption of goods and services. We cannot exist in isolation from one another, even after we cease to be infants dependent on our families for support. Just as we pigeonhole other people and adapt our own behaviour towards them, so too do they adapt to us, in a continuing creative process.

It is true, of course, that a very small number of people live as hermits, but such a tiny minority does not challenge our basic observation about our social nature. Even in the more common cases of people living as 'single-person households' – a growing trend in recent years – they still have contact with the outside world. Most people who 'live on their own' in fact work or study outside the home, in organisations. They do so in densely populated towns and cities, meeting other people as they buy food and clothes or engage in leisure pursuits, and indirectly connecting with other people by electronic and print media. Even if they live alone, many have family and relatives as a potential support. A feeling of loneliness is not the same as being alone or divorced from society, rather it confirms our social nature. The unfortunate cases where there is a real problem of isolation and too little human contact only prove the point that we prefer and expect to organise our lives on a collective basis of meeting with, and depending on, other people.

In practice, we lead our lives in social groups defined by what we have in common that is different from other groups – belonging to this one but not that one, in this society rather than another. Our personal sense of identity draws on how we routinely interact with the members of our groups: it is a social identity. We share sets of values and attitudes, a 'culture'. We take our cues for action from those who share that culture through membership of 'our' group, or against those who belong to the 'other' groups, with their rival values and beliefs.

It is not just being a member that counts: not being a member of another category is just as important. We define who 'we' are in terms of who we are not. Our encounters with 'others' point to their differences from 'us' and help us to identify our own distinctiveness. 'Our team', 'our gang', 'our kind of music', 'our part of the country' make sense in contrast – and sometimes active opposition – to 'others'.

This does not mean that we mix exclusively with other members of a particular category or that all social interactions with other people are the same. For instance, despite the mandatory cheerful 'Hello!' at the super-market checkout (resulting from recent research finding that customers prefer to be greeted as if they were individuals with a known identity, rather than treated as anonymous punters), our impersonal exchanges with shop assis-tants are not the same as the intense personal involvement with one's family. Acquaintances are not friends. Nonetheless, even the most minimal of social transactions are still orderly and governed by learned and regularised conven-tions. The social divisions that define both the shop assistant and us as customers (for example in terms of class, gender, age or ethnicity) set 'rules' for how we may interact.

We do not have to meet face-to-face for rule-driven constraints, inequalities and power to come into play. In the more usual situation where members of a social category do not meet or closely interact as a 'social group', the looser 'category' that is formed as part of the process of social division still imposes constraints on our individual actions. It places us inside a social structure. The common bond of a social identity, which is a mechanism for this, is not exclusively dependent on direct interpersonal interaction with other members of the category. It may also be a product of a more abstract awareness of shared circumstances and interests.

For example, when we talk about national identity or sexuality, we are dealing with social divisions that separate large numbers of people, are complex and extend well beyond the individual's direct personal experience. Over and above direct contact, we sense that we also belong to larger, notional categories of people who do not meet together. These 'imagined communities' provide us with identities in terms of which we define ourselves, and others define us (for example as belonging to a particular age group).

The connections between the large-scale and small-scale categories work both ways: just as we may experience the grand social divisions through localised contacts, so too do the divisions determine our often unconscious selection of friends and mates, careers and places to live. These are overwhelmingly chosen from people like ourselves, on one or more division (for example most marriages are between people from the same social class). Whatever our reactions to this fact, it is inescapable that we can most easily select for close relationships those whom we are most likely to meet. To the extent that societal arrangements define and physically separate young from old, men from women, upper class from working class and so on, it is simply more difficult to mix with people who are different from ourselves, even if that is what we want to do. The case of personal and sexual relationships between young adults, where members from different categories of the social divisions of gender and sexuality are meeting, mixing and mating, illustrates how difficult cross-boundary contact can be. Even at this most personal of levels, social interaction is still structured and segregated: mixing is still not an open and free process.

As this example also shows, when people from both sides of the social divide meet, their social interactions are rule-bounded. Indeed, not only are they rule-bounded, but the rules establish a social inequality between participants. Membership of a category offers social advantages or disadvantages vis-à-vis members of a matching category. This makes membership of some categories more desirable than others. What reader would seriously argue that it is less advantageous to be young, fit, white and upper class, than to be old, ill, black and working class? People on the 'right' side of the social division line take precedence over others, once their identities are known. Social divisions reflect the imbalance of power between categories: they are hierarchical. This is why some forms of social difference are more important than others and warrant the title 'social division'. Of course other kinds of social differences do exist and can confer a sense of identity, without being social divisions.

Thus the social divisions with which this book deals are not the small-scale ones, such as a gang, a family, or a work group, nor are all shared consumer lifestyles – like 'surfing' or 'clubbing' – counted as social divisions. Groups may thus be interesting for what they tell about wider processes, without being the core focus in a social division approach. This is not to ignore the fact that when major social divisions such as class or gender are encountered, they are normally experienced through membership of smaller collectivities. Divisions are often encountered indirectly, through participation in, say, a group of co-workers or students, and it is within such groups that we are likely to develop face-to-face relationships and social interactions based on the underlying principles of division. However, this process makes most sense when it is seen as the outcome of the underlying social division.

Social divisions as 'social rules'

Broader and less tangible social divisions share with smaller, more concrete groups the characteristics of recognisable behaviour patterns and sets of attitudes. For the most part, unwritten rules of conduct apply. 'The rich man in his castle, the poor man at his gate' of the Victorian hymn expressed the imperative that the lower orders should 'know their place' and keep to it. A more up-to-date set of rules for proper conduct, this time for older people, is suggested by Jenny Joseph's well-known poem in which the speaker imagines how, in later life, one might:

> wear purple,
> With a red hat which doesn't go, and doesn't suit me.
> And I shall spend my pension on brandy and summer gloves
> And satin sandals, and say we've no money for butter (Joseph 1987: 229)

In reading this description of how one older woman might think of behaving we can, as sociologists, see by implication the rules about how older women in general are expected to act. Older women should not run their sticks along the railings, spit, swear in the street, press alarm bells and so on. The poem is about how one might behave at a different age, not about gender. From a social divisions point of view, however, one might also note that behaviour at different ages will also be influenced by gender.

Similarly, in his fascinating book about life in a northern English city in the early 1960s (barely more than a generation ago), Jackson (1968) combines compassion with sociological insight to describe the details of the routine daily lives of 'ordinary people' working in the mill, getting into grammar school, meeting in the coffee bar or 'the club', standing on the terraces, or using gossip with family, friends and neighbours to express the right and wrong way of doing things. The book still makes a wonderful read, but it does so now as a social history. It is an account of a world we have lost. It tells us about living with greater certainties and more clearly patterned and predictable life experiences, governed by much sharper sets of social conventions specifying how people were expected to lead their lives. It shows how class and other divisions prescribed people's lives.

As post-modern writers have demonstrated, many such 'rules' have lost their force since the break-up of the old monolithic industrial social classes and their traditional ways. Even those rules and the more subtle ones that have replaced them should not be thought of as fixed, prescriptive, absolute laws of nature. They are there to be bent or broken. This operates at a variety of levels. Feminists have challenged male dominance, gay groups campaign for the lowering of the age of consent, patients ask for second medical opinions and young children try to stay up past their bedtimes. As groups and as individuals, people seek to change their social positions in major and minor ways.

That does not mean that rules do not exist, but rather that the codes of conduct around social divisions, although structured and constraining, will not always be encountered in a precise and rigid form. Sometimes they will be implicit and at others explicit. Conflicts of interests are sometimes played out in nationwide struggles to mobilise state support for particular pieces of single issue legislation, and subsequently in the courts. Equally, disputes can arise between two people from different categories whose lives together throw up contradictions in what they believe is 'the right thing' for 'people like us' to do. There is no uniform way to encounter the 'rules' that are intrinsic to social divisions.

Nonetheless, exploring social rules and their infractions helps us to identify boundaries and continuities in social divisions. A focus on social divisions offers an organised way of seeing and thinking about society; a 'perspective' for finding out what is going on and understanding social outcomes. It enables us to describe and explain our social world, starting from the position that society is not a neatly integrated, tidy, consistent and, in particular, simple thing. Nothing in human society is a 'given', fixed for all time or absolute. All social arrangements are worth examining, whether we are seeking explanations as specialists in sociology, or as students of health, welfare or social policy who want to use sociology's concepts and methods to situate our own work. Social divisions are important cleavages in society that affect us all. Social divisions are not just about society at a national or global level, but about what separates one individual from the next.

Social divisions in a post-modern world?

The relative importance of the various social divisions is then both situationally imposed by those around us and personally selected by ourselves. In the past there have been periods when the social behaviour expected as a result of major social divisions was more clearly defined and conformed to more uniformly. Although individual lives involved unique personal autobiographies, their broad shape was socially determined. Sons followed fathers 'down the Pit'. Daughters became wives and mothers. Old people did not wear purple with red hats.

These certainties (or constraints, depending on how one wishes to see them) are starkly illustrated by photographs of male workers in northern industrial cities, going home from the shipyards or factories in the 1930s and 40s, at trade union or political meetings, or 'on the terraces'. Their uniformity of social condition is symbolised in their 'uniform'. There is scarcely one that does not wear a flat cap and a 'muffler' (the muffler was a small scarf worn at the neck because British 'working men' – as distinct from 'white-collar' office workers or American denim-clad 'blue-collar' manual workers – could not wear collars on their weekday work shirts that would get dirty, worn and in any case be uncomfortable). Today, what we wear to and from work, or at leisure, is more likely to be an individual statement about how we want people to see us, in terms of more specific personal identities or memberships of other categories.

The older rigidities can be exaggerated. Not all workers lived in northern industrial towns, worked in heavy industry or followed their local football team. The upheaval of the late stages of the Industrial Revolution, two world wars, the Great Depression, massive technological changes in transport, housing and engineering production, the wholesale creation of new types of occupations, together with political and social welfare reforms, make it difficult to talk convincingly about a single period of 'modernity', even in the first half of the twentieth century. How much more difficult to see a coherent period reaching back to the fifteenth century (Kumar 1978; Hall et al. 1992). Calls to see our world as 'post-modern' are frequently based on an oversimplistic understanding of history.

Nonetheless, there are significant differences between an earlier 'modern period' of pre-war mass production and the social arrangements that went with it (see Chapter 2) and our contemporary society. In particular, it is generally accepted that, for most people, life in the first half of the twentieth century involved far fewer choices of behaviour. Our own society, with its media access to other cultures and ways of life and its greater separation of workplace, home and leisure, is less prescriptive. With national economies becoming increasingly interconnected in the process of globalisation, new possibilities have been opened up as our secure, localised little worlds and fixed positions in a traditional labour market have been eroded.

The shift from manufacturing production to a services economy destroyed old jobs and created new ones. As a result of this 'occupational transition', the proportion of people working in manual jobs has since halved. Most women with young children are now in paid employment. Most of us stay on in education well past the minimum school-leaving age, because more jobs now require advanced skills. Our experiences are broader and our encounters with different ways of life more common, but we have a greater sense of uncertainty about the future in the face of these new circumstances. The old localised and relatively rigid patterns have declined.

By contrast, the more fragmented society of our own times offers greater opportunities (and for most people, the money) to select from a multitude of styles, groups and identities. We have greater opportunities to select, from among the partial social identities that social divisions give, the particular version we want. Consumption and lifestyle can be manipulated. In a 'global society', we like to believe that we have a new freedom, that we can 'be what we consume', as we exercise a greater choice over what we consume or do, acting out our daydreams through our purchases and fashions.

We can distinguish two processes here. On the one hand, the contemporary world cannot be explained simply as a set of nations or localities, because multinational corporations have established a world economy of production and consumption as part of the boom in world trade since the mid-1960s. This has led to a homogenisation of our cultures and lifestyles. In this sense, we are less divided from each other: we are all consumers of a world economy, in which national differences are less important, although of course huge differences in per capita income and life expectancy remain between 'rich' and 'poor' nations.

On the other hand, our patterns of consumption provide ways of introducing new differentiations between ourselves. Within the underlying tendency for multinational corporations' products to be designed for global markets and more of our lives to be 'commodified' into patterns of consumption involving purchases under the influence of marketing, we can manipulate our own consumption to build and signal our identities. Better off groups can use 'positional' goods as markers to display their distinctiveness. Some writers, such as Saunders (1990) and Dunleavy (1980), have even suggested that new lines of social division can be drawn to mark 'consumption cleavages' between homeowners and renters, between those still dependent on core social welfare services (housing, state schooling, the NHS, welfare benefits) and the rest, and between those who work in the public sector and others.

Any new freedom of action has to be balanced by the recognition that choices operate within frameworks. Those in poorly paid, insecure, unskilled manual jobs cannot easily 'choose' to lead the life of, say, the mobile phone nerd or vacation tripper, let alone become cosmopolitan celebrities: these lifestyles cost money. The physically disabled are disabled from having access to vast tracts of the buildings in which consumption lifestyles are acted out. Women cannot simply behave like, and 'pass' as, men. These various social divisions may be complex but they remain powerful discriminators. Globalisation and consumption are important in their own right, but social life is still far from being totally homogenised.

Because we do still live in a fragmented world, our knowledge of others is necessarily incomplete. We may all be members of one 'society', but we live our lives as members of large, imagined categories or groups, with boundaries between them – middle class and working class, men and women, young and old. On the other hand, none of us belongs only to a single category: we belong to a whole series of such identities. While within limits we can manipulate these identities according to our particular circumstances of the moment, it is membership of, and identification with, groups that make up social life. Social divisions, then, blur not only because each is not a dichotomy, nor because a post-modern world offers a bedazzling variety of choices, but also because overlapping social divisions shape people's lives.

The complexity of social divisions

In *The Sociological Imagination* ([1959]1970), C. Wright Mills made two important distinctions: between 'personal troubles' and 'public issues', and between 'individuals' and 'history'. Mills is making the point that we can interpret what happens to us in life either on a personal basis or as part of a wider social process. For example, to be unemployed is a genuine problem for somebody, whether it is 'their own fault' or not. If we were talking about one unemployed person among a city population of 100,000 all in paid employment, we might look to personal circumstance to understand (and possibly remedy) the individual's misfortune. But in times of high and rapidly rising unemployment, such as the 1980s when Conservative government policies caused well over three million people to be unemployed, it is not credible to blame each person and expect each one to seek individual remedies.

Similarly, 'history' is not simply the record of kings and queens, but of social and economic movements and changes. Mills does not want us to forget the individual, but also to see the importance of the social processes that shape each life. He is concerned with systems, but sees systems as also made up of people with differing amounts of power. By addressing the interplay of systems and people, Mills ([1959]1970: 15–17) seeks to avoid the two extremes of a sociology exclusively of individuals and a sociology of social structures where the people are just pre-programmed robots.

The similarities between Mills' sociological perspective and the one outlined so far in this chapter are obvious. If anything, we have stressed the individual and small groups more than Mills did, but that will be balanced by what follows. The contributors to this book start from the powerful forces that tend to constrain and influence us, rather than the things that we can directly control ourselves. The emphasis tends to be on the patterned way we are shaped, rather than on the way we can modify our own actions. However, whereas Mills made his point in terms of two dichotomies, with a neat contrast between personal and public and between individual and history – which made them sharper, easy to remember and therefore all the more influential – the idea of social divisions is a little more complicated.

In the first place, we have seen that there are not one or two social divisions, but many. Mills' 'public issues' category is greatly subdivided. This book deals with 13 major social divisions, but there are others that could legitimately claim a chapter in a bigger volume: educational qualifications, consumer lifestyle, political affiliation or kinship, which are indeed discussed as aspects of the major divisions in later chapters. The 13 social divisions selected are a personal choice of topics central to the sociological curriculum, and other topics of greater significance than might at first appear obvious. These topics largely determine the patterns of difference in other potential divisions not included here.

For example, at first sight, it may seem surprising that there is no chapter in this book on 'social exclusion'. To be socially excluded sounds, on the face of it, to be something akin to being socially divided off from sets of other people and ways of life. However, when we unpack the notion of social exclusion, we soon discover that it is a political shorthand for the consequences of poverty, and the particular New Labour policy approach allegedly designed to provide 'joined-up' administrative solutions (Levitas 1998). In as far as we currently have explanations of exclusion, they are mainly couched in terms of employment, class, ethnicity, disability, gender, community structures and health inequalities (for example Hills and Stewart 2005). In other words, to explain social exclusion, we must first start with an understanding of the social divisions that produce it and are in turn reinforced by the processes of exclusion. There is therefore no chapter devoted to social exclusion, as the main topics for each chapter make up what are the major social divisions in contemporary society.

This means that the picture of a divided society we draw is a complex one. In practice, we can artificially simplify it by dealing mainly with one division at a time, bringing together ideas and evidence about its particular set of categories from the extensive specialist research carried out by sociologists in each of our selected areas. This enables us to explore each division in some depth and see the richness of its details.

The plan of the book

We can begin to demonstrate these points by looking at the titles of the chapters in this book, which indicate the range of key social divisions, starting in Section II with sociology's 'big three' of social class, gender and ethnicity, and going on in Section III to include religion, national identity, elites, age, childhood, sexuality and disability. Each of the chapters discusses the ideas we use to think about these divisions, together with the material, status and even mundane inequalities between the categories.

However, we shall also see that it is not possible to keep each division tidily in its own chapter. On the one hand, class, gender and ethnicity are themes running throughout the book. It is no accident that these three comprise Section II, and that each is longer than the later contributions. On the other hand, the chapters in Section IV on poverty, community, and health involve greater consideration of the other social divisions. While social inclusion or exclusion, rural and urban locations or health and illness are valid social divisions in their own right, poverty, community and health can also be seen as 'arenas' in which the consequences of the various social divisions are acted out and come together in people's lives. The effect these have on our various senses of social identity is not always straightforward. These topics are therefore grouped together in Section IV.

It is also the case that the social conditions we are trying to analyse have changed considerably, not least in the past few decades, a point that John Scott makes strongly in his discussion of class and stratification in Chapter 2. The vocabulary of 'social class' – the idea of upper, middle and working classes – did not emerge until the eighteenth and early nineteenth centuries. Manual workers have decreased from over 80 per cent of the workforce before the First World War to less than 45 per cent in the 1990s. The intermediate classes of professionals, managers and white-collar workers have grown and seen their work position radically changed, while what was called 'Society' – the exclusive, expensive social life of a small upper-class set – disappeared in the 1950s.

This does not mean that 'class is dead'. Drawing on an explanation of Weber's original conception of social stratification, Scott demonstrates continuing class differentials in material conditions, security of employment, health and life expectancy. Arguing that when most people today talk in popular parlance about 'class', they are actually referring to status and lifestyle, he presents a distinctive occupations-based account of the three main class groupings – the subordinate (manual, wage-paid) classes, the intermediate (salaried or self-employed) classes and the 'advantaged classes' (capital and property owners, and employers). This shows that despite social change, the social division of class survives in new forms. Occupational transition, culture, identity and consumption may blur the picture, but it is the underlying class situations that still determine life chances.

Occupations also loom large in Pamela Abbott's analysis of gender in Chapter 3, which she develops through a discussion of current patterns of work, education and poverty, and how they link with class and ethnicity. Work is pivotal to the position of women, representing both the public domain from which they have been largely excluded, an arena in which the struggle for equal pay and against the 'glass ceiling' is carried on, and in the form of unpaid, domestic work, representing much of the day-by-day oppression of women by men. She demonstrates a variety of gender-based material inequalities, concerning employment and pensions, state benefits, labour market access, 'home life' (in which mothers are the first 'to go without') and the poverty of the lone parent family, as the products of a patriarchal system of social division which, although more oppressive of women, constrains men as well.

The strength of her analysis is the integration of past and present ideologies and conceptions of female roles with contemporary social inequalities. This is exemplified both in terms of the development of sociological ideas, and in the way improving school performance by girls has recently been re-problematised as the declining performance of boys as a precursor to their youth unemployment. The 'natural' role of women and 'gender segregation' take on a particular significance when seen as related aspects of social division, interacting with ethnicity and class. As she comments in Chapter 3 on this interconnection, in the past:

> it was mainly middle-class women who were excluded from paid employment, while in the late twentieth century, African-Caribbean women are most likely to experience public patriarchy and Muslim/British women private patriarchy.

Thus, whereas at first sight one might expect gender to be exclusively a social division of two halves, Abbott unpacks much of the complexity of its categories. We have already observed that ethnicity is far more complicated than a simplistic dichotomy and Chapter 4, in which David Mason examines the notion of ethnic identity and demonstrates the differences between ethnic groups and their various experiences of discrimination, can be seen as a natural partner to the chapter on gender. It also draws a deliberate contrast to Scott's account of class: we cannot start from material circumstances, argues Mason, because:

> only in situations of extreme segregation will these kinds of information offer us good clues to people's ethnic status and, even then, few would argue that these characteristics represent the essence of their ethnicity. (Chapter 4)

In other words, while unemployment, earnings, type of work and location are important (and duly documented in his chapter), the real issue lies in the meaning of ethnic *identity*. This not only requires an appreciation of where, historically, ideas of 'race' and 'ethnicity' have come from and been adapted in this country, but also how discrimination has played a part in shaping identities. As the fourth Policy Studies Institute survey (Modood 1997) found, 'black' teenagers define themselves as much in terms of job, education or religion as any physical characteristics – but tend to think of themselves as 'black' when they are in contact with white people. Despite the disadvantaged positions of the minority ethnic groups that he describes, Mason is, on the whole, optimistic about the prospects for ethnic identity to be negotiable and open to change, not least as social conditions evolve and new senses of identity – the black woman, my religion, our specific minority ethnic group – enter the sociological and public consciousness.

This discussion of ethnic identity sets up the discussion of religion in Chapter 5. Religion is often closely linked with national identity, even in times and locations where, as Alan Aldridge shows, conventional patterns of religious observance may have given way to newer forms of religiosity. His account brings out the way in which beliefs can unite a group (for example a congregation), while being the basis for intense antagonisms towards other faith communities. One of the strengths of his analysis is the range of religions he covers and the concrete examples he draws from British society in particular. While religions do not sit neatly in a single hierarchy, their capacity to isolate minorities and manoeuvre for position shows how they operate as a social division.

Religion and ethnicity are also bound up with national identities but, as David McCrone shows in Chapter 6, this also needs to be seen in terms of political and historical processes. The physical boundaries of a society may be governed as a single state, but those living there may have a sense of identity with only one part of it. Using contemporary events, he asks under what conditions do people call themselves, say, 'British' rather than English, Welsh or Scots, or even say they are from 'Yorkshire' or 'the Highlands'. These expressions are markers of social division – so much so that they form the basis for political mobilisation – which are not so much to do with material differences as with cultural symbols and 'imagined communities'. McCrone is therefore less concerned with tangible material differentials across geographical areas than explanations that draw on political ideas. He locates the nationalism issue in the lack of fit between 'nation' and 'state', a problem of no small significance whether illustrated by governance and devolution, or the violence of civil unrest in Northern Ireland, Yugoslavia or other parts of Europe.

This political dimension is also evident in Chapter 7 on elites. Whereas class starts from issues of who owns what, and economic power, the idea of the division between 'elites' and 'masses' is based in who has political power and control of the state. Phil Stanworth traces the origins of theories of elites from just over a century ago with the work of Pareto and Mosca through to more recent discussions of democracy, pluralism and political parties. He shows how as new social formations developed in the middle of the 1900s, a new generation of writers (Burnham, Mills, Djilas) tried to account for the power accruing to alternative social groups. As well as bringing out the potential political dimension of social divisions, his recent research on the educational profiles of contemporary British elites illustrates how recruitment to groups underpins structures of difference and identity.

Chapters 8–11 present examples of social divisions that superficially seem to be physical or biological. In each case an alternative sociological analysis is developed, challenging common-sense assumptions and using the idea of social divisions to explore the current social positions of those in the less advantaged categories. In so far as these chapters can also be thought of as equivalent examples of social divisions, readers may choose to follow their own interests, by concentrating on particular topics.

Chapter 8 deals with age as a principle of social organisation, in particular with old age. All human societies have used age as a basis for distinguishing groups: we operate with a potentially confusing range of concepts – chronological age, cohort, generation, age group and so on. John Vincent draws on history and anthropology to explain the differences between these terms, and how demographic changes have set up new tensions within families between older and younger members. The divisions between the two, and among different groups of older people, are demonstrated through sharp contrasts of material circumstances. Together with his concerns with gender and class differences among the elderly, this connects directly into current social policy debates over how future pensions are to be financed. Vincent also addresses the social construction of ageism. His discussion of how our ideas shape our views of older citizens echoes that of disability in Chapter 11.

There is also a natural link to Chapter 9 on childhood, the other end of the age range. Here, too, the idea of 'childhood' is not taken as a given, but systematically explored as a social construction. Most earlier research (including that influential in the caring professions) has adopted a psychological development, or preparation for adulthood, model. This has not properly taken into account children's own experiences of being divided off into a subordinate position. Our pre-Industrial Revolution history, when children were more integrated into work, has been forgotten, which adds to our ethnocentric view of children as needing to be protected from 'growing up too fast', and the 'evils of the adult world'. Stevi Jackson and Sue Scott's sociological framework allows an extensive discussion of current issues about child safety, abuse, parental powers and the confusing transition points into 'maturity'. Together with the comparisons of ethnic and class differences in models of childhood, this chapter will be of particular interest to those with a vocational interest in the well-being of children.

The same authors develop a similar analysis in respect of sexuality in Chapter 10. Their first task is to dismantle the idea that heterosexuality is 'natural', 'normal' or universally the same. Sexuality is socially constructed, through institutions such as (male-dominated) marriage and the meanings and feelings that arise in and from social interactions. What is regarded as sexuality and sex depends on the society in which it exists: what is regarded as acceptable or deviant is largely a matter of power relations. Class and ethnic divisions mean there is no single shared 'normality'. Using examples such as sex education, the sex industry and current fashions to think of the 'successful self' in sexual terms, Scott and Jackson argue that normative heterosexuality, rather than being a simple biological process, makes more sense as a form of gender-based control. Instead of seeing sex as 'special area' of human life, it needs to be reintegrated into the mainstream of social life.

The idea of integration, together with access, dominates Chapter 11 on disability. The disabled 'have unique and particularly intense experiences of deprivation'; economically disadvantaged, excluded from mainstream social activities and stigmatised. In making a strong case for disability to be seen as a key social division, Mark Hyde argues that disabled people's social exclusion comes not from their disability, but from the way society interprets it primarily as a medical problem. An alternative social model, and different social arrangements, would release disabled people from the sharp social division they currently encounter. Access to education and jobs would reduce dependency on welfare and 'charity', and offer an escape from the poverty that is so frequently associated with disability. Access to the political process has the potential to bring about change, not least as a mechanism by which to challenge negative stereotyping. Access to places – and many disabled people do not fit the stereotype of being wheelchair-bound – would reduce the physical division between the disabled and not-disabled.

Section IV shifts the emphasis from single divisions towards the interaction of divisions. The three topics – poverty, community and health – can be treated as divisions in their own right, but are easier to understand as outcomes or processes in which many of the other divisions are also at work. That does not, however, mean that they are less important.

In Chapter 12, Lucinda Platt's account of poverty starts by disentangling the several threads of meaning in discussions about poverty. She rightly points out that as soon as one moves beyond a 'common-sense' view of what it means to be poor, poverty can be thought of in many ways: as a lack of income, a lack of the necessities that money can buy, or the state of deprivation and isolation that being poor produces. Even these three perspectives can be further differentiated by variations in definition and measurement, for example what exactly do we mean by 'necessities' and how much 'lack' marks the boundary of a division between tolerable disadvantage and intolerable deprivation. This careful analysis takes us beyond a simple absolute/relative dichotomy, providing the grounds for selecting some measurements and definitions over others, and for seeing how changes over time come into play. The second half of her chapter presents up-to-date data on the scale of contemporary poverty, which she uses to show how other social divisions come into play.

Chapter 13 on community also brings a fresh look at social divisions, rather than treating 'community' as a social division per se. In this sense, like the later health chapter, Graham Crow and Catherine Maclean's contribution differs from the earlier chapters, although they too bring out the importance of identity, conferred by membership of a community (whether of place, occupation or imagined community of attachment). Studies of place-based communities have richly documented the 'us' and 'them' divisions between incomers and locals over housing and local politics, which mobilise class, ethnic and gender identities. But as with the other chapters, the authors try to escape conventional wisdom, drawing attention to the normative pressures of 'community', the prevalence of migration, and the significance for identification of the contacts with the outside world. Because community tends to bring together many facets of human life, they are able to show the shift and play of social divisions during the dynamics of daily living.

The purpose of Chapter 14, as with Chapters 12 and 13, is not simply to show that divisions exist, but to demonstrate the interplay of social divisions and how there can be competing explanations of what people experience in their everyday lives. Health is a topic with a long history of social inequality research, with an extensive debate about how health and (particularly class-based) inequality are related. Judy Payne, Geoff Payne and Matthew Bond set this discussion in the context of 'the new public health', arguing that a medical or 'lifestyle' approach fails to address the connections between illness and the poverty, unemployment, bad housing and poor services that make up the daily experience of the more disadvantaged sector of society. They also attempt to extend the idea of social division from this structural and material view, considering the divisions between health workers and their clients, and between the ill and the well. The interconnection with the other social divisions runs through the analysis.

Chapter 15 revisits the core idea of a social division approach. Using the earlier chapters, it establishes a formal definition of social division and addresses the questions of cohesion and continuity that divisions pose. A contrast is drawn between this and other perspectives from sociological theory. This is a more conceptual chapter, and while there is an element of reprise, no new data on divisions are introduced.

Social divisions begin to make sense once we know what is being divided, how it is divided and what the results of the divisions are for our lives. This collection of essays testifies to the range and quality of contemporary sociological research, demonstrating the relevance of sociology for understanding contemporary social conditions. It also helps us to escape from the narrow confines of small sociological compartments into a broader view. The point of sociological analyses is to promote a better understanding of society and social processes, so that we can operate more effectively. As Albrow (1993: 241) has observed, sociology has no reason to be ashamed in 'staking its claim to enhancing the competence of its students to meet the demands of living and working'.

Discussion Questions

1. Why is 'my gang' not a social division?

2. List the differences between social division, social inequality, social differentiation and social exclusion.

3. How do we become aware of our own social identities?

4. What is it about *contemporary society* (compared with the 1950s) that makes a social divisions perspective so useful?

5. Write a brief scene from an imaginary novel in which three characters meet: one is white, male, middle class, fit and under 25; one is black, female, working class, unwell and over 50; and the third is chosen by you using the social divisions mentioned in this chapter.

SECTION II

Three Core Social Divisions

CHAPTER 2

Class and Stratification

JOHN SCOTT

This chapter will provide you with a broad critical understanding of the following issues in social class as a source of social division:

- The difference between everyday and sociological understandings of 'class'
- The key sociological definitions of class, status and social stratification
- The relationship between class and inequality
- The grounding of class relations in relations of property and employment and the occupational division of labour
- The foundations of status in prestige and social honour
- The role of social mobility in the formation of social class boundaries
- The ideas of class consciousness and class identity
- The various class schemas devised by Wright, Goldthorpe and the Office for National Statistics
- Trends in the size and composition of the principal social classes over the last century
- Variations in the life chances associated with social class membership
- The idea that social inequalities have moved in a 'post-modern' direction
- The transformation of the 'working class'
- The growth and expansion of the 'middle classes'
- The structure of advantage and the propertied classes

In our everyday lives many of us use the language of class to refer to a social hierarchy in which everyone 'knows their place'. Class is seen as a matter of 'breeding' and social background. It is reflected in our attitudes and lifestyles, our accents and ways of dressing. For this reason, class has also come to be seen as something that is outmoded and old-fashioned. Class distinctions are tied to a world of tradition and subordination that no longer exists, and the language of class is incompatible with contemporary attitudes and values. Many journalists and social commentators hold this view. These writers see the persistence of class-ridden attitudes and the continued use of the word 'class' itself as evidence that Britain has failed to adopt the more modern – or perhaps 'post-modern' – approach to life found in such apparently classless societies as the US.

On the other hand, sociologists have more often used the word 'class' to describe *economic* divisions and inequalities, especially those rooted in *property* and *employment* relations: in other words a particular kind of social division. This has led them to question whether Britain actually is any more, or any less, of a class society than the US or the countries of Continental Europe and other parts of the world. All these societies are unequal societies – they show vast and continuing differences in income, wealth and property ownership – and so all can be described, in these terms, as class societies. Other differences of culture, attitudes and lifestyle are not disregarded, but they are seen as pointing to quite different kinds of social division. In sociological analyses, therefore, the economic relations of class are often contrasted with cultural differences of 'status', those more visible 'styles of life' led by people which affect their standing in the community. What non-sociologists describe in the everyday language of class, sociologists describe in the language of status.

Not all sociologists take this point of view, of course. There are few things on which sociologists are unanimous. For some, especially in the US, class is seen as a matter of culture and identity, not a matter of underlying material inequalities. According to these sociologists, cultural change has indeed undermined the power and relevance of the language of class. 'Class is dead', it is a thing of the past, even though economic and other inequalities may persist (Kingston 2000).

Even if it were true that class is dead and that a new framework of analysis is needed, we would still need to know what class was supposed to have been before we could consign it to a historical grave. Unfortunately, as we have already noted, class does not mean the same thing to everybody. A considerable task of clarification is necessary before we can make an informed judgement on the importance – or lack of importance – of class as a social division.

Indeed, linguistic confusion is a recipe for misunderstanding in any field. If progress in sociological understanding is to be made and sociologists are to contribute to public debates, there needs to be some common ground in the language and concepts that they use. We need concepts that will help us to understand the many inequalities in resources, health and education that exist in contemporary societies. This will help us to see how they relate to other social divisions, in particular, gender, sexuality, ethnicity and age. We must also agree about which aspects of these inequalities can legitimately be described and analysed as aspects of class relations. Only then would it be possible to investigate whether these class inequalities and class differences are increasing or declining in importance in particular societies. This kind of investigation raises the relationship between the *facts* of class and their *interpretation* by commentators and those who experience them in their everyday lives.

This chapter therefore begins with a conceptual exploration of the terms required to make some sense of this kind of social stratification. This exploration returns to the works of the classical sociologists, not for reasons of 'ancestor worship', but in order to recapture the important distinctions they recognised, which have been lost in many contemporary debates over class and stratification.

Conceptualising class and stratification

Social inequalities are central to any understanding of social stratification but social stratification itself consists of more than simply inequalities in life chances. The concept of social stratification as a particular form of social division emphasises the idea that individuals are distributed among the levels or layers of a social hierarchy because of their economic relations. These layers or 'social strata' are real social groupings, forged together through both their economic relations and their associated social relations and interactions; groupings that are able to reproduce themselves over time. Work in similar occupations, marriage, kinship and informal interaction connect individuals together and build up boundaries that close one stratum and divide it from another.

Social strata are not simply statistical categories defined in an unequal distribution of resources, such as the 'top 10 per cent' or 'bottom 30 per cent' of a distribution of income and wealth. Social strata are a kind of social grouping. They are a particular form of what Chapter 1 called the 'categories' that comprise a social division. In this sense, social stratification is a typical social division, but differing from others in that it is solidly based in economic relations.

The inter-connections between social stratification and other divisions like gender, sexuality, ethnicity and age are complex. Social inequalities are invariably structured by all these social divisions: inequalities are gendered, sexualised, racialised and aged. On the one hand, each division has an independent importance in sociological analysis, as do relations of social stratification. Social exclusion and discrimination on the basis of gender and ethnicity, for example, generate inequalities in life chances.

On the other hand, this often operates through a process that combines exclusion in one division with exclusion in another, so that these other social divisions can become crucial conditions for the formation of social strata. This comes out clearly in the other chapters in this book, particularly in the chapters on health and community that deal with how social divisions interact in ordinary life. However, this does not mean that the social inequalities arising from other divisions should simply be equated with stratification. As referred to in this chapter, 'social strata' exist only when the economic and social relations of people tie them into larger, more complex and more permanent structures that take the form of a system of 'social stratification'.

To develop these arguments, I want to return to some distinctions made by Max Weber ([1914] 1968, [1920] 1968) in his comparative investigations into economy and society, where he set out an argument that has been massively influential in contemporary sociology. He identified three distinct aspects or dimensions to the distribution of power within societies. These are class, status and authority or command. Weber's discussions concentrate on class and status and their relationship to 'party', which has led to the common misunderstanding that his three dimensions were class, status and party. However, his third dimension is better understood as 'authority', as I shall shortly show. This misunderstanding is not, however, my main concern here: a more extensive discussion of this particular point can be found in Fulcher and Scott (1999: Ch. 15) and in Scott (1996: Ch. 2). My main concern is to distinguish Weber's core ideas on social stratification and the ways in which they can inform our understanding of social divisions.

For Weber, class, status and authority are aspects of power, each of which has a separate effect on the production of life chances. He defined *class relations* as those that result from the distribution of property and other resources in capital, product and labour markets. It is the possession or non-possession of economic resources that gives people a specific capacity or power to acquire income and assets and, therefore, to enhance their life chances in all sorts of ways. Company shares yield an investment income and can be sold at a profit on the stock market, while educational credentials or technical expertise may give people the opportunity to earn a higher income in the labour market. The distribution of economic resources, defines the various class situations that individuals can occupy in a society. A class situation exists wherever the distribution of resources is such that a particular category of individuals have similar abilities to secure advantages (and disadvantages) for themselves through the use of their marketable resources. A person's class situation is a causal component in determining both their life chances and the interests that they have in protecting and enhancing these life chances.

In setting out his view of class, Weber quite deliberately sought to build on Marx's work, much of which he took as valid. Marx saw property ownership, especially property in the means of production, as the basis of class relations.

For him, it was the ownership or non-ownership of factories, machines and land that determined people's life chances and shaped their actions. Marx recognised just two principal class situations in contemporary societies – capitalists and proletarians. Capitalist class situations rest on the ownership and control of capital. Their occupants include industrial entrepreneurs, bankers and landowners, as well as those who simply live on an income from company shares. Proletarian class situations involve a lack of ownership and are based on the exercise of labour power as an employee. They include those of people involved in skilled work, manual labour or office work, in other words, people involved in sets of similar types of occupation.

Debates largely within Marxism have modified this basic picture of two classes, leading to the recognition of lines of differentiation among capitalists and proletarians, and the identification of a whole array of 'intermediate' class situations. The proletarian class, being larger, has more obviously been subdivided, and arguments about the relative merits of how this subdivision should be carried out, and which resulting classification scheme of class situations is best, have been extensive. The most important of these debates are around the recent work of E. O. Wright (1985, 1989, 1997). These debates are in line with Weber's suggestion that it is necessary to recognise a great variety of class situations in any society. In later sections, I will show how it is possible to build on these ideas to investigate contemporary class divisions.

Differentiating class, 'status' and 'authority'

One of the things that Weber objected to in Marxism was its economic determinism. He pointed out that non-economic factors were important, alongside the economic, in determining life chances and shaping patterns of social stratification. The first of these non-economic factors he discussed was status. He saw divisions of status as originating in the distribution of prestige or social honour within a community. People judge one another as superior or inferior in relation to the values they hold in common and so a person's status is their standing or reputation in the eyes of others. When people act in conformity with these values, they build up a good reputation and a high status in their community. Those who deviate from these values are accorded a lower status and may be excluded from the benefits and advantages given to others.

Most typically, a person's status follows from what Weber called the 'style of life'. The ways that people carry out the tasks associated with their occupations and sex/gender roles and the customs and practices they follow as members of ethnic and other social groups define their particular and distinct styles of life (Chapter 4). Thus, manual workers, women or Asians may have a low status because of the way their style of life is perceived and evaluated. 'Dirty' or routine work may be seen as undesirable or demeaning, a feminine style of life may be valued less highly than a masculine one or the Asian way of life may be devalued.

What Weber called 'status' corresponds closely to what is often referred to as 'class' in everyday life. A style of life involves specific types of dress and bodily adornment, types and sizes of house, areas of residence, clothing, accent, methods of cooking and eating and so on. These markers of social identity – symbols of status – are often very important. Much public discussion of 'class', however, tends to highlight status and concentrate on its relatively minor and superficial aspects, disregarding and disguising economic class.

However, for a more sophisticated, sociological analysis, we need to recognise that inequalities in life chances must be seen as reflecting the effects of *both* class and status situations. Status situation, like class situation, is a causal component in life chances. Class situations comprise the property and employment relations through which control over marketable resources is organised, while status situations are the communal relations through which prestige is given to a particular lifestyle. Both operate to determine the life chances of individuals. An occupation, for example, involves both specific employment relations in the labour market *and* a particular level of occupational prestige (Parkin 1971). These two aspects of occupational position operate interdependently in determining life chances and their separate effects can be difficult to disentangle. To claim that class and status should be seen as two separate and distinct dimensions of stratification is not to prejudge their relative importance. This is always an empirical matter. The distinction does, however, allow questions about the salience of class to be formulated with greater clarity than is the case in much discussion of the subject.

Weber's third dimension of stratification is to be found in his discussions of authority and bureaucracy. Authority relations in states and business enterprises, he argued, involve relations of command in which one person is empowered to give orders to another. What Weber had to say on this can best be understood by introducing the concept of a 'command situation' to parallel his concepts of class situation and status situation. A command situation is a causal component in life chances that results from differentials of authority in formal organisations.

Weber's analysis of domination and authority gave him an acute understanding of the formation of ruling minorities in the top command situations of political, economic and other hierarchies, but, for all his insights, the conceptualisation of ruling minorities was one of the least developed parts of his sociology. His insights were independently developed, so far as social strat-ification is concerned, by Mosca (1896, 1923) and Pareto ([1916] 1963: 1430). Their particular view was that the crucial social division was between a dominant minority and a subordinate majority. In other words, there were essentially two groups, a small one at the top of society and a large one below it. They believed that this was an inevitable consequence of any social organ-isation of authority and that authority relations involve the formation of ruling minorities or what they called 'elites'. While we do not have to adopt their model of a society based on elites and masses, it illustrates how the delin-eation of class situation, status situation and command situation is the crucial basis for any analysis of the patterns of social inequalities that comprise social stratification. A more detailed discussion of elites and their power can be found in Chapter 7. This chapter concentrates on issues of class and status.

Occupations and social stratification

In distinguishing class, status and command in contemporary societies, I have already noted that occupations are central to the analysis of class and status situations. Occupations also lie at the core of structures of command. Occupations are positions in economic and social organisations in which each occupation has a different degree of authority, or lack of authority, over others. In all companies, government agencies or charities, people in some occupations direct and manage the work of those in other occupations. Any particular occupation also rests on specific marketable skills or resources and has a particular level of occupational prestige. A sociological analysis of the class, status and command situations of contemporary societies is, for many purposes, a mapping of occupational structures. Investigating social inequal-ities involves assessing the relative importance of class, status and command in the life chances that are associated with particular occupations and groups of occupations.

Sociological research has used a variety of 'class schemes' to represent this, taking occupation as an indicator of class situation, in order to study classes as 'employment aggregates' (Crompton 1998: Ch. 4). This work is extremely important – and I make use of it below. It is sometimes held that the useful-ness of particular class schemes and their advantages over others are to be judged on purely pragmatic grounds: whichever has the best *predictive* capacity for dealing with whatever is being studied is to be preferred (Erikson and Goldthorpe 1993. See the criticism in Morris and Scott 1996). However, the implication of my argument is that class schemes must by judged on theo-retical as well as empirical grounds, and they must be seen as more or less adequate attempts to offer a coherent and operational concept of class. It is Weber's framework that offers the best basis for this latter requirement.

A system of social stratification can be thought of as consisting of a number of separate social strata, layered one above another. Each social stratum contains people in similar distinctive class, status and command situations. Each stratum is a social group with boundaries marking off those inside from those outside. The group contains a cluster of social positions, with individuals moving between these social positions and interacting (or 'associating') with each other as they do so. They may modify their own and their children's social position by marriage or changing jobs ('circulating' within the boundary of their group). Through kinship and close intimate interactions such as leisure time socialising and club membership, they associate with other people like themselves who make up their social stratum. For these reasons, both occupational mobility and patterns of association must be seen as central to strata formation.

These movements of individuals from one occupation to another and interactions among those engaged in particular occupations, define the key boundaries within a system of social stratification. Occupational categories are a part of the same social stratum if there is easy and frequent movement between them. This might involve the lifetime mobility of individuals between types of occupations (called *intra*-generational mobility), or it might involve occupational movement between generations, for example from father to son (*inter*-generational mobility: see Payne 1989). Equally, it might involve frequent intermarriage between those in similar occupations or their interaction with one another in leisure activities. Whenever these relations of circulation and association reinforce one another in such a way as to create regular and established patterns of connection among the people working in a set of occupations, the connected occupations form part of a single stratum.

Occupations fall into the same social stratum when they are connected through chains of frequent and relatively easy circulation and association. They fall into different social strata when they are connected – if at all – only through infrequent circulation and association. Boundaries between social strata exist wherever patterns of circulation and association produce divisions between categories of occupations. In sociological research, individuals are allocated to the occupations that combine together various class, status and command situations; rates of mobility and social interaction must be examined in order to uncover how those occupations are clustered together into social strata.

Marx held that the occupants of capitalist situations form a distinct social stratum because they circulate freely around the different forms of capital, they are involved in extensive networks of intermarriage and their children are able to inherit accumulated capital and enjoy the advantaged life chances that it generates. In the same way, he saw the occupants of proletarian situations as forming a separate social stratum because they move from one type of work to another similar type, and from work to unemployment, they marry other workers and their children have no choice but to try and enter paid employment.

One perennial topic in studies of stratification has been the question of whether the individual or the family household should be taken as the unit of analysis (Goldthorpe 1983; Abbott and Sapsford 1987; Scott 1994a). This debate has been fired in recent years by feminist criticisms of those conventional approaches to stratification that have allocated women to social classes according to the occupational position of their husbands (Stanworth 1984). Proponents of this approach claim that women's class attitudes and behaviour can be adequately 'approximated' by this method (Erikson and Goldthorpe 1993). This pragmatic argument offers little theoretical purchase on class, and its critics have rightly argued that women's work must be considered independently of men's work and must play an equal part in determining positions in a system of social stratification.

When considering the class, status and command situations of individuals, it is important that each individual is classified on the basis of his or her own occupation. However, this is not the end of the matter. When considering the formation of social *strata* (rather than just the occupancy of class, status and command *situations*), the social relations among members of family households cannot be ignored. Marriage and intimate partnerships connect or divide occupations from one another, and the question of which social stratum a person (man or woman) belongs to cannot be decided without reference to their various family and domestic relations. Households are formed through marriage or cohabitation and it is within households that the educational and other opportunities that shape occupational mobility are generated. Households are also the bases for the organisation of much free time interaction. In all these ways, household membership is central to the allocation of individuals to social strata.

Class societies

Class, status and command operate alongside one another, but their relative importance can vary a great deal. In contemporary capitalist societies, they operate in and through the occupational division of labour and the associated system of property relations. One of the central features of the development of capitalist societies has been the way in which class situations have become, through the occupational system, the fundamental determinants of all other aspects of stratification. Status relations and command relations are, to a considerable extent, consequences of or reflections of class relations. It was for this reason that Weber thought it appropriate to describe contemporary capitalist societies as 'class societies'. A class society is one in which class situation is the most important determinant of the life chances of individuals. Weber contrasted class societies with 'status societies', where the most important determinants of life chances and the overall pattern of social stratification were status situations. Similarly, we can recognise 'command societies', where command situations are of paramount importance. These distinctions are important for comparative investigations, but they need not concern us here.

In a class society, social strata take the form of what Weber called 'social classes'. A social class is a cluster of households whose members owe their life chances principally to their property ownership or employment relations. It has been argued that the language of 'class' developed in the eighteenth and nineteenth centuries as an attempt to grasp the new social relations that emerged with the increasing salience of class situations in capitalist industrial economies. The language of class was central to the recognition of 'social classes'. By the early nineteenth century, it was widely recognised that capitalist societies contained three social classes – upper, middle and working.

The final conceptual point that needs to be made concerns class consciousness and class identity. All of us attempt to interpret and understand the social world in which we live, and a central part of this social understanding is the attempt to interpret the social inequalities that we experience. Where people have life experiences in common, they are likely to develop a shared awareness and outlook on those experiences. Those who occupy the same class, status or command situation and the members of a social stratum are likely to develop a shared understanding of patterns of social stratification and the boundaries of social strata. This common awareness is most likely to result when people work together, live in the same neighbourhood and engage in the same leisure activities. It is also influenced by the imagery conveyed in the mass media, although this is often mediated by personal, face-to-face contacts. This consciousness of social stratification (whether strong or weak) forms a central part of overall images of society, those cognitive maps that guide us in our relations with others.

What Marx and Weber called 'class consciousness' is that form of class awareness that develops in social classes and, at its fullest, defines the interests that their members have in maintaining or enhancing their life chances. This will shape their political outlook and may lead them to form what Weber called 'parties' – conflict or interest groups of various kinds that give voice to their interests in political struggles. It is also likely to shape individual political action, and even in the absence of strong, class-based parties, a class consciousness may, for example, bring about a close association between social class position and voting.

The formation of a class consciousness is by no means automatic, as the awareness of social stratification may be only weakly developed or may be outweighed by other elements in social experience. One important aspect of investigations into social stratification, therefore, is the extent to which people's social imagery actually does centre on a sense of class identity. This means that we can add to the concepts we have set out so far – principally those of social stratification based on economic relations, the differences between class, status and command situations, and the way occupations have been used to define strata – the ideas of identity and actions. One thing to have emerged from the debate on the alleged death of class is the fact that economic divisions of class may persist and even deepen, although people may no longer adopt class identities as ways of defining themselves or engage in collective, class-based action.

Mapping classes

I observed earlier that to understand class fully, clear concepts and a coherent way to operationalise them in research are needed. The ideas just discussed have underpinned, often without being made explicit, the extensive discussion on how the class situations and social classes of contemporary Britain can be mapped into clear and reliable categories. Many different official and unofficial schemes have been proposed, by sociologists and non-sociologists alike. In these schemes, the number of classes and their composition vary quite considerably. In most cases, the theoretical basis of the scheme is not spelled out, and few have been constructed along explicitly Weberian lines. It sometimes seems as if there is a huge gap between stratification theory and empirical research on social stratification, with the latter showing a bewildering variety of class maps. This has led some sociologists to suggest a radical revision of how stratification is conceptualised and measured. The Cambridge approach, for example, sees stratification as involving a continuous scale rather than discrete categories (Prandy 1991; Blackburn and Prandy 1997).

The range of disagreement can be seen quite clearly in the differences between two of the leading class schemes, those of E. O. Wright (1985) and Goldthorpe (1980). Wright's scheme – the most developed of a number he has produced – contains 12 distinct class categories. These categories are defined by ownership and control of property, organisational assets of authority and skills and education. These 12 categories are seen by Wright as a halfway house between the detailed listing of class situations and a briefer listing of real social classes, and they were intended to grasp broad differences in life chances in a large comparative study. Marshall et al. (1988) applied Wright's scheme to British data and showed that the classes ranged from a 'bourgeoisie' of property owners, accounting for 2.0 per cent of the population, to a 'proletariat' containing 42.9 per cent of the population. Between this bourgeoisie and proletariat was a whole range of propertied and non-propertied classes covering those working in various kinds of managerial, supervisory and technical work.

Goldthorpe's scheme was an attempt to move closer to a true social class map, and he allocated class situations to seven separate categories. The extremes of this scheme were a 'service class' containing 25 per cent of the population and a class of non-skilled manual workers containing 22 per cent of the population (Erikson and Goldthorpe 1993). Unlike Wright, Goldthorpe did not incorporate substantial property ownership into his scheme, on the grounds that there were too few large property holders to figure in any national sample survey. Nevertheless, he recognised that, for some purposes, it was sensible to try to distinguish an 'elite' of property owners that would amount to a fraction of one per cent of the population. Goldthorpe has also modified his basic scheme in order to use it in the wide range of different societies that he has investigated in comparative research. This enlarged scheme is less useful for investigations of any one society. Neither Wright nor Goldthorpe can be taken as having produced a completely accurate map of the class structure of contemporary Britain. Nevertheless, a wealth of secondary evidence suggests that Goldthorpe's basic scheme – modified by the inclusion of his eighth 'elite' category – does provide a remarkably accurate mapping of contemporary social class boundaries.

The older and rival 'official', that is government-produced, schemes, however, are still widely used for a variety of purposes related to the investigation of life chances and lifestyles and are likely to continue in use for some time. In much of this chapter, these categories will therefore be the ones used. In many studies and especially in official statistics, two alternative sets of 'official' class categories have been used. These are the so-called 'Registrar General's scheme' and the SEG (Socio-Economic Groups) scheme. These are far from having the plausibility of the Goldthorpe scheme (not least because their origins and subsequent changes of detail were not grounded in a systematic sociological analysis), but they are nevertheless useful bases for mapping contemporary differences in life chances and lifestyles. Their particular attraction is that for many years they were the only schemes available to access data collected by the government's large-scale social surveys.

The basic Registrar General's scheme contains five social classes, in which Class III is divided into manual and non-manual sections. In its most developed form, therefore, the Registrar General's classification contains six social classes. This scheme attempts to see class differences in terms of the skill and employment relations of occupations, and it combines this with an assessment of the social standing of the various occupations. The 17-category SEG scheme is more systematically economic in its basis, and in its 'collapsed' version also contains six social classes. These boundaries, however, are drawn at different points and do not correspond to the Registrar General's categories in a one-to-one way. The SEG scheme has sometimes been converted into a 7-category scheme by the subdivision of white-collar workers by their grade. With numerous qualifications, it is possible to summarise the relationship between the various schemes as in Table 2.1.

Table 2.1 Social class schemes

Social class		Goldthorpe categories	Registrar General categories	SEG categories
Advantaged classes				
	Capitalist class	'elite'		
	Service class	I, II	I	1, 2
Intermediate classes			II, IIIn	3a, 3b
	Petty bourgeoisie	IV		
	White-collar workers	III		
	Blue-collar elite	V		
Subordinate classes				
	Skilled manual	VI	IIIm	4
	Unskilled manual	VII	IV, V	5, 6

A significant advance in sociological research techniques was the introduction of a new official social class scheme that extends the Goldthorpe classification and integrates it with the Registrar General's and the SEG schemes. This scheme is the NS-SEC, produced by David Lockwood and David Rose (see Rose and O'Reilly 1998), which allows a far more effective integration of official and sociological research into social class. For the first time, official and sociological maps of class structure have converged and, in the future, it will be possible to make far more accurate comparisons of census and survey data than ever before. The most common version of this scheme is shown in Table 2.2, where it can be seen that official estimates see these classes ranging in size from 10 per cent of the British population in the highest class of employers and top professionals to the 33 per cent in the classes of routine and semi-routine workers. It should be noted that, for practical reasons related to sample sizes, the NS-SEC did not attempt to differentiate the 'small capitalist' class from the larger Class 1 of employers, managers and higher professionals in the scheme.

Table 2.2 The NS-SEC social class classification

Social class		% in GB population, 2002
Advantaged classes	1.1 Large employers and higher managerial	10
	1.2 Higher professional	
Intermediate classes	2. Lower managerial and professional	22
	3. Intermediate occupations	13
	4. Small employers	8
	5. Lower supervisory and technical	10
Subordinate classes	6. Semi-routine occupations	18
	7. Routine occupations	15
	8. Never worked or long-term unemployed	5

Source: For population distribution *Living in Britain* (ONS 2002a), Table 3.14.

Changing class relations

We can use these class schemes to map the shape and size of classes and how these evolve. Class relations have not stayed the same in British society. The structure of class relations itself is subject to change, and these patterns of change cannot be reflected in a fixed scheme of social classes. Nevertheless, the use of these categories in historical research does give some indication of how class relations have altered. A key element in this is the declining significance of the subordinate classes of manual workers. The subordinate classes amounted to over 80 per cent of the population in 1911, and in 1951 they still accounted for almost three quarters of the population. By 1981, however, they represented only just over a half of the population. Ten years later, they made up just 45 per cent of the population.

The decline in the number of manual workers, both skilled and unskilled, has been matched by a growth in the number of non-manual workers employed in the new service industries that have grown massively over the course of the twentieth century. Between 1911 and 1951, non-manual workers increased from just over 12 per cent to around a quarter of the population. By 1991 they made up 55 per cent of the population.

These figures, like all official statistics, must be treated with caution. However, they do give a general impression of the principal change in the system of social stratification. The key to understanding this change is what

Payne (1987a; see also Clark 1940) has described as the 'occupational transition'. This term refers to the shift in occupational structure that occurs with developments in technology and the division of labour. Industrialism involved a shift from a structure of primary sector occupations (in industries such as agriculture and mining) to one in which secondary sector occupations (those involved in the manufacturing of machinery and consumer goods from the products of the primary sector) played the leading part. Developments in manufacturing technology, however, led to the growth of technical and specialist occupations that require high levels of education and training. These occupations grew at the expense of purely manual work and, at the same time, there was an expansion in the tertiary sector of public service and commercial occupations concerned with distribution, banking and insurance. The occupational transition is one in which, successively, the primary, secondary and tertiary sectors have been the most important bases of occupational differentiation.

The implications of these changes in the occupational division of labour have been widely discussed. For many observers, the changes point to a long-term development from an 'industrial' to a 'post-industrial' society, while others have described it as one aspect of a transition from a 'modern' to a 'post-modern' society. Whatever might be concluded about this, it is clear that the occupational transition has been associated with the development of forms of social structure in the second half of the twentieth century that are radically different from those that existed in the first half. The old pattern of social classes, their boundaries and forms of consciousness have all been transformed. The large, cohesive social classes that existed in the early twentieth century have developed into the more fragmented and divided classes of the new millennium.

These changes in class relations will be discussed later in this chapter, but I would first like to look in some detail at the distribution of life chances across the social classes as they exist today. This will establish a benchmark from which the social changes of the twentieth century can be assessed.

Class and life chances in contemporary society

Figure 2.1 shows the distribution of income, in which a clear class gradient is apparent. Using broad statistical measures of income distribution – a relatively crude approximation to class divisions – Figure 2.1 shows that all classes have shown an increase in real income over the period 1971–2001, although the growth has been greatest for those at the top. Thus, the higher classes have increased their income far more than the lower classes, resulting in a growing class division between top and bottom. Median disposable income in 2001 was £293 a week, but those in the top 10 per cent of the population had typical incomes of £599 a week, while those in the bottom 10 per cent received only £148 a week. A national survey in 1996 found that most people thought that a weekly income of £211 was necessary to avoid poverty, and it can be seen that the average disposable income for the bottom 25 per cent of the population was below that level. (See Chapter 12 for more detail on poverty and low income.) More detailed measures by occupational group show that the middle levels of the scheme do not form a neat and clear-cut hierarchy. Skilled manual workers, for example, earn slightly more per week than routine non-manual workers.

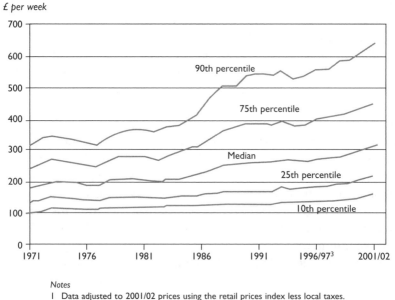

Notes
1 Data adjusted to 2001/02 prices using the retail prices index less local taxes.
2 Equivalised household disposable income before housing costs.
3 Data from 1993/94 onwards are for financial years; data for 1994/95 onwards exclude Northern Ireland.

Figure 2.1 Distribution of real[1] household disposable income[2] in the UK (2001)

Source: Social Trends, **34** (ONS 2003), drawing on data from the Institute for Fiscal Studies.

These differences are reflected in such measures as the ownership of shares and membership in pension schemes. Almost three-quarters of professional men and two-thirds of professional women are in private pension schemes, compared with just under a half of unskilled men and a quarter of unskilled women. The level and continuity of income determines the chances that a person has to purchase property and, in addition to inequalities in income-generating shares, there are marked inequalities in home ownership. Rates of home ownership are much lower for semi-skilled and unskilled workers than they are for all other classes. The rate for unskilled workers is half that found among professionals.

Unemployment is a life experience that can push people into poverty, and all the evidence shows that unskilled workers are especially likely to become unemployed. The data in Figure 2.2, relating to broadly defined occupational categories, show the significant differences that exist between routine and manual occupations and all others. It is notable that the unemployment rates for male workers are almost uniformly higher than those for female workers. Rates of unemployment are almost five times as high for unskilled manual workers than they are for professionals and managers, and unskilled workers are also far more likely to remain unemployed for a year or more.

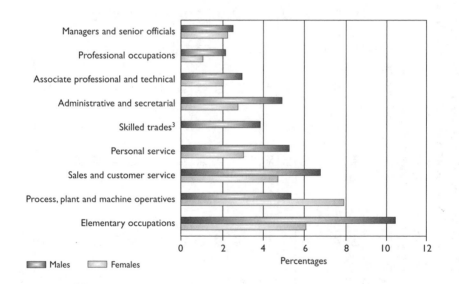

Notes
1 These estimates are not seasonably adjusted and have not been adjusted to take account of the recent Census 2001 results.
2 Bases for rates are calculated by adding those currently employed in each occupational group to those who are now unemployed but whose last job was in that occupational group.
3 Sample size for females too small for reliable estimate.

Figure 2.2 Unemployment rates[1] by previous occupation[2] (2002) in the UK

Source: Labour Force Survey (ONS 2003); *Social Trends* **33**, Figure 4.21.

Table 2.3 Percentage of households with consumer durables, central heating, home internet access and cars by social class NS-SEC (2002)

	Large employers and higher managerial	Higher professional	Lower managerial and professional	Intermediate	Small employers and own account	Lower supervisory and technical	Semi-routine	Routine
Television								
colour	100	98	99	99	99	100	98	99
digital	37	30	35	30	38	41	32	30
Telephone (fixed or mobile)	100	100	100	99	100	100	99	99
Central heating	100	98	95	92	93	92	92	90
Washing machine	99	98	98	95	97	96	95	96
Deep freezer/fridge freezer	97	96	97	96	96	97	96	96
Video recorder	97	94	95	95	93	96	93	93
CD player	98	97	96	94	90	93	87	88
Microwave oven	93	89	89	89	91	94	93	92
Home computer	89	88	80	65	67	64	53	47
Access to internet at home	82	83	70	52	58	51	36	33
DVD player	60	49	43	38	43	48	36	37
Tumble drier	71	63	61	60	63	59	56	56
Dishwasher	59	56	43	28	44	27	19	18
Car or van – more than one	61	50	43	31	54	32	21	24

Source: *Living in Britain* (ONS 2002a), Table 4.20.

Table 2.3 presents some evidence on how incomes are spent in different groups. It can be seen that certain consumer durables (television, telephone, washing machine, freezer) are owned by almost all households, with central heating, video recorders, CD players, and microwave ovens being almost as common. Even in these areas, however, it is the lower classes that are less likely to own these basic goods. Home computers and internet access, however, are far more unequally distributed, as are DVD players, tumble dryers and dishwashers. Multiple car ownership, which occurs in over half of higher class households, is found among just a quarter of those in routine occupations.

These class inequalities are reflected in inequalities of health, life and death, some of which are documented in Figures 2.3 and 2.4 and Table 2.4. A clear, although far from perfect, class gradient is apparent in all such data. Rates of obesity vary from 16 per cent among higher managerial and professional workers to between a quarter and a third of routine workers. Mental health, too, is class-related. Using direct income measures, Figure 2.4 shows that neurotic disorders are between four and five times more common among those with low incomes than they are among those with high incomes.

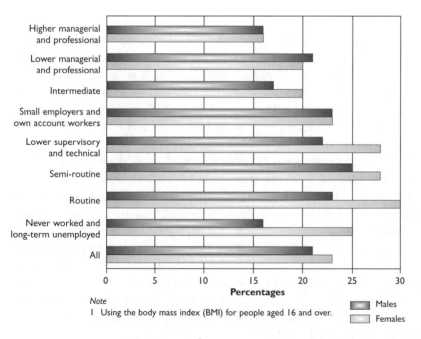

Note
1 Using the body mass index (BMI) for people aged 16 and over.

Males
Females

Figure 2.3 Obesity[1] among adults in England (2001)

*Source: Social Trends, **34** (ONS 2004a), Table 7.12, drawing on Health Survey for England (DoH).*

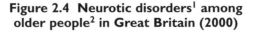

Notes
1 Includes depression, anxiety, obsessive compulsive disorder, panic disorder and phobias.
2 Those aged 60 to 74 years living in private households.

**Figure 2.4 Neurotic disorders[1] among
older people[2] in Great Britain (2000)**

Source: Social Trends, **34** (ONS 2004a), Table 7.20, drawing on the Psychiatric Morbidity Survey.

Rates of neonatal and infant mortality vary by class, regardless of how births and deaths are recorded, or whether actual numbers or rates are considered. The proportion of babies with low birth weight, rates of child mortality and life expectancy all show the same class gradient, and these differentials in life chances persist into adulthood. Even less crucial aspects of health like long-term illness, eye, ear and tooth problems (see also Chapter 14) show this class gradient.

In addition to these demographic life chances, class situation appears as a clear determinant of both housing and education. The proportion of those living in overcrowded housing or without central heating shows the familiar gradient. The same pattern is also found in measures of educational achievement. Table 2.5 shows that the attainment of five or more GCSEs at grades A to C is more than twice as high among children of professional parents as it is among children of parents with routine occupations. Rates of attendance at private schools, where attendance depends on income, are predictably unequal, so also are rates of higher education and the proportion of those leaving school with no formal educational qualifications of any kind.

Table 2.4 Live births[1] and sudden infant death in England and Wales[2] (2003)

NS SEC	Numbers				Rates[3]		
	Births	Deaths					
Three-class version	Live births	Neonatal	Post-neonatal	Infants	Neonatal	Post-neonatal	Infants
All	54,539	25	119	144	0.00	0.02	0.02
Inside marriage							
All	34,774	17	45	62	0.05	0.13	0.18
Managerial and professional	17,162	5	9	14	0.03	0.05	0.08
Intermediate	6,737	5	6	11	0.07	0.09	0.16
Routine and manual	10,875	4	21	25	0.04	0.19	0.23
Outside marriage joint registration							
All	19,765	8	74	82	0.04	0.37	0.41
Managerial and professional	5,072	0	3	3	0.00	0.06	0.06
Intermediate	4,126	1	12	13	0.02	0.29	0.32
Routine and manual	10,567	5	38	43	0.05	0.36	0.41
Inside/outside marriage joint registration							
All	54,539	25	119	144	0.05	0.22	0.26
Managerial and professional	22,234	5	12	17	0.02	0.05	0.08
Intermediate	10,863	6	18	24	0.06	0.17	0.22
Routine and manual	21,442	9	59	68	0.04	0.28	0.32

Notes
1 Figures for live births are a 10 per cent sample coded for father's occupation.
2 Information on the father's occupation is not collected for births outside marriage if the father does not attend the registration of the baby's birth.
3 Neonatal, post-neonatal and infant deaths per 1,000 live births.

Source: Health Statistics Quarterly, **23**, Autumn 2004.

Table 2.5 Educational attainments[1] in England and Wales, percentages (2002)

	5 or more GCSE grades A*–C	1–4 GCSE grades A*–C[2]	5 or more GCSE grades D–G	1–4 GCSE grades D–G	None reported	All
Higher professional	77	13	6	–	3	100
Lower professional	64	21	11	2	2	100
Intermediate	52	25	17	2	4	100
Lower supervisory	35	30	27	4	4	100
Routine	32	32	25	5	6	100
Other	32	29	26	4	9	100

Notes
1 For pupils in year 11. Includes equivalent GNVQ qualification achieved in year 11.
2 Consists of those with 1–4 GCSE grades A*–C and any number of other grades.

Source: Social Trends, **35** (ONS 2004a), Table 3.9, drawing on the Youth Cohort Study.

Inequalities of life chances in education of the kind shown in Table 2.5 are especially important, as these are central to the reproduction of class relations. The chances of entering highly paid occupations are closely related to educational achievement, which is, in turn, related to class situation as measured by occupation. This is the most striking result of research into social mobility (the movement between classes), the consequences of which are shown in Table 2.6 and Figure 2.5. Data from the 1972 Nuffield study, relating to the generation born after the Second World War and maturing during the 1960s and 70s, show high levels of self-recruitment in each class.

Table 2.6 Social mobility in England and Wales, 1972: row percentages

Father's social class	Respondent's social class (Goldthorpe scheme)							Total
	I	II	III	IV	V	VI	VII	
I	46	19	12	7	5	5	7	100
II	29	23	12	6	10	11	9	100
III	19	16	13	7	13	16	16	100
IV	14	14	9	21	10	15	16	100
V	14	14	10	8	16	21	17	100
VI	8	9	8	6	12	31	26	100
VII	7	9	9	6	13	25	32	100

Source: Goldthorpe (1980), Table 2.2.

Of the men born with semi-skilled or unskilled fathers, over half remained in manual work, with only 16 per cent entering professional or managerial work. Conversely, almost two-thirds of those born into professional and management families remained there, only 12 per cent taking up manual work. Despite apparently high levels of social mobility, class inequalities in chances of mobility remain strong, and they closely follow the other documented inequalities in material life chances.

Using more recent data, Payne and Roberts (2002) were able to look at trends in social mobility since the 1970s. They show that patterns of mobility have altered considerably over that period. Focusing on the advantaged (or service) class, the intermediate class and the working class of the Goldthorpe scheme, they show that about a third of all men had been upwardly mobile between 1972 and 1997, and only one-sixth had been downwardly mobile. These were long-term trends, although there was some evidence that the increase in upward mobility had fallen somewhat in the years 1992–97. The manual working class is shrinking and becoming more homogeneous, while the service class is becoming larger and more diverse in its composition. The service class, nevertheless, remains highly self-recruiting, with little tendency for any sons of service class men to be downwardly mobile.

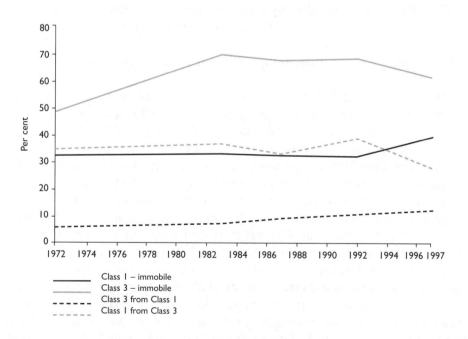

Figure 2.5 Trends in social mobility

Source: Payne and Roberts (2002).

These figures on inequalities in life chances are illustrative only – such inequalities are documented more comprehensively in Reid's (1998) summary and in many recent issues of official publications such as *Social Trends*. My purpose in using them is to demonstrate that class situation, however this is measured, remains an important determinant of life chances in contemporary Britain. For a number of key measures, there is a clear class gradient and this has to be recognised in any discussion of the relevance of class analysis. Class differences persist and have, in many respects, become sharper. However, these are far less directly reflected in distinct differences of social status and so are less directly reflected in sharp differences of attitude and outlook. Class consciousness, at least as conventionally understood, is no longer a central feature of contemporary class relations. The traditional status values that for so long defined the character of British class relations have decayed. This has undermined the everyday use of the language of 'class', which I showed to rest, in fact, on 'status' differences in accent, dress and social background.

Cannadine (1998) has convincingly shown that the language of stratification in Britain has drawn on three distinct and often contradictory images, which he terms the hierarchical, the triadic and the dichotomous. People draw on these to varying degrees and according to their social position (Lockwood 1975). They are rhetorical and interpretative devices that allow people to construct an understanding of the complex social structures in which they live. When thinking about the social stratification of their society, people are 'silently and easily shifting from one social vision to another' (Cannadine 1998: 165).

Hierarchical imagery has been dominant in social thought, especially in the form of a status hierarchy focused around traditional distinctions of education, dress, accent, ancestry and other aspects of style of life. This imagery began its long-term decline in the inter-war years, when a tripartite imagery of upper class, middle class and working class consolidated its position in the popular mind. For many in the working class of subordinate manual workers, this shaded into a dichotomous opposition between 'us' and 'them'.

In the second half of the twentieth century, social imagery became more complex and less clear-cut. The traditional imagery continued to decline as traditional and deferential values generally decayed with the decline of empire and the sense of 'greatness' that went with it. The growth of consumerism and the encouragement of a greater diversity in lifestyles fragmented the tripartite and dichotomous images and encouraged the formulation of new hierarchical images in which spending power and consumption were the central elements. Such 'money models' of society established new and highly flexible forms of status division that mask, rather than solidify, underlying differences in economic resources. Class, as defined by Marx and Weber, remains the crucial determinant of life chances and shapes the opportunities that people have for pursuing particular lifestyles, but it is less visible to people, who tend to define their positions in status terms.

Having sketched the persistence of class differences, it is now possible to look in more detail at each of the classes in turn. This will involve taking a broadly historical perspective, examining the most important social changes that have taken place at the various levels of the system of social classes. Only on this basis is it possible to understand contemporary patterns of stratification and recent debates about these. I will start with the subordinate, manual classes, followed by the intermediate or 'middle' classes, before discussing the 'advantaged' or upper classes.

Subordinate classes

The employment relations that define the social position of the subordinate manual worker are those of the wage labour contract. Manual workers are engaged to work in exchange for a wage that is supposed to compensate them for their labour time. Most typically, this kind of work has been paid on a weekly basis, although large numbers of manual workers are employed on a part-time or casual basis for shorter periods. The limited autonomy allowed or expected for manual workers is apparent in the fact that their wages are generally calculated on an hourly basis, with employers exercising controls over both the time and pace of their work.

The market situation of the manual worker depends on the skills they can bring to the labour market. Those skills that are in the greatest demand are likely to command a higher rate of pay than skills that are less in demand, and a significantly higher rate than unskilled labour. The major source of internal division within this class has tended to be along the lines of skill.

The employment relations of manual workers also involve them in distinct work situations. Within the occupational division of labour of the enterprise that employs them, they are in a subordinate position and are subject to managerial authority in all aspects of their work. Manual workers in large organisations, such as car plants, engineering works, chemical plants, local authorities, banks and so on (and formerly in now declining industries such as shipbuilding and coal mining) are subject to an extensive managerial hierarchy, the top levels of which may be far removed from them socially and physically. Manual workers in smaller organisations, typical in light industrial and building work, farm work and domestic service, are employed in smaller work groups and may have closer and more immediate contact with the managers and owners who supervise their work. Cross-cutting the lines of skill is a secondary line of internal division between those involved in large-scale and those in small-scale work situations.

Similarities in their conditions of employment – their involvement in a wage labour contract and their subordination to managerial authority – form these workers into a distinct class at the economic level. Unless lines of division by skill and work situation become particularly sharp, workers will form what Marx referred to as a 'class in-itself'. They are united by the shared economic conditions of propertylessness and subordinate employment, and the life chances with which these are associated. Where internal divisions become marked and are reflected in differences in life chances – and I have documented some evidence for this in the previous section – it may make more sense to identify a number of different subordinate classes, or subclasses, at the economic level.

The identification of economic class boundaries, however, is merely the first step towards the identification of social class boundaries. Those in various economically defined class situations form a single social class, it will be recalled, whenever mobility and association are easy and frequent among them. When a class in-itself is forged into a social class through the relations of mobility and association of its members, it is on the way to becoming what Marx described as a 'class for-itself'. In its fully developed form, a class for-itself not only has a real existence as a clearly bounded social class, but also has a consciousness of its own position and its interests relative to other social classes. The class for-itself is most likely to act politically in pursuit of its collective interests.

For much of the nineteenth century, manual workers formed neither a class in-itself nor a class for-itself. They were, for the most part, employed in relatively small workshops where there were few opportunities for them to develop a consciousness and solidarity of themselves as members of a single class. At the same time, they were greatly divided by differences of skill (Thompson 1968). From around the middle of the century, however, the scale of production began to increase and workers were brought together in larger and larger productive settings. The discipline of the factory became the common experience for manual workers (Foster 1974). Within large-scale factory systems of production, the occupational division of labour brought workers with different skills into closer contact with each other, and many forms of craft work underwent a process of de-skilling. Manual workers, while still differentiated by their skills, became more homogeneous in terms of their market and work situations.

This gradual forging of manual workers into a class in-itself was matched by high levels of mobility and association across the lines of skill within the working class during the nineteenth and early twentieth centuries. Manual workers were sharply separated from non-manual workers and were internally unified as a distinct social class. Very few manual workers or children of manual workers entered non-manual work, even at its lowest levels, and there were very few marriages across manual/non-manual lines (Savage and Miles 1994). On the other hand, skilled workers whose jobs disappeared with technological change had little option but to take up unskilled work. Consequently, unskilled workers and their children could sometimes enter semi-skilled work through on-the-job training, especially in times of economic growth and relative prosperity.

These relations of mobility and intermarriage closely linked workers in a particular locality to one another, although they were far less closely linked to similar workers in other localities. As a result, the great industrial towns and inner cities each became distinct, but structurally similar, communities of families dependent on manual work. It was in these conditions that the idea of a 'working class' took root. The proletarian communities were fertile seedbeds for sentiments of class solidarity and the forging of a shared consciousness of class.

By the inter-war years of the twentieth century, this process was well developed. Contemporaries could refer to 'the working class' and everyone would know what this meant. Manual workers themselves embraced the label wholeheartedly and took it as their basic marker of social identity. The social institutions and agencies of the working-class community sustained this identity. The dense networks of kinship and friendship that tied together neighbourhood and place of work (Young and Willmott 1957) had a more formal expression in the shared leisure time involvement in pubs and clubs, cinemas and dance halls with which they were associated (Dennis et al. 1956; Jackson 1968), and in participation in trade unions, co-operatives and the Labour Party. Through the first half of the century, the electoral strength of the Labour Party grew in parallel with the crystallisation of these working-class communities. Support for the Labour Party was seen as a natural reflection of the stronger and deeper rooted local solidarity of a working-class community.

The degree of unity found in the working class until the middle of the twentieth century should not be exaggerated. Skill differences persisted, associated with differences in life chances, and they could often undermine class solidarity. Highly skilled male craft workers – those who had served an apprenticeship or some similar period of training – could generally command higher wages and had greater job security than the semi-skilled and unskilled. Many were also able to exercise a degree of authority at work as the foremen and supervisors of other manual workers. Their relatively high wages and involvement in authority meant that there was a tendency for them to see their interests as distinct from those of unskilled workers (Gray 1981). As an 'aristocracy of labour', they were especially likely to be committed to ideals of self-help, getting on and respectability. One aspect of this respectability was that their wives withdrew from the labour market and took on full-time responsibility for domestic work and family obligations.

In a similar way, the persistence of small-scale production, often in small towns, meant that large numbers of manual workers were isolated from the mainstream of the labour movement. Their work situation encouraged a greater sense of identification with, or at least accommodation to, their employers and managers. Isolated from the supportive institutions of the oppositional subculture, they were more likely to defer to the authority of their employers (Stacey 1960; Newby 1977).

At the other end of the scale, there were large numbers of manual workers who lived in poverty and experienced long periods of unemployment. Casual work, lack of a skill, old age and illness all made people susceptible to economic downturns that could push them below the poverty line (Booth 1901–2; Rowntree 1901). Poverty was the fate that could all too easily befall any manual working family. Once forced into poverty, their lives were degraded and demoralised and they became the targets of moralising attack by respectable society – manual and non-manual alike – which saw them as the 'rough' and 'undeserving' members of society. The poor were not, however, a distinct social class, they were the lower level of the working class. The rise and fall of families across the poverty line ensured that there was no sharp separation between the poor and the rest of the working class (see Chapter 12).

The mainstream of the proletarian working class, therefore, coexisted with the small-town working class of deferential workers and workers who aspired to improve themselves within the system (Parkin 1971; Bulmer 1975; Lockwood 1975). The lower levels of this working class formed a poor working class that amounted to 30 per cent of the whole population at its peak. The cultural division between the 'rough' and the 'respectable' working class, rooted in real economic differences, became a persistent theme in national politics.

Although there have been great changes, not everything has changed significantly since the middle of the twentieth century. Many of these changes had their roots in the early years of the century, while others are only just beginning to make themselves felt. It is undoubtedly the case, however, that the mid-century marked a watershed in the history of the working class.

The subordinate classes today

Manual workers, as I have shown, have come to account for a much smaller proportion of the population than was the case a century ago, and the economic boundary between manual and non-manual work has become less sharp and less salient. Changing technology has transformed much manual work. It has led to the collapse of whole industries and, through the resulting migration of workers in search of work, it has undermined and caused the disappearance of the stable working-class communities with which they were associated. The sociologists who first commented on these changes tended to see them as a process of 'embourgeoisement': a process in which manual workers, and society as a whole, were becoming more 'middle class' in character and outlook and, as a result, were abandoning old patterns of class solidarity and class politics (Zweig 1961; Klein 1965). These claims involved a serious overstatement of their case and many of the changes that were occurring were misinterpreted. They did, nevertheless, highlight the quite critical changes in class structure that were taking place.

Manual workers were not becoming middle class, but many of them were becoming far better off than earlier generations. The 1950s and 60s saw a real growth in manual worker incomes, and the general improvement in economic conditions allowed many more people to buy domestic consumer goods that were, in the past, available only to the privileged or were simply not available at all. 'Affluent' workers were able to buy houses, washing machines, cars and televisions, and they were able to furnish their homes in more comfortable ways than before.

This partial homogenisation of standards of consumption between manual and non-manual workers (apparent in Table 2.3) was not matched, however, by changes in their property and employment relations or their life chances more generally. The conditions of work for manual workers remained inferior even to those of routine non-manual workers. Their work was dreary and monotonous, it was not a source of intrinsic satisfaction, they had less security of employment, inferior pension and holiday provision and few opportunities for promotion. They often had to move long distances to obtain this work. It was tolerated only because of the size of the pay packet – the higher their pay, the greater their willingness to tolerate their inferior working conditions (Goldthorpe et al. 1969: see also Lockwood 1960; Goldthorpe and Lockwood 1963; Goldthorpe 1964; Devine 1992a).

Most importantly, consumer goods were acquired because of the opportunities that they opened up, not because they were the status symbols of a middle-class lifestyle. It is still worth making the obvious point that people buy washing machines to wash clothes, televisions to provide entertainment and cars to provide them with mobility. These things are not accumulated simply in order to make a claim to higher status. Indeed, status divisions, like class divisions, remain sharp. Manual workers do not regularly and frequently entertain non-manual workers at home, nor do they engage in many common forms of leisure time associations with them. They have, in fact, been forced to become more 'home-centred', more concerned with the life chances and lifestyle of their own family, as they no longer have extensive working-class communities to support them in times of need.

'Affluence' was a cyclical phenomenon, not a permanent state, although levels of consumption have remained much higher than in the past. For a significant minority, however, poverty conditions have persisted (Townsend 1979). For some commentators, the poverty of the postwar period has been seen as indicating the emergence of an 'underclass' separate from the social class of subordinate manual workers (Murray 1984). The evidence does not support this claim.

In the first place, poverty is associated with other social divisions, particularly gender, age and ill health, as we shall see in Chapters 3, 8 and 14. Equally, as in the past, poverty remains an ever-present possibility for all manual workers, and its incidence is generally beyond their individual control. The collapse of a firm or an industry in an area of high unemployment can throw workers at all levels of skill into protracted periods of poverty. On the other hand, those living in poverty are not necessarily condemned to a life of poverty. Many are able to obtain employment or better paid work after a period of poverty, and there is, overall, a substantial turnover among those in poverty (Morris 1995). Those who do persist in poverty are, in particular, the aged and the infirm, whose families and friends often do not themselves live far enough above the poverty line to help them out. Poverty is a real and important problem in contemporary society, an inevitable consequence of the way that it operates, but the poor do not form an underclass that exists separately from the rest of the class of subordinate manual workers (Scott 1994b). Poverty is not a class situation per se, although aspects of it can be thought of as arising from many poor people's lack of opportunities to sell their labour in the market (Payne et al. 1996). These issues are discussed further in Chapter 12.

Changes in consumption and spending have largely concerned the extent to which a class of subordinate manual workers can be regarded as forming a class for-itself. Their market and work situations, and their associated life chances, remain distinct from those of other workers, and patterns of mobility and association still form them into a distinct social class, but these ties are neither so strong nor so intense as they were in the past. There is not the institutional support for the degree of class solidarity and cohesion that characterised the period before the Second World War and persisted into the 1950s.

Instead of a class consciousness rooted in common cultural and political traditions and participation in the labour movement, manual workers today are more likely to see their society, and their own position within it, in terms of a more open and flexible 'money model' of society that stresses relative spending power rather than political power. A focus on consumption and spending has made traditional class and status distinctions less relevant and has replaced them by new distinctions rooted in differences in consumption. To the extent that they see the language of class as relevant – and most will use it if given some encouragement by a researcher – it is not regarded as the sole or even the most relevant way of describing themselves.

People are likely to report themselves as being members of a large class that contains virtually the whole of society, only the very rich and the very poor falling outside it. Within the main class, people make distinctions on the basis of the income and standards of living that they believe people to have achieved. Their knowledge of the true extent of income differences, however, is generally poor, and the correspondence between real conditions and perceived conditions is slight. Most manual workers feel that those who are better off than themselves are not that much better off, and so they look for only relatively modest improvements in their economic situation. They see the less well off as being not much worse off than themselves, often tending to be unsympathetic towards welfare payments. For some, this central class is described as a 'middle class', while for others it is a 'working class'. For yet others – perhaps a growing number – it is a sign of 'classlessness': if almost everybody is in a single class, then 'class' distinctions are no longer relevant (Savage 2000).

Subordinate manual workers, therefore, no longer live class in the same way as their counterparts did in the working-class communities of the past. This makes it more difficult to use the term 'working class' to describe them. They are a more fragmented social class than before, the differences between 'rough' and 'respectable', skilled and unskilled, proletarian and 'deferential' having become more visible and, at the same time, submerged in a larger and diverse pool of social identities. Despite the inferior life chances that were documented earlier in this chapter, manual workers have neither the solidarity nor the consciousness that is needed to sustain a strong commitment to collective class action. This declining sense of class identity is one of the most important factors underlying the decline in the traditional Labour vote from the 1940s to the 1990s. If a greater percentage of manual workers now support Labour than at any other time in the postwar period, this is evidence not of a resurgence of class consciousness but of the transformation of the Labour Party itself. New Labour's commitment to the 'classless' society commits the party to mobilising the support of those who see themselves in the large central class through pursuing the politics of the centre.

Intermediate classes

Just as the subordinate classes can be thought of as either a single block or as subdivided, the middle classes cover a range of positions. The three main segments of the intermediate classes comprise those who are employed in professional, managerial, administrative and technical occupations; those who are self-employed; and those with small-scale property. The employment relations of the latter are distinguished from those of subordinate workers by the much greater autonomy and involvement in authority that their work situations involve and, for those at the more senior levels, by the possession of a longer term 'service' contract of employment rather than a time-based labour contract. They are contracted to employ their skills in the service of an employer – generally a large-scale organisation – and they have a great deal of autonomy and discretion as to when and how they provide these services (Goldthorpe 1980). They are paid on a monthly, salaried basis, with significant additional benefits over and above their basic salary.

Self-employed workers, such as lawyers, accountants, doctors and many business consultants, whether working alone or in partnership, exchange their professional services for a fee paid by their clients. By virtue of their self-employment, they also have considerable discretion and autonomy over the conditions under which they carry out their work, with leeway in determining the level of their own fees. Small-scale property owners involved in the running of manufacturing or service businesses may, legally, be employees of their own businesses or self-employed. In practice, however, it is their property that defines the petty bourgeoisie's market situation and allows them to earn an income.

These differences in market situations have meant that the intermediate classes have never had quite the degree of economic homogeneity achieved by subordinate manual workers. Nevertheless, there was a sharp economic gulf between the two classes. The intermediate classes were more closely linked to each other than they were to those who stood below them in the economic structure. This was matched by the sharpness of the social imagery that, for most of the nineteenth century, separated the 'middle class' – often called the 'middle classes' – from the mass of society.

The middle classes were the leading elements in the towns and cities, occupying positions of power in local councils and running a whole array of church, civic, charitable and other voluntary associations (Morris 1990). Around the formal associations were formed extensive networks of interlocking committee memberships, informal meetings and leisure activities. Their economic circumstances and lifestyle sustained a cultural and political individualism that precluded any collective action except that in pursuit of sectional professional privileges and business interests. Individuals were to help themselves and not expect the state to act on their behalf, although this self-help often involved the mobilisation of the informal social networks that abounded within the middle classes. In small towns across the country, this pattern persisted into the 1950s (Stacey 1960).

Internal differences within the intermediate classes did, however, sharpen towards the end of the nineteenth century. The numbers of doctors, lawyers and teachers grew only slowly in the years leading up to the First World War, as did the numbers of small property owners. However, there was rapid and substantial growth in the number of managerial and clerical workers: the number of clerks was almost three times as high in 1911 as it was in 1880. Clerks accounted for 0.8 per cent of all male employees in 1851, but by 1911 they accounted for 5.7 per cent. By 1951, they formed 10.5 per cent.

While these clerks did not have the long-term service contract and the autonomy enjoyed by the old middle class, they did enjoy conditions of employment that were far superior to those of subordinate manual workers. They were generally recruited through the interpersonal connections that they or their families could mobilise, and their promotion depended on their maintaining good personal relations and loyalty to their employers (Lockwood [1958] 1993). These employment conditions secured them clear advantages in income and status over manual workers. Like the similarly expanding numbers of shop assistants, commercial travellers and technicians, however, they remained at some distance from the established middle classes and tended to be defined as 'lower middle class' (Crossick 1977).

The continued growth in the numbers of clerical and managerial workers in the twentieth century further increased the diversity of the 'middle classes'. A growth in the scale of management in large business enterprises produced a growing 'service class' of managers who became increasingly sharply separated from the equally large number of clerical workers whose working conditions were being transformed. Instead of being dependent on the mobilisation of personal contacts, clerks were more dependent on the educational qualifications they could secure. The expansion of management was also associated with a mechanisation of office work, which progressively devalued the skills that these qualifications signified. Office work became more routine and, in many respects, more 'manual' than 'mental' in character (Braverman 1974). Promotion opportunities for clerks declined, while the work itself became more feminised (Holcombe 1973; Anderson 1976). By 1951, over half of all clerks were female. The women who entered clerical work were often the wives or daughters of manual workers, further reducing the significance of the boundary between clerical work and manual work. Clerks were no longer so unambiguously 'middle class' as they had been in the nineteenth century, while the middle classes had become more exclusively professional and managerial in character.

The transformation of the middle classes, therefore, began much earlier than the changes experienced by subordinate manual workers. Nevertheless, the middle of the twentieth century does mark an important point of transition for the intermediate classes also. Economic competition meant that small businesses came under greater pressure from the large enterprises (in which the vast array of managers were employed), and consequently the position of the petty bourgeoisie was much weakened. Small business owners also had high levels of self-recruitment, and correspondingly much lower rates of mobility in and out of other intermediate class situations (Scase and Goffee 1982). The growth of large-scale enterprise also transformed the position of many managerial and professional workers, forcing many of them to convert from self-employed to employed positions (Johnson 1972). Those in service locations became more diverse. Particularly significant was the growth of the public sector and the 'semi-professionals' (teachers, social workers, nurses and so on) employed within it. The vast growth of financial services in the 1980s led to an expansion in the numbers of non-traditional service workers in insurance, pensions and estate agency. At all levels, then, the intermediate classes have been tied to bureaucratised conditions of employment.

The class cohesion of the middle classes was always rather low: they formed a clearly bounded social class in relation to the working class, but they were internally divided by the relative difficulty of moving from propertied to employed and self-employed positions. Savage et al. (1992) have argued that this separation became more marked in the second half of the twentieth century, and that the managerial, professional and propertied sections of the intermediate classes are now sharply distinct from each other. The intermediate layers of the class structure have, like its subordinate levels, become more fragmented. This fragmentation at the intermediate levels has been along the lines of organisational assets, educational assets and property assets.

As a result, traditional middle-class individualism and civic power have weakened (Stacey et al. 1975). Those in the vast managerial bureaucracies – especially those in the public sector bureaucracies – are more likely to consider collective action in pursuit of their interests. In place of the individualism of the old middle classes, the collectivism of the new middle classes has emerged.

The term 'middle class', however, may be less useful as a designation for those in these intermediate employment and property relations. The term 'middle class' as a self-description, as I have already shown, is as likely to be used by manual workers as it is by non-manual workers. Large bureaucracies, with their extensive professional and managerial hierarchies based on entry by educational qualification, technical competence, measured performance and competitive promotion, form the bases of intermediate class situations. This encourages their occupants towards the social imagery of an ostensibly open and 'classless' society. Intermediate class situations still exist and they still enjoy life chances that divide them from subordinate manual and routine non-manual workers, but their self-perception – even when it employs the phrase 'middle class' – is not one that emphasises either their traditional status or a solidaristic class identity.

Advantaged classes

The advantaged classes are those who are involved in property and employment relations that give them ownership and/or control over large amounts of capital. Whether in the form of land, buildings, machinery or financial securities, property is the key to their power. In some cases, this involves the direct personal ownership of substantial property. This might be as the exclusive or part-ownership of a large integrated block of capital (such as a landed estate or large business enterprise) or it might be the holding of diversified portfolio investments in a large number of different types of capital. In other cases, the class situation might involve an employment relation that defines a position of control over these kinds of assets. The chief executives of large enterprises, their part-time directors and the investment managers of large financial enterprises are all able to use their control over capital to secure, directly or indirectly, significant advantages for themselves. This view of a *class* determined by their ownership or control of property contrasts with that of *elites* who occupy positions of political power (see Chapter 7).

For much of the nineteenth century, there was a sharp separation between land and manufacturing as sources of class advantage. Landowners – closely linked to the financial sector – saw themselves and were seen by others as forming an 'upper class', rooted in the aristocracy and, more narrowly, in the peerage. Landed wealth was the source of the biggest fortunes (Rubinstein 1981), and it was the landowning upper class that dominated the political machinery of the state (Guttsman 1963). Manufacturing capitalists, often provincial in their origins, became an increasingly significant category of wealth, but they were barely distinguished by their contemporaries from the vast mass of the middle classes. The social imagery of upper, middle and working class made manufacturing capitalists virtually invisible as a class. Towards the end of the nineteenth century, land and industry came closer together. Peers and other landowners, who were experiencing a fall in the returns on their estates, became more willing to invest in industrial enterprises and sit on the boards of the large business enterprises that were formed from the 1880s onwards in banking, insurance and railways, as well as in manufacturing. A 'lord on the board' was an important marker of stability and probity in a more complex business environment. Through these connections, and through mobility and intermarriage, manufacturing capitalists came grudgingly to be accepted as part of the upper class (Thompson 1963; Stone and Stone 1984; Scott 1991).

At the turn of the twentieth century, the advantaged class numbered just under 40,000 people, approximately 0.1 per cent of the population. Its position in society was confirmed more by its status than by any widespread recognition of its economic resources. The popularity of the royal family was central to this, as the monarchs were, as major landowners, core members of the class. Victoria, Edward and the two Georges were well integrated into the advantaged class and, through the ceremony and glamour that was attached to royalty, they ensured that the social class as a whole received a high level of public approval and at least overt deference. The cement that held together the increasingly diverse upper class as a distinct status group was the round of 'Society' activities: the dances, dinners, parties and salons held by the aristocracy and other prominent families in their London and country homes (Weiner 1981; Rubinstein 1993; McKibbin 1998).

As it became less exclusively aristocratic, Society became more ostentatious and more focused around glamour and frippery. The relaxation of traditional standards helped to weld the diverse elements of the upper class together, but in the long run Society was incapable of preventing the disintegration of the class in the face of this diversity. The institutions of Society became more open to sheer wealth and less able to impose a single lifestyle on all its members. This is clear in the informal social networks that were rooted in kinship and friendship and sustained through attendance at public schools and prestigious Oxford and Cambridge colleges. These networks were important bonds of solidarity for the male members of this upper class, who could rely on the mobilisation of the social capital of their 'old boy networks'. As the century progressed, these networks became weaker. They could no longer guarantee success for landowning families, although they were still highly successful in the social placement of the sons of the aristocracy, and they could not meet the needs of those who were closer to the margins of the class. Advantaged class situations were becoming ever more business-based in character and less exclusively landed. In parliament and government, public schools and old universities, and the top levels of the military and civil service, the upper class was beginning to lose its distinctiveness and its cohesion (see Chapter 7).

By the early 1950s, Society had virtually ceased to operate in its traditional form, its demise having been hastened by wartime conditions. The advantaged classes could no longer really be defined as an 'upper class'. Instead, they formed a diversity of overlapping cliques and sets, an 'upper circle' rather than an 'upper class'. These cliques were diverse. Some followed traditional country pursuits, some were involved in the media and entertainment, some were members of a 'jet set', and others simply kept to themselves and made their money (see Chapter 7).

This decay in the traditional status of the upper class – the death of the upper class – was the counterpart of the growing economic complexity of property and its management. The middle decades of the twentieth century saw a transition from the direct personal ownership of land and business that had prevailed in the nineteenth century to more indirect and impersonal forms of corporate ownership. The number of large personal shareholdings in major companies declined and there was a corresponding growth in the proportion of shares that were owned by financial enterprises such as insurance companies, banks and pension funds (Scott 1997). In this situation, it was the directors and top executives who controlled the capital embodied in these enterprises.

These directors and executives were recruited disproportionately from those who were, individually, property owners, although new channels of mobility to advantaged class situations had been opened up. Wealthy families had diversified their assets by taking stakes in a large number of enterprises and entrusting the management of these assets to the growing financial enterprises. At the same time, they were able to ensure their continuing control over the assets that generated their wealth by taking top board and management positions in them. Whether as rentiers, who depended passively on the management of their capital by others, or as active finance capitalists and finance executives, the propertied were able to secure a continuation of their advantaged life chances. Indeed, the demise of Society made their privileges far less visible and therefore less open to attack than in the past (Scott 1997: Ch. 8).

This trend has been described as a 'managerial reorganisation' of the capitalist class (Mills 1956). Business enterprises have become ever more closely tied together through the interweaving shareholdings and interlocking directorships of the big financial investors. The directors and executives of these enterprises are overwhelmingly drawn from a propertied background, although with a growing influx from management and the professions, and their children are, thereby, able to become the propertied inheritors of the next generation. The capitalist class of today combines personal wealth with top-level participation in corporate management.

Conclusion

I have tried to show that a Weberian approach to social stratification – especially his distinction between class and status – allows us to understand both the contemporary contours of class division and the long-term processes that have brought them about. There has been a move away from a stable tripartite system of social classes (upper, middle and working) to a more fragmented class structure in which the advantaged, intermediate and subordinate levels are no longer so directly defined in status terms. It was the close association of class and status from the 1880s to the 1950s, underpinned by the economic conditions of the period, that allowed the formation of a stable system of social classes. In these circumstances, the members of the various classes readily accepted this in their own social imagery, class consciousness and political action.

Economic change and the demographic changes that have gone along with it have destroyed this structure. These changes have long roots, but they have been especially marked since the 1950s. Class divisions still exist, but they are no longer so easily mapped into a tripartite imagery of social classes. There is still a sharp gradient of life chances, as shown in the evidence on health, mortality, housing and education presented in this chapter, but it is no longer so obvious exactly where the real social boundaries are to be drawn on this gradient. Boundaries are more fuzzy, less distinct. Indeed, it is not clear whether it is more useful to focus on the broadly defined advantaged, intermediate and subordinate classes or their internal divisions along the lines of their property and employment relations.

In this sense, class as a social division is a complex one that does not divide society neatly or conspicuously into two, three or even half a dozen categories. It is also true that, certainly compared to the past, many more individuals can move between classes during their lifetimes (Payne 1992). Other social divisions, not least gender and ethnicity, have become increasingly important to our sense of identity, as will be seen in Chapters 3 and 4. However, 'fuzziness' of boundaries and complexity in the structure of subdivisions do not necessarily invalidate the idea of social divisions.

The new complexity of multiple class situations should not disguise this fact. It would be wrong to mistake contemporary society's increased individual capacities to manipulate the cultural trappings of identity as meaning that class actually no longer matters. No amount of personal choice to 'mix and match' consumption behaviour or symbolic life goals will remove the underlying constraints of class situations. The fact that we encounter so much political rhetoric about 'classlessness', the importance of individual choice or the latest fashion in 'achievement' does not mean that class has disappeared.

Everybody does not have to believe in the existence of class or constantly think of themselves in terms of class identity for class to be a social division. The system of class situations is not dependent on people's awareness of, or faith in, it. Differences in health and mortality, for example, exist as material facts, independently of what people may, or may not, think about them. Social divisions do not always lead systematically to a sense of distinctive group identities, or to action with others on the basis of such shared personal social identities.

Despite lacking in visibility, and however imperfectly measured in the existing social classifications, class divisions remain central to social life in contemporary Britain. Of course, we recognise that in contemporary society, people are less likely spontaneously to describe their own experiences in the language of class. They search for more direct and specific determinants of their life chances to put alongside their recognition of class, and they recognise the independent part played by age, gender and ethnicity. We do not live in a 'classless' society, although we do live in a society whose members no longer spontaneously and unambiguously use the language of class as the obvious, taken-for-granted way of describing social inequalities. Class is not dead, but perhaps the monolithic social imagery of class has, indeed, had its day.

Discussion Questions

1. To what extent do people today identify themselves as members of a particular social class? Has class consciousness declined in the face of a growing consciousness of gender, ethnicity and other sources of social division? Draw on evidence from other chapters in this book to consider this question.

2. Is it still appropriate to see the working class as the source and basis of radical political action aimed at changing the structure of inequality? To what extent has the transformation of the working-class and the declining salience of working class identity undermined the basis of radical political commitments? Are there new sources of opposition to class inequalities?

3. Does the growing significance of consumption and consumerism point to a new source of social division distinct from that of class relations based in production? To what extent is consumption inde-pendent of production? Have the consumer identities promoted through advertising become more important than traditional class identities?

4. Can we still see modern societies as dominated by a propertied, capitalist class? What kind of evidence is needed to assess the continuing
   inequality in property ownership? Is there evidence that such a class
   also dominates the state as a 'ruling class', as depicted in Marxist
   theory?

FURTHER READING

The most comprehensive overview of data on class differences is Ivan Reid's *Class in Britain* (London: Polity Press, 1998), although now a little dated. More detail can be found in the various editions of *Social Trends* and other publications (now available online). Geoff Payne's *Mobility and Change in Modern Society* (Basingstoke: Macmillan – now Palgrave Macmillan, 1987) is an excellent summary of the debates and trends in social mobility, while *Class and Cultures: England 1918–1951* (McKibbin, R., Oxford: Oxford University Press, 1998) is a social history of earlier class differences that adds some life to the statistical bones. A useful balanced summary of the theoretical debates can be found in Crompton, R. *Class and Stratification* (Cambridge: Polity Press 1998, 2nd edn), while empirical material is well covered in Ken Roberts' *Class in Modern Britain* (Basingstoke: Palgrave – now Palgrave Macmillan, 2001). A useful recent overview that pays particular attention to recent changes in lifestyle and outlook is Mike Savage's *Class Analysis and Social Transformation* (Buckingham: Open University Press, 2000).

CHAPTER 3

Gender

PAMELA ABBOTT

This chapter will provide you with a broad critical understanding of the following issues in social class as a source of social division:

- The social construction of gender
- Changing gender relationships in western societies
- Social as opposed to biological explanations for gender inequalities
- Gendered power relationships
- Gender differences and inequalities in education
- Gendered patterns of and inequalities in paid employment
- Gender and poverty across the life-course

Since the 1970s, sociology has attached greater importance to the distinctive positions of women and men. Assumptions about gender and gender differences are now seen as embedded in the structures and institutions of British and other societies, in our way of thinking and talking, our beliefs and attitudes, and in employment, education, politics, the family and leisure. In identifying gender as an important social division, sociologists are going beyond arguing that men and women have *different* roles in society and are typically found performing different jobs. We are concerned with explaining them – to provide theoretical accounts based on the idea that these differences are *structural*, are predominantly *social in origin*, and that men, as a category, have more power than women as a category. While there are considerable differences in these various theoretical accounts (see the discussion on 'patriarchy' below), men are seen as able to use their power to control resources, maintain their position of dominance vis-à-vis women and so are able to exploit women. However, although men are thus in a position of advantage, they are also structurally constrained by ideas of masculinity and what is expected as the correct way for a 'man' to behave.

Underlying gender divisions, there continues to be a (generally unspoken) view that the sexual division of labour and the inequalities between men and women are natural and immutable. This is reflected not only in the assumption that women should be responsible for domestic labour and child care, but in the occupational roles that are available to women, or indeed those from which women continue to be excluded. There continues to be a view that women are naturally good at caring, service work, secretarial work and so on, and an expectation that when men do this work they will do it differently to women. The assumed natural basis for women being able to perform these occupational roles is also used to justify the low pay of female occupations compared with male occupations, whether they are routine, non-manual or professional. Inequalities between men and women persist across the life-course, from girls and young women being denied the freedoms enjoyed by their brothers, through inequalities in the labour market, to the poverty and dependency on the state for income and care that many older women experience (Chapters 8 and 12).

Gender identity is fundamentally ascribed at birth and structures our experiences from birth and the expectations that others have of us. Generally, the first, or at least second, comment made on delivery of a baby is its gender. This is marked in the hospital by the colour of band that is placed on the baby's wrist. In UK hospitals, boys have a blue band and girls a pink band. From that point on, they are regarded as fundamentally different and as boys or girls. This ascription at birth of gender is reflected in the clothing that they are subsequently dressed in, which in turn is a fundamental basis for our cues for social interaction and our expectations dependent on the assumed gender of the person with whom we are interacting.

Sociologists have challenged the view that gender divisions can be explained by biological differences between men and women. They argue that biology is an inadequate explanation and we must look to social, cultural and structural reasons for the differential access that men and women have to power, wealth and privilege in modern industrial societies. Smith (1979) has argued that there is a distinct female life experience that is a reflection of the essentialist notions of what it is to be male or female. The notions of what femininity is and what masculinity is are used as the basis for interacting with girls/women and boys/men, both in terms of expectations and the behaviour that is encouraged or discouraged and punished. Boys/men are expected to be domineering, aggressive, noisy and active, whereas girls/women are expected to be caring, quiet and less assertive. These very characteristics are then those that are seen to differentiate men and women in terms of employment. Characteristics associated with men are those that are said to be necessary for management positions within non-manual occupations and skilled positions within the manual classification, whereas the 'natural' qualities of girls/women are seen to suit them for occupations which are accorded lower status and lower economic remuneration, such as, nurses, teachers, care workers, waitresses, domestic workers, and so on.

These differences between men and women now seem so obvious that it is easy to forget that until the 1970s, sociologists rarely considered gender divisions to be significant, focusing mainly on class and status differences. Indeed, it is possible to go beyond criticising sociology for ignoring the importance of gender divisions and argue that often women were ignored. Much sociological research focused on boys and men. Women were not even included in many samples and, when they were, gender was not seen as a significant variable for analysis. Even when differences between men and women were noted, these were usually seen as 'natural', that is, as the outcome of biological differences. As Hartman (1978) indicated, sociology was at best sex-blind and at worst sexist.

Changes in gender relations?

This chapter argues that gender inequalities persist as a significant social division and illustrates this by focusing on three areas; education, work and social exclusion. The ascriptive principle of gender – our genders are something that we are born with – continues systematically to disadvantage women and deny them freedom and equality with men. In other words, structural constraints continue to limit the opportunities available to women in a masculine culture. At the same time, although men benefit from this relationship, the same masculine culture also imposes constraints on men.

This not to deny recent changes in men's and women's roles, as the latter have moved from the private sphere of the home into the public sphere of work and wider social involvement. However, there continue to be different expectations of the role of men and women – in particular, continuing evidence that women's entry into the public sphere actually increases their burden, that is, they are expected to take on more roles – worker as well as domestic labourer and mother – whereas men's major role remains that of breadwinner. A Eurobarometer poll (1997) found that nearly 50 per cent of men but only 30 per cent of women thought that 'the jobs that need to be done to keep a home running such as shopping, cooking and cleaning' were shared equally between themselves and their husband, wife or partner.

As women move into the public sphere, control by men in the home is replaced by control in the workplace or the state (Abbot and Ackers 1997). This is exemplified in the role of office wife/secretary (Pringle 1988), mother/primary schoolteacher (Burgess 1990) and wife/mother/tart/female flight attendant (Tyler 1997). In other words, the servicing work that women have traditionally undertaken for men in the private sphere becomes part of the work they are expected to perform in the public sphere. Men employed in the same jobs are not expected to undertake this work. So secretaries are expected to perform wifely duties for their male bosses, primary school-teachers have to 'mother' their classes of children, while flight attendants are seen as being there to 'serve' the needs of male passengers. Women are expected to relate to men in the public sphere in the same way they do in the private sphere.

This is not to suggest that women are passive victims. Women do struggle to resist male power and this is evidenced by the considerable gains that women have made in the past 20–30 years, not least in western societies. Gender relations have been transformed: girls are now doing as well, if not better, in the educational system than boys. Women (including married or cohabiting women) are increasingly in paid employment, with some women challenging men for the 'top' jobs. Women are no longer largely confined to the domestic sphere – they are part of the 'public sphere' of paid employment and politics.

One reaction to this has been a concern that male dominance, that is, masculinity, is being challenged. Working-class boys are taking on new masculine identities in situations where the normal transition for boys is from work to (un)employment, where they see their male relatives without paid employment and their mothers as the breadwinner often engaged in low-paid service work. In this situation, some of the most powerful 'truths' about gender – that men are breadwinners and women are housewives and mothers and economically dependent on men – have been exploded. In the face of this uncertainty about what it is to be a man, there is now a variety of masculinities rather than one hegemonic understanding.

Many areas with high levels of social deprivation have witnessed the construction of an exaggerated masculinity where to 'be a man' is to engage in activities such as binge drinking, joy-riding, burglary and arson. Nevertheless, there remains a value on maleness which involves the routine harassment of girls and women, homophobia and a rejection of what are seen as female characteristics (Mac an Ghail 1994). Boys continue to take on masculine identities within which they see themselves as dominant, more powerful than, and controllers of, women. In particular, working-class lads continue to be 'sometimes/always sexist, homophobic and often explicitly racist' (Dixon 1996). For middle-class boys, the role adopted is one of intellectual masculinity – an apparent effortless success (Power et al. 1998). The culture of masculinity also perpetuates a kind of domineering manhood – the definition of masculinity that boys take on has femininity as the subordinate term. Boys therefore 'need' to dominate girls in order to demonstrate that they are 'real men'.

An alternative position has suggested that women are increasingly rejecting their 'natural' roles as wives and mothers. This is seen as an important factor in explaining male unemployment, the rise in crime and divorce rates and the lower educational achievement of some young men. However, feminist sociologists have argued that these New Right and 'Christian sociologists' – Murray, Marsland, Cox, Dennis – are doing no more than simply blaming women for social problems (Abbott and Wallace 1992).

Although the initial focus of much feminist sociological work was considering gender divisions, they have also come to recognise the importance of divisions amongst women (and men) based on race, ethnicity, age, social class and sexuality (Phizacklea 1983; Crompton and Mann 1986; Arber and Ginn 1991). As Guillaumin (1995: 17, 19) has pointed out:

> women, blacks and other dominated social groups are not categories existing of and by themselves ... they are constituted in the context of social relation and dependence and the process of sexualisation and racialisation ... functions so as to allocate humans within specific social categories and positions.

In recent years, it has been increasingly argued that differences between men and women are no longer as great as they were. Young women are doing as well, if not better, than young men in the formal education system, and women are competing on more equal terms with men in the labour market. However 'in Europe inequalities between women and men remain substantial in a large number of areas', not least in employment and public policy (Eurobarometer 1997: 3; Wallace et al. 2004).

Feminist sociologists have pointed out that these inequalities apply within academic circles as well as outside. The work of nineteenth and early twentieth-century female sociologists, in particular that which recognised the centrality of gender analysis, has been erased from the sociological cannon (Lengermann and Niebragge-Brantley 1998). Who now has regard for Harriet Martineau, forgotten as the first translator of Comte; Marianne Weber, a sociologist in her own right but reduced to the status of Max Weber's wife; Jane Adams and the other Chicago sociologists who published in the *American Journal of Sociology*, but who came to be regarded as 'social workers'; or Beatrice Webb, whose own contributions became merged with her husband as 'The Webbs'? These are examples of the way in which the power of men in privileged positions can be used to determine what is to count as important and significant knowledge, while in the process the work of women is discounted. This process has been referred to as the construction of a 'man-made world' – knowledge produced by women has either been ignored, marginalised or erased from history (Abbott et al. 2005).

Nineteenth and early twentieth-century sociologists accepted biological explanations for gender division, or rather, in the terms of Sydie's (1987) book title, *Natural Women, Cultural Men*, attributed female behaviour to women's physical characteristics, whereas men were seen as dealing in logic, reason, intellect, and so on. Contemporary sociologists have generally sought to replace this gendered explanation of gender by *sociological* explanations. An important starting point for this was the distinction between sex, meaning biological differences – anatomical and hormonal – and gender, meaning socially constructed expectations and behaviour:

> Gender refers to the varied and complex arrangements between men and women encompassing the organisation of reproduction, the sexual division of labour, cultural definitions of femininity and masculinity. (Bradley 1996: 203)

Beck (1992) refers to the 'omnidimensionality' of the inequality between men and women.

Gender is a social category – a lived relationship between men and women – which structures every aspect of our daily lives. It is both cultural and material. Men are able to control women not only by marginalising them in discourse, but by the exercise of political, economic, social and physical power. Gender is also a 'script' – we have to learn how to *do gender*, that is, behave in gender-appropriate ways. All gender behaviour is an act, a performance. As Jan Morris (1974: 140) has said about her own transition from male to female:

> There seems to be no aspect of existence, no moment of the day, no contact, no arrangement, no response, which is not different for men and women.

Explaining gender divisions

I have already pointed out that gender divisions have traditionally been seen as natural, inevitable and therefore immutable. This acceptance that different roles, associated statuses and access to scarce resources are based on natural differences went unquestioned, not only by the founding male sociologists, but in academic sociology until the 1960s. Whilst some sociological work did explicitly accept the biological argument, most omitted a gender analysis – assuming either that men and women experienced the social world in the same way, or that gender differences were natural and/or of no interest or importance. As Simone de Beauviour ([1949]1972: 16) has pointed out, women have been defined as 'other':

> She is defined and differentiated with reference to men and not he with reference to her. She is the incidental, the inessential, as opposed to the essential. He is the subject, he is the Absolute. She is the Other.

However, in the 1960s and 70s, women began to express a dissatisfaction with sociology; to argue that the sociological imagination was a male one – it did not speak to the experiences of women. Despite its claim to neutrality, sociology had a male bias. Smith (1979) argued that this was because women's concerns and experiences were not seen as authentic but subjective, whilst men's were seen as the basis for the production of 'true' knowledge. Consequently, sociological knowledge portrayed women through the eyes of men and male-made theories.

In this way, sociology, along with other disciplines such as biology and anthropology, was implicated in maintaining the subordination of women by providing a scientific justification for it. Mainstream sociological theories underpin and justify the subordination and exploitation of women by claiming to be factual. They have framed what is considered to be the subject matter of sociology – what should be studied, how studies should be undertaken, what questions it is important to seek answers to, what variables are significant and inform the conceptualisation and interpretation of the research findings. Feminist sociologists have therefore argued that it is necessary to re-conceptualise sociology, not just to add women, but to develop adequate theories for explaining the exploitation and subordination of women – ones which will enable us to make sense of women's and men's positions in contemporary society.

Kuhn (1970) has argued that theories are not just rejected because they have been shown to be inadequate. Theories are only replaced when more adequate theories have been developed, ones that can explain more adequately than the existing ones can. Whilst feminists in the 1960s and 70s were concerned to demonstrate the inadequacies of existing sociological theories, carry out empirical research in areas of interest to women and argue for the inclusion of gender as a variable in research, they also began to develop theories to explain gender divisions. There was not a single feminist theory, but a number of theories that challenged mainstream theoretical explanations for gender divisions and the exploitation and subordination of women.

Thus, on the one hand, feminist sociologists were united in their rejection of mainstream theories, being concerned with explaining how a male monopoly of knowledge and positions of power is exercised, how social relations are structured around gender and how women can challenge man's privileged position. On the other hand, differences began to develop. The feminist theories developed in the 1960s and 70s had been 'totalising' theories that saw oppressive power as located in the structure of society, such as the capitalist economic system. However, there was a division between 'realist' feminists who argued that gender divisions had an existence in society beyond the lives of individuals who made them up, and those who argued from a 'social constructivist' position that gender relations were bound up in our personal beliefs and how these were acted out in our day-to-day interactions with other people. The early feminist theories were mainly concerned with theorising gender divisions, but throughout the mid-1980s the need to recognise that race, class, age, disability and sexuality also structured the experiences of women has been increasingly acknowledged (Abbott et al. 2005; Chapters 2 and 14 in this volume).

More recently, feminists' accounts influenced by post-modernism and post-structuralism have been concerned to explain the operation of power through institutional arrangements and how social control is exercised through agencies that discipline the body. Post-modernism has been particularly problematic for feminists. On the one hand, feminist sociologists' critique of mainstream sociology has been seen as an important element of the development of post-modernism within sociology. However, the post-modernist claim that there is no valid or verifiable knowledge and the death of the subject – that knowledge is about control not liberation – is problematic for feminists who are concerned to uncover the systematic disadvantage of women and produce the knowledge that will enable them to liberate themselves. Whilst recognising that it is important to ask how we think about male power, it is also necessary to recognise the reality of the exercising of male power, which is a constant force within society, and its impacts on women's lives. Male power has a real existence outside of the 'discourse' of theoretical discussion, for example in rape, domestic violence and sexual harassment.

Feminists are more ambivalent about the post-modernist claim that society and social relations are too complex to be understood through totalising theories. Some (for example Walby 1990) maintain that it is possible to have a theoretical explanation for the subordination and exploitation of women, whereas others (for example Doyle 1995) argue that, despite differences, there are shared commonalities in women's experiences. Barrett and Phillips (1992), among others, argue that it is no longer possible (if it ever was) to have universal theories and that the concern must be with explaining, understanding and theorising the local and the particular – the world as experienced by women and men in their everyday lives.

Gender and power

The key concept developed by feminists to describe male power was 'patriarchy'. This term, originally meaning 'rule of the fathers' was used in a specific sense in social anthropology to describe a kinship system in which males had dominant positions with respect to their female relatives. It was then adapted by feminists to mean any kind of male domination of women – at the level of society or within households. Although intended as an explanation of the multiple disadvantages experienced by women, patriarchy in this looser second sense has not been an unproblematic term, because it is such an all-encompassing, general idea that it does not enable us to identify the causal elements that make up the patterns of gender divisions. Power relationships between men and women vary both historically and geographically, so to describe these just as 'patriarchy' is too universalistic and abstract. It also rules out the possibility of a society in which men and women are equal.

Furthermore, the term has been used in a variety of ways. The main difference is between 'realist' and 'social constructivist' explanations. The former sees patriarchy as embedded in economic structures (for example the labour market, the family), that is, the ideology of patriarchy justifies the inequalities rather than gives rise to them. For example, Hartman (1978: 11) uses the term to refer to *male control of the female labour force:*

> The material base upon which patriarchy rests lies most fundamentally in men's control over women's labour power. Men maintain this control by excluding women from access to essential productive resources (in capitalist societies for example, jobs that pay living wages) and by restricting women's sexuality.

However there are a variety of realist explanations. Firestone (1974) sees the material base of patriarchy as being men's *control of reproduction*, while Delphy (1984) places it in the *domestic mode of production,* that is, the ways in which the structure of the family means that women provide domestic services for husbands and children.

In contrast, social constructivists see patriarchal control as emanating from men's aggression and use of sexual power in rape, domestic violence and sexual harassment, all designed to keep women in their place. Men's superordinate position is maintained by an ideology which values men's 'natural' characteristics of aggression and competitiveness over those of women – cooperation and caring. Radical feminists see men as dominating and controlling women in their day-to-day *relationships*, whereas the realist feminists (Marxists, materialists and dual systems) see patriarchy as a *system* that dominates women.

The most developed analysis of patriarchy from a realist perspective is that of Sylvia Walby (1990: 20) who defines it as 'a system of social structures and practices in which men dominate, oppress and exploit women'. She indicates that it exists in six structures: paid work, domestic labour, sexuality, the state, violence and culture. She rejects the view of patriarchy as unchanging, and argues that the system is integrated with capitalism and is dynamic. In particular, she points to the move from private patriarchy in the nineteenth century, when women were controlled within the private sphere, to public patriarchy in the twentieth century, where women are controlled within paid employment and by the state. However, many feminists argue that even this more dynamic version of patriarchy is inadequate to take account of the complex power relationships between men and women and between women and women.

Influenced by Foucault, post-modernist feminists have replaced the idea of patriarchy, that is, top-down power, with an interest in analysing gendered power and the way in which power is embedded in everyday practices and relationships at every level of society. This involves exploring how 'discourses' create particular forms of control and surveillance. 'Discourses' are groups of statements (which can change over time) which provide a language for talking about, and representing knowledge or 'truth' about, a topic. Discourses exist as dominant ways of framing what we believe, and men and women use them in their day-to-day lives every time they think or talk about each other. As a result, gender relationships are routinely re-affirmed and re-constructed in a way that enables male power to be perpetuated.

Discourses of masculinity and femininity powerfully control and regulate female behaviour, for example controlling the lives of young women as they try to avoid being seen as a 'slag' or 'easy lay' (Halson 1991; Lees 1993). Young men are similarly controlled as they strive to become seen as 'real men' (Mac an Ghail 1994). The difficulty with this approach is that we are left with analysing local narratives of a particular context, such as young black women in school, and the view that if discourses are changed, men's domination of women will cease. It is possible, however, to recognise the importance of the deconstruction of women and men as categories and develop more adequate understandings of how different men and different women are placed within the dynamics of gender inequalities.

Thus, Holland et al. (1998) have argued that it is important to recognise that there are layers of power within which gender power is experienced and each layer must be analysed. They suggest that power is:

● Institutionalised and hierarchical
● Embedded in and represented in language, ideas, beliefs, norms, values and so on, for instance the belief that men are 'naturally better at science than girls'
● Embedded in and represented in agency and action; women's freedom to go out at night is curtailed by fear of rape and violent attack from men
● Embedded in 'embodied practices', that is, lived gender/how we do gender, also reproduces power relationships
● Historically specific and subject to change.

Holland et al. (1998: 11) argue that whilst individual men may lack power, Britain is still a male-dominated society but point out that this controls men as well as women:

Individual men may reject, resist or ignore the demands and constraints of dominant masculinity. Yet in their first sexual relationship, they and their partners continue to be aware of, and subject to, the exercise of its surveillance power articulated through the male peer group and the efficacy of sexual reputation and both young men and young women live by these rules or take the personal and social consequences of social transgressions.

Men, they suggest, have more access to power than women and are both oppressors and oppressed. Hegemonic masculinity controls men and there are powerful pressures on men to conform. Women do resist male power, for example by challenging male dominance, by resistance and by celebrating rather than conforming to male expectations of behaviour. However, their overall conclusion is summed up by the title of their book *The Male in the Head*. As Bartkey (1990: 72), says: 'in contemporary patriarchal culture, a pan-optical male connoisseur resides within the consciousness of most women; they stand perpetually before his gaze and under his judgement'.

Nevertheless, gender cannot be adequately represented solely as a single hierarchical division between men and women. As Lees (1993) points out, relationships between men and women and structured gender relationships are changing – they are not static, but gender remains as an important dimension of stratification. The structures of opportunities available to men and women remain unequal, but not fixed. Women do have 'agency' (self-determination and choice), but this agency is constrained by structures – unequal and controlled access to opportunities. There are also divisions between men and between women in their access to opportunity structures based on race, social class, age, sexuality and geographical location (as other chapters in this book show). The next section develops the ways in which young men negotiate their masculine identity in the face of changing labour market opportunities, which mean that 'real men's jobs' (Willis, 1977) no longer exist for the lads.

Gender and education

The educational process is central to an understanding of contemporary manifestations of gender. It is through the schooling process that identities are developed, and it is on the basis of educational outcomes that subsequent access to types of employment opportunities are determined. One might even argue that educational experience and qualifications are so important as to almost constitute a social division in their own right. Education therefore merits consideration in some detail.

Until recently, sociologists were mainly concerned with understanding why girls did not achieve as well as boys at school and in the education system more broadly. However, in the 1990s, the question was revised and the concern now is why young women are achieving *better* results than young, particularly working-class, men in public examinations. Indeed, there is a widespread concern about underachieving boys, which amounts to a 'moral panic'.

This is seen as one of the most disturbing problems facing the education system. Media headlines continue to express concern about girls outclassing boys, especially each summer when the results of public examinations are published. At meetings that I have attended at local education authorities, continued concern has been expressed about the underachievement of boys and how to develop strategies to reverse the increasing tendency for boys to become disaffected with schooling. However, whilst girls are outperforming boys, more boys than girls tend to score at the extremes, gaining either very good or very poor results in examinations. Sociologists are also aware that race (Chapter 4) and social class (Chapter 2) interact in complex ways with gender in terms of educational achievement.

The main changes that have taken place since the mid-1980s in the relative achievement of boys and girls come in the late secondary and post-compulsory school years. Up to the 1960s, girls outperformed boys in the primary and early secondary years, before boys caught up with and outperformed them in public examinations at 16+. Since the early 1980s, girls now also outperform boys in GCSE examinations at 16+ and A levels (and Highers in Scotland) at 18+ (see Table 3.1). In the same period, there has been a considerable improvement in the proportions of young men and women gaining educational qualifications. In 1983, 26 per cent of boys gained five or more GCSEs grade A-C. By 2002/03, this had risen to 47.9 per cent, while in the same period, girls' performance improved from 27 to 58.2 per cent.

Similarly, the proportion of young people passing A levels has increased dramatically since the mid-1980s, with girls' performance improving at a faster rate than boys. In 1983/4, more boys than girls achieved three or more A level passes; 11 per cent compared to 9.5 per cent. By 2002/03, 34 per cent of boys were gaining two or more passes, but 43 per cent of girls. There are also differences in the subjects that boys and girls choose to study after the age of 16 when it becomes possible for students to decide which subjects they will

Table 3.1 Examination results of pupils in UK schools by gender (2002–03)

Two or more A levels[1]		Five or more GCSEs[2] Grade A* to C		No graded GCSEs	
Males	Females	Males	Females	Males	Females
34	43	47.9	58.2	6.3	4.1

Notes

1 Pupils aged 17–19 at end of school year in England, Wales and Northern Ireland as percentage of 18-year-old population. For Scotland, figures relate to pupils in years S5/S6 gaining three or more SCE Higher passes as a percentage of the 17-year-old population.

2 Pupils aged 16 at end of school year as percentage of 15-year-old population at start of school year. Scottish pupils are in year S4.

Source: ONS (2004e).

specialise in. Boys' subjects are computer studies, mathematics, physics and economics, while girls' subjects are humanities, arts, social studies and languages, as Table 3.2 shows. This broad pattern of girls specialising in arts subjects and boys in science and technology is even more marked in the choice of higher education (Abbott et al. 2005). However, what are seen as appropriate subjects for one gender or the other can change over time. Until comparatively recently, chemistry and medicine were seen as boys' subjects, whereas now, in terms of the proportion of girls and boys choosing to study them, they are gender-neutral.

It is often assumed that subject choice is determined by the natural differences in the academic ability of boys and girls, with boys being better at mathematics, science and engineering than girls. There is no marked difference in performance between boys and girls in the primary and early secondary stages, except for English where girls markedly outperform boys (see Table 3.3). Subsequently, girls who choose to take boys' subjects do as well as boys. In the past, boys outperformed girls in science and mathematics at 16+ examinations and A level, but in the 1990s, girls achieved the same level of performance as boys in these subjects (ONS 1999, 2004e).

At university, proportionately more women than men complete their undergraduate programme and are awarded a degree. However, more men get first class and third class degrees than women, and more men than women go on to study for higher degrees by research, but roughly the same numbers take postgraduate taught degrees. Twice as many women as men study for a postgraduate teaching qualification.

Table 3.2 Girls' and boys' subjects

Girls' subjects		Boys' subjects		Not gendered	
A level[1]	Degree[2]	A level	Degree	A level	Degree
Biological sciences	Biosciences	ICT		Geography	Medicine Dentistry
Psychology	Social, economic and political sciences	Computer studies	Computer science	History	Agriculture
Communication studies	Library and information sciences	Maths	Maths	Business studies	Business and admin
Media, film and TV	Subjects allied to medicine	Physics	Physical sciences	Chemistry	Humanities
Home economics		Economics			Creative art and design
Foreign languages	Languages		Architecture, building and planning		
English and English literature	Education Teacher training		Engineering technology		

Notes
1 Calculated from A level entries in 2002–03.
2 Calculated from numbers studying for a first degree in 2003.

Source: ONS website, HESA website.

Further education and vocational training is also gendered. Young women tend to study social sciences, subjects aligned to medicine or the creative arts. Women's subjects in further education are hairdressing, secretarial studies and health and social care. Men are more likely to study mathematics, agriculture, engineering and technology. The proportion of young women and young men participating in youth vocational training is roughly the same. However, young men are more likely to be working towards a higher level qualification and be paid a wage, while young women are more likely to be on youth training because they could not find a job or gain a college course of their choice. A slightly higher proportion of Advanced Modern Apprenticeships are held by men (58.6 per cent). Conversely, women hold 53 per cent of Foundation Modern Apprenticeships. Modern apprenticeships are also gendered, with nearly 100 per cent of apprenticeships in the motor industry, construction and electrical installation engineering going to young men.

Table 3.3 Pupils reaching or exceeding expected standards (%) (2003)

		Boys	Girls
Key stage 1	Mathematics	89	91
Key stage 2	English	70	80
	Mathematics	73	72
	Science	86	87
Key stage 3	English	61	75
	Mathematics	69	72
	Science	68	68

Source: ONS (2004e) Table 3.6.

Young women predominate in hairdressing and business administration, while there is a rough gender balance in retailing and hotels and catering (Table 3.4).

Given that the changes in the relative performance of boys and girls in the education system are recent, sociological explanations are only just beginning to be developed and empirical evidence is limited. Researchers have pointed to two key questions: why are boys underachieving in the education system and why has the performance of girls improved so dramatically in the last 20 years? Those who focus on the former question tend to assume that boys are disadvantaged in the education system – that schools are failing boys. They argue that schools are not 'boy-friendly' and need to become so. In other words, it is suggested that in meeting the earlier criticisms that schools were not 'girl-friendly', the changes have gone too far and it is now boys who are disadvantaged. One example cited is the move towards coursework for public examinations, which is said to favour girls; another is the feminisation of teaching, with a majority of primary and secondary schoolteachers being female and the consequent lack of role models for boys – although the majority of secondary school heads are male as are academics in higher education.

However, concern about the underachievement of boys and young men at school is not new. Cohen (1998) traces commentary on the poor performance of boys back as far as worries expressed in John Lockes' treatise *Some Thoughts Concerning Education* ([1693]1989). The Taunton Commission (1868) also found that girls outperformed boys in reading, spelling, geography and history; in arithmetic, algebra and Euclid, girls did better than boys when they had been prepared for the same examinations. Cohen (1998) also quotes a government report of 1923 which expressed concern about girls outperforming boys

(*The Teaching of English*, Board of Education). She points out that boys' under-achievement is explained by factors external to them, for example the education system, whereas their success is seen to be intrinsic – high ability is seen as natural for boys. Conversely, girls' success is explained by extrinsic factors, or low status internal characteristics such as neatness and conformity. Failure in girls is seen as natural – girls are seen as 'naturally less able' than boys.

Table 3.4 Modern apprenticeships by gender and sector (2002–03)

Sector	Women		Men	
	AMA[1] %	FMA[2] %	AMA %	FMA %
Accountancy	63.1	63.6	36.9	36.4
Business	81.1	76.1	18.9	23.9
Call handling	66.0	68.6	34.0	31.4
Construction	1.9	0.7	98.1	99.3
Customer service	68.4	67.9	31.6	32.1
Early years care and education	97.5	97.0	2.5	3.0
Electrotechnical engineering	0.4	1.0	99.6	99.0
Hairdressing	92.8	92.3	7.2	7.7
Health and social care	87.7	90.0	12.3	10.0
Hospitality	49.0	52.1	51.0	47.9
IT and electronic services	13.2	17.2	86.8	82.8
Management	61.7	50.0	38.3	50.0
Motor industry	1.4	1.4	98.6	98.6
Plumbing	0.6	0.7	99.4	99.3
Retail	64.2	67.4	35.8	32.6
Sport and recreation	39.7	37.1	60.3	62.9
Telecommunications	16.1	26.8	83.9	73.2
Travel services	89.9	82.5	10.1	17.5
All[3]	41.4	53.0	58.6	47.0

Notes
1 AMA = Advanced Modern Apprenticeship.
2 FMA = Foundation Modern Apprenticeship.
3 Includes those not shown separately.

Source: Equal Opportunities Commission (2004).

Those who focus on the second question, why has girls' performance improved, tend to assume that in the past schools failed girls and they under-achieved, whilst now girls' achievement is more in line with their potential. They point out that in the 1950s and 60s, the pass grade for the 11+ was set higher for girls than for boys (to ensure that more of the slower developing boys were able to pass), so that it was more difficult for girls to gain selective grammar school places. The move to comprehensive secondary schooling has removed this barrier. They see no evidence that schools themselves have become more girl-friendly. Indeed, they argue that while there has been some reduction in the bias against girls, girls are still at a disadvantage in schools. For example, in terms of teaching, 48 per cent of secondary schoolteachers are male and the majority of senior posts are held by men (ONS 1999: 50).

Indeed, some researchers have argued that schools in fact continue to be boy-friendly, in that boys continue to dominate the classroom and teachers do little to challenge this (Skelton 1993; Jackson and Salisbury 1996). Lees (1993) argues that mixed comprehensive education has increased sexism in schools and teachers rarely challenge the sexual harassment that girls experience. There is evidence that teachers continue to believe, or at least work on the assumption, that boys are more academically able than girls. Textbooks and other teaching material continue to divide men and women into stereotypical sex roles. It follows that explanations for the rapid improvement in the educational performance of girls in public examinations, and the slower rate of boys, must be sought in factors outside the school, for example the decline in manual jobs for boys and the increasing labour market opportunities for women. In other words, we should ask why girls do as well as they do in the education system, given that girls still underestimate, and have less confidence in, their ability compared with boys, get less teacher time and have to tolerate the disruptive behaviour of boys in the classroom?

Among answers to this question are several based on notions of the masculine role. On the one hand, teaching staff are more tolerant of disruptive behaviour, poor performance and lack of effort by boys than girls. Because more boys are disruptive in the classroom than girls, they lose more time and are more likely than girls to be permanently excluded from school. On the other hand, parents control their sons less than their daughters, meaning that boys are less likely to do homework. Furthermore, boys think that they can 'muck around' in the early years in secondary school and catch up later but they fail to do so. This is especially the case in their inability to catch up with and complete coursework for GCSEs (Abbott et al. 2005).

It is also important to ask the question, which boys underachieve and, indeed, which girls do well? There is considerable overlap in the performance of boys and girls in school. Whilst many boys underachieve at school, many others do very well. Underachievement of boys is a strongly classed and racial phenomena (see Table 2.5 and Chapter 4). For young men and women, social class is the major determinant of success (or otherwise) in school examina-tions. While there are differences between schools in their examination results, the best predictor of a state school's position in a league table is the LEA's position on the index of deprivation (DETR 1998).

The decline in masculine jobs, as contemporary society moves ever more to an economy based on the services sector, means that working-class young men, living in areas of high unemployment with no tradition of education, see few prospects for their future. This results in what is known as the 'new lad' culture, an alternative culture, in which 'lads' attempt to construct a positive self-image and draw attention to themselves by laddish behaviour and aggres-sive macho posturing. For many the instrumental orientation to school, a limited compliance in order to get a job, no longer holds. In many deprived estates, especially in the north of England, the response to lack of opportunity has been a rejection of schooling.

Indeed, the concern about boys' underachievement is closely related to the concern about the high levels of unemployment amongst low-achieving males in areas of industrial decline. It is not that these young men are achieving less well at school than their fathers did, but that the unskilled and semi-skilled jobs that their fathers took when leaving school no longer exist. To the extent that there are employment opportunities in these areas, they require credentials that these young men have failed to acquire, or are seen as cissy jobs – not jobs for real men. Rather than making the transition to 'adult man' in terms of full-time paid employment, marriage and fatherhood, they are said to become dependent on welfare benefits and 'fiddly' jobs (cash in hand employment taken whilst registered as unemployed). The restructuring of the labour market means that there are more jobs available for educationally low-achieving young women, who also have the 'option' of becoming lone mothers. When concern is expressed about teenage lone mothers, the pathway to this status is rarely directly related in public debates to underachievement in education.

Given all the arguments for why boys underachieve, it is important to remember that boys' performance has actually *improved* in recent years. After all, while *some* boys may be underachieving, overall their levels of education and achievement have markedly improved in the last 20 years, even if girls have improved their performance at a faster rate than boys. It is this improve-ment in girls' performance that needs to be explained. One explanation is that the gap between the educational achievement of working-class and middle-class boys has widened, while the gap in performance between girls of different socio-economic backgrounds has not. The reason for this is that the women's movement has widened the aspirations of young women in general, so that the majority now expect to have paid work as well as being wives and mothers. There are more employment opportunities for girls than in the past and many occupations that girls from all backgrounds aspire to require post-16 educational credentials at least equivalent to A levels and often higher education ones. Nursing, for example, is now a graduate profession and administrative and clerical positions often require higher educational credentials. The occupations that boys from manual backgrounds often aspire to such as skilled and craft occupations do not require the same level of educational credentials. Beyond this, girls are more controlled by their parents and consequently do homework and complete coursework.

Furthermore, it is important to recognise that not all girls conform to the demands of the school system or succeed in it. In the same ways that schooling is an important element in boys learning appropriate masculinity, so the majority of girls take on an appropriate feminine identity. School is centrally important to the process by which girls take on a complex identity that is feminised, racialised and located within a class system. Lees (1993) has suggested four strategies that girls adopt in secondary school:

1. The *pro-school, academic* orientation of white girls from middle-class backgrounds who aspire to academic success and an occupational career.
2. The *anti-school, pro-work* orientation typical of some African-Caribbean girls who reject the racist attitudes of the school system, but are nevertheless committed to academic success and an occupational career.
3. The *pro-school, anti-work* orientation of some working-class girls who reject the discipline and academic elements of school, but see school as a place to have contact with friends.
4. The *anti-school, anti-work* orientation of some working-class girls who want to leave school at the earliest opportunity and see their future major role as wife and mother.

Girls' orientations are crucially mediated by class and race, which informs their expectations for their future careers. While most young women expect to combine motherhood and marriage with paid employment, it is only academic girls, mainly from middle-class backgrounds, and some African-Caribbean girls, who expect careers. Mirza (1992) found that African-Caribbean girls anticipated a career, but that Irish girls saw their future as home-makers, child carers and part-time workers. Working-class girls anticipate having part-time employment that fits in with their domestic responsibilities. As we shall see, schoolgirls' anticipations of 'work' are often misplaced.

Gender, 'work' and domestic labour

One of the major contributions of feminist sociology in the area of work was to redefine the term. In malestream sociology, work was used to mean paid employment, with priority given to full-time, lifelong employment and the (male) breadwinner role. Feminists have challenged this, pointing to both the domestic labour and emotional work that women undertake, saying that this is real work. Glucksman (1995: 68) has indicated that work refers to all 'activity necessary for the production and reproduction of economic structures irrespective of how and when it is carried out'. By opening up the black box of the family, feminists have been able to demonstrate not only the persistence of the gendered inequality of power in the private sphere, but also the long hours of unpaid work that women undertake in the home, doing the bulk of caring for the household, children and other dependent relatives, in addition to their paid employment – working the 'double shift'.

In looking at gender and work globally, Seager (1997) indicates that time diaries show that both men and women do more total work than conventional measures suggest, but that while most of men's work is paid, most of women's is not. Women and girls have the major responsibility for domestic labour. She concludes that not only do women work more than men, but they also perform a greater variety of tasks and have less rest. Similarly, in Britain, women do more unpaid work than men, and while men do more paid work than women, they also have more leisure time than women (ONS 2004e). In 1995, the monetary value of unpaid work in Britain was estimated to be between £341 and £739 billion. The lower value was more than the value of the UK manufacturing sector and the higher value was equivalent to 120 per cent of the GDP (Murgatroyd and Neuburger 1997).

When men become unemployed, some take on more responsibility for domestic labour, but most tasks remained gendered – cooking the main meal and thorough cleaning remain exclusively female tasks, while washing the clothes and ironing are done predominantly by women, as is shopping and handling the household budget. The predominant male tasks are mowing the lawn, doing household repairs and taking out the rubbish. The British Social Attitude Survey (Park et al. 2002) found that women were more likely to claim the main responsibility for tasks than men, who were likely to describe tasks as shared with their partners. Even allowing for this, the only domestic task done mainly by men (80 per cent men/65 per cent women) in households headed by a married or cohabiting couple was making small repairs about the home. The only other task not seen as mainly the responsibility of women was shopping for groceries, where nearly half of men and women indicated that it was a shared task although nearly half the women said they were mainly responsible (49 per cent). Women were mainly responsible for doing the laundry (75/81), looking after sick family members (46/62), household cleaning (55/65) and preparing meals (55/62). Less than ten per cent of men said they were mainly responsible for any task except household repairs (ONS 2004e). As Delphy and Leonard (1992) point out, men do household work, but few are obliged to do family work.

Women continue to take the major responsibility for child care and looking after children, especially young children. Fathers do, however, take on some responsibility for child care. Half the men interviewed in a survey in the UK in the early 1990s said that they would take on more responsibility for child care if they had the time. Clift and Fielding (1991) found that the nearer the wife's earnings were to a breadwinner's, the more equally domestic labour and child care were shared. Women expect, and are generally expected, to take time out of the labour market when they have children (or considerably to reduce the hours of paid work they undertake) and, as their children grow older, to take paid employment that fits in with child care responsibilities.

In Sweden, where both part-time paid work and child care leave are equally available to wives and husbands, mothers are much more likely to take leave and/or part-time employment (Dryler 1998). Women are still seen primarily in their roles as wives and mothers and domestic responsibilities are expected to be given priority. The Eurobarometer survey (1997) found that 60 per cent of women but only 30 per cent of men said that they were prepared to give up their job to look after children, and about 55 per cent of women (and 30 per cent of men) said that they would be prepared to give up paid employment to look after a dependent relative.

Despite married women's increased participation in employment, there is little evidence that men have taken on significantly more responsibility for domestic labour and child care. The traditional domestic bargain – that women take on responsibility for child care and domestic labour and men the breadwinner role – is still the predominant ideal, even if not every family is able to live up to this. Women continue to be seen not only as the main performers of domestic labour, but the ones mainly responsible for ensuring that it is carried out. This means that women are trapped in a cycle of dependency – they are not expected to be a breadwinner and are often not trained for an occupation that provides a breadwinner's wage. Taking time out of the labour market to have children further reduces a woman's economic potential and her opportunities for career advancement and promotion. Women continue to be dependent on men for part of their livelihood. As Joshi (1990: 52) notes:

> The traditional domestic bargain does not work to the advantage of all women. It involves loss of earnings, future earning potential and pension rights. It can involve social obligations, loss of autonomy and self and social esteem and, perhaps most importantly, loss of security.

Gender and the labour market

Despite the 'traditional domestic bargain', there has been a steady increase in women's participation in the labour market in Britain especially since the Second World War. The most dramatic increase has been in married women in paid, especially part-time, employment outside the home. The majority of women (including married women) are in paid employment for the majority of years that they are of employment age. The time that married women take out of employment for child care has also reduced significantly. The employment pattern for women in Britain was, until the 1980s, an inverted M-shaped curve, rising as more women came onto the labour market in their late teens and then falling as the vast majority of married women took a break from paid employment whilst they had young children. The curve then rose again, as they returned to work when their children became more independent, before dipping again as women withdrew from the labour market as they neared 60 years. Now it is more of an 'inverted U', the same as for men – the majority of women, including those who have children, do not take a break from paid employment (Abbott and Ackers 1997). The male–female activity gap halved between 1984 and 2003 – from 22 percentage points to 11.

At the same time that the participation rate for women in the labour market (albeit mainly in part-time jobs) has been going up, it has been declining for men. In 2003, 71.2 per cent of men were economically active compared to 55.6 per cent of women. The comparable figurers for 1988 are 75.7 per cent for men and 52.2 per cent for women (Table 3.5). In 1971, for example, just over half of women aged 25–44 years, the period during which women are most likely to take a break, were economically active (in paid employment or seeking work); by 2003, over three-quarters of women in this age group were economically active. In comparison, 98 per cent of men aged 45–54 years were economically active in 1971, but by 2003, this had fallen to 92 per cent. This is partly because of an increase in men, especially in their fifties and sixties, on long-term sick leave, taking early retirement or being made redundant and unable to gain further employment and partly because of the increase in female employment. It is predicted that the gender gap in economic activity will continue to narrow. The economic activity rate for women may indeed underestimate their rate because it does not take undeclared homework into account.

Table 3.5 UK economic activity by employment status and gender (1988 and 2003)

	1988		2003	
	Males %	Females %	Males %	Females %
Full-time employees	53.3	25.1	50.9	27.6
Part-time employees	2.8	18.6	5.3	21.0
Self-employed	9.8	3.5	10.6	3.7
Others in employment[1]	1.4	0.9	0.4	0.4
All in employment	68.7	48.1	67.3	53.1
Unemployed[2]	7.0	4.3	4.0	2.5
All economically active	75.7	52.2	71.2	55.6
Economically inactive	24.3	47.8	28.8	46.4
Population	21,400,000	23,200,000	22,600,000	24,300,000

Notes

1 On government training scheme and, in 2003, unpaid family workers.

2 Based on ILO definition, that is, those 16 years and over who are without a job, or available to start work in the next two weeks, who have been seeking work in the last four weeks or are intending to start a job.

Source: ONS (1999), Table 4.2.

The reasons for non-employment also vary by gender. The main reason in 2003 for women being economically inactive was that they were engaged in non-remunerated work; 45 per cent looking after a family or home. The main reasons for men were that they were in full-time education or training (28 per cent), or that they were long-term sick (38 per cent). Only 6 per cent of men were looking after a family or home (ONS 2004e). Non-employment is of course also connected to other factors, such as level of qualification, disability and ethnicity. However, even here, gender interacts with other social divisions. Thus differences in unemployment rates among women from different ethnic groups and women with different levels of educational qualifications are also marked (see Chapter 4; Abbott and Tyler 1995; Iganski and Payne 1996; Iganski et al. 2001).

The majority of married women, even those with young children, are economically active: in 2003, 60 per cent of married or cohabiting women whose youngest child was under five years and 82 per cent of those whose youngest child was 11–15 years were in or seeking paid work. This compares with 77 per cent of married or cohabiting women who had no children – this latter group will include women in their fifties who have taken early retirement (ONS 2004e: Table 4.5). However, the majority of employed married or cohabiting mothers work part time – although the proportion of those in full-time employment increases as the youngest child gets older, from just over one-third for those whose youngest child was under five years old, to just under half for those whose youngest child is 11–15 years old. Married or cohabiting women with no children are twice as likely to be in full-time as part-time employment (52 per cent compared with 25 per cent).

Lone mothers are also more likely to be employed as their children grow older, 28 per cent of those with children under five are economically active, compared with 72 per cent of those whose youngest child is aged 11–15 years. The proportion working full time also increases as children get older – from less than a third of those in employment with children under five years to a marginally higher proportion working full time for those whose youngest child is age 11–15 years (35 per cent working full time and 32 per cent part time). Single, divorced and widowed women with no children are much more likely to work full time than part time, 46 per cent compared with 21 per cent. In contrast, being married or having a child has no impact whatsoever on men's labour market activity (Abbott and Ackers 1997).

Gender also affects the kind of paid employment available, with women more likely than men to be in non-manual occupations. However, as Table 3.6 shows, men are more likely to be employed in the more 'desirable' (higher status and higher remuneration) occupations as managers and professionals, and women are more likely to be in lower paid and less attractive routine, non-manual work and caring professions (Abbott et al. 2005). Similarly, within the manual category, men are more likely to be categorised in skilled occupations than women. Despite over 20 years of equal opportunities legislation, there is still clear evidence that the 'glass ceiling' (a barrier to women's upward mobility into the higher level positions) and the 'glass wall' (a barrier to women entering occupations defined as male) still act as barriers (Payne and Abbott 1990).

We have seen that the choices that young men and young women make, about which subjects to study in formal education (especially post-16 years) and the training schemes that they enter, remain gender stereotyped. Education influence the job choices that are made on leaving formal education, despite the changes in the relative educational success of young men and women. Occupations are still heavily gendered, especially manual occupations in the declining industrial sectors of manufacturing. In 2003, 20 per cent of men were employed in manufacturing, compared with 7 per cent of women; in construction, the figures were 8 per cent of men, compared with 1 per cent of women. Women were mainly employed in 'other services' (42 per cent of all employed women compared with 20 per cent of employed men) and distribution, hotel, catering and repairs (26 per cent of all employed women, compared with 22 per cent of employed men) (ONS 2004a: Table 4.13).

**Table 3.6 UK employment by occupation – employees
and self-employed aged 16 years and over (2003)**

Occupational Group	% FT female	% PT female	% FT male	% PT male	% women in occupation FT	% women in occupation PT
Managers and senior officials	15.1	4.2	19.8	5.8	29.0	72.2
Professional	9.7	7.2	13.5	11.2	34.9	70.1
Associate professionals and technical	17.2	10.4	13.9	9.5	40.0	79.8
Administrative and secretarial	23.8	20.7	4.7	5.5	73.0	93.2
Skilled trades	2.1	1.9	20.6	8.9	5.1	4.3
Personal services	12.0	15.4	1.9	5.1	77.4	92.0
Sales and customer services	7.2	18.6	3.0	16.5	56.4	80.0
Elementary	5.6	20.0	9.7	28.9	23.5	71.5
Process, plant and machine operatives	3.4	1.7	12.9	8.5	12.3	42.3
All occupations[1] thousands	6,932	5,492	12,966	1,511	34.8	78.4

Note
1 Includes those not stating an occupation.

Source: Equal Opportunities Commission (2004).

The largest employment category for women remains clerical and secretarial work, although the percentage of women employed doing this kind of work has declined slightly from 29 per cent in 1991, to 24 per cent in 2003. The single biggest employment category for men remains skilled trades, with 21 per cent of men engaged in this category. Employers clearly have a view of what is appropriate work for women and women generally share this view (Chaney 1981; Yeandle 1984; Beechy and Perkins 1986). Many 'female' occupations, clearly regarded as using the 'natural abilities' women are seen to require, are in the private sphere: caring for young children, nursing, preparing and serving food and in general securing the needs of others – 'emotional labour'. Thus, there is continuing evidence that women find it difficult to obtain employment in traditional male occupations and that men continue to be reluctant to move into traditional female ones (Table 3.7).

Table 3.7 Occupational segregation – selected occupations (2003)

Female occupations	% women	Male occupations	% women	Neutral occupations	% women
Sales assistants	73	Taxi driver	8	Solicitors, lawyers, judges and coroners	42
Waiters and waitresses	73	Security guard	12	Shelf fillers	48
Cleaners and domestics	79	Software professional	14	Chefs and cooks	49
Retail cashiers and checkout operators	82	ICT manager	16	Secondary teachers	55
General office assistants and clerks	83	Police officer – constables and sergeants	22		
Primary and nursery teachers	86	Marketing and sales managers	25		
Care assistants and home carers	88	IT technicians	32		
Hairdressers and barbers	89	Medical practitioners	39		
Nurses	89				
Receptionists	96				

Source: Equal Opportunities Commission (2004).

There is evidence, for example, that it is still virtually impossible for young women to get training places in the traditional male craft and related occupations, while those who do succeed then experience discrimination and sexual harassment. In terms of entry to middle management, women are less likely to be promoted than men, and those who are, are often promoted to positions that do not give them the necessary experiences to be seen as promotable to the next positions up. Examples include women police officers being promoted within the Domestic Violence Unit, women managers in the NHS running health centres, rather than positions in the central NHS administration, and female teachers promoted to pastoral posts, rather than the management of resources (Abbott et al. 2005). Savage (1992) found that female bank managers were generally employed in specialist units where they used specific expertise and were rarely promoted to managerial jobs involving the exercise of client control and/or authority. In her study of women engineers, Devine (1992b) found that they were promoted to managerial positions where they managed women, rather than men. Women who are promoted to these middle-level managerial posts are often unable to gain the experiences seen as necessary for further promotion.

In addition, men are often seen to have the skills and competence necessary for senior managerial positions, whereas women are perceived to have the characteristics necessary for the caring roles. There is some evidence that women may choose these types of positions where specific expertise dominate because they enable them to cope with the conflicting demands of family life and 'organisation' woman (Evetts 1994). Crompton and Le Feuvre (1996) found female pharmacists in jobs in which expertise or professional technique were predominant, as this was more flexible than those in which the exercise of organisational power was the main function.

There is also clear evidence that the glass ceiling remains, albeit some cracks may be beginning to appear. It is true that there are now more female head teachers, vice chancellors, women professors and managers, but they still remain in the minority in the first decade of the twenty-first century. Only 12 per cent of vice chancellors are female, 9 per cent of national newspaper editors, 7 per cent of senior police officers, 1 per cent of senior officers in the armed forces, 14 per cent of chief executives of national sporting bodies, 21 per cent of directors of museums and galleries and 18 per cent of MPs. There are no female Lords of Appeal, only 6 per cent of High Court judges are female and in total only 15 per cent of judicial appointments were female in 2003 (EOC 2004). The private sector is no better, with only 5 per cent of directorships held by women and four out of five firms having no female directors (Chapter 7).

The glass ceiling exists at a number of different levels, not just as a barrier to women entering top jobs. Organisations are dominated by masculinities, and femininities are subordinated. There is a denial of emotional life in organisations (Pringle 1988). Women often feel uncomfortable in the masculine environment and sexual harassment is one way in which men subordinate and control women in the workplace. It is one of the tactics used by men in restricting and resisting moves towards sexual equality in organisations (Cockburn 1990).

Despite the implementation of the 1970 Equal Pay Act, in 1975 women still earned less than men. The gender pay gap in 2003, for example, between male full-time and female part-time workers was 41 per cent, a figure that has barely changed since 1975 (EOC 2003). The gap between men and women's pay increases with age, and this is partly because men's average pay does not peak until they are in their fifties, whereas pay for women peaks in their thirties. Younger women are better qualified than older ones, which is part of the explanation for this. Differences in pay are partly accounted for by differences in labour market positions and partly by hours worked but there is a gender pay gap at every qualification level. The gender pay gap in hourly earnings is 18 per cent but 25 per cent in weekly earnings. This is because on average women engage in paid employment for fewer hours a week than men – the majority of women work less than 45 hours a week and over 40 per cent work less than 31 hours, whereas nearly a third of men work over 45 hours a week and only 10 per cent work less than 31 hours (ONS 2004a: Table 4.17). Even when women are in full-time employment, they work, on average, for fewer hours than men – 40.7 hours compared with 45.8 hours a week. This is partly because men are more likely to work overtime than women, and partly because of differences in basic hours of work in predominantly male and female occupations.

There is, however, clear evidence that even when they are in similar jobs, women earn less than men – the 'gender premium'. A recent survey of the earnings of lecturers in higher education, for example, found that the gender pay gap was much the same as the national average figure (see also EOC 2003). Thus, despite formal access to employment in Britain for women since the Second World War, the Equal Pay Act 1970 and the Equal Opportunities Act 1975, women have not achieved equality with men in the labour market.

The labour market remains vertically and horizontally segregated, with women occupying the lower strata, less well-paid levels within all strata and concentrated in particular industrial sectors. Women are less likely to be promoted than men and are concentrated in jobs that have fewer opportunities for career progression than men. Even in female professions such as social work, nursing and primary schoolteaching, men are proportionately more likely to be promoted than women. Routine non-manual, service and manual occupations are more clearly and specifically gendered than professional and managerial ones.

As with professional and managerial occupations, the movement of women into an area of employment tends to result in a decline in its status and relative remuneration. This process is clearly evident in the history of clerical work. It is not self-evident, however, that any less skill is involved now than was the case in the past, even if the skills required may be different, which contrasts with the ways in which male printers have retained their high status and remuneration with the move from typesetting to computers.

Explanations of women's labour market participation

Feminist sociologists argue that the major factor explaining the segregated labour market is structural (Crompton and Le Feuvre 1996). However, Hakim 1991, 1995) has argued that in exploring their patterns of labour market participation, insufficient account has been taken of women's orienta-tion to paid employment and work commitment. She argues that there are three main groups of women:

1. The *home-centred* – 15–30 per cent of women who prefer not to work and whose main priority is children and family.
2. The *adapters* – 40–80 per cent of women who are a diverse group including women who want to combine work and family and those who want to have paid employment, but are not committed to a career.
3. The *work-centred* – 10–30 per cent of women who are mainly childless and whose main priority is paid employment.

Hakim suggests that there are also two extreme groups of women, those who are childless from choice and those who see motherhood and domesticity as their destiny. Professional managerial women are, Hakim argues, a minority who cannot provide the basis for a general theory of women's employment choices. She develops what she calls 'preference theory', arguing that women can now choose whether to have an employment career or not. She argues that the majority of women who combine domesticity with employment ('the uncommitted') seek part-time work even when it is concentrated in the lower grades and is less well paid than other work. Contrary to feminist sociologists who have argued that women's employment patterns are the outcome of struc-tural factors and the exclusionary tactics used by men, Hakim argues that women positively choose low-paid, low-status, part-time work that fits in with their domestic and familial roles, which they themselves see as the priority. Tam (1997) found that female part-time employees are generally satisfied with their employment, although younger and well-qualified ones are less so.

However, Crompton and Le Feuvre (1996), arguing on the basis of their study of women in banking and pharmacy employment in both Britain and France, conclude that there is little empirical evidence to support the view that there are different categories of women as far as work commitment is concerned. They suggest that there is no evidence, even when these profes-sional women work part time, to suggest that they are not committed to their paid employment. Martin and Roberts (1984) provided some information on women's attitude to work. They did find that social and domestic circum-stances had a considerable influence on the way women thought about it. Some, for example, found it difficult to cope with paid work and domestic responsibilities. However, the type of work and employment situations also affected women's orientations to work. Contrary to popular opinion, they found that the majority of women, including married women, were highly dependent financially on their wages from work and the majority of women were fully committed to work but this varied over the life cycle. The most highly committed were childless women older than 30 years (see also McRae 2003a, b; Hakim 2003).

Further support for this argument is provided by the findings from a study of 1182 part-time female workers in Australia (Walsh 1999). Walsh argues that female part-time workers are not homogeneous in terms of their characteristics or orientations and there were a variety of reasons for women working part time. Whilst a majority of women in her sample were content with their current situations, a substantial majority wanted to return to full-time work in the future. She questions Hakim's view that a majority of female employees are not committed to a career and suggests that female employees' commitment to the labour market varied over the life-course. Women are expected, however, to cope with the 'double shift' and this influences their ability to demonstrate total loyalty to the job in the way in which men can. They have to juggle their responsibilities to their families and their employers in ways that men rarely have to do. Furthermore, working in paid employment part time does not prove a lack of commitment to that employment or to a career.

In order to understand women's position in the labour market, and their experiences of paid employment, we need to understand the ways in which patriarchy and capitalism work together to subordinate and exploit women. The essence of patriarchy is that women should be subordinated to and serve the needs of men, including their sexual needs, whereas capitalism as an economic system can only function with a flexible, cheap labour force. It is in the interest of patriarchal relations to keep women in the domestic sphere and in capitalism's to employ them in the labour force. In terms of employment, this has meant a move from strategies designed to exclude women from paid employment to segregationalist and subordinating strategies. Women's participation in the labour force and the way the labour market is segmented into jobs for women and jobs for men are not only driven by the economic forces of supply and demand for labour. They are also driven by family and sexual ideologies. The search for profit in the capitalist system of production is not incompatible with the power of men to exploit women and define skills (Phillips and Taylor 1980; Walby 1986).

The relationship between capitalism and patriarchy is a dynamic and changing one and it impacts differently on different groups of women. In the nineteenth century, it was mainly middle-class women who were excluded from paid employment, whilst in the early twenty-first century, African-Caribbean women are most likely to experience public patriarchy and British Muslim women private patriarchy (see also Chapter 4). Patriarchy and capitalism have competing interests but reach accommodation. Thus men (as husbands) clearly benefit from the additional income generated by their wives' paid employment – especially as research suggests that women retain the major responsibility for child care and domestic labour. Conversely, employers have been able to create jobs that use the assumed 'natural' skills of women, justifying the low wages they are paid. Men benefit from the servicing and emotional labour that women provide in the public sphere as well as enjoying and controlling women's sexuality, where employers are able to sell goods and services by exploiting women's sexuality and potentially disruptive men are controlled by women's sexualised servicing, as, for example, in the case of the female flight attendant.

Finally, it is essential to remember that women choose to combine their commitments to both unremunerated (and often undervalued work) with paid employment. The choices they make, and their orientation to both, are the outcome of the socially constructed expectations of women's roles and women's responsibilities. For example, highly qualified women in managerial and professional occupations can pay for quality child care and domestic help and avoid the criticisms often directed at working mothers or wives of neglecting their children and husbands.

Gender, poverty and the family

The (assumed) social and economic dependency of women on men means that women are more vulnerable to poverty than men (for an extended discussion, see Chapter 12). In couple households, men's income accounted for two-thirds of total family income. In her work on money management in marriage, Pahl (1983) found that joint or male management of finances was the norm in households with average and above-average incomes but in low-income households, women were expected to manage the household's resources. Pahl (1985) and Graham (1987) found that household resources are not necessarily shared and that some women in households with average and above-average incomes have little or no access to these resources.

Indeed, in the last 25 years, sociologists have pointed to the feminisation of poverty, although women have always been more vulnerable than men. Twenty-five per cent of the female population live in households with incomes below 60 per cent of the median income compared with 22 per cent of men, but it is women who usually bear the brunt of poverty when they live in poor households, being the ones 'to do without', and having to manage the scarce financial resources. Middleton et al. (1997) have pointed to the sacrifices that many mothers make, 'often' or 'sometimes' going without clothes and shoes, holidays and entertainment in order to provide things for their children. Lone mothers on income support are more likely than other mothers to go without each item and go without more of the items. These mothers are 14 times more likely to go without food than mothers in two-parent families not on income support. Glendinning and Miller (1992: 60) have suggested that:

> women bear the burden of managing poverty on a day to day basis whether they live alone or with a partner, on benefits or low earnings, it is usually women who are responsible for making ends meet and for managing the debts which result when they don't ... As more women and men lose their jobs, as benefits are cut or decline in value, women are increasingly caught in a daily struggle to feed and clothe their families ... usually at considerable personal sacrifice.

Women are also more likely than men to feel poor, to be on income support and lack two or more socially perceived necessities (EOC 2003). Women's vulnerability to poverty is the outcome of their restricted roles in the private sphere and the weak position they hold in the labour market. Women earn less than men (as we have seen above), have breaks in employment to care for children and elderly relatives and not only live, on average, longer than men but also, given the tendency of women to marry men older themselves, outlive their partners. Women are especially vulnerable to experiencing poverty when they are caring for children and in old age. The groups of women most vulnerable to poverty are lone-parent mothers, women caring for children who are married to men in low-paid jobs or who are unemployed and women in later life. In 2003, 40 per cent of one-parent households (9 out of 10 female headed) were in the bottom fifth of the income distribution and 33 per cent in the next fifth. Those households in the bottom two-fifths are heavily dependent on state benefits in cash and kind.

Over the last 25 years, there has been a growing divide between 'work rich' households and 'work poor' households. Married or cohabiting women in paid employment generally have a partner who is also in employment. The wives or partners of unemployed men rarely have paid employment because the benefits system is a disincentive to do so. There is then an increasing gulf between households in employment (and young pensioner households with occupational and/or personal pensions) and those dependent on welfare benefits. Furthermore, in a substantial proportion of two-earner households, women's earnings contribute to keeping the family out of poverty. Households with a male breadwinner and a female home-maker have between a four and six times higher risk of being in the bottom income quintile than those in households where both partners have paid employment.

Women who are lone parents are especially vulnerable to poverty. There has been a dramatic increase in one-parent families in the last 40 years. In 1961, 2 per cent of households comprised a lone parent with a dependent child or children. This has now risen to 7 per cent. This is mainly because of the increase in the divorce rate. The main route to lone parenthood is divorce – 72 per cent of one-parent families are headed by a divorcee, whereas only 18 per cent are the result of the birth of a child outside a relationship. Despite the introduction of the Child Support Agency to enforce the absent parent to pay towards the cost of child support, the normal consequence of divorce is that the absent parent (generally the father) is financially better off and mothers with custody are less well off than before the separation. Children are generally looked after by their mothers when parents divorce: the assumption that children should be cared for by their mother is deeply embedded in cultural and legal attitudes and values, and only about 9 per cent of one-parent households are headed by a man.

Poverty and older women

Older women are especially vulnerable to poverty – and women are a majority of those 65 years and over – and the proportion of older women to men increases with age (see Chapter 8). While around three-quarters of men over 65 live with someone, only around a half of women do so (Winquist 2002). Fifty-five per cent of women expect their husband or partner will provide for them in retirement (*The Sunday Times,* 19 October 1997) but women outlive their partners on average by about ten years. Two-thirds of all people aged over 75 years and three-quarters of those over 85 years are women. Older women are much more likely to live in single-person households than older men: 43.5 per cent of women (35 per cent of these being widows) do so compared with 21.8 per cent of men. While 64.8 per cent of men aged 75–84 years and 41.4 per cent of those aged 85 live as a married or cohabiting couple, only 29.6 per cent of women aged 75–84 and 19 per cent of those over 85 do so.

Retirement from paid employment for both men and women and the households in which they live means reduced economic and other resources. The average income of women over 65 years living alone is 51 per cent of that of people below 65 years, while for men living alone it is 62 per cent. Forty-four per cent of women aged over 65 years live in households with incomes below 60 per cent of median income compared to 33 per cent of men – one of the largest gender gaps in the EU (Winquist 2002). Women are less likely than men to have an occupational private pension. Over two-thirds of men over 65 years have an occupational private pension, compared with 43 per cent of women (including widows receiving occupational pension income from a deceased spouse's pension). Only 28 per cent of married women over 65 years receive an occupational pension compared with 74 per cent of men. The average private pension income of all women over 65 years is 53 per cent that of men and for married women it is only 37 per cent. Even when women do have an occupational pension, its final value will be considerably reduced by the time they reach very old age (Arber and Ginn in ONS 2004a). Men's occupational pensions often cease, or their widows only receive a considerably reduced pension, when they die and, again, the 'real value' declines with increasing age.

Married or cohabiting women are also less likely than men to have a state pension in their own right. Many older women did not have paid employment in the past and therefore have no entitlement to a state pension whilst others chose to pay the married women's contributions (an option that was abolished in 1976) and therefore also do not have a state pension in their own right. Furthermore, many married or cohabiting women who have been in paid employment will often have worked too few hours a week over extended periods to pay NI contributions and therefore have no entitlement to a pension, or have a reduced pension when they retire. Four-fifths of the 2 million employees who have weekly earnings below the NI lower earnings limit (McKnight et al. 1998) and 3.1 million of the 3.5 million pensioners who do not qualify for basic pension are women (Baroness Hollis of Higham's statement in the House of Commons: *The Times*, 18 October 1997).

Women in old age, then, are more likely than older men to be dependent on means-tested state benefits and less likely than men to have an employer's or private pension and even when they do, because women on average earn less than men, it will be considerably smaller. Three-quarters of pensioners on income support are women (1.5 million women: *The Times*, 18 October 1997) and many more women than men live on incomes just above the poverty line. Three in five older women are not married and must rely on their own meagre income.

Whilst sociologists and others now frequently talk about the third age – a period of relative affluence and good health after retirement enjoyed by pensioners in countries like Britain – this is not the case for all. Women are much less likely than men to enjoy this third age for a number of reasons. They are less likely than men to have the economic resources, they are more likely than men to have to care for dependent relatives (including their male partner), domestic labour does not cease on retirement and older women are more likely to have chronic health or disability problems. Furthermore, older women are more likely than men to live into the fourth age of increased dependence and have to live on a low income – including those who may have lived in a relatively affluent household when their partners were alive.

When the Labour government came to power in 1997, it made tackling poverty and inequality a major concern. It has, however, focused on social exclusion, raising educational standards and getting people into employment as the major strategies – tackling the causes of poverty, rather than compensating people for its effects. The core approach recognises that poverty is part of wider social exclusion, a more inclusive term that takes in health, housing, employment and so on. Whereas a sociological analysis of social exclusion is concerned with the dynamic processes by which individuals and communities come to be disadvantaged and raises questions about the role of social institutions, including the welfare state, in generating these problems, New Labour terminology was really an attempt to signal an inter-departmental collaborative style of seeing social exclusion.

However, the policies are not based on consideration of the differences between men and women in terms of their role in the community or the family – they are gender-blind. Single parents (mainly women) are encouraged to take paid employment with child care and wage subsidies provided to make this possible. This takes no account of the difficulties of being a lone-parent mother and combining this with paid employment. Policies designed to encourage community participation take no account of the different ways in which men and women involve themselves in the community. While women tend to play a greater role, it is generally on an informal basis, helping neighbours and other members of the community. When men become involved in the community, it is normally in formal organisations. Agencies working with communities are more likely to work with organisations and therefore men are likely to be over-represented in consultation and empowerment exercises, thus marginalising women.

Conclusion

In this chapter, I have examined gender divisions in modern Britain – the persistence of inequalities between men and women. Despite equal opportunities and equal pay at work legislation, there has been little improvement in the overall situation of women vis-à-vis men in paid employment. The majority of women continue to be dependent on men because legal changes do not change relationships between men and women in the private sphere, where women are expected to provide care for children and other dependent relatives. Nor do they provide help for women in carrying out the informal care for which they are seen as responsible. Whilst the welfare state has challenged patriarchal power – enabling, for example, women to leave men who beat them up – it has replaced private patriarchy with public patriarchy.

Gender is a key aspect of social division and classification in modern industrial societies. It is not just that there are differences between men and women, but that there are inequalities that are built into the structures of society. Gender is a fundamental way in which every aspect of our lives is organised. It is the key category through which we make sense of our social and natural world and our experiences of that world. There are inequalities in the distribution of wealth, power and privilege between men and women. Gender inequalities are ordered and consistent in type, although in the longer term there are changes. Gendered relationships exist outside the ways in which we categorise men and women, although the categories affect the ways in which gendered relationships evolve.

Nevertheless, gender as a concept is a social construct that is used to define, explain and justify inequalities and, as such, is unstable and contestable. The structured inequalities and the socially constructed discourses of gender work together to perpetuate gender inequalities in hierarchies. Everyday struggles to change and resist the discourses of gender take place within the context of the pre-existing structural relationships within which men, on the whole, have more power, more ability to control and more access to scarce resources than women. Historically, women have resisted men's power and fought to gain equality and men have resisted the attempts of women to improve their situation vis-à-vis men.

Despite the gains of women over the last two centuries in terms of achievement of the right to vote, laws against rape, laws to protect women from domestic violence, equal opportunities and equal pay legislation, women on the whole continue to be subordinate to men within contemporary industrial societies. However, we should not lose sight of the fact of the fragmentary nature of social stratification and social divisions within contemporary societies. Men and women's experiences are structured not only by gender, but also by class, ethnicity, age, sexuality and so on. At the same time, gender remains an important and fascinating element of social division in its own right.

Discussion Questions

Public institutions including universities and colleges will have a duty to promote gender equality. This means that where inequalities exist they will have a duty to take positive action to eliminate the inequalities. Write a briefing paper for the head of your institution, setting out:

1. The reasons why the institution should audit programmes across the institution for gender representation.

2. The partners that the institution would need to work with if it were to develop positive actions to reduce gender imbalances.

3. The research that would need to be undertaken in order to develop positive action recommendations.

FURTHER READING

Abbott, P., Wallace, C. and Tyler, M. *An Introduction to Sociology: Feminist Perspectives* (London: Routledge, 2005) offers a broad introduction to gender inequalities in contemporary Britain and feminist explanations for them. Bradley, H. *Fractured Identities: Changing Patterns of Inequality* (Cambridge: Polity, 1996) offers a comprehensive introduction to past and current theories of stratification and inequalities, with a major focus on gender. A more specialist edited collection, dealing with gender inequalities and ageing, is Arber, S. and Ginn, J. (eds), *Connecting Gender and Ageing: A Sociological Approach* (Buckingham: Open University Press, 1995). A selection of articles that considers and analyses the debates about the changing outcomes of education, as based on gender can be found in Epstein, D., Elwood, J., Hey, V. and Maw, J. *Failing Boys? Issues in Gender and Achievement* (Buckingham: Open University Press, 1998) and Skelton, C. and Beck, F. (eds) *Investigating Gender: Contemporary Perspectives in Education* (Buckingham: Open University Press, 2001). The Equal Opportunities Commission website (www.eoc.org.uk) provides a range of up-to-date briefing papers on gender, and the most recent edition of *Social Trends* as well as relevant statistical information can be accessed via the government website.

CHAPTER 4

Ethnicity

DAVID MASON

This chapter will provide you with a broad critical understanding of the following issues in ethnicity as a source of social division:

- The origins of the concept of ethnicity
- The relationship of ethnicity to other concepts such as class and race
- The relational character of ethnicity
- British conceptions of ethnicity
- Problems of measuring ethnic difference and disadvantage
- Problems of categorisation and identity
- The broad demographic profile of minority ethnic groups in Britain
- Patterns of ethnic advantage and disadvantage in the British labour market
- Discrimination
- The dynamics of ethnic divisions in Britain
- Changing ethnic identities
- The intellectual and political challenges of recognising diversity and change while measuring disadvantage and tracking social divisions

As we saw in Chapter 2, the analysis of class divisions has characteristically been concerned first to map and explain the causes of underlying material inequalities and then investigate their implications for people's conceptions of themselves and how this affects their relations with others. In other words, people's identities and their relationship to others' identities are usually second order questions in the study of class. Ethnicity, by contrast, presents us with a different problem. Ethnic differences are not constituted by material inequalities, even if they may frequently be marked by them. We cannot know people's ethnicity by seeking information about their occupations, income, wealth or housing circumstances. Only in situations of extreme segregation will this kind of information offer us good clues to people's ethnic status and, even then, few would argue that these characteristics represent the essence of their ethnicity in the way that is common in class analysis. Thus, if we are to understand the implications of ethnic differences for social divisions, we must ask some rather different questions.

Specifically, we must start by considering what constitutes ethnic difference. Then we need to map the patterning of that difference in the societies we are studying. Only then can we proceed to ask what patterns of material inequalities are to be observed among the groups concerned. In other words, when we begin to consider ethnic differences, we may find that these divisions are manifested in ways other than simple material inequality.

Some conceptual ground-clearing

Thus far we have spoken of ethnic differences as if the concept of ethnicity were unproblematic and uncontested. Unfortunately, this is far from being the case. Before we can proceed, therefore, we need to consider what we mean by this term. As in the case of social class, we shall rapidly discover that 'ethnicity' is used in a variety of different ways and has been subject to a range of different theorisations. Moreover, the term is not one confined to sociological discourse but is widely used in lay debate and policy formulation in ways that considerably complicate our task in this chapter. Not only that, but the concept is related in complex ways to other commonly used terms such as 'race' and 'minority'. Indeed, in order to understand the origins and character of the concept of ethnicity, it is necessary briefly to consider its relationship to the concept of 'race'.

The first thing to say about both the terms 'race' and 'ethnicity' is that they are distinctively modern. By that I mean that they are products of what Kumar (1978) has called 'The Great Transformation' of European societies and particularly the global expansion of European societies from the late fifteenth century onwards. As they explored other parts of the world, Europeans came into contact with other human societies with unfamiliar patterns of social organisation and populated by persons whose physical appearance was noticeably different from their own. Europeans' encounters with other societies rapidly turned to conquest and annexation, while they adapted the ancient institution of slavery to the new requirements of colonial expansion and capitalist production (Davis 1984). Against this background, not only the striking differences between themselves and those whom they met and conquered but also apparent European superiority seemed to require explanation. The result was the emergence of a distinctive way of thinking about and explaining human variation – 'race'.

The modern concept of race emerged between the end of the eighteenth and the middle of the nineteenth centuries (see the discussions in Banton

1967, 1977, 1987, 1988; Stepan 1982). By the middle of the nineteenth century, race science was characterising human diversity in terms of divisions between fixed, separate and hierarchically ranked races, rooted in biological difference and a product of divergent ancestries. The differences between them were seen not merely as markers of current status but as determinants of their past history and future potential. By the turn of the century, this view, expressed increasingly in terms of 'Social Darwinism', was being harnessed to the justification of conquest and war as the age of high imperialism dawned in the wake of the 1885 Congress of Berlin (Mason 2000: 7).

By the end of the Second World War, as the horrors of the Holocaust were revealed, race science was becoming discredited. At the same time, modern genetics was undermining notions of biological fixity. The result was a gradual disappearance of the concept of race from natural science debates (Montague 1964, 1974; Banton and Harwood 1975). Nevertheless, biological notions persisted in both political discourse and popular conceptions of human variation. As a result, even those, such as sociologists, who were convinced by the evidence that races in the biological sense did not exist found themselves having to confront the persistence of the concept. However uneasily, sociologists found themselves continuing to use the concept on the basis that social actors treated it as real and organised their lives in terms of it (van den Berghe 1967). Only in the last twenty years or so have writers such as Miles (1982, 1993) challenged this usage, arguing that it serves to legitimise an ideological category, naturalising divisions that are really the outcome of exploitation and oppression. One result of this challenge has been the tendency for recent sociological writing to substitute the problematic of 'racism' for that of 'race' (see for example Solomos and Back 1996). Readers wishing to pursue further the issues raised by this ongoing debate may find the fuller discussions in Mason (1994, 2000) a useful starting point.

In what follows, I shall not use the term 'race' except where this is unavoidable in referring to the work of others. Nevertheless, if we are to understand the status of the concept of ethnicity – the focus of this chapter – it is necessary to grasp the extent to which it has emerged, and continues to appear, in dialogue with that of race. This is so, despite the fact that the concept of ethnicity represents an attempt to replace an emphasis on physical difference with stress on cultural variation. Moreover, the concept of ethnicity entered sociological and policy discourse partly as a reaction to the perceived inadequacies of race. It is frequently seen as more legitimate because it avoids biological determinism and appeals, at least in part, to the self-definitions of members.

Despite this, the terms 'race' and 'ethnicity' are widely used interchangeably in both policy and academic discourses, as well as in everyday speech.

Thus we have policies to counter the 'racial' harassment of 'ethnic minorities', while the term 'race' is enshrined in law itself – in the title and content of the Race Relations (Amendment) Act 2000. Moreover, even in places where one might anticipate a little more conceptual rigour – such as undergraduate textbooks in sociology – the terms are frequently used interchangeably, even when an attempt is made conceptually to distinguish them (see the discussion in Mason 1996).

In many ways this is a peculiarly British phenomenon. In the US, where the concept of race is perhaps even more entrenched in the national consciousness and political and administrative life, there is nevertheless a well-established understanding that the concepts are not identical. There are all sorts of intellectual problems with the way the distinction is made in the USA but at least it is made. In Continental Europe, outside a few far right political movements, the concept of race is scarcely encountered at all, other than when incorporated into the term 'racism' which is used generally as a term of disapproval for particular political attitudes and movements.

I suggest that the widespread interchangeability of the concepts of race and ethnicity in Britain is intimately bound up with the colonial roots of Britain's immigration experience, with the distinctive visibility of those who came to be seen as quintessential 'immigrants', and with the persistence of a subtext of biological thinking about human difference that experiences periodic public resurgences (see the discussion in Mason 1994). Indeed, as Modood (2003) and others have suggested, the racialisation of ethnic difference is a key to understanding some of the ways in which British conceptions of ethnic diversity have developed.

Matters are complicated further because, as a result of the range of theoretical traditions from which ethnicity can be approached, there is no universally accepted definition of the term. It is probably true to say that, if pressed for a definition, most academics and policy makers would stress some sort of cultural distinctiveness as the mark of an ethnic grouping. For example, Smith (1986: 192) defined an ethnic unit as 'a population whose members believe that in some sense they share common descent and a common cultural heritage or tradition, and who are so regarded by others'.

Nevertheless, there are considerable differences of view among sociologists about how negotiable ethnicity is. How much freedom do social actors have to define themselves and their relationships to others? To what extent can people choose their ethnicity? For some, there is a primordial element to ethnicity that explains the fervour of commitments to particular cultural identities. For others, ethnicity is little more than a symbolic resource to be used instrumentally (Jenkins 1986a, 1997; Mason 1986; Yinger 1986: 26–31, 1994).

One influential approach places emphasis on the processes by which ethnic boundaries are drawn. Whether and how social boundaries are erected is an empirical question and not one that can be simply read off from the existence of cultural difference (see the discussion in Jenkins 1997; see also Barth 1969; Wallman 1986). In this view, ethnicity is *situational*. Whether or not members of a group celebrate cultural markers to distinguish themselves from others depends, in part, on their immediate objectives – including political and economic ones. This perspective also allows us to recognise that people may have different ethnic identities in different situations. Thus it is possible to be simultaneously English, British and European, stressing these identities more or less strongly in different aspects of daily life. Similarly, the same person might identify him or herself as Gujerati, Indian, Hindu, East African Asian or British, depending on the situation, immediate objectives and responses and behaviour of others.

The responses of others are important, of course, because they too are making identity choices and constructing and maintaining their own boundaries. In other words, as well as being potentially situational, ethnicity is also, and fundamentally, *relational*. As a result, no one's identity choices are unconstrained. This point has a particular significance in a British context, because nowhere are these constraints more significant than in relation to public policy and its capacity to frame and shape the opportunity structures in which people play out their lives. In this context, a key role is played by the processes by which ethnic difference is defined and measured.

In Britain, in much popular and, indeed, official parlance, the term 'ethnic' is used to refer only to those who are thought of as different from some assumed indigenous norm of 'Britishness' (see Chapter 6). It is frequently used as a synonym for those thought of as culturally different. Talk of an ethnic 'look' in the world of fashion is only one, relatively trivial, example of the way white British people are apt to see ethnicity as an attribute only of others – something that distinguishes 'them' from 'us'. This is exemplified by the way in which in Britain the term 'ethnic' is usually qualified with the word 'minority'. We almost never hear mention of an ethnic *majority*.

Matters are, however, more complicated still. Not every group having a distinctive culture and constituting a minority in the British population is normally included in the designation. Instead, in order to qualify for designation as an ethnic minority, a category of people must exhibit a degree of 'difference' that is regarded as significant. In practice, a mixture of skin colour and distinctive culture is the criterion that is usually thought to mark off 'ethnic minorities' from the 'majority' population in Britain. At the same time, 'ethnic minorities' are frequently seen to have more in common with one another than with the 'majority'. The term thus often seems to de-emphasise *diversity among* minority ethnic groups while exaggerating *differences from* the white population. Even those who argue that 'ethnic minorities' are united by a common experience of racism often fail to be sufficiently alert to the diverse ways in which racism may impact on different communities or, within them, on men and women (Field 1987; Modood 1988, 1990, 1992; Yuval-Davis and Anthias 1989; Anthias and Yuval-Davis 1992; Mason 2003a).

Ethnic differences in Britain: some problems of measurement

We have seen that the term 'ethnic minority' and, by extension 'ethnicity', has a particular resonance in Britain. Despite the fact that Britain's population is one forged from successive historical migrations, the term characteristically refers to people descended from the populations of the countries of the former British Empire – the so-called New Commonwealth. Indeed it is interesting to note that, until recently, the term 'immigration' was automatically associated in popular parlance with the immigration to Britain of people whose origins lay in these countries.

A key reason for this lies in the rapid growth of this population in the years following the end of the Second World War. At the end of the war, the British Empire was still largely intact. It provided a ready source of potential labour until the period of immigration control was initiated with the passing of the Commonwealth Immigrants Act in 1962 (for a discussion of the history of immigration control to Britain, see Layton-Henry 1992 and Mason 2000).

Due to a number of factors, a severe labour shortage developed in post-war Britain. Partly this was a result of the need to engage in post-war reconstruction. At the same time, British industry was becoming increasingly large scale and capital-intensive, with a growing demand for skilled workers. In addition, new employment opportunities were opening up in the rapidly growing service industries and in the public sector which was expanding as a result of the new welfare state established by the Labour government. Increasingly, British workers, and in particular those of the first generation to receive secondary education, had access to avenues of upward social mobility as they moved into newly created and more desirable occupations. This process left a pool of hard-to-fill unskilled and routine semi-skilled jobs at the lower levels of the labour market. These were often dirty, poorly paid and involved unsocial hours like night shiftwork. Many were found in declining industries where cheap labour was an alternative to capital investment or collapse (see Fevre 1984; Duffield 1985). Given Britain's labour shortage in a period when women had been encouraged to leave the labour market and raise families, these vacancies could best be filled by substantial immigration.

From an early stage, then, Britain's new minority ethnic citizens found themselves differentiated from the rest of the population, first by socio-economic situation and later by immigration status. These characteristics established the conditions in which early attempts to measure the size and growth of the minority ethnic population were made. However, over time, the sources of data about Britain's ethnic diversity have changed and developed in the light of changing policy concerns, changing political priorities (both within government and outside) and changing patterns of political struggle, including the demands of minority ethnic communities themselves. The same is true of the categories in terms of which members of different groups are categorised. One consequence of this is that tracking changes over time is extremely difficult.

Early discussions of Britain's growing ethnic diversity were framed within debates about immigration. As a result, until recently, most official estimates of the size of the minority ethnic population were based on the place of birth of those born outside the UK, in the 'New Commonwealth'. The term 'New Commonwealth' is a euphemism for the countries of the former British Empire populated by people whose skin colour is not white. The New Commonwealth is thus distinguished from the Old Commonwealth of countries thought of as having predominantly white populations. The term 'New' was justified largely on the grounds that these countries attained independence after the Second World War, in contrast to Australia, Canada and New Zealand which had been granted effective self-government much earlier. The convolutions entailed in this usage are well illustrated by the fact that when Pakistan left the Commonwealth in 1972, it was necessary to revise the term to 'New Commonwealth and Pakistan', often rendered as 'NCWP'.

Counting those born in the New Commonwealth made some statistical sense in the early days of immigration but it became increasingly unsatisfactory as a growing proportion of the New Commonwealth-descended population was actually being born in Britain. The initial solution was to count those living in households where the 'head of household' had been born in the New Commonwealth. Yet again, this could only ever be a temporary solution until the children of initial migrants began to establish their own households. Nevertheless, until data from the 1991 census became available, estimates of this kind based on the censuses of 1971 and 1981 were the main sources for both official and academic purposes.

For the first time, the 1991 Census asked respondents to classify themselves in ethnic terms. The following schema was the one finally adopted:

White	Pakistani
Black – Caribbean	Indian
Black – African	Chinese
Black – Other (please specify)	Any other ethnic group (please describe)
Bangladeshi	

The census categories were also adopted by the Commission for Racial Equality (CRE) as those that it recommended for ethnic monitoring purposes. This increasing standardisation offers the future benefits of comparability between data sources and over time. As we shall see, however, these features are not without their problems when faced with the realities of changing ethnic identities.

In the 2001 census, the categories were revised further to respond to a number of emergent problems. These included the difficulty that many minority ethnic citizens found in locating a category that adequately matched their own self-identity, the absence of opportunities to affirm differentiated white identities and a failure to keep pace with the rapid increase in the numbers of people wishing to record 'mixed' origins or 'hybrid' identities. The 2001 census also introduced a question on religion that, it was hoped, would allow further fine-tuned disaggregation of the population.

Nevertheless, it remains the case that underlying the 2001 census question is still a sense that the most significant ethnic differences are those associated with the conventional British conceptualisation of 'ethnic minorities' described above, one that is, above all, racialised. The result is that, increasingly sophisticated attempts to disaggregate the minority population notwithstanding, there is still a tendency to conceptualise this population as relatively unchanging in terms of both its boundaries and the problems to which it is thought to be victim. For a fuller discussion of some of the key problems of measurement, see Mason (2003b).

In addition to figures derived from the census, there have been some other sources of data. The most important, and widely used, are the periodic surveys conducted by the Policy Studies Institute (PSI, formerly Political and Economic Planning) (Daniel 1968; Smith 1974; Brown 1984; Modood et al. 1997) and the results of the annual Labour Force Survey (LFS) conducted by the Office for National Statistics. Both have utilised self-classification measures of ethnicity. However, there are technical differences not only between one another but also with those used in the census, so that comparisons are fraught with difficulty, particularly where they involve attempts to measure change over time. In the rest of this chapter, much of the discussion will rely on data from the 2001 census and the 2001/02 LFS. Additional material has been drawn from analyses of earlier sweeps of the LFS (Jones 1993) and the fourth PSI survey (Modood et al. 1997).

Minority ethnic groups in Britain

Table 4.1 reproduces results from the 2001 census, which indicate that there are now more than 4.6 million people of minority ethnic origin resident in the UK. They make up 9 per cent of the total population in England, 2 per cent in both Scotland and Wales, and less than 1 per cent in Northern Ireland.

Table 4.1 Population of the UK by ethnic group (April 2001)

	Total population		Non-white population
	Number	*%*	*%*
White	54,153,898	92.1	–
Mixed	677,117	1.2	14.6
Indian	1,053,411	1.8	22.7
Pakistani	747,285	1.3	16.1
Bangladeshi	283,063	0.5	6.1
Other Asian	247,664	0.4	5.3
All Asian or Asian British	2,331,423	4.0	50.3
Black Caribbean	565,876	1.0	12.2
Black African	485,277	0.8	10.5
Black other	97,585	0.2	2.1
All black or black British	1,148,738	2.0	24.8
Chinese	247,403	0.4	5.3
Other ethnic groups	230,615	0.4	5.0
All minority ethnic population	4,635,296	7.9	100.0
All population	58,789,194	100.0	

Source: Office for National Statistics, National Statistics Online.

As Figure 4.1 shows, this population has an uneven geographical spread, concentrated as it is not just in England but also overwhelmingly in the most densely populated urban areas. Around 45 per cent of the minority ethnic population lives in London, 13 per cent in the West Midlands, 8 per cent in each of the southeast and the northwest and 7 per cent in Yorkshire and the

Humber. By contrast, less than 4 per cent live in the northeast and the southwest, comprising only 2 per cent of each of these regions' populations. The largest proportions of both black Africans (78 per cent) and black Caribbeans (61 per cent) are resident in London, as are a small majority of Bangladeshis (54 per cent.) Other minority groups are more dispersed with, for example, 19 per cent of Pakistanis living in London, 21 per cent in the West Midlands, 20 per cent in Yorkshire and the Humber and 16 per cent in the northwest.

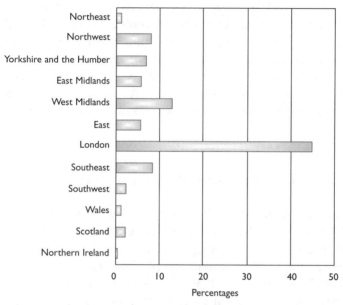

Note
1 Non-White is the term used in the original source of these data. It includes all minority ethnic groups but not White Irish or Other White groups.

Figure 4.1 Regional distribution of the Non-White[1] population (April 2001)

Source: Office for National Statistics, National Statistics Online.

Over a lengthy period, there has been a tendency for the minority ethnic population to become more spatially concentrated (Brown 1984: 59; Owen 1992: 9–10, 2003). It is important to note that within this overall pattern, the distribution of individual ethnic groups varies widely. For at least some groups, this concentration in areas of initial settlement has important implications for their economic and other opportunities (see Mason 2003c).

As we have seen, ethnic differences are not, in themselves, constituted by material inequalities. However, to the extent that ethnicity is a source of social division, it would be surprising if ethnic differences were not associated with such inequalities. Indeed, access to economic resources is usually a key to people's ability to control other aspects of their lives and, for most of Britain's citizens, income from employment represents the major economic resource for day-to-day living. As a result, it is appropriate, in the next part of the discussion, to focus on labour market placement.

Research from the 1960s into the 1980s (Daniel 1968; Smith 1974; Brown 1984) consistently showed that people from minority ethnic groups were clustered in particular industries and occupations, over-represented in semi-skilled and unskilled jobs and frequently excluded altogether from the labour market. More recent evidence reveals both continuity and change from earlier periods. We should remember, however, that material inequalities have other dimensions (some, but not all, directly related to the control of economic resources). They include housing status and access to health and healthcare. For an introduction to these issues, see Mason (2000, 2003a) and Modood et al. (1997).

Employment, unemployment and poverty

Successive studies (Smith 1974, 1981; Brown 1984; Jones 1993; Owen 1993; Mason 2003c) have revealed that persons of ethnic minority origin are at a consistently higher risk of unemployment than white people. There is evidence that unemployment among people from minority ethnic groups is 'hypercyclical' (Jones 1993: 112; Berthoud 2000). In other words, it rises faster than white unemployment in times of recession and falls more rapidly when the economy recovers. Over an extended period, however, we can say that the rate of unemployment among minority ethnic men has tended to be roughly double the rate for white men. Figure 4.2 presents data from the 2001/02 LFS which show that unemployment rates for minority ethnic groups were higher than those for white people, for both men and women, although, in contrast to earlier periods, it seems that unemployment rates for women were generally lower than those for men.

We should, however, note that there are marked variations in the experience of different groups and of men and women. The LFS data show that Bangladeshis had the highest male unemployment rate in Great Britain, at 20 per cent – four times that for white British or white Irish men – while, at 7 per cent, the rate for Indian men was only slightly higher than that for white British or white Irish men at 5 per cent. Unemployment rates for all other minority ethnic men were between two and three times higher than those for white British or white Irish men. Among women, Bangladeshis again had the highest unemployment rate of all, at 24 per cent, six times greater than that for white British or white Irish women at 4 per cent. The rate for Indian women was slightly higher than for white women at 7 per cent.

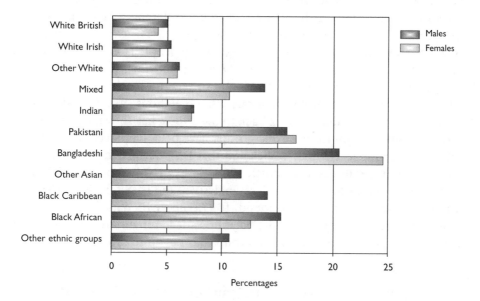

Figure 4.2 Unemployment rates by ethnic group and sex (2001/02)

Source: Annual Local Area Labour Force Survey, 2001/02, Office for
National Statistics, National Statistics Online.

Among young people, who represent a relatively larger proportion of minority ethnic groups than of whites, there are similar variations as among the economically active as a whole. While, for all ethnic groups, unemployment was highest among young people under 25, rates were consistently higher among minority ethnic groups. Thus young white British men and women experienced unemployment rates of 12 per cent and 9 per cent respectively. By contrast, over 40 per cent of young Bangladeshi men were unemployed, while young black African men, Pakistani men and women, black Caribbean men and women and men belonging to the mixed group had unemployment rates in excess of 20 per cent. Once again, these data reflect relatively longstanding patterns (compare Jones 1993: 113; Owen 1993: 7; Modood et al. 1997: 88–93). Moreover, the true position may also be masked by the higher post-compulsory educational participation of minority ethnic young people (Modood 2003).

There are also regional variations in unemployment rates, with a number of important areas of minority ethnic residence in the north and Midlands of England exhibiting high levels of unemployment. At the risk of oversimplifying, we can note that while levels of minority ethnic unemployment are consistently higher than the white rate, these differences are larger outside Greater London. In these areas, even groups such as African Asians are likely to experience higher unemployment than white people (Jones 1993: 113–14; Owen 1993; Modood 1997b: 88–93). Having said this, it is not clear that geographical distribution itself can be said to account for differences between white and minority unemployment rates (see Fieldhouse and Gould 1998).

A long series of studies, dating back to the 1960s, has shown that in general terms members of minority ethnic groups have been employed in less skilled jobs, at lower job levels than whites and that they have been concentrated in particular industrial sectors (Daniel, 1968; Smith, 1974; Brown, 1984). More recent data such as Jones's (1993) re-analysis of the LFS for 1988, 1989 and 1990, the fourth PSI survey (Modood, 1997a) and LFS data for 2001/2 have, however, begun to suggest that the position is becoming more complex as the experience of members of different groups has begun to diverge.

Table 4.2 Job levels of men (employees and self-employed)

Socio-ecomic group	White %	Caribbean %	Indian %	African Asian %	Pakistani %	Bangladeshi %	Chinese %
Professionals, managers and employers	**30**	**14**	**25**	**30**	**19**	**18**	**46**
Employers and managers (large establishments)	11	5	5	3	3	0	6
Employers and managers (small establishments)	11	4	11	14	12	16	23
Professional workers	8	6	9	14	4	2	17
Intermediate and junior non-manual	18	19	20	24	13	19	17
Skilled manual and foremen	36	39	31	30	46	7	14
Semi-skilled manual	11	22	16	12	18	53	12
Unskilled manual	3	6	5	2	3	3	5
Armed forces or n/a	2	0	3	2	2	0	5
Non-manual total	**48**	**33**	**45**	**54**	**32**	**37**	**63**
Manual total	**50**	**67**	**52**	**44**	**67**	**63**	**31**

Source: Modood et al. (1997).

Table 4.2 suggests that male members of some minority ethnic groups are beginning to experience employment patterns increasingly similar to those of white men. This is true of African Asian, Chinese and, to a slightly lesser extent, Indian men, where the proportions approximate or exceed the proportions of white workers in each of the top two categories. However, these figures conceal important variations since, although African Asian and Chinese men are more likely to be professional workers than white men, they are considerably less likely to be represented among senior managers in large enterprises. Among those of African-Caribbean, Bangladeshi and Pakistani descent, there is much less evidence of progress in the top category (although there is some convergence in the 'intermediate and junior non-manual' category). Bangladeshi men in particular, 53 per cent of whom are in semi-skilled manual occupations, remain concentrated in the lower echelons of the labour market. In addition, we should note that some groups display marked bipolarity. Thus both Indian and Chinese men are found in large numbers in both the highest and lowest job categories. Jones (1993: 70) argues: 'This may suggest that men from these two groups enter a relatively narrow range of occupations, either at the top or bottom end of the job market' (see also the discussion in Heath et al. 2000).

Table 4.3 Job levels of women (employees and self-employed)

Socio-ecomic group	White %	Caribbean %	Indian %	African Asian %	Pakistani %	Chinese %
Professionals, managers and employers	16	5	11	12	12	30
Intermediate non-manual	21	28	14	14	29	23
Junior non-manual	33	36	33	49	23	23
Skilled manual and foremen	7	4	11	30	9	13
Semi-skilled manual	18	20	16	16	22	9
Unskilled manual	4	6	4	1	4	2
Armed forces or n/a	0	1	1	1	0	0
Non-manual total	**70**	**69**	**58**	**75**	**64**	**76**
Manual total	**29**	**30**	**42**	**24**	**35**	**24**

Source: Modood et al. (1997).

Table 4.3 presents comparable data for women. It shows that women of all groups are less likely than men to be in the top category and, for all groups, the largest concentrations are to be found in the 'intermediate' and 'junior' non-manual categories, followed by 'semi-skilled manual'. This finding matches that of the 1982 PSI survey (Brown 1984) and Jones's (1993) re-analysis of

LFS data. Both of these studies offered a similar explanation, that is, that women are already disadvantaged in the labour market relative to men and that, as a result, there is limited scope for an additional disadvantage arising from ethnicity. Despite detailed variations between groups, therefore, there is some evidence that 'gender divisions in the labour market may be stronger and more deeply rooted than differences due to race and ethnicity' (Modood 1997b: 104; see also Iganski and Payne 1996; Iganski et al. 2001).

So far as distribution between employment sectors is concerned, the data suggest both continuity with, and some changes in, the previously established pattern of concentration of the ethnic minority population in particular employment sectors. That concentration to some degree reflected patterns of settlement and demand for labour at the time of initial settlement. However, major economy-wide changes in the 1980s, associated with the decline in manufacturing employment and the growth of the service sector, led to significant changes for members of all groups. It might be thought that, given their patterns of initial settlement and their concentration in semi-skilled and unskilled manual occupations, the descendants of New Commonwealth migrants to Britain would have fared rather badly in these transformations. In fact, the evidence suggests that, continued disadvantage and exclusion notwithstanding, minority ethnic groups were not disproportionately negatively affected (Iganski and Payne 1999).

The LFS data for 1988, 1989, 1990 (Jones 1993) and 2001/02 (ONS 2004b) suggest that the largest proportion of all groups, including white employees, are now to be found in distribution, hotels, catering and repairs. Within this broad pattern, people of South Asian origin are rather more likely than white people to be employed in retail distribution, while those of Chinese and Bangladeshi origin are markedly more likely than white people to work in hotels and catering. Pakistani men are particularly likely to be found in the transport and communication sectors, with one in six working as cab drivers or chauffeurs by 2001/02. By the same date, half (51 per cent) of black Caribbean women worked in the public administration, education or health sectors. Indeed there is a marked concentration of women of all groups in the service sector, reflecting the general pattern of segregation of women in employment (Jones 1993: 66–8; compare Rees 1992; Iganski et al. 2001).

Some caution has to be exercised in interpreting the data that are available. Apparently similar proportions of groups in the same occupational category may conceal important differences in status, the kinds of enterprises worked in or the working conditions enjoyed by members of different groups. Thus it appears that even successful members of minority ethnic groups may have greater difficulty in accessing high status positions in major companies. This in turn may help to explain the enthusiasm of minority ethnic students for the professions where opportunities exist for the establishment of independent practices. A good example is the law, where minority ethnic groups are increasingly over-represented among students registering with the Law Society while remaining under-represented in large firms of solicitors and the higher reaches of the legal profession (Home Office 1998: 37–8).

In this connection, it is sometimes argued that self-employment represents an escape route from disadvantage and discrimination in employment and that this accounts for its prevalence among minority ethnic groups. This characterisation may, however, owe as much to popular stereotypes – notably the thriving corner shop – as to real evidence of high levels of minority ethnic self-employment. In this context, it is worth noting, therefore, that the results the 2001/03 LFS reveal some important changes over time in the levels of self-employment among different ethnic groups. They show that Pakistanis and Chinese increasingly stood out as those among whom self-employment was likely to be significantly higher than other groups (for a fuller discussion of this issue, see Mason 2003b).

The data reviewed above suggest a variety of experience, with widespread discrimination and disadvantage coexisting with significant upward mobility for some. Modood's analysis and census data appear to show an increasing similarity of experience between white people and at least some minority ethnic groups (Owen 1993; Modood 1997a). The growth of a middle class of professional and managerial workers in some ethnic communities, and the entry of these groups into the service sector, has led some to suggest that a convergence is underway in the class structure of minority ethnic groups towards that of the white population (Iganski and Payne 1996, 1999; Iganski et al. 2001; Platt 2003a). Moreover, some recent evidence also suggests that these patterns of upward occupational mobility are being matched by a diminution in earning differentials (Leslie et al. 1998: 489, 503–4). However, the patterns are complex and need to be approached with caution (see Mason 2003b).

The first point to note is that there are significant differences between members of different ethnic groups. We have seen that those of Caribbean, Pakistani and Bangladeshi descent in particular tend to occupy the lowest positions in the labour market and also experience the highest levels of unemployment. Indeed, patterns of exclusion altogether from the labour market must be taken into account when considering the successes of those in work. The same is true for the differences between the experiences of women and men.

We should also remember that upward mobility is not incompatible with continued occupational segregation or discrimination. We know, for example, that there may be important differences of level within broad occupational categories, such as between senior and middle management (compare the experience of women in this connection: Cockburn 1991; and see Chapter 3).

Members of all minority ethnic groups are under-represented among managers of large enterprises. The kinds of enterprises in which people work may also have significant implications for their opportunities and earnings. These may even be reinforced by patterns of self-employment if their result is to increase opportunities for advancement by other members of the same groups. This suggests that there are significant patterns of ethnic segregation to be discerned in the labour market.

Finally, we should reiterate the extent to which experience in the field of employment is in some ways the key to overall life chances. The labour market situation of minority ethnic groups has had knock-on effects in other fields, such as health and housing. There is, however, one further source of information about material inequalities that we must consider. This is the evidence on household incomes and standards of living.

The fourth PSI survey (Modood et al. 1997) attempted for the first time to produce an analysis of the household incomes of minority ethnic groups. This is important because the household is commonly used as the unit of analysis in studying living standards and economic well-being. As we have seen, there is some evidence that patterns of upward occupational mobility are beginning to be matched by changes in individual earnings. It is a plausible assumption that individual earning differences would be likely to feed through into household differences but the manner in which this takes place is not clear. Among relevant factors influencing outcomes will be relative household size, the number of wage earners, the number of dependants and the availability of source of income other than earnings.

The analysis undertaken for the PSI reveals that the outcomes are complex and influenced by a range of factors. It also shows that, while some of the patterns revealed by analyses of employment continue to hold, there are other patterns that differ. Among key findings, we should note the extent of poverty (defined as incomes below half the national average) among Pakistani and Bangladeshi households (Chapter 13). As Berthoud (1997: 180) puts it:

> Name any group whose poverty causes national concern – pensioners, disabled people, one-parent families, the unemployed – Pakistanis and Bangladeshis are poorer.

The data also show that only Chinese households had incomes close to those of whites. Caribbean, Indian and African Asian household were all more likely than whites to experience poverty and less likely to have large family incomes. These results lead to an important qualification to the evidence on upward occupational mobility. When household incomes are taken into account, African Asians and Indians fare less well than those of Chinese descent, while Caribbeans are much better placed than Pakistanis and Bangladeshis (Berthoud 1997: 180). These data thus provide further reasons to be cautious in assessing the significance of occupational mobility and the relative labour market placement of groups.

Explaining ethnic disadvantage – discrimination

A variety of explanations for the disadvantage suffered by members of minority ethnic groups in the labour market have been reviewed by the various studies conducted under the auspices of the PSI or its predecessor Political and Economic Planning (Daniel 1968; Smith 1974; Brown 1984; Jones 1993; Modood et al. 1997). All have shown that when matters such as language competence, skill levels and qualifications are controlled for, there remains a residue which is not explained by such factors. As a result, it is difficult to avoid the conclusion that discrimination on the part of employers plays a significant part in the labour market placement of minority ethnic groups (Mason 2003b).

In this context, it is interesting to note that the fourth PSI survey found that a large majority of all respondents believed that discrimination was widespread. Indeed, white respondents were the most likely to hold such a belief (Modood 1997b: 129–35). This belief is consistent with the findings of an overwhelming body of research evidence which has exposed direct, and apparently intentional, discrimination in employment selection decisions (Daniel 1968; Hubbock and Carter 1980; National Association of Citizens Advice Bureaux 1984). A common research method has been to submit job applications from candidates matched in every way except ethnic origin. Using this method, Brown and Gay (1985) revealed systematic discrimination, despite the many years of race relations legislation: white applicants were more than 30 per cent more likely to be treated favourably than those of minority ethnic origin. Moreover, when compared with the results of earlier studies dating back to the early 1970s, Brown and Gay (1985) found no evidence of a diminution in the level of racial discrimination and concluded that a major reason was the fact that employers were unlikely to be caught in the act of discrimination.

Research of this kind, capable of uncovering clear evidence of discrimination, has become less common in recent years. One example, conducted some dozen years ago, concerned research into the fate of speculative employment inquiries made to some of Britain's major companies (Noon 1993). Matched letters of inquiry were sent to personnel managers at the top one hundred UK companies identified from the Times 1,000 index. The letters were signed by fictitious applicants called Evans and Patel. They were presented as MBA students who were about to qualify and already had relevant experience. The research compared both the frequency of responses sent to the two applicants and their quality in terms of the assistance and encouragement offered. It found that, overall, companies were more helpful and encouraging to white candidates. Moreover, Noon concluded that, even in companies ostensibly sensitive to equal opportunities issues, direct discrimination was taking place on a routine basis.

Equally serious a problem is posed by indirect discrimination, where selection criteria are applied equally to everyone but where they are such that they disproportionately affect members of particular groups. A good example is where there are occupationally unnecessary dress requirements that members of some groups cannot comply with for religious or other reasons. Indirect discrimination may be deliberate but it may also frequently be unintentional and unrecognised. Jenkins (1986b) has argued that many selection decisions are based not on whether candidates have the right qualifications for the job but on whether they are thought to be likely to 'fit in' to the workplace without causing any trouble. Such judgements are applied equally to everyone but become discriminatory when they are consciously or unconsciously informed by managers' stereotypes of minority ethnic groups.

Jenkins' research and other studies (Jewson et al. 1990) revealed that negative stereotypes were widespread among managers responsible for recruitment decisions. Even ostensibly positive stereotypes can be disadvantageous: Gray et al. (1993) found that employers' characterisations of Asian women workers as loyal, hardworking and uncomplaining could work against them in a situation where qualities demanded of employees were increasingly those of flexibility, ability to exercise initiative and readiness to carry responsibility and acquire new skills. These examples reveal how easy it is for the taken-for-granted routines of everyday working life to disadvantage minority ethnic groups unintentionally. Of course they also make it easy to hide intentional discrimination as the unplanned and accidental results of impersonal forces.

Ethnic inequalities in Britain: changing social divisions and identities

In the preceding sections, we have reviewed some of the evidence of material inequalities among Britain's varied ethnic communities revealed in official and other data sources. These material inequalities are changing in often complex and subtle ways such that any generalisations about the patterning of divisions based on those inequalities are fraught with difficulty. One source of difficulty lies in changes in official categorisation and measurement practices. As we saw, for example, the 2001 census disaggregated a number of formerly used ethnic categories. These revised categories have also been adopted in other official data sources. As a result, patterns have been revealed that may variously reflect actual change, previously unrecognised complexities or some combination of the two. A good example is provided by the disaggregation of the 'white' category.

We saw above that many recent analyses have identified patterns of upward occupational mobility among some minority ethnic groups that suggest a convergence with the white population. When the white category is disaggregated, however, a more complex picture is revealed. Figure 4.3 shows the distribution of people in professional occupations in Great Britain as measured by the 2001/02 LFS. It reveals a pattern, matched also by managerial occupations and 'senior officials', which complicates somewhat earlier analyses suggesting convergence. Measured in these terms, the greatest convergence is found among those from the Indian, Chinese, white Irish and other non-British white groups. By contrast, white British people had relatively low rates of people working in professional occupations, with only black Caribbeans, Bangladeshis and Pakistanis exhibiting lower rates. It is not clear whether this pattern is a new phenomenon or merely one previously concealed by the use of an undifferentiated 'white' category. It certainly complicates, however, our understanding of patterns of ethnic disadvantage in Britain, challenging a number of previous oversimplifications, including those relating to unambiguous 'white' advantage.

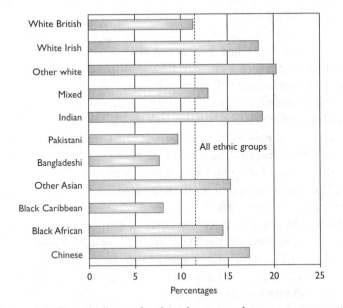

Figure 4.3 People in professional occupations as a percentage of all in employment by ethnic group (2001/02)

Source: Annual Local Area Labour Force Survey, 2001/02, Office for National Statistics, National Statistics Online.

In this connection, we may note that the civil disturbances that took place in a number of towns in the north of England in 2001 revealed, all too clearly, the potential consequences of unchallenged deprivation (see the discussions in Mason 2003a). They also illustrated how, in many deprived areas, the 'white' population frequently also experiences exclusion, albeit differently mediated and labelled. As the events of 2001 show, this can easily fuel damaging inter-ethnic conflict, particularly when it is exploited by far Right political parties. It points to the dangers of conceiving ethnic difference in a way which fails to recognise the diversity of the 'white' population or that aspects of their experience may be shared with those who are ostensibly ethnically different. It reinforces the need, in particular, to make greater efforts to understand the interactions among class and ethnicity as well as the relationship of both of these to gender. The success of 'other white groups', in particular, may well be a reflection of a key feature of the recent immigration history of the UK, where there is clear evidence that a substantial proportion of economic migrants come from Europe, the Old Commonwealth and the US to take up high skilled positions in an economy suffering chronic skills shortages. As a result, about half the overseas-born population is classified as white. It is also interesting to note that this is a population exhibiting high levels of turnover, with about 50 per cent re-emigrating within five years (ONS 2004c).

A further innovation in the 2001 census was the introduction in mainland Britain of a question on religion. This revealed evidence for some previously suspected patterns that may have significant implications for the ethnic landscape of twenty-first-century Britain. The data show that Muslims represented the second largest religious group and made up more that half of those who affirmed a non-Christian religion. They exhibited the highest rates of social disadvantage across a range of aspects of social life, including unemployment, education and health, with Muslim women faring worse than men (*Guardian* 2004a). Muslims also had the largest households, the youngest age profiles and the largest proportion of their population born outside the UK. We have already noted the high levels of disadvantage to be identified among Bangladeshis and Pakistanis. It is, therefore, no surprise to note that Muslims accounted for 92 per cent of members of these groups. There are, however, also significant Muslim minorities among both the Indian and black African populations, a fact that may be relevant to some of the polarities of experience to be identified in these groups.

We have noted that material inequalities, manifested primarily in labour market placement and household incomes, are overlain by a complex of advantages and disadvantages in a variety of other aspects of social life (see the discussions in Mason 2003a). As Scott (Chapter 2) observes, it is not just the direct differences in income, wealth or power that define social class divisions. It is the location of people in class situations that shapes their life chances, even to the extent of setting the length of life and probable cause of death (Chapter 14). Shared social experiences generally follow from a structured sharing of material circumstances.

As we noted at the outset, however, the understanding of social divisions cannot rest simply with the mapping of material differences. In addition to the question of whether we can discern social categories on the basis of 'objective' structural characteristics, there is also the question of whether the people so discerned think of themselves as constituting a group and act in terms of this perception. This brings us back to the question of identity, a concept, as we have seen, that is central to ethnicity.

Ethnicity is a matter both of self-identity ('us' statements) and categorisation ('them' statements). Moreover, identity and categorisation do not proceed entirely independently of one another. In most societies, some groups and individuals have a greater capacity than others to define the terms under which categorisations are made. As a consequence, self-identification takes place in contexts where others' categorisations to some extent constrain the choices that can realistically be made. In other words, if others do not accept one's identity choices in practice, it may be difficult, if not impossible, to act out the implications of those choices.

These kinds of constraints may take the form of subtle social cues and messages that constrain behaviour. They may, however, take more concrete forms. An example of some importance in modern Britain has been the operation of immigration law. From the outset, the increasing restrictions on inward migration that followed the introduction of the 1962 Commonwealth Immigrants Act have targeted potential migrants whose skin colour was not white. Indeed, the term 'immigrant' has often been a synonym for 'person of minority ethnic descent'. A continuing source of grievance in many minority ethnic communities has been the way they, their relatives and often their legitimate visitors and business contacts are more likely than their white counterparts to have the legitimacy of their residence questioned, or experience difficulties at passport control when entering the country (Mason 2000: 123–4). Once again, the subtle message received by many of Britain's minority ethnic citizens is that they are second-class citizens. Such messages are further reinforced by the nature of press coverage of scares about illegal migration and allegedly bogus asylum seekers (Gabriel 1998: 97–128). Most recently, attempts by the two major political parties in Britain (Conservative and Labour) to position themselves in the run-up to the 2005 general election have led to the publication of competing proposals to, in popular parlance, 'get tough on immigration'. These proposals have, more or less explicitly –

and perhaps intentionally – conflated the issue of how to deal with claims for asylum with the issue of whether or not additional controls are required on immigration. Much of the discussion has failed to take cognisance of the actual profile of immigration into Britain (see above) and has, instead, seemed to draw on popular fears and confusions by stressing the need for quotas based on skill shortages and checks on health status.

There is not space here adequately to dissect these political discourses. What is clear, however, is that they carry messages that equate 'immigration' with a threat of alien swamping and the potential overwhelming of public resources. In the process, they help to reinforce longstanding messages about the relationship of migrant and minority ethnic status. As a result, they implicitly challenge the citizenship claims of the long-settled descendents of earlier migrants. Paradoxically, therefore, even as the diversity of ethnic identities becomes ever more apparent, so these political discourses help once again to reinforce a simplistic division between undifferentiated ethnic majorities and minorities.

We noted above that the 2001 census had revealed evidence of significant deprivation among Muslims. It is no accident, perhaps, that 2001 saw the participation of significant numbers of Muslim young men in urban disturbances in cities in the north of England with significant Muslim populations. Although this was not an entirely novel phenomenon, it fuelled an already emerging process of demonisation, in terms of which young Muslim males began to replace young black men as the object of white fears. There is also some evidence that, in the context of a continuing popular tendency to be unable to differentiate their fellow 'Asian' citizens, members of other communities have been caught up in hostility to Muslims. These processes had already been given some momentum by the 1991 Gulf War and the Salman Rushdie affair (see the discussion in Mason 2000: 113, 141–2). They were to be given even greater impetus by the events of September 11 2001 and the war in Iraq in 2003.

One of the consequences of these developments, as well as of changes in the activities of the police and security services in the context of the so-called 'war on terror', has been an increasing sense among British Muslims that they are not trusted and their Islamic faith is incompatible with British citizenship and identity. Nevertheless, it is interesting to note that, notwithstanding their concerns about not being respected by their fellow citizens and government, a significant proportion of those interviewed in recent research expressed a commitment to a British identity alongside a commitment to a Muslim one (*Guardian* 2004b).

The message of these kinds of experiences is frequently that, notwithstanding their formal entitlement to full citizenship rights, many members of Britain's minority ethnic communities experience a sense of exclusion from the identity 'British'. Of course, there is a variety of different characteristics that go to make up the identity of all of us including, crucially, gender. Evidence from the fourth PSI survey shows that Britain's minority ethnic citizens call on a wide variety of cultural and other characteristics in defining their ethnic identities.

In order to explore this issue, the PSI survey adopted the strategy of asking respondents to rank in importance a range of characteristics in terms of which they might describe themselves to strangers. These included nationality, skin colour, country of origin, age, job, education, height, colour of hair or eyes, level of income and father's job. In other words, they included a range of more or less visible personal characteristics and attributes, only some of which are conventionally associated with ethnicity. In particular, characteristics often used in the measurement of social class, such as job and education, scored highly among all minority ethnic groups. In addition, religion was of great significance, especially among members of the Asian groups. Put another way, it is clear that in constructing their identities, the respondents in the PSI survey utilised a range of physical, positional and lifestyle characteristics in combinations which both varied between groups but which also exhibited considerable similarities (Modood 1997c: 290–338).

Nevertheless, there is also evidence that these identifications are made in the context of a recognition that others categorise them in a way that constrains the choices they themselves can make. A number of persons of Asian descent who responded to the PSI survey indicated that they were inclined to think of themselves as 'black' in situations where they were in contact with white people. Among the reasons given was the belief that this was how they were defined by whites – in other words, they felt their choices were constrained (Modood 1997c: 295–6). It is in this context that subtle messages about what constitutes 'Britishness' exercise exclusionary pressures that limit choice.

Having said this, it would equally be a mistake to believe that identities are static or that Britain's minority ethnic citizens are simply passive victims in the face of economic exclusion and racist attitudes and behaviour. There are myriad examples, ranging from self-help community organisations through to various forms of political mobilisation, of Britain's minority citizens challenging their exclusion. More subtly, there is considerable evidence of a process of continuous change in the ways the identities of all Britain's varied citizens are constructed and negotiated. Modood has attempted to capture the ways in which, for second and third generation members of minority ethnic groups in Britain, subtle and complex changes in patterns of ethnic identification have occurred. His analysis suggests that there is no straightforward relationship between 'the cultural content of an ethnicity and strategies of ethnic self-definition' (Modood 1997c: 337). The result is a shift from what Modood calls 'behavioural difference' to an emphasis on 'associational identity':

> for many the strength of their ethnic identity was owed to a group pride in response to perceptions of racial exclusion and ethnic stereotyping by the white majority. The consequent sense of rejection and insecurity was instrumental in assertions of ethnic identities, often in forms susceptible to forging new anti-racist solidarities (such as 'black') and hyphenated (such as British-Pakistani) or even multiple identities. (Modood 1997c: 337)

Modood is at pains to argue that the resultant identifications are not weaker than those of the first generation but differently constructed. They are much less taken for granted (based on shared cultural values) and more consciously chosen, publicly celebrated and debated, and part of a contested arena of identity politics. As a result, they are potentially fluid and may change with political and other circumstances. In the process, they may either revive old cultural practices or generate new ones (Modood 1997c: 337).

We should also note that, just as the disaggregation of the 'white' ethnic category offers the potential to reveal hitherto unacknowledged patterns of advantage and disadvantage, so there are processes afoot which are increasingly challenging many of the things we have come to take for granted about white British ethnic and, for that matter, national identities. One does not need to subscribe to the 'break-up of Britain' thesis (Nairn 1981) to recognise that the process of devolution has led to a reinvigoration of longstanding national identities among both the Scots and the Welsh. Hand in hand with devolution is a growing regional agenda, at both national and EU levels, which has the potential to reawaken regional identities which have long appeared dormant. An interesting byproduct of these developments has been the way in which Englishness as an identity has been increasingly problematised (Chapter 5; McCrone and Kiely 2000). As the dominant national group in Britain, until recently it was not necessary for most English people to reflect on the relationship between English and British identities. With the increasing assertiveness of other national identities within Britain, however, the English are being forced to confront the question of what exactly marks them off. This has been reflected in a flurry of recent television programmes and press commentary on the question 'who are the English?' (Paxman 1999). These processes parallel and interact with the changing identities of minority ethnic citizens, offering yet further scope for hybrid identities that may challenge still further what was until recently an apparently unproblematic national category.

At this point, it is appropriate to note that much recent work in sociology has argued that, in the modern world, all identities are more fluid, provisional and multifaceted than some more traditional characterisations of cultural difference would suggest. We may identify two broad bodies of literature from which these kinds of arguments have developed. The first is a feminist critique and the second writing in the post-modern and post-structuralist schools of thought.

One of the earliest challenges came from feminist scholars and activists who, from the early 1980s onwards, began to challenge the idea that women constituted a single, undifferentiated category sharing a common set of interests. Some of these criticisms came from black feminists who contested what they saw as the dominance of white middle-class perspectives and argued that patriarchal oppression was mediated by racism in ways that made the experience and opportunities of black and white women quite different. Other writers in the feminist tradition have challenged the essentialisation of ethnic difference, arguing that ethnicity is gendered in ways that differentiate the experience of men and women but which are also constitutive of ethnic difference (Anthias and Yuval-Davis 1992: 113–15).

A second source for the recognition of the provisionality and negotiability of identity is to be found in post-modernist and post-structuralist writing. According to this view, old-style, modernist explanations of the social world in terms of large-scale and relatively stable social categories do violence to the complexity of individuals' everyday experiences. Instead, it is argued that the pace of change in the post-modern world creates conditions in which individuals are increasingly free to make multiple identity choices that match the purposes (or even the whims) of the moment (Rattansi and Westwood 1994; Bradley 1996: 21–7).

It will be apparent from what was said above about the relationship between choice and constraint that we are sceptical about the more extreme versions of this kind of perspective. Nevertheless, we have shown there is some evidence that Britain's young minority ethnic citizens do perceive a wider range of identity options than some of the more rigid characterisations of ethnic difference may suggest.

Understanding social divisions, difference and diversity

It is difficult to deny the power of accounts that recognise the dynamism of ethnic identity in modern Britain. They are, after all, consistent with the conception of ethnicity (discussed above) that recognises the significance of the boundary process. Moreover, they also challenge the simplistic victimology that has all too frequently characterised discussions of ethnic inequalities in Britain. On the other hand, they present a potential problem. When we take these insights together with the evidence reviewed above about increasing social mobility, it is all too easy to make the mistake of assuming that social divisions based on ethnicity are, if not a thing of the past, at least on the way to a solution. However, when measured by material inequalities and differences of treatment, this is far from being the case.

The difficulty arises not simply because of a debate about the meaning of the evidence or even the pace of change. There is a more fundamental difficulty arising from the clash of modernist and post-modernist perspectives. As the example of traditional class analysis shows, concern with social divisions based on material inequalities is firmly located within a modernist world view. From whatever theoretical perspective it is approached, there is an implicit acceptance that social divisions are problematic. This may be because they are thought to undermine some minimum common standard – expressed in such notions as equality or human rights. Alternatively, it may be because they are perceived to threaten social cohesion by either undermining shared value systems (anomie) or encouraging political dissent. Thus, whether inequalities are to be challenged or justified, there is a common belief that solutions are available in the form of political and social action.

By contrast, for post-modernist writers, the old meta-narratives underpinning these traditional approaches are no longer tenable in a world characterised by diversity, fluidity and fragmentation. Abandoning faith in such certainties, post-modernism is more likely to move to a celebration of difference rather than detect in it signs of social decay. In its extreme forms, post-modernism represents a celebration of choice and the triumph of style. Even in its less triumphalist guise, however, in the diverse identity options open to individuals in the modern world, it identifies the opportunity to challenge the stereotyping and categorisation all too often characteristic of the behaviour of 'ethnic majorities' (Jenkins 1997: 29–30). It thus celebrates rather than problematises difference. At the same times it challenges the essentialisation of the ethnic categories that are central to the process of measuring and tracking social inequalities, conventionally defined.

The difficulty with this is that while it may be easy to agree that ethnic diversity in modern Britain should be viewed positively – as something contributing to the richness of the lives of all citizens – all too often difference has been seen as problematic. Indeed, as we have seen, even when it gives rise to positive assertions of identity, 'difference' has frequently been a product of exclusionary processes and practices. Is there a solution to this apparent impasse? Modood (1997c: 358) has suggested that the way forward lies with a conception of equality that recognises 'the right to have one's "difference" recognised and supported in both the public and the private spheres'. He argues that this implies common rights and responsibilities and, in the end, a renewal of concepts of Britishness within which currently negative views of difference are framed. We need 'to develop a more plural approach to racial disadvantage, and to formulate an explicit ideal of multicultural citizenship appropriate to Britain in the next decade and beyond' (Modood 1997c: 359).

But herein lies the dilemma. Without the capacity to measure the patterning of material inequalities and differences of treatment among Britain's minority ethnic groups, how will it be possible to know whether progress has been made in reducing disadvantage? Such measurement must, by definition, use some set of categories in terms of which data can be collected. However sensitive we seek to be to people's self-definitions, any category system runs the risk of failing to capture the richness and complexity of people's identity choices. There is a danger, then, that we may reproduce the very divisions we seek to problematise.

I have tried to show in this chapter that there are very real social divisions in modern Britain arising from ethnic difference. They are, however, neither static nor unchallenged. Moreover, they interact in complex ways with sources of social differentiation based on class and gender, to the extent that not only are their effects difficult to disentangle but they may be thought of as mutually constitutive.

Discussion Questions

All British citizens regularly encounter occasions on which they are required to complete ethnic monitoring questionnaires. They all, therefore, regularly have to make decisions about 'which box to tick'. This chapter has argued that the categories they are offered are a result of a mix of historical accident and changing policy preoccupations. They do not always keep pace with the real-world dynamics of ethnic divisions and identities. Thus claims and attributions of ethnicity involve a complex process in which people's choices are constrained, provisional and contested. In light of this:

1. What do you consider to be your ethnic identity?

2. What leads you to this choice?

3. To what extent do you think your answer provides a satisfactory representation of the 'real you'? What are your reasons for your answers?

FURTHER READING

David Mason *Race and Ethnicity in Modern Britain* (Oxford: Oxford University Press, 2nd edn 2000) seeks to provide a comprehensive introduction to race and ethnicity in modern Britain. It links conceptual and theoretical debates to detailed empirical evidence of ethnic stratification in a range of areas of social life. Andrew Pilkington *Racial Disadvantage and Ethnic Diversity in Britain* (Basingstoke: Palgrave – now Palgrave Macmillan, 2002) is another wide-ranging introductory overview of key debates and research on race and ethnicity in contemporary Britain. Mason, D. (ed.) *Explaining Ethnic Differences* (Bristol: Policy Press, 2003), comprising contributions from a number of key experts in the field, offers a more advanced and detailed discussion of several of the themes of this chapter as well as providing analyses of patterns of changing ethnic disadvantage in a wider range of aspects of life in modern Britain. Modood, T., Berthoud, R., Lakey, J., Nazroo, J. et al. *Ethnic Minorities in Britain* (London: Policy Studies Institute, 1997) reports the results of the Fourth National Survey of Ethnic Minorities conducted by the Policy Studies Institute. It represents one of the most comprehensive sources of data on the current situation of Britain's minority ethnic groups, while providing detailed comparisons with the results of earlier surveys dating back to the 1960s. John Solomos and Les Back *Racism in Society* (Basingstoke: Macmillan – now Palgrave Macmillan, 1996) is an accessible introduction to some of the key contemporary debates surrounding racism in modern societies. Mohan Luthra *Britain's Black Population: Social Change, Public Policy and Agenda* (Aldershot: Arena, Ashgate, 1997) is the third in a series with the same title which presents evidence of ethnic inequality in a range of areas of social life in modern Britain. The author's background combines experience as both an academic and a practitioner and the volume reflects this by providing a sustained attempt to identify the social policy implications of the trends identified.

Other Major Social Divisions

CHAPTER 5

Religion

ALAN ALDRIDGE

This chapter will provide you with a critical understanding of the following aspects of religion as a source of social division:

- The relevance of religious divisions to the secularisation thesis
- The relationship between religion and the nation-state
- Divisions within faith communities
- Religious conflict in Northern Ireland
- Cultural bias and the legal position of different religions and faith communities
- The rights of religious minorities in multi-faith societies
- Anti-Catholic prejudice and the decline of Catholic subculture
- Islamophobia and cultural racism
- Religion and social disadvantage
- The relationship between religious and ethnic identities
- Problems with essentialist approaches to religion
- Religion as a cultural resource

The persistence of religious divisions

The place of religion in the modern world was a central concern of the great theorists who founded the discipline of sociology in the early nineteenth century. For all their theoretical, methodological and ideological differences, most of these classic founders took the view that religion was losing its place at the heart of social, cultural and political life. The modern world was, they believed, undergoing secularisation – a profound transformation captured in Wilson's (1966: xiv) concise definition: 'the process by which religious thinking, practice and institutions lose social significance'.

In a similar vein to Wilson, Berger (1967) distinguishes three different facets of the secularisation of the Christian world. The first is socio-structural: Christian churches, at least in the West, have lost functions (such as educa-

133

tion, law making and law enforcement) which are now performed by secular agencies. Equally important is the *cultural* aspect: the natural and social sciences relentless promote a secular perspective on the world, while the religious content of western art, music, literature and philosophy has drastically declined. This secularisation of society and culture brings a secularisation of *individual consciousness*: quite simply, fewer people use religious categories to understand the world and guide their own actions within it. Perhaps this last facet of secularisation has been exaggerated; thus Davie (1994) argues that 'believing without belonging' persists as a significant feature of contemporary societies, despite the decline of traditional religious institutions. Against this, Bruce (2002) contends that the secularisation of individual consciousness has been an inescapable corollary of the secularisation of society and culture. Religious belief has declined, together with religious belonging; each succeeding generation is more secularised than its predecessors.

If the secularisation thesis is valid, then we should expect religion to become less and less important as a source of social division. That was certainly the view that Wilson took in his early work. Religion would survive and even flourish among minority religious movements ('sects' and 'cults'), but what this showed was not so much the continued vitality of religion as its consignment to the margins of society. Minority religious movements were protests against the secularisation of the wider society; their marginality and lack of impact was evidence not against but in favour of the triumph of secularity. In support of this, Wilson (1966: 81) argued that 'the marked loss of religious fervour in Northern Ireland in the decades since the end of the Second World War, and its diminished consequence in political terms, illustrates the declining relevance of religion for politics'. The pattern of events in Northern Ireland since Wilson wrote those words raises profound questions about the nature and significance of social divisions based on religion (Chapter 6).

Religion rarely stands alone as a cause of conflict and division, but is usually bound up with other dimensions, in particular ethnicity, 'race', language and nationality. Given that it affirms a source of meaning and authority that transcends human desires and social conventions, religion has the capacity to provide the ultimate justification for social conflict, violence, liberation struggles and war. When nation-states are created or destroyed, religion is almost invariably a focus of unity or conflict. Take the case of the Kingdom of Serbs, Croats and Slovenes, which was founded in 1918 after the end of the First World War and in the wake of the fall of the Ottoman (Muslim) and Austro-Hungarian (Christian) empires. It was renamed the Kingdom of Yugoslavia in 1929, and became a Communist state in 1945. When Communism collapsed in the 1990s, Yugoslavia broke up into smaller states: the Union of Serbia and Montenegro, which is predominantly Serbian

Orthodox; Bosnia-Herzegovina, mainly Muslim although with a large Eastern Orthodox minority and significant Roman Catholic presence; Croatia and Slovenia, both predominantly Roman Catholic; and Macedonia, predominantly Eastern Orthodox. There is no prospect of reunification; on the contrary, further divisions may occur, such as the breakaway of Montenegro from Serbia. Part of the justification for its desired secession is Montenegro's claim to be, in implied contrast to Serbia, a tolerant multi-faith society.

The partition of India in 1947 has left its own religiously-inflicted conflicts, including Sikh claims against Pakistan over the Punjab, and Pakistani claims against India over Kashmir and Jammu, where Muslims are in the majority. The recurring conflicts in Ireland were not solved by the partition in 1921, when the Irish Republic gained its independence from British rule, while the 'six counties' – Antrim, Armagh, Down, Fermanagh, Londonderry and Tyrone – were constituted as the UK province of Northern Ireland. Although Protestants often refer to Northern Ireland as 'Ulster', the historic Ulster was made up of nine counties, including Cavan, Donegal and Monaghan. These three were predominantly Roman Catholic, which is why they were allocated to the Irish Republic, preserving a Protestant majority in the North. Within what became Northern Ireland, territorial segregation between Catholics and Protestants has become more pronounced over time, particularly in the working-class areas of Belfast and Derry, where Catholics have been driven out of Protestant areas and vice versa.

These examples show the potential for division not only between the world's religions but also within them. The main divide within Islam is between Sunnis and Shi'ites, the repercussions of which are currently being played out in Iraq, where the majority Shia community had been oppressed under Saddam Hussein. Christianity has a tripartite division between Catholics, Protestants and Orthodox, with numerous subdivisions in the Protestant tradition. Christianity has been more bitterly divided on doctrinal grounds than any other of the world's major religions. Clashes over doctrine and heresy have gone together with conflicts over authority: what is the correct relationship between the authority of scripture, the church, and human reason? Where is authority located (in the Pope, for example?), and who may exercise it? Contemporary divisions over the ordination of women to the priesthood or the place within the church of lesbians and gays are testimony to Christianity's continuing preoccupation with authority.

Even allowing for secularisation, the contemporary vitality of these conflicts shows that religious identity remains a powerful source of social division, not just confined to one part of the world or Britain. The UK national census, conducted every ten years, is a useful source of information about religious affiliation. Census data on religion have been regularly gathered in

Northern Ireland; in the 2001 census, a voluntary question on religious affiliation was asked in the rest of the UK – the first time this had been done since 1851. The results are shown in Table 5.1.

Table 5.1 Population of Great Britain by religion (April 2001)

	Numbers	*Percentages*
Christian	41,014,811	71.8
Muslim	1,588,890	2.8
Hindu	558,342	1.0
Sikh	336,179	0.6
Jewish	267,373	0.5
Buddhist	149,157	0.3
Other religions	159,167	0.3
No religion	8,596,488	15.1
Religion not stated	4,433,520	7.8
Total	**57,103,927**	

Source: Office for National Statistics, *Focus on Religion*, October (2004d).

On these data, Britain appears to be quite clearly a Christian country. Almost 72 per cent of those answering the question gave their religion as Christian; the next highest figure was the 15.1 per cent who said they had no religion. Turning to other faiths, the Muslim community is markedly larger than any other, as shown in Figure 5.1.

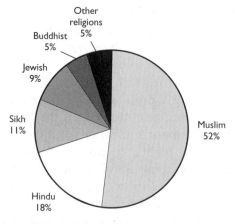

Figure 5.1 Distribution of non-Christian religions in Great Britain (April 2001)

Source: Calculated from Census 2001, ONS (2003).

In addition to the major world faiths, the census returns show that 32,000 respondents were Spiritualists, 31,000 Pagans, 15,000 Jains, 7,000 Wiccans, 5,000 Rastafarians, 5,000 Bahá'ís and 4,000 Zoroastrians.

The distribution of religious affiliation is markedly different in the various parts of the UK. The figures for Northern Ireland show, by comparison to the rest of the UK, an overwhelming preponderance of Christians. The census questions reflect this. In England and Wales, respondents were simply asked: 'What is your religion?', and were offered the following response categories:

- None
- Christian
- Buddhist
- Hindu
- Jewish
- Muslim
- Sikh
- Any other religion (please write in)

People in Northern Ireland, in contrast, were first asked a filter question: 'Do you regard yourself as belonging to any particular religion?' Those who replied 'yes' were then asked: 'What religion, religious denomination or body do you belong to?' The response categories were:

- Roman Catholic
- Presbyterian Church in Ireland
- Church of Ireland
- Methodist Church in Ireland
- Other, please write in

Perhaps the most striking difference is that whereas in England and Wales the major faith communities – Buddhist, Hindu, Jewish, Muslim and Sikh – are listed alongside Christianity, the census in Northern Ireland treats all religions apart from Christian denominations as falling into the category 'other'. This differing approach reflects the patterns of religious affiliation in Northern Ireland, where, on the census figures, 86 per cent of the population identify themselves as Christian.

In Scotland, the census asked: 'What religion, religious denomination or body do you belong to?' The results, as depicted in Figure 5.2, show that 65 per cent of Scots identify themselves as Christian, with the Church of Scotland accounting for 42 per cent of the population. Faith communities other than Christianity – including Muslims, Jews, Hindus, Sikhs and Buddhists – only total 2 per cent.

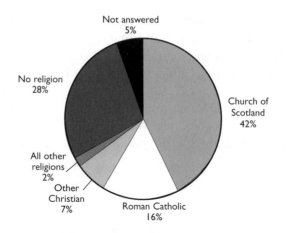

Figure 5.2 Religious affiliation in Scotland (April 2001)

Source: Calculated from Census 2001, ONS (2003).

These considerable differences between England and Wales and Scotland and Northern Ireland are closely connected to the distribution of ethnicity in the UK. Ethnic minority groups account for only 2 per cent of the population of Scotland, and less than 1 per cent in Northern Ireland.

Table 5.2 Religion by ethnic group, England and Wales (April 2001)

Religion	Row percentages by selected ethnic group						
	White	Indian	Pakistani	Bangladeshi	Black Caribbean	Black African	Chinese
Christian	96.33	0.14	0.02	0.00	1.11	0.88	0.13
Buddhist	38.79	1.30	0.13	0.12	0.67	0.24	23.75
Hindu	1.31	84.46	0.10	0.31	0.30	0.18	0.03
Jewish	96.81	0.26	0.14	0.05	0.21	0.09	0.04
Muslim	11.62	8.51	42.52	16.79	0.29	6.22	0.05
Sikh	2.09	91.48	0.11	0.03	0.04	0.12	0.02
No religion	94.54	0.23	0.05	0.02	0.82	0.14	1.55

Source: Census 2001, ONS (2003).

Table 5.2, which relates to data on England and Wales, shows religion broken down by ethnic group (Chapter 4). The correlations are striking. Ninety-six per cent of Christians and 97 per cent of Jews are white; 84 per cent of Hindus and 91 per cent of Sikhs are Indian. Compared to the other Asian faiths, the Muslim population is more ethnically diverse: 12 per cent white, 9 per cent Indian, 43 per cent Pakistani, 17 per cent Bangladeshi and 6 per cent black African – a pattern reflecting Islam's history as a conversionist faith. As far as having no religion is concerned, it is predominantly a white affair.

When ethnicity is broken down by religion (Table 5.3), strong correlations are equally apparent. White people are predominantly Christian (76 per cent) or have no religion (15 per cent). Pakistanis are overwhelmingly Muslim (92 per cent), as are Bangladeshis (also 92 per cent). People giving their ethnic identification as black Caribbean are predominantly Christian, as are black Africans (with a significant Muslim minority). Indians are the most religiously diverse, with sizeable percentages of Hindus, Sikhs and Muslims, as well as a smaller percentage of Christians. Having no religion is, strikingly, a majority option only for the Chinese respondents.

Table 5.3 Ethnic group by religion, England and Wales (April 2001)

Selected ethnic group	Row percentages by religion						
	Christian	Buddhist	Hindu	Jewish	Muslim	Sikh	No religion
White	75.69	0.12	0.02	0.53	0.38	0.01	15.34
Indian	4.89	0.18	45.00	0.06	12.70	29.06	1.73
Pakistani	1.09	0.03	0.08	0.05	92.01	0.05	0.50
Bangladeshi	0.50	0.06	0.60	0.05	92.48	0.04	0.43
Black Caribbean	73.76	0.17	0.29	0.10	0.79	0.02	11.23
Black African	68.87	0.07	0.21	0.05	20.04	0.09	2.31
Chinese	21.56	15.12	0.07	0.05	0.33	0.03	52.60

Source: Census 2001, ONS (2003).

Cultural bias and the law

The complexity of national identities in the UK, discussed in detail in Chapter 6, is graphically illustrated by the legal position of the Christian churches. In England, the church 'by law established' is the Church of England; it has enjoyed a privileged position since Henry VIII severed the English Church from Rome in 1534. Since that date, the British monarch has been required to be a Protestant; no heir to the throne can be Roman Catholic or, even more controversially, be married to a Roman Catholic.

Establishment means that the Church of England is not a voluntary society, such as a golf club or political pressure group, formed as a result of contractual agreements between its members. The Church has a unique relationship to the state. The reigning monarch is Supreme Governor of the Church of England. Its ecclesiastical laws and courts are part of the English legal system. Twenty-six senior bishops of the Church of England, including the Archbishops of Canterbury and York, sit as of right in the House of Lords, the upper chamber of the British Parliament. People living in England have a legal right to be married in their parish church and have their children baptised by a member of the parish clergy. The Anglican clergy are also required to conduct funeral services if requested to do so. These obligations were less problematic when England was a predominantly Christian culture, but the decline in church attendance and the transition to a multicultural society have put them under strain. A growing number of Anglican clergy resent these obligations, feeling themselves compelled to offer the sacraments 'cheaply' to people who have at best a 'nominal' commitment to the Christian faith.

While culturally dominant in England, the Anglican tradition was always a cultural minority in Northern Ireland and Wales, a fact reflected in the eventual disestablishment of the Church of Ireland in 1869 and the Church of Wales in 1914 (with a symbolic change of name to the Church in Wales). Scotland has an established church, but it is not the Scottish Episcopal Church, which is Anglican, but the Presbyterian Church of Scotland (known to Scots as the Kirk). Presbyterianism (the word presbyter comes from the Greek *presbuteros*, meaning 'elder') has its origins in the Protestant Reformation, specifically in the teachings and forms of church governance instituted in the sixteenth century by John Calvin in Geneva and John Knox in Scotland. Presbyterians played an active part in the War of Independence of Britain's American colonies.

The British sovereign takes an oath, upon accession to the throne, to uphold the legal rights and Presbyterian government of the Church of Scotland. The Queen is Supreme Governor of the Church of England, but when she and other members of the royal family visit Scotland, they are ministered to by the Church of Scotland. Occasionally, this can have unexpected benefits. The Church of England has been opposed to offering a church wedding to divorcees, on the grounds that divorce was condemned by Jesus himself. When Princess Anne remarried, the ceremony was held in Scotland, in a kirk; no controversy ensued.

To people from other countries, these peculiarities seem puzzling. In Britain, they pass almost without comment – they have become non-issues. From a historical point of view, they are the residue of once bitter religious conflicts: the persecution of Roman Catholics under Edward VI and Elizabeth I, the persecution of Protestants under Mary Queen of Scots and the penalties suffered by members of the Free Churches who dissented from the Anglican supremacy. Arguably, what remains from the history of bigotry and oppression is a warm afterglow of quaint practices that demonstrate not conflict but mutual accommodation. Britain, on this view, has moved towards the American situation of 'denominational pluralism', in which mainstream religious institutions no longer insist on their own monopoly of the truth but instead see themselves, in Wallis's phrase (1976: 13), as 'pluralistically legitimate' – that is, simply one among many valid paths to salvation.

In contrast to this agreeable portrait of denominational pluralism, one can point to the decline of liberal Protestant denominations such as Episcopalians, Presbyterians and Methodists, and the ascendancy and political mobilisation of fundamentalist Christian groups that are hostile to tolerant liberalism, which they see as permissive, degenerate and ungodly. The political platforms of Presidents Jimmy Carter, Ronald Reagan and George W. Bush all appealed to the conservative heartlands. Although the USA is a vast and culturally diverse society, many Americans live their lives encapsulated in local, homogeneous, mono-cultural milieux (Bruce 1996: 143). These stable communities are frequently breeding grounds for xenophobia, bigotry and intolerance, directed against sex education, birth control, stem cell research, abortion, homosexuality, the theory of evolution, Godless Communism and selected foreign regimes that are presented as a threat to peace and liberty. Christian fundamentalism is intolerant towards both other people's religious beliefs with which they disagree, and the social and political stances of more secular people.

If denominational pluralism is benign, then the establishment of the Church of England, far from being a problem for other churches and faith communities, might be seen as an asset. As secularisation proceeds, the established Church of England may be uniquely positioned to represent faith in its struggle against unbelief, rationalism and secularity. Muslims, Jews, Sikhs, Hindus and others do not seem to be pressing for disestablishment, still less for a secular state on the French model. Tellingly, the most vocal advocate of disestablishment and the complete separation of Church and state is an *antireligious* organisation: the National Secular Society, founded in 1866 by the atheist Charles Bradlaugh.

On the other hand, the notion that, in an increasingly multi-faith society, the Church of England can act as principal advocate for all faiths is likely to come under challenge. It may be a stage in the transition to multiculturalism, but can scarcely be the end point. A relevant case is prison chaplaincy (Beckford and Gilliat 1998; Beckford 1999). The British state expects Anglican chaplains to play a leading role in enabling prisoners of whatever religion to practice their faith while in prison; this is enshrined in the Prison Act of 1952. The act was passed in an era before the expansion of migration to Britain from the 'New Commonwealth', following which the country's Muslim, Hindu, Sikh, Jain and Buddhist communities rapidly expanded.

Their predicament is captured by Beckford (1999: 7):

> In return for abandoning claims to equality of treatment or equality of opportunity to influence chaplaincy policies, minority faith communities can rely on Anglican chaplains to defend their interests and facilitate their access to prisoners. Pragmatism takes precedence over principles of equality.

Within British prisons, minority faiths may be 'tolerated', but they are scarcely accorded equal rights, as demonstrated by their dependency on the goodwill of 'the' (Anglican) chaplain.

Until relatively recently, British law presupposed a society that was Christian, with the established Church of England at the core of the worshipping life of the nation (if we forget Scotland, Wales and Northern Ireland). For example, under the Burial Laws Amendment Act 1880, it is an offence to 'bring into contempt or obloquy the Christian religion, or the belief or worship of any church or denomination of Christians, or the members or any minister of any such church or denomination, or' – the law somewhat obscurely adds – 'any other person'. Similarly, the Offences Against The Persons Act 1861 makes it an offence to use

> threats or force, obstruct or prevent or endeavour to obstruct or prevent, any clergyman or other minister in or from celebrating divine service or otherwise officiating in any church, chapel, meeting house, or other place of divine worship.

It would seem that, despite the use of the Anglican term 'clergyman', the phrase 'divine service' implies that the law would cover all mainstream Christian denominations. What, though, of polytheistic religions such as (arguably) Hinduism, or non-theistic religions such as (arguably) Buddhism, or religious communities such as the Quakers, who have no ministers at all?

Most contentious of all have been the laws on blasphemy and blasphemous libel. These were used twice in the twentieth century. In 1921, the secularist John William Gott published a pamphlet insinuating that Jesus's entry into Jerusalem on a donkey made him look like a circus clown. Gott was successfully prosecuted by the state and, despite public uproar, sentenced to nine months' hard labour. As the years passed, many people persuaded themselves that the last had been heard of the laws on blasphemy, until, in 1977, Mary Whitehouse, an evangelical Christian and founder of the National Viewers' and Listeners' Association, brought a successful private prosecution against the magazine *Gay News* for publishing a poem depicting a Roman centurion's homoerotic feelings for the crucified Christ. In his summing-up, the judge said:

> Blasphemous libel is committed if there is published any writing concerning God or Christ, the Christian religion, the Bible, or some sacred subject, using words which are scurrilous, abusive or offensive and which tend to vilify the Christian religion (and therefore have a tendency to lead to a breach of the peace). (quoted by Ruthven 1991: 49)

With the passage of the Human Rights Act 1998, which came into force in 2000, it is virtually certain that these antiquated laws are no longer effective. The Human Rights Act, which makes the provisions of the European Convention on Human Rights enforceable in British courts, forbids discrimination on the grounds of religion. Any attempt to invoke laws such as blasphemy and blasphemous libel, with their protection only for Christianity in general and the Church of England in particular, would therefore be struck down by the court.

Until recently, British law offered scant protection to religious minorities. Some communities, notably Jews and Sikhs, have been able to secure legal protection of their rights, but only because the law has recognised them as ethnic groups, which means they are covered by legislation governing race relations. The Jewish and the Sikh faith are not conversionist; they are religions of a people defined ethnically as a community sharing a sense of a common descent and common culture (Fenton 2003: 3). Conversionist faiths such as Christianity and Islam are not ethnic religions, and this has produced a series of legal anomalies that have caused growing resentment, particularly among Britain's Muslim community. Muslims are left exposed as potential targets for racists, who can seek to evade prosecution by claiming that they are not unlawfully attacking an ethnic group or 'race', but are mounting an entirely lawful critique of a religion.

Membership of the EU has already brought about a radical shift in UK law, above all with the passage of the Human Rights Act. After years in which UK law treated religion under the heading of ethnicity, discrimination on grounds of religion is gradually being explicitly criminalised. At the time of writing, the latest example of this process is the government's stated intention to introduce legislation forbidding incitement to religious hatred, in parallel to the existing laws against incitement to racial hatred. As discussed above, the aim is to extend protection to communities such as Muslims, whose faith cannot be characterised as an ethnic religion. A secondary aim is to prevent extremists from claiming a platform to speak for persecuted religious minorities. Religion is firmly on the political agenda.

The erosion of Catholic subculture

Until the 1960s, Roman Catholicism in Britain formed a distinctive subculture, with its own characteristic beliefs, symbols, rituals and lifestyles. For many Catholics, their faith was experienced as an ascribed identity, similar in many ways to that of an ethnic group: a religion not simply of choice but of birth and birthright, often referred to as 'cradle' Catholicism.

At the organisational level, the Church set itself up as a bastion, 'Fortress Rome', defending itself against the perceived threats presented by secular culture and Protestantism. Nationally and locally, many Catholic leaders drew back from close ecumenical cooperation with other Christian churches that had 'separated' from the Catholic fold; shared communion with such churches was strictly forbidden. The Catholic Church cultivated its own organisations – schools and convents, parish clubs and Catholic associations. Catholics were encouraged to pray for the conversion of Britain to the fullness of faith embodied in the one true Church founded by Christ.

During this period, the Church was successful in inculcating traditional values and disciplines into its members. Catholics were encouraged to socialise with and marry Catholics. Catholics who married Protestants were expected to hold the wedding in a Catholic Church, bring their children up as Catholics and try to convert their partner. 'Marrying out' could cause family conflict, and some relatives would refuse to have anything to do with people who had formed a 'mixed' marriage.

The Catholic priesthood possessed considerable authority over parishioners. Disciplines such as Friday abstinence from meat (popularly referred to as 'fish on Friday'), regular attendance at mass, individual confession of sins and rejection of any artificial means of contraception were widely respected. Catholic were socialised into a guilt-ridden culture marked by anxiety about mortal sin and fear of eternal damnation. The Catholics' strong sense of their own distinctive identity was reinforced by anti-Catholic, anti-papal and anti-Irish prejudice in the wider society which drew on a stock of derogatory terms and negative stereotypes.

The subcultural Catholicism of Fortress Rome presented itself to the faithful as all of a piece. Hornsby-Smith (2004: 47) suggests that many Catholics probably did not draw distinctions between the various elements that made up the subculture:

- *credal beliefs*, such as belief in the Holy Trinity
- *non-credal beliefs*, such as papal infallibility
- *moral teachings*, such as marital fidelity and avoidance of artificial contraception
- *disciplinary rules*, such as the obligation to attend mass and confess sins regularly to a priest.

As the 1960s progressed, this subcultural Catholicism fell apart; collective 'cradle' Catholicism gave way to a faith that has been chosen. Some critics saw the collapse of Fortress Rome as a wilful act of self-destruction perpetrated by the Church authorities through the reforms introduced by the Second Vatican Council (1962–65). Not only did the Church relax its insistence on such distinctive disciplines as Friday abstinence, it ruinously abandoned the glory of the Latin Mass (the Tridentine Mass, named after the Council of Trent, 1545–63) in favour of an insipid 'modern' version. Others would argue that the Church had to engage in this programme of 'updating' *(aggiornamento)* to secure its future in the modern world.

A wealth of evidence shows that Catholicism has been transformed socially and culturally. Instead of treating all the elements of Catholic culture as equally binding, more and more Catholics draw a distinction between the core, credal beliefs – eternal truths that cannot be challenged – and cultural symbols and practices that reflect traditional customs rather than the unchanging gospel. Priests may seek to impose the old disciplines, but their parishioners quietly disobey – an open secret being the use of contraceptives. Catholics feel less tightly bound by the Church's authority, less anxious and guilt-ridden; their identity is more a matter of individual choice and is no longer defined in opposition to the wider culture. If use of contraceptives stands as evidence of the weakening of the Church's once unquestioned authority, the growth and increasing acceptance of 'mixed marriages' points unequivocally to the erosion of Catholic subculture.

We have evidence of similar processes occurring among Catholics in Northern Ireland. Boal et al.'s study (1997, cited by Mitchell 2004), which surveyed churchgoers in Belfast, showed the growth of individualism in the Catholic community. They reported an increased tendency, particularly among young people, to pick and choose among Catholic doctrines and disobey religious disciplines, a position justified on the ground that the individual's own conscience should take priority over the formal teaching of the Church.

Cultural racism: the case of Islamophobia

'Islamophobia' was famously defined in Parekh's report for the Runnymede Trust (1997: 4) as an 'unfounded hostility towards Islam, and therefore fear or dislike of all or most Muslims'. As with any definition of a key term, it is controversial. To speak of a phobia may suggest something irrational and beyond the control of the persons afflicted with it; thus arachnophobes, who have an irrational fear of spiders, are to be seen not as perpetrators of an evil but innocent victims of a mild psychopathology. People suffering from a phobia typically avoid and flee from the source of their fear; they do not aggressively attack or persecute it.

This is just one of a number of reasons why some writers have suggested alternative terms to replace Islamophobia. Halliday (1999) argues that, although its advocates are liberal and well intentioned, the concept of Islamophobia plays into the hands of extremists. It puts forward Islam as an undifferentiated abstract essence, ripe for attack by those who hate Muslims, and for defence by radical Islamists seeking to impose Islamic culture in particular nation-states or even across the globe. Islamists construct Islam as an essence; in their hands, culturally variable and invented traditions are transformed into the eternal truths of the Qur'an and the life and teaching of the Prophet Muhammad. Islamophobia lends credence to the contention that there is a deep-seated and inevitable conflict between Christian and Islamic civilisation. The concept of Islamophobia, Halliday argues, distracts attention from the enormous cultural diversity within and between Islamic communities and the social and cultural currents of change that have swept through them. Islamophobia misrepresents the target of hostility, which is not the faith that is Islam but the people who are Muslims. Halliday (1999) therefore proposes, by analogy with anti-Semitism, the term 'anti-Muslimism' – a term which has not, however, gained wide currency.

Modood (1997a) argues that the concept of 'cultural racism' captures the social realities that 'Islamophobia' allows to escape. Cultural racism must be considered a form of racism, because it uses such physical characteristics as skin colour and physiognomy as markers that indicate supposedly 'racial' groups; racists proceed to impute inferiority to these 'races'. Unlike the Nazis, however, cultural racists do not see racial inferiority as *biologically* determined; instead, it is the product of the racial group's *culture*, as expressed in its history, traditions, values, norms of conduct and, most acutely, in its religion. In a historical perspective, Modood argues, nineteenth- and twentieth-century biological racism is the exception; cultural racism has been far more prevalent, manifesting itself specifically in anti-Semitism and hostility towards Muslims, and more generally in ideologies based on the 'problem' of assimilating 'backward' colonial peoples into the refined civilisations of the West. Confronted with legislation forbidding incitement to racial hatred, cultural racists tend to offer spurious disavowals of racism, made superficially plausible by their focus on culture rather than biology. Their racism may be encoded and sanitised as cultural critique, but it would be foolish to be taken in by it. The targets of racial abuse are typically Muslims from the Indian subcontinent, people who are easily identified by superficial physical characteristics (phenotypes) such as skin colour, which are falsely taken to indicate a different biological race (a genotype). For all the power of cultural racism, it is perhaps premature, as Mason points out (2000: 10), to pronounce the demise of racism based on biology.

The debate about terminology is significant; it points to the intersection of overlapping of a family of key concepts – religion, ethnicity, 'race' and nation. For all the doubts raised about it, 'Islamophobia' persists as a term that is widely used, not least by Muslims who feel themselves to be the targets of it. The term has the merit of signalling that religion is a salient badge of identity and a source of social discrimination and hostility in a society that is frequently taken to be secular. While Halliday is right to say that religion is not the only thing of significance, it should not be discounted. What becomes crucial, then, is the way in which Islamophobia has been measured and assessed.

The Runnymede Trust report (1997) identified four aspects of Islamophobia:

● *prejudice*, institutionalised in the mass media and pervasive in everyday social interaction
● *discrimination* in employment practices and the provision of services such as education and health;
● *exclusion* from employment, management and positions of responsibility, and from politics and government
● *violence*, whether in the form of physical assaults, the vandalising of property or verbal abuse.

The report is most famous for its identification of Islamophobia as a 'closed' rather than an 'open' view of Islam. It is 'closed' in eight respects:

1. Islam is seen as monolithic and static. It is intolerant of internal diversity and debate, and unreceptive to new cultural and scientific developments.
2. Islam is perceived as entirely 'other'. It has little in common with other cultures, refuses to be affected by them and therefore exerts little influence upon them.
3. Islam is seen as inferior to Western faiths and philosophies. It is unenlightened: primitive, barbaric, oppressive, irrational and sexist. None of this is worthy of our respect.

4. Islam is seen as a violent, aggressive religion that lends comfort, support and legitimacy to terrorists. It poses a grave threat to our values and way of life. We are parties to a 'clash of civilisations', in which Islamic states are not partners but enemies.
5. Islam is not a genuine faith sincerely practised by its followers, but a political ideology manipulated by autocratic regimes for political and military advantage.
6. Islamic criticisms of the West have no validity and are dismissed as worthless.
7. Hostility towards Islam serves as justification for discrimination against Muslims and their social exclusion from mainstream society.
8. Anti-Muslim and anti-Islamic ideas and practices are accepted as natural and normal.

This closed view constructs Islam in essentialist terms and opposes it to an equally essentialised and mythologised Britishness, an indiscriminate compound of culture, history, ethnicity, 'race' and religion. The opposition constructs Islam as an enemy and Muslims as potential traitors to Britain (Ansari 2004). Muslims are said to have their primary loyalty to the *umma*, the worldwide Muslim community, not to the British nation-state; they are supposedly taught to see the world as divided between *dar al-Islam*, the house of Islam and governed by Shari'a law, and *dar al-harb*, the house of war; they are allegedly bound by a sacred obligation to wage *jihad* or holy war in defence of Islam, irrespective of the national interests of the host society; and – a view lent colour by the attacks of September 11, 2001 – they venerate martyrdom in the cause of Islam, even if it involves carnage and self-immolation. In Ansari's words (2004: 8): 'The West has constructed and stigmatised an Islam with little resemblance to anything that is of value in ordinary Muslim lives.'

Islamophobia has deep roots in British culture. Two Gulf Wars, Western intervention in Afghanistan to oust the Taliban regime and the carnage of September 11 did not create Islamophobia, but they have undoubtedly intensified it. They appear to have strengthened xenophobia and racism, creating a climate of fear and hatred, which neo-Nazi and other extremist groups have sought to exploit. This has given a public platform to some of the most radical Islamist leaders, to the alarm of most of the Muslims for whom they claim to speak. An accumulating body of evidence shows that Britain's Muslim communities feel more vulnerable to prejudice, discrimination, exclusion and violence than any other social group. These fears have been experienced throughout Europe (Allen and Nielsen 2002). Muslims have been increasingly subjected to verbal abuse, harassment and aggression. Women wearing the *hijab* (covering for the head and face) have been particular targets, as have men wearing turbans, most of whom are in fact Sikhs.

Mosques have suffered graffiti and vandalism, as well as arson and bomb attacks. Visual identifiers of Islamic 'otherness' are a focus of abuse; where these are not apparent, Muslims have been relatively free from harassment. An example of this is Finland's long-established Tatar community: Muslims of Turkish descent who are well integrated into Finnish society and display few if any visual markers that they are Muslim. The Tatars have escaped abuses to which other Muslims in Finland have been subjected.

Official statistics bear out the disadvantages from which British Muslims suffer (ONS 2004e). Almost a third of Muslims (31 per cent) working in Great Britain have no formal qualifications at all – the highest proportion for any religious group. They are also the least likely to have university degrees. The unemployment rate among Muslims is higher than for any other religious group; this is true both of male and female unemployment. Young Muslims aged 16–24 have the highest unemployment rate of all, 22 per cent, almost exactly twice the figure for Christians of the same age. Muslims share with Sikhs the fate of being the most under-represented faith communities in professional and managerial occupations, and the most likely to be working in poorly paid, low-skilled jobs. The pattern of disadvantage shows itself in housing: 32 per cent of Muslim households are officially classified as 'overcrowded', the highest figure for any religious group. This may be accounted for, in part, by cultural preferences for larger families and a strong commitment to caring for elderly family members. Such cultural factors do not, however, explain the fact that Muslim households are less likely than any other to have central heating, sole use of a bathroom or be self-contained. This pattern is replicated across the country. What is true of employment and housing is also true of health (Chapter 14). After taking account of the age structures of the various religions (the Muslim community has a relatively high proportion of children and young people), rates of disability are highest among Muslims. It is not surprising, in the light of these indices of deprivation, that Muslims report higher rates of ill health than any other faith community. Muslims may share such disadvantages with other groups – the elderly, less skilled workers, the poor – but their identity tends to be articulated both by themselves and others in terms of their religious distinctiveness.

'Religion' as a troublesome category

'The Northern Ireland conflict is a religious conflict', as Bruce (1986: 249) pointedly reminds us. It is not purely about religion (religion in practice is never pure) nor is it mainly theological (theology is of concern to only a tiny minority of academics and clerics). In Northern Ireland, religion coincides with other bases of social division, including ethnicity, language, nationality, education and social class. This does not mean that religious conflict can be explained away as being 'really' class conflict, or nationalism, or tribalism. If there was any doubt that social divisions based on religion are complex, the case of Northern Ireland puts the matter beyond question.

In Bruce's interpretation, the conflict in Northern Ireland is marked by a basic asymmetry. Republicanism is nationalist and fundamentally secular. Many Catholics in the North look for the reunification of the six counties with the Irish Republic; enthusiasm for a united Ireland is notably greater among Catholics in the North than in the Republic itself. Ulster Loyalists, in contrast, do not identify straightforwardly and unequivocally with Britain. Their loyalty is to the symbol of the Crown, not the government in Westminster. They cherish a highly romanticised and nostalgic vision of Britain as it might once have been, not the social realities of the contemporary nation-state, still less its membership of the EU.

Although he describes conflict in Northern Ireland as religious, Bruce maintains that religion is not simply about humanity's relationship to the divine. People use churches and religion to signal ethnic identifications and draw boundaries around them; in doing so, religion is invoked not simply to mark ethnicity but to construct and reproduce it (Mitchell 2004: 248). This is particularly striking as far as Protestants are concerned. They regard themselves as possessing a distinctive culture, with a shared history, traditions, values, beliefs, lifestyles and symbols. The culture embodies a sense of what Max Weber called 'ethnic honour', incorporating an opposition between Protestant virtues and Catholic vices – a contrast which is used to explain and justify the relative advantage enjoyed by Protestants, particularly in the field of employment.

According to Bruce (1986: 262), the evangelical Protestantism espoused by Loyalists is 'the only identity that can make sense of their history and that justifies their separation from the South'. Hostility towards Catholicism is built into this identity. In Foucauldian terms, anti-Catholicism is a *discursive formation* that encodes in linguistic form, through ritualised codes and slogans ('ye must be born again', 'remember 1690'), a sense of Protestant identity and identification with a sacred history in which 'Bible Protestants' have triumphed over 'Papists'.

Following Brewer and Higgins (1999), we can distinguish four modes of anti-Catholicism. The first two are apolitical: the *passive* mode, that is, a cultural backdrop of taken-for-granted stereotypes and prejudices; and the *Pharisaic* mode, in which Protestants, while recognising Catholics as fellow Christians, confidently assert the theological superiority of their faith and its firm biblical grounding, as a vantage point from which to critique the distortions and errors of Catholic theology.

These two modes are not without social significance; in analysing social divisions, however, we need to focus on anti-Catholicism in its politicised forms. The first of these is *secular*: it holds firm to the Union with Britain and rejects Irish nationalism and Republicanism. The Catholic Church is criticised as an anti-democratic conspiracy that threatens political and civil liberties and puts economic prosperity in jeopardy. Even though secular anti-Catholics are deeply suspicious of the motives of Catholic and Republican leaders, it may be politically expedient to negotiate with them.

The second mode of politicised anti-Catholicism is not secular but theological; Brewer and Higgins call it *covenantal*. The Catholic Church is vilified as a heretical, anti-Christian organisation, a view justified by appeal to biblical prophecy and the Book of Revelation. The mission of Protestants is to save Ulster from the clutches of the evil conspiracy that is Catholicism. Not only can there be 'no surrender', there can be no political dialogue with Catholics. The covenantal mode predominates in the Free Presbyterian Church and the Democratic Unionist Party.

The secular and covenantal modes are very different, but they share the capacity to legitimise social divisions that disadvantage and marginalise Catholics politically, economically and socially. They are a cultural resource through which passive anti-Catholicism can be mobilised into political action.

In Britain itself, as abroad, Northern Ireland is typically viewed as an exceptional, pathological case of abnormal politics fuelled by sectarian religion – a throwback to a pre-industrial era in which conflicts within and between societies were indeed wars of religion. Such an interpretation can lead to overlooking commonalities between Northern Ireland and the rest of the UK.

The case against such a view is put sharply by Mitchell (2004: 251): 'Contemporary Britain is only beginning to face the task of formulating policies to cater for a religiously plural society. It should not ignore the experiences of religious division and change in its own backyard.' A leading example is provided by education. The question of faith-based schooling, a salient feature of Northern Ireland, is high on the political agenda in the rest of UK, principally because of the debate about state funding of Muslim schools (Tinker forthcoming).

A vast array of interested parties have addressed the issue from many angles, arguing about identity, gender, authority, multiculturalism, citizenship, social equality, social justice and human rights. Religion lies at the heart of these debates and underpins the social divisions they seek to erase or perpetuate. The part played by religion in creating and perpetuating social divisions is displayed graphically in religious sects. In a sociological perspective, sects are culturally deviant religious minorities that regard themselves as having a monopoly of the truth. They have a strong sense of their own unique identity and typically have strict rules of performance which they enforce rigorously, expelling sinners in order to keep the community pure (Wilson 1970).

The Exclusive Brethren provide an instructive case. This sect broke away from the wider Brethren movement in the 1840s under the leadership of John Nelson Darby. The Exclusive Brethren are required to avoid worldly practices and minimise contact with non-members. So, for example, Exclusive Brethren are not permitted to watch television, listen to the radio, read newspapers, read works of fiction, attend the theatre or cinema, use computers, mobile phones or the internet, attend university, join a trade union or professional association or vote in a political election. Their places of worship have no windows through which outsiders might observe them and they live in detached houses because they are not allowed to share any facilities with outsiders. If a family member leaves the movement, they have to move out of the family home.

The Exclusive Brethren's deliberate segregation from the wider society is justified by several key biblical texts, in particular the advice given by St Paul to the fledgling Christian community at Corinth: 'come out from among them and be ye separate'. Paul's instruction to 'remove the wicked person from amongst yourselves' justifies the practice of 'withdrawing from' – that is, completely ostracising – people who have violated the sect's strict codes of conduct.

The case of the Exclusive Brethren highlights a distinguishing feature of religion as a source of division. On the one hand, it can be argued that in the contemporary world, religion is something that we as individuals choose for ourselves. Britain, like other First World countries, is a multicultural, multi-faith society. Unless one is the reigning monarch or heir to the throne, there is no legal impediment to joining the religion of one's preference. In apparent contrast to the other social divisions discussed in this book, religion is fundamentally something that we choose, a status that in sociological terms is achieved rather than ascribed. This point has recently been used to question the wisdom of legislation against incitement to religious hatred, on the grounds that it would jeopardise freedom of speech. Surely, the argument runs, people's religious beliefs and practices are a legitimate target of satire; why should religion be protected as a special case in a way that secular and political philosophies are not?

Against this, it is important to see that, like ethnicity, religious affiliation involves powerful constraints as well as choices. Someone who was born into the Exclusive Brethren but who chooses as an adult to leave them is forced to abandon the community and their own family. Many who leave find life outside the community unbearable; not only do they fail to integrate into the wider society, they also feel guilty at having deserted their family and friends. The family, above all other institutions, is unique, given, irreplaceable. For all the problems of life within the sect, some who leave find they have little real choice but it rejoin it.

The interplay between choice and constraint is equally acute in religions such as the Jewish, Hindu and Sikh faiths, where religion and ethnicity are inextricably linked. Ethnic identification on the basis of shared descent and common culture is overlaid with religious significance. Apostasy (renunciation of one's faith) is viewed as a serious offence, not a legitimate consumer 'choice'. With its reference to an ultimate, transcendental source of meaning and authority, religion has a unique character that sets it apart from secular belief systems.

Whether or not we subscribe to the secularisation thesis, there is a good case for Beckford's (1989: 170–2) claim that religion remains a cultural resource on which individuals and social groupings can draw for identity, motivation, mobilisation and legitimacy. As religion has lost social significance so, paradoxically, it has gained cultural significance as a powerful but increasingly volatile and unpredictable resource that can be deployed to promote social cohesion or social division.

Discussion Questions

1. How does your own religious or non-religious identity relate to your ethnic identity? Are there any conflicts between them? To what extent would you say that you have chosen your own religious or non-religious identity?

2. Why is religion given special protections under the law, when other belief systems are not? How are such protections justified? Should they all be abolished?

3. Is there a cultural bias against religious minorities? Is it typically based on hostility towards their beliefs and/or their practices? How would you distinguish between religious hostility and racism?

4. If the secularisation thesis is true, why do religious divisions persist? Are they 'really' religious?

FURTHER READING

Aldridge, A. *Religion in the Contemporary World: A Sociological Introduction* (Cambridge: Polity, 2000) provides a broad overview of sociological work on religion. For a balanced account of religion in the British context, see Davie, G. *Religion in Britain since 1945: Believing Without Belonging* (Oxford: Blackwell (1994). Among many expositions of the secularisation thesis, Bruce, S. *God is Dead: Secularization in the West* (Oxford: Blackwell, 2002) stands out as trenchant and thought provoking. Beckford, J. A. *Social Theory and Religion* (Cambridge: Cambridge University Press, 2003) can be recommended as a sophisticated treatment of sociological theorising about religion.

CHAPTER 6

National Identity

DAVID MCCRONE

This chapter will provide you with a broad critical understanding of the following issues in national identity as a source of social division:

■ The difference between national identity and state identity in the UK
■ The variations between the different countries of the UK with regard to these forms of identity
■ How being British evolved in the context of other territorial identities in these islands
■ Why there is no single or simple way of being British
■ The relationship between national identity and citizenship
■ The problematic nature of 'nation-state' as a concept in the modern world
■ Why nationalism is an inherent ideology in modern societies
■ The strengths and the weaknesses of being British today

Who are you? If you are asked what nationality you are, what do you say? If you live in the archipelago of islands called the 'British Isles', think about it for a moment. Would you say you are British? English? Scottish? Welsh? Irish? None of these? How do you decide? You may say you are British because you are a citizen of the UK. But strictly speaking that terms refers to people who live on the British mainland. The state, after all, is the United Kingdom of Great Britain and Northern Ireland. So we are UK-people – 'Ukanians' in Tom Nairn's ironic term (1977) – who live together in the same state but who have not bothered to find a proper name for ourselves. While virtually all modern states have problems defining who 'nationals' are, it is instructive to focus first on people in these islands where such issues are especially problematic. By focusing on these, we can begin to understand just how complex and changing national identity is in the new millennium, and also what we mean by 'nationality' in more general terms, together with 'citizenship, 'nation' and 'state', which is what we will try to do in this chapter.

Let us try another tack. What do you call the country you live in? The 'United Kingdom' sounds too stilted. Britain? Great Britain? England? Scotland? Wales? Ireland? Northern Ireland? Ulster? To many foreigners, this is England (even to the English), but the Scots, Welsh, and Northern Irish know that it is not so. So who is right? Let us try some elementary algebra. Formally, the United Kingdom = Great Britain (the big island) + Northern Ireland, where Great Britain = England + Scotland + Wales. The problem with that (correct) formulation is that it does not correspond with sociological reality, that is, how people see themselves. The non-English peoples – the Scots and Welsh in particular – define their nationality (their 'nation-ness') as Scottish and Welsh, while recognising that their citizenship – their state identity – is British. In Northern Ireland, on the other hand, being 'British' is a political statement that you do wish to belong to the UK – that you are a 'unionist'.

Indeed, Northern Ireland provides us with the starkest home-grown example of why national identity is such an important principle of social division. Hundreds of people who were ordinary 'citizens', living in a territory that, as an accident of history and constitutionality is part of the UK, have killed or been killed in an internal war over nationality, state and culture. Social divisions do not come much sharper than that (except in the scale and intensity of fighting elsewhere in Europe, as the Balkans have shown us). In Northern Ireland, when about two-thirds of Protestants say they are British, it is no casual observation, just as when the significant minority (about three in five Catholics: Curtice 1990) assert that they are Irish, they are expressing a powerful counter-identity. Catholics and Protestants do not just divide on national identity or religious grounds. They live in different areas, go to different schools, often work in separate organisations and mix with 'their own people', who share similar experiences of good or poor housing, education, occupational opportunity or exclusion (Chapters 4 and 12). Those who lead the most separate lives in this way are also the most likely to express a distinctive sense of nationalism (Breen 1998).

Although the sense of difference is not so extreme in Scotland, Scottish 'social arrangements' are not the same as in England, as many media correspondents seemed to discover for the first time in the run-up to elections for the Scottish Parliament in 1999. Scotland has its own legal system; a less selective and subject-special education service; unique churches; separate organisation of trade associations, banks, charities and political parties; and media production systems that ensure a diet of news coverage about Scotland that even Wales with its distinctive language, and certainly no mere regional service, can match. For some sociologists, Scotland is just as suitable a 'unit of analysis' as is the more conventional, mirror image way of thinking about the size and geographical spread of what we research; namely the area usually defined as 'England and Wales' (Payne 1987b; McCrone 1992).

These nuances in parts of the UK have in the past been lost on the majority people, the English, who make up 85 per cent of the UK state's population. This distinction between national identity and state identity in these islands is not one they usually make, although in recent times flying the English flag of St George rather than the Union Flag of the UK, notably at football events such as Euro 2004, appears more common than it once was. Anthony Barnett, who helped to found Charter 88, the pressure group for constitutional change, commented:

> What is the difference between being English and being British? If you ask a Scot or a Welsh person about their Britishness, the question makes sense to them. They might say that they feel Scots first and British second. Or that they enjoy a dual identity as Welsh-British, with both parts being equal. Or they might say: 'I'm definitely British first.' What they have in common is an understanding that there is a space between their nation and Britain, and they can assess the relationship between the two. The English, however, are more often baffled when asked how they relate their Englishness and Britishness to each other. They often fail to understand how the two can be contrasted at all. It seems like one of those puzzles that others can undo but you can't: Englishness and Britishness seem inseparable. They might prefer to be called one thing rather than the other – and today young people increasingly prefer English to British – but, like two sides of a coin, neither term has an independent existence from the other. (Barnett 1997: 292–3)

Since Barnett wrote that, it does appear that people in England are more willing to say that they are English. For example, in 1997, the British Social Attitudes Survey (an annual series which is invaluable in charting changes over time) asked people to indicate what they considered their most important identity. The same proportions – 24 per cent – said they were British as said they were English. By 2001, 20 per cent said British and 30 per cent English. People in Scotland are far more likely to say they are Scottish (77 per cent) than they are British (16 per cent). If anything, in Scotland, there has been a move away from being British (38 per cent gave it as their 'best' identity in 1979, compared with 56 per cent who said Scottish: Park et al. 2004).

Simply asking people to choose between identities is crude, and over the years we have evolved a five-point scale ranging from one extreme at which national identity (being English, Scottish, Welsh) is everything and state identity (British) is nothing, to the reverse of that, with dual identities in between. This method gives the results shown in Table 6.1.

Table 6.1 National identity by country

	Scotland %	Wales %	England %
X not British	36	23	17
More X than British	30	22	13
Equally X and British	24	29	42
More British than X	3	11	9
British not X	3	11	11
None of these	4	4	8
Sample sizes	1605	1085	2786

Note
X=Scottish/Welsh/English.

Source: British Social Attitudes (2001).

What the data in Table 6.1 suggest is that there are considerable national differences. People in Scotland are ten times more likely to give priority to being Scottish than to being British (points 1 or 2 on our scale – either 'Scottish not British', or 'more Scottish than British'). The Welsh are twice as likely to say they are Welsh than British. In England, marginally more say that they are English than that they are British. Here, of course, Barnett's health warning applies: we cannot be sure that people in England make the distinction between England and Britain, between national and state identity, as do people in Scotland and Wales. Nevertheless, they do appear to feel more comfortable claiming to be English, and the survey of 2003 indicated that twice as many people in England said they were English not British (17 per cent) than said so in 1997 (8 per cent).

How, as sociologists, are we to make sense of this confusion? This is, we might say, a meaningful error. There is a puzzle about Britishness. In Cohen's helpful metaphor (1994), it is 'fuzzy', that is, blurred and opaque. (Cohen is making the analogy with 'fuzzy logic' in mathematics by which a solution is reached by way of eliminating the uncertain edges to a problem.) This fuzziness is a legacy of history and sociology in these islands and at its heart is the confusion of nationality and citizenship.

At this point in our argument, you may be asking yourself why any of this matters. After all, you may say, I do not actually think it matters much what nationality I am. Let me press you on this point. If you go abroad, do you feel yourself more or less 'national'? During the football World Cup, or for that matter most international sporting occasions, which team do you support? Well, you may reply, I do feel patriotic, but not nationalistic. That is a fairly common answer. It implies that feeling pride in one's country is not the same as hating, even killing, other people. Indeed not, but can we be sure that this is a valid distinction we are making between patriotism and nationalism? Most of us in the UK today are too young to remember the Second World War – you would need to be about 80 to have been an adult in 1945 – but most people in those days had little difficulty going and fighting, and even dying, for what they felt was right. Perhaps the problem we have in thinking that we are not susceptible to feelings of patriotism and nationalism – because, in truth, they are the same thing – is that we have not been confronted by the need to do so. Those who are so confronted often feel they have no alternative.

Perhaps part of the issue here is that, as Barnett made clear above, for the most part English people are not very aware of their Englishness, compared, for example, with the Scots, the Welsh and the Irish, all of whom have historically looked to the English as the 'other' against whom they define themselves. For English people, however, there is a more fundamental confusion with being British. Let us now explore that in some depth.

Making Britain

There are two historical parts to our puzzle: how the British state was created in the eighteenth century; and how modern citizenship evolved in the twentieth. The creation of Great Britain in the early eighteenth century before the wave of modernising states transformed our world is the key. The British state managed to contain within it quite distinct self-governing 'civil societies', which coexisted within its formal boundaries quite contentedly as long as a fairly high degree of limited autonomy was afforded them. By 'civil society', we mean that social sphere between the individual and the state; the domestic world, economic relations, cultural activities and even legal institutions which are organised by private or voluntary arrangements and largely outside the control of the state. We can now see with hindsight that by the middle of the twentieth century, the relationship between the state and these civil societies had been radically altered in such a way that peaceful coexistence was no longer logically possible. Above all, the generic shift between the boundaries of the state and civil society in the modern world created particular difficulties for relations between the British state and its constituent civil societies.

The central relationship is the one between England and Scotland because that was the basis of the creation of the new state of Great Britain in 1707, and is and always has been the most problematic and intriguing one. Of course, other civil societies existed within the state – notably those in Wales and (after 1801 when the state became the United Kingdom) Ireland, as well as local and regional ones within England itself. However, their relationships to the political centre were different. On the one hand, the national societies of Wales and Ireland had been the subject of successful conquest by England from the thirteenth century and had elements of colonial status attached to their civil and political institutions. On the other hand, regional autonomy within England did not have to contend with competing national identities and institutional residues of historical statehood like those north of the English border.

How did Scottish (or Welsh) civil society develop in the context of the unitary British state since 1707? Given that all formal political power resided in Westminster, how much (or little) autonomy did these nations continue to have? There was a consensus of political opposites on this issue. For nationalists, Scotland had ceased to exist in 1707 when it was incorporated into greater England. Their project was and is that Scotland should rise and be a nation again (in the sense of being an independent state). For unionists, on the other hand, a new, integrated society was born called Britain (or the UK), and they argue that it would be disastrous if the whole was unscrambled into its weaker constituent parts. The problem with these two stark representations is that they play fast and loose with history as well as sociology.

At this point it is useful to clarify some of our terms. The 'state' refers to the institutions of governance, and includes not simply parliament, but the legal system and the civil service. It is in essential terms a 'political' concept. The 'nation' on the other hand refers to the 'cultural' realm, to what people see as their shared characteristics, most usually language, religion and/or common history. In Anderson's useful term (1996), a nation is an 'imagined community' of people who believe themselves to belong to the same cultural group, and which has the right of self-determination. The important aspect to grasp here is that 'state' and 'nation' belong to different spheres, even though they are frequently treated as the same, and linked together as in the term 'nation-state'. As we shall see later in this chapter, there is nothing inevitable about linking the two together, and it is becoming increasingly problematic to do so in the modern world. How does this apply to the UK?

What is nearer the truth is that Scotland, while ceasing to be an independent state, did not stop being a nation or a civil society in 1707, nor was it incorporated into greater England. The Treaty of Union in 1707 did create something new. Greater England it was not. Instead, Scots took full advantage of the opportunity that England and the Empire provided. As Colley has pointed out, a genuine sense of Britishness was 'forged', with reference to two related aspects: war with France, and Protestantism (Chapter 5). Britishness was invented in the long period of virtual or actual warfare with France from 1707 until 1837. These wars were religious wars and perceived as such on both sides. The overthrow of the Catholic Stuarts in 1689 and their replacement with the Protestant William of Orange reinforced the political-religious nature of the settlement. Britain, Colley (1992: 5) says:

> was an invention forged above all by war. Time and time again, war with France brought Britons, whether they hailed from Wales or Scotland or England, into confrontation with an obvious hostile Other and encouraged them to define themselves collectively against it. They defined themselves as Protestants struggling for survival against the world's foremost Catholic power. They defined themselves against the French as they imagined them to be, superstitious, militarist, decadent and unfree.

This struggle against the French may seem like an integrating mechanism, a forging of a new national identity, but Colley (1992: 6) argues that 'Britishness was superimposed over an array of internal differences in response to contact with the Other, and above all in response to conflict with the Other'. It worked with rather than against the grain of older national identities that were to persist and outlast the later British one. Britishness sat lightly on top of the constituent nations as a kind of state identity. This is the key to understanding state–society relations in the UK. The British state was quite unlike later state formations that sought to integrate political, cultural and economic structures in the classical 'nation-state' outlined above. These formations demanded the lining up of state, nation, society, economy and culture in such a way that 'national identity' ran through all these institutions. Being a citizen in these nineteenth-century modern states demanded allegiance, and in return the state was made accountable, and its sovereignty limited, often by means of the doctrine of popular, rather than Crown/parliamentary, sovereignty, as in Britain.

The British state, on the other hand, as a 'nightwatchman state' was content to concern itself with matters of defence, foreign policy and maintaining a stable currency. It was a state externally oriented to managing its dependent territories and arranging their defence. Above all, it left civil society to its own devices and only intervened where it perceived a threat to social and political order. This it did most notoriously after the Jacobite Rising of 1745, and only at the behest of, and largely by the hands of, lowland Protestant Scots.

The point here is that the British state sat lightly on civil society, whereas Continental European states were thoroughly interwoven with theirs. The unreformed quality of the British state has been commented on by many writers. Marquand, for example, has called the UK an 'unprincipled' society because its state structures are fundamentally deficient. Marquand (1988: 152) observed:

Thanks to the upheavals of the 17th century – thanks in particular to the victory of the English landed classes over the Stuart kings – one cannot speak of a 'British state' in the way that one speaks of a 'French state' or in modern times of a 'German state'. The UK is not a state in the continental sense. It is a bundle of islands (including such exotica as the Channel Islands and the Isle of Man which are not even represented at Westminster), acquired at different times by the English crown, and governed in different ways.

Its inhabitants are not citizens of a state, with defined rights of citizenship. They are subjects of a monarch, enjoying 'liberties' which their ancestors won from previous monarchs.

Marquand's point is not that the British state suffers from a form of arrested political development. It was a minimal state with a small bureaucracy that was clearly suited to market-driven adjustment in the eighteenth century, but which failed to make the transition to full modernity in the late nineteenth century. At its root lies an ethos of market liberalism, which has survived long after the doctrine that created it has been abandoned.

A similar point is made by Colley (1992), who points out that for a time the British state (at the turn of the nineteenth century) was one of the most modernised and democratic in Europe. Its Protestant 'ethic' gave it a commitment to civil and economic liberalism that helped to make it the premier power until the late nineteenth century. The problem was, she comments, that whereas the reforms of 1832 established a high degree of civil and democratic rights, by 1865 it had been overtaken by most Continental powers. Its political development had been arrested, possibly because its route to modernisation was more conservative than is usually made out, that a thoroughgoing reform of political and constitutional structures, with, for example, a written constitution and bill of rights, did not take place.

You may by now have noticed an important omission in describing who the British are. What, you may ask, about the Irish? Was Ireland not incorporated into the United Kingdom of Great Britain and Ireland in 1801? Constitutionally speaking, this is correct. However, if we take Colley's point that Protestantism was a prime shaper of Britishness, then as Catholics, most of the people on the island of Ireland could not and, indeed, were not allowed to be British in this sense. To be British was to be a Protestant which in turn made one loyal to the British Crown. That is the origin of the term 'loyalist', and the reason why in Ireland over the last two centuries religion is less a matter of theology and more a matter of constitutional politics.

In Northern Ireland today, issues of national identity are framed by this nexus between politics and religion, in so many ways, one being a proxy for the other. Hence, over 60 per cent of Catholics in the Province give their nationality as 'Irish' and two-thirds of Protestants say they are 'British' (Northern Ireland Life and Times Survey, 2001). Just over a fifth of Catholics and just under a fifth of Protestants lay claim to being 'Northern Irish' (see also Chapter 5). These figures show relatively little change since 1988, suggesting that 'confessional' identities are more important for both communities than territorial ones.

Making British citizens

The second piece of our puzzle about British nationality and citizenship is to be found in the second half of the twentieth century: how modern citizenship in these islands was made. The inhabitants of the UK attained formal citizenship by a legislative sleight of hand under the 1948 Nationality Act as 'citizens of the UK and the colonies'. Prior to that date, the inhabitants of the British Isles and the British Empire were formally 'subjects' of the Crown. Hitherto, Britain was not so much a geographical entity; it was perceived in terms of those who owed allegiance to the Crown, and included those who inhabited the far-flung territories of the Empire. In other words, there was something unusual about the relationship between the British state and its inhabitants.

In essence, Britishness had grown up as an imperial identity, although a fuzzy one, defined more by an allegiance to the Crown than residence in these islands. Britain, in other words, exists (or existed) as an imperial state – with colonies and dominions that came to embody its identity. It took Pocock (1975), a New Zealander, to define 'British' history as something quite different from English, Scottish, Welsh and Irish history, and also something that belonged to those living beyond these shores. Whatever else it was, Britain was not England. It evoked an imperial identity, much as in the Roman Empire. 'Civis Britannicus Sum' was the nineteenth-century equivalent of 'Civis Romanus Sum'.

The post-1945 crisis arose because former parts of the Empire such as Canada and India wished to redefine citizenship for immigration purposes, and so a separate status was necessary for the remaining inhabitants of the UK. The preferred position of the British government was that people in Commonwealth countries were subjects of the British Crown first and citizens of individual states second, but it quickly became obvious that newly independent countries balked at this constraint on their sovereignty. The British political parties reflected the confusion. In the post-imperial age, the Labour Party sought to encourage a 'traditional', that is, non-ethnic, definition of 'Britishness' to encompass the Commonwealth, while supporting colonial peoples in their liberation struggles (Goulbourne 1991). The Conservative Party for its part developed an 'ethnic' definition – 'those groups which consider themselves to be British, and also the indigenous and/or white population' (Goulbourne 1991: 245). This was reflected in the 1962 Commonwealth Immigration Act, the 1971 Immigration Act and the 1981 Nationality Act, and an ethnic definition was reinforced ideologically under the influence of right-wing politicians like Enoch Powell and Margaret Thatcher (see Chapter 4). The politicisation of ethnic identity has helped to highlight the racial context of the debate over the last 30 years. By the 1981 Act, patriality – the right to settle in the UK if one had at least one grandparent born here – drew on the law of blood *(ius sanguinis)* rather than the law of territory *(ius soli)*, so that ethnic definitions of Britishness are at least as important as civic ones. We will return to this important distinction between 'blood' and 'soil' later.

This brief overview of how 'Britishness' has come to be redefined in the postcolonial age provides a context for important shifts in national identities within the UK itself. If British identity is externally fuzzy, so too is its meaning within these islands. Until Ireland became a republic in 1948, its citizens remained formally 'subjects' of the British Crown (reinforced by the new republic leaving the Commonwealth a year later, largely to break finally with this colonial legacy). A number of other key confusions remained, notably that between 'Britain' and 'England', a distinction that was rarely made in the UK's largest country as well as overseas. It was the norm to describe the UK as a 'nation-state', an extension of England. Although the Scots and the Welsh worked within a more logical model, whereby their national identities were nested in the broader British state identity, the unitary nature of that state, with a single, sovereign parliament, seemed to reinforce the equation of Britain and England, and the tendency to see the UK as 'greater England'.

We have, then, in these islands a complex set of national political identities. Following Cohen's idea of 'fuzzy frontiers', we can identify the following:

● between the English, the largest nationality, and the Scots, who were jointly responsible for founding the 'Great Britain' in 1707
● the relationship between the English/Scots and the other Celtic peoples – the Welsh on the one hand and the Irish on the other (most of whom are citizens of an independent republic, but with voting and residence rights in the UK – leaving aside the complications in Northern Ireland)
● the (white) Commonwealth or former 'Dominions' such as Australia, New Zealand and Canada, which are politically independent, but genealogically, culturally and legally linked (via 'patriality' rights of settlement)
● the (black) Commonwealth, with a history of postwar settlement (defining 'ethnicity' in the UK)
● European links (via but not exclusively with the EU), which also imply rights of settlement and residence to 'non-British' people

● Anglophones (especially via cultural and historical links with the USA).

The result, in Cohen's words (1994: 35), is that:

> British identity shows a general pattern of fragmentation. Multiple axes of identification have meant that Irish, Scots, Welsh and English people, those from the white, black and brown Commonwealth, Americans, English-speakers, Europeans and even 'aliens' have had their lives intersect one with another in overlapping and complex circles of identity-construction and rejection. The shape and edges of British identity are thus historically changing, often vague and, to a degree, malleable – an aspect of the British identity I have called 'a fuzzy frontier'.

The issues of ethnicity and nationality, then, in the UK are especially 'fuzzy'. Britishness is a political identity, roughly equated with citizenship, but growing out of a pre-modern prior definition of people as 'subjects' of the Crown, and even applying to those who do not live in these islands. As this older sense of Britishness declines (after all, those entering pensionable age in 1998 were not even in their early teens when the Second World War ended), it is tempting to predict its demise.

Citizens and the nation-state

Let us next take a broader and comparative view of the making of modern states and nationality. It is part of our vocabulary to talk of 'nation-states'. Why does the term nation-state have such strong currency in the western world? The answer lies in the fact that the term was captured by the process of state-building, which has shaped Western Europe over the last two centuries. If states were not actually 'nations' too, then they could be imagined as such either now or in the future. Essentially, the state is a political concept, whereas the nation is a cultural one. So successful is this alignment between state and nation that it is part of our common sense, our taken-for-granted political and cultural world (McCrone 1998). Does it matter that we align state and nation, the political and the cultural? Most certainly, because it gives a fundamental legitimacy to the modern state without which it could not function. After all, the modern state derives its legitimacy from its claim to speak on behalf of 'the people'.

In his study of citizenship and nationhood in France and Germany, Brubaker (1992) argued that definitions of citizenship in these states result from the fact that whereas in France the unitary state was established before the concept of nation took hold there, in Germany it was the other way round;

the 'nation' preceded the 'state'. In France, the monarchy held sway over a fairly defined and gradually expanding territory, and promoted the concept of citizenship based on *ius soli*, the law of soil or territorial jurisdiction, in such a way that whatever their ethnic or geographical origins, all residents on French soil could in principle be subjects, later citizens, of the French state. Peasants had, of course, in Eugene Weber's phrase, to be made into Frenchmen, but this formulation neatly expresses the prior existence of the state over the sense of nation, at least in popular terms.

In Germany, by contrast, the unitary state did not arrive until 1871, and the nation had to be defined differently. Since members of the German nation might be subjects of different kings – Bavaria, Saxony, Prussia, even Austria and Russia – national identity was based on *ius sanguinis*, the law of blood, so that anyone with German blood was German and thus after 1871 eligible to be a citizen of Germany, whether or not they actually lived on German soil.

As a result of these different routes to 'nation-statehood', the interpretation of nationality differs. In France, according to Brubaker, it is state-centred and assimilationist, so that anyone living within the territory of the French state became a French citizen. In Germany, on the other hand, it is nation-centred and differentialist. Anyone who could prove German ethnicity was counted as 'German', but the definition differentiated among those living within Germany itself so that some were counted as ethnically German and others, such as people of Turkish origin, were not, until the law was changed as late as 1998. Brubaker (1992: 3) comments:

> The state-centred assimilationist understanding of nationhood in France is embodied and expressed in an expansive definition of citizenship, one that automatically transforms second-generation immigrants into citizens, assimilating them – legally – to other French men and women. The ethnocultural, differentialist understanding of nationhood in Germany is embodied and expressed in a definition of citizenship that is remarkably open to ethnic German immigrants from Eastern Europe and the Soviet Union, but remarkably closed to non-German immigrants.

Further, as Cobban (1994: 245) points out: 'during the early modern period ... the word nation changed its significance: it lost its linguistic and acquired an almost wholly exclusively political meaning'. In general, there has been a progressive downplaying of the cultural component in modern definitions of the state. Held (1992: 87) comments:

> All modern states are nation-states – political apparatuses, distinct from both rulers and ruled, with supreme jurisdiction over a demarcated territorial area,

backed by a claim to a monopoly of coercive power, and enjoying a minimum level of support or loyalty from their citizens.

We might be surprised that the cultural component is downplayed and operates merely as a loyalty device for the state, but this view of the 'nation-state' is the dominant one. In like manner, Giddens (1981: 190) virtually reproduces this definition, but without any cultural component being mentioned. The nation-state, he comments, is:

> a set of institutional forms of governance maintaining an administrative monopoly over a territory with demarcated boundaries, its rule being sanctioned by law and direct control of the means of internal and external violence.

Giddens (1985: 120) sees the 'nation' as a 'bordered power-container', which can exist only 'when a state has a unified administrative reach over the territory over which its sovereignty is claimed'. Max Weber well understood the distinction between state and nation and defined the key characteristics of the modern state as follows: territoriality – having fixed and defensible borders; control of the means of violence – both internally and externally; an impersonal structure of power – the idea of a sovereign and impersonal political order; and legitimacy – requiring the loyalty of its citizens (Held 1992).

Does this reduction of the nation to the state matter? My argument is that it does, because the concepts actually operate on different planes and lead us to imagine that modern states have captured political and cultural power. This is problematic because the ideal-typical process always had a more messy reality lying behind it.

Particularly in the early twenty-first century, the concepts are coming apart. The (con)fusion of nation and state is a common one, and requires to be taken seriously rather than as an unfortunate error. What it signifies is that the cultural and the political have become so closely allied in the modern state that we usually treat their outcomes – nation and state – as synonyms. In its conventional expression – the nation-state – it is expected that the 'people' who are governed by the institutions of the state are by and large culturally homogeneous in having a strong and common linguistic, religious and symbolic identity. We see, more clearly than most, the 'impending crisis of the hyphen' (Anderson 1996: 8). Some scholars have pointed out that very few so-called nation-states are actually such. Connor (1994) claims less than ten per cent in 1971, and historical sociologists like Tilly (1992: 3) distinguish between 'nation-states' and 'national states' that are governed by common political and institutional structures. He comments that very few European states have ever qualified as nation-states (possibly Sweden and Ireland), and that 'Great Britain, Germany and France – quintessential national states – certainly have never met the test'.

Whether we use 'national' or 'nation-state' matters because it frames the world as it is meant to be, not how it is. Strictly speaking, 'nation-state' implies that all self-governing political units – states – correspond with culturally distinctive units – nations – so that the world appears as a giant jigsaw of such entities. Of course, the pieces do not fit. Not only are most states not culturally and ethnically homogeneous, but many, even most, nations are, in formal terms, 'stateless', such as Scotland and even England.

We might ask, then, why it is that the term nation-state has such strong currency in the West. It is one thing to fret about the inexactness of the term, but more interesting to ask why it has such hegemony in describing the contemporary world. The root of the answer lies in the process of state-building, which also shaped Western Europe over the last two centuries. If states were not actually 'nations' too, then they could be imagined as such or at least aspired to. So successful has this alignment between state and nation been that it is part of our sociological 'common sense', our taken-for-granted political and cultural world. Does it matter? Most certainly, because it gives a fundamental legitimacy to the modern state without which it could not function.

The problem with this formulation is that, on the one hand, the covert influence of nation-state building in the nineteenth, twentieth and twenty-first centuries dominates politics, sociology and history alike. On the other hand, societies bounded in geographical and social space are less and less likely to be unified totalities in the early twenty-first century when economic, political and cultural forces have eroded the homogeneity of states.

The key changes that impact on the relationships between state, society and nation in the early twenty-first century can be characterised as follows. On the one hand, and contrary to expectations, nationalism has waxed rather than waned in importance over time. Nationalisms have arisen in regions or territories that wish to break away from existing states. When we think of nationalism in the West, we think of its rise in Scotland, Wales, Catalonia and Quebec and other formally 'stateless' nations (McCrone 1992). Nationalism has become an active basis for social divisions within states.

We need however, to recognise that, in the postwar period, there has also been a core form of nationalism that is frequently implicit. As the modern state became the appropriate instrument for guaranteeing the life chances of its citizens and ironing out social inequalities, governments became major actors in economic competition between states in the quest for economic growth 'in the national interest'. This is 'state nationalism' expressed in economic and political competition. Nationalism, in this form, became more, not less, common in this process of postwar international competition. This nationalism of the 'core', that is, existing states such as the UK, Spain and Belgium, developed alongside counter-nationalisms on the periphery among stateless nations within core states (such as Scotland, Catalonia and Flanders), which sought to redraw the limits and responsibilities of central state power and, in many cases, secede from it.

And yet, just as nationalism was growing in importance, so the 'nation-state' appeared to be losing its powers. The growing interest in nationalism coincides with the apparent decline in the powers of the state. This is one aspect of a wider process known as 'globalisation', whereby economic, cultural and political influences increasingly operate at a world or global level. After all, we live in a world of global economic markets, with its cultural products like Coca-Cola, and supra-state institutions such as the EU, the IMF and the World Bank. All these forces would seem to have eroded the power of the independent state. Why then has there been an increase in national movements wanting a state of their own? How is it possible to explain this apparent contradiction?

One possibility is that the sovereignty of the nation-state was always a trick of the eye. In the words of Tamir (1993: 3):

> The era of the homogeneous and viable nation-states is over (or rather the era of the illusion that homogeneous and viable nation-states are possible is over, since such states never existed) and the national vision must be redefined.

Nowhere is this more obvious than in the British Isles where, as we have seen, nationality and citizenship have evolved in an idiosyncratic way. The British are not at all like the French, in that their civic republican tradition defines (possibly overdefines) who is to be French and how one is to behave as French. The British, we might say, are underdefined. There is no common football team, no rugby team (the British Lions includes all the Irish, most of whom quit this state over 70 years ago). Sport is a good indicator of nationality. After all, you are a 'national' if you play for the national side. In the 1980s, the Conservative politician Norman Tebbit provoked controversy when he talked about *his* 'cricket test'. How could people of Caribbean and Asian origins be considered English, he implied, if they opted to cheer for the West Indies, India or Pakistan against England? What he failed to notice was the 'fuzzy' nature of national identity (that England was not Britain). In recent years, an important debate has started in England about whether or not black people can be 'English' rather than simply 'British'. In many ways this is a debate about ethnic (being English by lineage or 'blood') versus civic definitions (being British by residence and citizenship). Black footballers and brown cricketers playing for England help to highlight the issue.

There is a related matter that is worth exploring at this point in our argument, and that is the issue of regional identity. When English people are asked to describe their nationality, it is not uncommon for many to echo the views of the person who replied: 'I'm not English. I'm from Yorkshire.' In strict terms, of course, being from Yorkshire (or Lancashire and so on) is a regional not a national identity. However, the speaker is possibly reacting to what could be perceived to be the 'capture' of Englishness by a southern, 'home counties' version. (In passing, it is interesting to note the revealing terminology of English geography. The cultural core is 'the home counties' (not the Midlands) and the peripheries are described as 'the North' and 'the West'.) It would be difficult to argue, however, that, with few exceptions, any English region has the cultural wherewithal – language, history, institutions – to turn regionalism into nationalism (in 2004, voters in northeast England declined the opportunity of moving towards regional devolution). Perhaps the only real region is Cornwall, where there is an embryonic 'national' movement based on precisely these cultural markers.

Being British today

What, then, does it mean to be British? We know that being British was 'forged' in Colley's (1992) apt word, in the eighteenth century as a result of war with France and, relatedly, being Protestant in contradistinction to Europe's greatest Catholic power. 'Forgery' of course implies not simply something beaten into shape on the blacksmith's anvil, but a counterfeit, a subterfuge. It was nevertheless a convincing one because it created Britons (who were also Scots, English, Welsh – but only rarely Irish, most of whom were too Catholic to be British). We can measure the success of this creation by the huge number of Britons who died for their country. *Dulce et decorum est pro patria mori*, perhaps, but the 'patria' in question was undoubtedly British and it even encompassed others in the far-flung Empire, as a visit to any war graveyard will show.

What makes people British these days? By and large the same criteria that are used by other states: where you are born, your legal citizenship, being resident in the country, speaking the language, respecting the country's political institutions and the law and generally feeling a national citizen. In these respects, they are no different from other Western Europeans. The British appear to have above-average levels of national pride. In the International Social Survey Programme survey, they scored more highly on national pride than other comparable countries such as Germany, Spain and Sweden, when asked a battery of questions on national pride (McCrone and Surridge 1998). What marked the British from citizens of these other countries was the disproportionate pride they took in their history and the armed forces, compared with the Germans, for example, who had much higher scores on pride in economic achievements and the social security system.

These findings are broadly in line with those of the late 1980s, when the British cited the monarchy as the national institution they took most pride in, compared with the West Germans (as they were then) who were most proud of their system of Basic Law (Topf et al. 1989). Again, Northern Ireland is more complex (Dowds and Young 1996). Those who define themselves as 'British' are broadly in line with their mainland counterparts in terms of pride in British culture and heritage, whereas those who say they are 'Irish' have low levels of pride in being British.

There are, of course, also important social differences in these matters. Older people and those with the minimum levels of education are most likely to rank highly on national pride, whereas younger people and those with a university education score significantly lower. There appear to be little significant gender differences. On the other hand, pride in the monarchy in the 1989 survey was highest among older women with basic education who were members of the Church of England. Scots, Catholics and university-educated younger people were those least likely to claim pride in the monarchy as a national emblem.

What we are able to identify in such surveys is evidence for a proto-English nationalism. Englishness differs from Scottishness, Welshness and Irishness, in so far as it does not look to these 'Celtic' identities to provide the necessary 'other'. Instead, we would have to look to Continental Europe – France and Germany in particular, and possibly 'Europe' as a whole – for that alter ego against which being English can be constructed. We can see this most easily in the right-of-centre opinion that is hostile to the EU, held by those who commonly – and revealingly – are referred to as 'Little Englanders' (not, of course, 'little Britishers', for there is perhaps more of a 'greater England' perspective on these matters in right-wing circles). Such opinion also tends to be hostile to devolution for Scotland and Wales, and we might speculate that opposition to Europe as well as to constitutional change in these islands provides a solid platform on which a right-wing version of English nationalism might emerge in the early decades of the twenty-first century.

That, however, is to look too far ahead. Instead, we might ask: how significant is national identity as a source of social division and differentiation in modern Britain? There is a strong case for saying that there is no single 'national' identity in these islands, and that, if anything, it is likely to get even weaker than it currently appears to be. The UK is a de facto (but not as yet de jure) multinational state, which is likely to grow more diverse in constitutional terms as the different nations develop their own parliaments and assemblies. What is the prognosis for Britishness? One scenario would be that the political, religious and cultural conditions that created and sustained it – war, empire, religion and the welfare state – no longer operate to hold the British together. An alternative scenario is to say that the loose, umbrella-like identity of being British is best suited to adapt to the multicultural – ethnic as well as national – conditions that now exist in these islands. The last 50 years have seen the growing importance of nation and ethnicity as markers of social identity. The next 50 years are likely to see an expanding sense of European-ness, with greater political and economic integration. One key task for sociology is to make sense of the new identity politics that this new era will bring.

Discussion Questions

1. To what extent, and why, does being English differ from being British?

2. Is national identity stronger or weaker than state identity in the countries of the UK?

3. Why is nationalism a taken-for-granted ideology in modern societies?

FURTHER READING

McCrone, D. *The Sociology of Nationalism* (London: Routledge, 1998) reviews the various contemporary manifestations of nationalism, while Colley, L. *Britons: Forging the Nation* (New Haven, CT: Yale University Press, 1992) is the key text on how 'being British' was manufactured from the eighteenth century. A useful analysis of ethnic and national identities in the UK can be found in Cohen, R. *Frontiers of Identity* (Harlow: Longman, 1994). Brubaker, R. *Citizenship and Nationhood in France and Germany* (Cambridge, MA: Harvard University Press, 1992) is an elegant review of the different nationalisms of the two countries.

CHAPTER 7

Elites

PHILIP STANWORTH

This chapter will provide you with a broad critical understanding of the main features of elite analysis including:

- Pareto, Mosca and Michels' ideas on the origins and character of elites
- Burnham's theory of the 'managerial revolution'
- Schumpeter's thoughts on the links between leadership and democracy
- The incorporation of the concept of elites into pluralist theories of democracy
- The development of a power elite in the USA as proposed by C. Wright Mills
- Djilas's theory of the 'new class'
- The Miliband/Poulantzas debate on the use of elite analysis in Marxist accounts of contemporary capitalism
- Giddens' clarification of the main dimensions of elite analysis: recruitment, structure and power
- The importance of situating elite analysis in the wider socio-economic and political context
- A comparison of the educational profiles of selected contemporary British elites
- Detailed examination of the educational profiles of the political, civil service and army elites

Even in social democracies, the familiar sight of presidential or prime ministerial motor cavalcades, with their key players cocooned in heavy security, is a dramatic representation of the idea of elites as a separate political group, ruling over and divided from the great masses to which the rest of us belong. The commonly expressed sense of public alienation from political participation – 'my vote won't change anything: politicians are all the same' – is another testament to the gulf that is perceived to exist between rulers and the ruled. The social division between elites and masses is not only stark, but clearly demonstrates the social processes that provide the foundations of division more generally. The distinctive dimension of difference in elites is that of organisational, usually political, power.

The origins of elite theory

The concept of elites entered the sociological lexicon through the work of three major figures: Pareto (at the beginning of the twentieth century), Mosca and Michels. Whereas Pareto used the term 'elite' to refer to the small group he believed dominated all complex societies, Mosca preferred the term 'political class'. However, he later also used the term 'ruling class', which should not to be confused with the different meaning that Marx and Weber gave to the same expression (Chapter 2). Michels tended to use 'leadership' and 'oligarchy' rather than 'elites', although, as with Pareto and Mosca, the focus of his attention was ruling minorities. To clarify their similarities and differences, we need to look in more detail at each of their contributions.

Pareto and Mosca became embroiled in an argument about whose work had precedence in the exploration of elites, but, of the two, it was indisputably Mosca (1896) who first developed the idea of minority rule. A conservative exponent of the cause of the upper middle class, Mosca had two principal targets. On the one hand, he challenged the central claims of socialism, especially the promise of a class-free, stateless society, and, on the other, the overambitious extension of parliamentary democracy in Italy, which he believed had produced a decline of civic morality and the rise of the Left. His commitment to the idea of elite rule derived from Saint-Simon's observation (1825) that an organised minority would always hold sway over a disorganised majority and was a necessary feature of any complex society. It was Mosca's hope that this minority would be a civilised, benign, patrician political elite of 'superior persons' although he recognised that this was not always so.

All societies, he contended, consisted of two classes, the rulers and the ruled, this division expressing a universal trait in human beings – the unending struggle for power. Although this conflict resulted from the unchanging psychological structure of men, in Mosca's view dominance itself resulted from cultural, intellectual and moral attributes rather biological superiority. Even though force was a factor in minority rule, of far more importance was the 'political formula' by which those in power legitimised their position. Such a ruling myth was constructed out of values, beliefs and habits, and rooted in the specific historical conditions and culture of a society. A feature of all stable rule was the carefully cultivated adherence to this formula amongst the masses in order to secure their compliance and acquiescence. A political class could maintain its position peaceably only when its rule was the expression of a unified culture and morality, which encapsulated 'real' social forces.

Pareto developed an interest in sociology after first studying engineering and later economics. He was an adherent of free-market economic theory and policies of free trade, yet found classical economic theory lacking. As he observed, in contradiction of his intellectual convictions, protectionist policies were often associated with strong economic growth. Something, Pareto concluded, must be missing from liberal economic theory, and that something was the recognition that a large proportion of human activity was 'non-logical' rather than the outcome of reasoning and rationality. Pareto's sociology was therefore an inversion of his economics, in that it analysed the irrational, rather than rational, pursuit of self-interest as the key feature in the struggle for power.

Pareto's first major book of sociological significance was a critique of socialism, *Les Systems Socialistes* (1902), rumoured to have given Lenin sleepless nights. Pareto's conclusion was that socialism was fundamentally flawed in its aspiration to build a classless society, since all societies were, and always would be, divided between those who held power and the masses they dominated. Marxism failed to acknowledge the irredeemable inferiority of the masses and the psychological and social superiority of elites. The existence of elites reflected the differential distribution of talents amongst the population. All forms of social activity, from art, music, cooking and governing, display different levels of performance, from incompetence to excellence. The elites that dominated society did so by demonstrating their force of character, capacity to command and elemental and general superiority over those they dominated.

Pareto linked the social character of elites to the 'residues' they encompassed. Most of social life, Pareto asserted, derived from relatively unchanging 'residues' – givens in human behaviour that had the quality of biologically based building blocks of social life. These instinctual elements in behaviour were overlain by more readily observable, but less significant, 'derivations' – the varying rationales, justifications and explanations that legitimated conduct. Pareto distinguished between six types of residue, most importantly between Class 1, the 'Instinct for Combinations', which he associated with inventiveness, ingenuity, originality and progressive change, and Class 2, the 'Persistence of Aggregates', which concerned continuity, convention and the conservative tendencies in human life.

Each of these residues was dominant in different types of elite. Those elites that relied on cunning, persuasiveness and originality – 'foxes' – manifested the instinct for combination. Those characterised by force and strength of purpose – 'lions' – evidenced the persistence of aggregates. History consisted of the circulation of elites, in which the manipulative foxes would eventually concede too much to the masses, to be replaced by lions willing and able to establish their authority by means of violence. In time, their rule would stagnate and decline, only to be replaced by scheming foxes.

Michels' ([1911]1962) analysis is perhaps the most sociological of the three, yet his complex analysis of the emergence of oligarchies has a place for inherent human psychology and a conception of fixed human nature. Michels' basic idea was that all large-scale organisations, including political parties, develop bureaucratic structures that concentrate power at the top. They were, therefore, oligarchic and undemocratic. Michels argued that the increasing complexity of political organisations favoured those with the specialist knowledge and skills associated with leadership and reduced the possibility of widespread participation in decision-making. Leaders were able to control flows of information and discipline dissidents, further strengthening their position. They became more practised in the use of power and arts of manipulation. As political organisations matured, leadership was consolidated and further alienated from the rank and file as it absorbed the lifestyle of other metropolitan elites. In contrast, subordinates for the most part, indeed the masses in general, were perennially incompetent, incapable of self-organisation and generally content to be led.

Although Michels focused on the social processes of organisational life in explaining the emergence of oligarchy, such concentrations of power were also an expression of an immutable tendency to regard power as a personal possession. The vagaries of upward and downward mobility (Chapter 2) might account for some change in the personnel comprising elites, but the tendency to manipulation and self-interest would remain the same. These were the factors that sapped the revolutionary ideas of socialist parties and produced their conservative leaderships, more concerned with furthering their own interests than those of the people they claimed to represent.

Michels maintained that the 'iron law of oligarchy' was a major problem for any political organisation that aimed to create a democratic society, especially a classless society, and which claimed to be democratic in its own procedures. This was a particular concern for Michels, a supporter of the socialist movement in Germany at the time he wrote *Political Parties* ([1911]1962). His disillusionment marked the beginning of a political journey towards the Right.

Although there were important theoretical and terminological differences between Pareto, Mosca and Michels, the object of their attention was broadly similar – the organised and self-interested minorities that, they asserted, ruled all complex societies, utilising a combination of force and fraud. It would be going too far to claim they offer a coherent school of thought but their work has certain elements in common. All viewed the fundamental division in society as that between a ruling minority, an elite, and the masses who were the vast majority of the population. Elites, they claim, are driven to monopolise power whilst the masses are portrayed as typically incompetent, unorganised and inchoate. Ruling elites are characterised by the three Cs, group consciousness, internal coherence and conspiracy (common intentions).

Mosca, Pareto and Michels argued that governing minorities are composed of people of proven 'superiority', with regard to their intellects, organisational abilities, cultural attributes and capacity to rule. Such elites are required if society is not to descend into disorder. Their superiority and associated desire for power was, for Pareto, primarily innate in origin. Mosca and Michels gave more, but not exclusive, weight to social and cultural factors.

This classical conception of elites placed political manipulation and power at the centre of attention and stood in contrast with the Marxist stress on the economy and control of the means of production. For Pareto, Marx's class conflict is but a subspecies of the universal clash between elites and those who aspire to replace them. To Michels, class revolution always would end in the creation of yet another oligarchy, a view he expressed prior to the Bolshevik revolution.

These writers shared a rejection of Marxism, particularly the promise of a classless society and opposed the ambitions of the Socialist and Communist movements in Italy, particularly after the First World War. They were also sceptical about the claims to participation and representation made on behalf of parliamentary democracy. In this case, the specific object of their criticism was the weakness, vacillation and corruption of the Italian political system in the late decades of the nineteenth and early years of the twentieth centuries, prior to the rise of Fascism.

Mosca, Pareto and Michels witnessed the rise to power of Mussolini, the Fascist dictator of Italy. Pareto was an enthusiastic supporter and took the rise of Fascism to be confirmation of his theories. Appointed senator by Mussolini, he died within a year of the March on Rome. Mosca surveyed Fascism with the reluctant disdain of an intellectual confronted by the vulgarity of the rabble. He became a leading conservative critic of Fascism and hoped for a limited form of democratic rule under the leadership of an enlightened political class. Michels welcomed Fascism as right for Italy, in that it brought a 'forceful' clarity to a society in danger of collapse. Whilst he hoped an elitist form of democracy might eventually emerge, he accepted a chair in political science in Turin, whose purpose was the promotion of Fascism, and became a member of the Fascist Party.

The development of elite theory

Perhaps the most direct heir of classical elite theory was James Burnham, initially a supporter of Trotsky and the revolutionary Left, who moved to the political Right to become a neo-conservative of some influence. In *The Managerial Revolution*, published in 1941, Burnham argued that managers, by virtue of their control of large-scale organisations and indispensable technical function, were taking over the world, regardless of the social, economic and political character of the societies in which they operated. For Burnham, factual control of the means of production was more important than mere legal ownership and therefore the rise of the Bolsheviks, the Nazis and indeed the so-called 'propertyless managers' in free-market democracies were all manifestations of the same phenomenon, the rise of organisational elites. This claim was quite in line with elite theory, although what Burnham purported to discern was the rise of a new class, rather than a new elite. Burnham's ideas on management had some influence on Crossman and Crosland – luminaries in the 1950's Labour Party.

Burnham's affinity with classical elite theory was made explicit in *The New Machiavellians* published in 1944. In reviewing the work of Mosca, Pareto and Michels, Burnham adapts an amalgam of their approaches to the analysis of power. Politics is portrayed as being about unceasing struggle, non-logical in character and based on instinct. Rulers always rule in their own interests by combining force, fraud and political formulations to supply the cultural foundations of power.

Schumpeter, influenced by Weber, developed the links between leadership groups, competitive elites and the prospects for democracy in his book *Capitalism, Socialism and Democracy* (1942). After a brilliant early career as an economist (three major books and finance minister in Austria in 1919 by the age of 35), Schumpeter also made a considerable impact in sociology and political science. In his ruminations on democracy, elites were regarded not as inherently at odds with representative democracy (as with Pareto and Michels) but as key elements in the modern democratic system, albeit a system in which the main political duty of the general population was to elect its leaders and little else. Thus, circulating elites and leadership groups linked to different interests competing for influence and power were conceived to be among the principal constituents of democracy. Schumpeter placed particular importance on the manipulation of symbols and the values that elites espoused. He feared that such pluralistic democratic systems would produce forms of democratic socialism and the ideal elite would be one of talent and civilised ideals able to contain such tendencies.

Schumpeter's rather conservative notion of democratic rule was an influence on the ideas of the 'pluralist' political theorists of the 1950s. Pluralists argued that the democratic systems of modern societies were characterised by the diffusion of power rather than its concentration in the hands of a dominant class or group. Picking up certain elements of Burnham's approach, they accepted that class structure was decomposing and a business elite of professionalised, propertyless managers was taking over the corporate sector. In the view of pluralists, such leadership groups and elites were linked to widely differing interests and pressure groups and competed for control of the policy-making apparatus at the local and national levels through the electoral process. In associating the concept of elites with the diffusion rather than accretion of power, pluralists were using the term in direct reversal of the ideas of the classical elite theorists.

However, the idea of elites as the locus of concentrated power re-emerged in Mills' critique of pluralism, although shorn of assumptions of inherent superiority or inevitability. Mills had reviewed Burnham's *The Managerial Revolution* and rejected its central argument, on the grounds that technical indispensability (the management function) was no guarantor of power. In his own book *The Power Elite* (1956), Mills also rejected the Marxist idea of a ruling class, arguing that it assumed too close an identity of economic and political power and the subordination of the latter to the former. The term 'power elite' was more appropriate, in that a good deal of its authority derived from the characteristics of complex organisations in modern societies rather than control of the means of production. The class society of eighteenth and nineteenth-century USA, Mills stated, was being replaced by a more concentrated, and, in some senses, less democratic configuration of power.

Mills identified three, initially distinct, components of power, the political, the military and the industrial/business sectors. He argued that there had been a complex process of consolidation occurring throughout the twentieth century, accelerated by the Second World War, in which a developing 'military-industrial complex' (a term used by President Eisenhower) was melding with the political sphere to produce a consolidated power elite. This elite controlled the masses in part through the manipulation of the media. Mills feared that the plurality of diverse interests that had characterised American history was increasingly unable to act as a restraint on the elite and that the community of publics was being replaced by a mass society, with grave consequences for democracy.

Mills' *The Power Elite* was heavily criticised, especially by those of pluralist persuasion, including Talcott Parsons, who focused on Mills' insecure 'zero-sum' conception of power. However, what is notable is Mills' attempt to analyse the social origins, career paths, affiliations and connections between the occupants of elite positions. He places these sociological attributes of elite people (exclusively men in fact) within an analysis of institutional change in the USA, and in so doing concentrates on the intersection of biography and history – the essential task of the sociologist in Mills' view.

Mills' analysis of the USA, in which a class society had given way to elite domination, mirrored Milovan Djilas's analysis of Tito's Yugoslavia in the 1950s. In *The New Class* (1957), Djilas suggested that the Communist Party's political power as a political elite was metamorphosing into the birth of a new class, a position that cost him years in jail. Thus, whilst Mills maintained that the USA was moving from class to elite, Djilas was tracking the shift from elite to class in Yugoslavia. So, ironically, Mills, who had little sympathy with the politics of the classical elitists, used the term in some sense as they did to express the concentration of power of a minority over a manipulated mass. However, there is no suggestion that this had always been or would always be the case, was desirable or that rule is based on inherent or civilisational superiority. Mills was indeed a vocal critic of the elite he portrayed, so much so that the FBI kept track of his activities after Mills' defence of the Cuban Revolution.

Mills visited Britain, mixing with the emerging New Left and certainly influencing the Marxist Ralph Miliband. Yet in contrast to Mills' doubts about class analysis, Miliband linked the terms 'class' and 'elite' in his book *The State in Capitalist Society* (1969). This was intended to both extend Marxist analysis of the state and reject pluralist claims about the nature of contemporary capitalist societies. In attempting to demonstrate how the state served, defended and consolidated the interests of capital, Miliband explored, briefly, the social and educational background of those holding elite positions within the state and other organisations. He hoped, thereby, to establish the manner in which class factors influenced the recruitment and training of elites in further consolidation of the capitalist system.

For some Marxists, this use of the concepts of class and elites in this way was unacceptable, not least because of the historic link between the concept of elite and Fascism. Poulantzas (1969), for instance, argued that Miliband's attempt to establish empirical links between the dominant class and the composition and operation of various institutional elites was theoretically flawed and subjectivist. It was not a matter of who occupied such positions but how the positions were arranged and functioned.

Thus, by the 1970s, there were at least four different major conceptions of elites operative in sociology:

1. Elites are leadership groups, representing different interests, competing for power and influence. They are a central feature of the democratic process and integral to a political process that ameliorates social division (pluralists such as Parsons, Dahl).

2. Elites represent necessary concentrations of power and are fundamental to social order in all complex societies. They are the key feature of the major social division between elites and masses (Pareto, Mosca, Michels, Burnham).
3. Elites reflect the interests of the dominant class but have a degree of relative autonomy. Class is the central social division of contemporary capitalist societies (Miliband).
4. The power elite has developed a complex logic of its own, serving the amalgamated interests of capital, the political establishment and the military hierarchy, and is the fundamental enemy of democratic processes however the rhetoric of democracy is deployed. The central social division in modern society (at least the USA in the 1950s and 60s) is between the elite and the masses (Mills).

Giddens' (1974) intervention in the debate at this stage aimed to remove some of the confusions patrolling elite analysis. He defined elites as holders of senior positions of formal authority in major social institutions and the state (for example MPs, the Cabinet, senior civil servants, chairs and chief executive officers in major corporations, high ranking military officers and so on). Giddens made a number of still useful distinctions between three dimensions of elite analysis – recruitment, structure and power.

The analysis of recruitment concerned the gender, social origins and educational experience of elites, and avenues of occupational and professional advancement that lead to elite positions. Here the issue is of the channels of entry, some highly formalised (military, judiciary), others involving a large element of custom and practice (politics). With respect to recruitment, much has been made of the high proportion of those entering British elites (the vast majority men) over the past 1500 years who have been educated in public schools and attended Oxford or Cambridge universities. However, of equal significance are the professional, occupational and less formal processes of career *socialisation* experienced by future holders of elite positions that facilitate the accumulation of the appropriate types of cultural and social capital associated with elites. For instance, army officers subscribe to the officer and gentleman ethos, regardless of their social and educational origins, due to the impact and efficacy of officer training at Sandhurst.

Giddens' notion of structure embraces two elements: patterns of social and organisational interaction and linkage within an elite – its *social structure*; and the values and orientations that characterise an elite – its *ethos*. Investigating the social structure of an elite involves attempting to discern whether there are networks of friendship, kinship, formal and informal association which embroider the formal organisational activities of elites within and between their different spheres of operation. Casual acquaintance may be as significant as strong ties in facilitating flows of information, getting things done and generally operating effectively. Some elites (the Cabinet for instance) constitute a demo-graphic group, in that they meet and work in close proximity. Others (business leaders) never meet or act as a socially constituted group as such, although sharing various forms of formal and informal contact. The analysis of the values of elites incorporates questions such as whether, and to what extent, elites possess a distinctive *ethos*, and the extent to which different elites may share certain value orientations. Important studies of elites in the military, the police and the civil service, for instance, have noted their distinctive cultural character and elements of change and continuity in their core values.

The third and most important of Giddens' dimensions is the complex problem of *power*, including issues of the extent to which elites exercise power within their own institutional domains and are able to influence affairs in other areas of activity. Giddens is emphatic that formal authority should be distin-guished from effective power, although it may be an important source of such. Consequently, the issue of the extent to which elites are able to transform their formal authority into decision-making and operative policy is an empirical question, not to be settled a priori by assuming that elites are, by definition, all-powerful. Nor should the examination of elite power be confined only to decision-making, for there are aspects of the powers of elites that go beyond the decisions and policies in which they are implicated and which require examination, including control of what is publicly discussed by 'agenda-setting' and selecting personnel who will join and, in some cases, replace them.

These analytically distinct dimensions should always be placed within an analysis of broader society in order to understand the configuration of economy, state and sociocultural structures within which elites operate and which provide the context for their formation, reproduction and operation. For instance, the structural and organisational changes characterised as the move from 'organised' to 'disorganised capitalism', the impact of globalisation and the emergence of so-called post-modern culture have significance in the general setting and context within which elites are formed and operate.

The kinds of questions that can be approached using these distinctions are the degree of openness of elites in socio-economic, gender or ethnic terms, the extent of their social and cultural cohesion, the range or scope of issues over which the elite has influence, the degree to which elites monopolise power within their institutional domain and the extent to which the power of an elite may extend into other spheres of activity. In this way, elites throw light on the ways in which social divisions operate in contemporary society. For example, the simple observations that women and most ethnic minorities are seriously under-represented in British elites and that there is a well-defined and long-established pattern of educational selectivity are revealing of the structure of opportunity and, perhaps, ambition in the UK over the past three decades or so.

Education and elites in Britain

The tradition of investigating the educational backgrounds of holders of elite positions in the UK has been chiefly concerned with the relative importance of public schools and Oxford and Cambridge in educating elites. This type of analysis provides purchase on the question of the possible economic, political and sociocultural consequences resulting from the historical predominance of these institutions. Whilst attendance at certain types of school (for example independent schools, particularly the most prestigious) has often been used to infer social background, William Rubinstein (1993) has demonstrated that the connection between social origin and educational experience in the case of many elite position holders has been far less straightforward than often assumed. That is, whilst it may be fair to say that children at independent schools are in general drawn from the more prosperous sections of the population, there are many particular cases of people from lower middle-class and even working-class backgrounds who have reached elite positions after attending such schools (perhaps on scholarships). For instance, as recently as 1999, 17 per cent of the first year intake at Cambridge University was drawn from the Registrar General's social classes 3B, 4 and 5 (parental background being routine, poorly paid, white-collar or manual worker), one-third of whom were educated privately. Thus, the social background of elites (which is often difficult to research) should be established independently of education. Nor will an examination of education reveal how the people comprising elites will behave or the values to which they will adhere when they achieve their position. Without recourse to other data, educational background reveals only the extent to which there are clear paths of educational achievement associated with *entry* to elites, how they differ *between* elites and the extent they have *changed over time*. Possession of a particular educational experience does not in itself cause a person to become a member of an elite (Payne 1987b: 122–43).

Most of the information on the backgrounds of elites can be found in the publicly available directories, such as *Who's Who*, *Dods Parliamentary Companion* and *The Whitehall Directory*. The internet is also a valuable source of information. However, given the changes in the organisation and status of many schools, especially during the 1960s and 70s when comprehensive schools were introduced, it is important to ascertain the position of a school with regard to the state/private distinction at the time the person being investigated was attending. For instance, rather than be transformed into comprehensive schools, a number of state grammar schools moved to the independent sector. Thus, persons holding elite positions today may have attended a school that is now in the private category but was a state school 35 years ago when they attended it. The terms 'public', 'private' and 'independent' schools are used interchangeably here to refer to schools that lie outside the state sector.

During the past 30–40 years independent schools have educated approximately 5–7 per cent of the school population and 15–18 per cent of 16–18-year-olds. The vast majority of men who attended public schools and are represented in the following data attended Headmasters Conference (HMC) schools. At present, HMC schools number 247 – and 220 in the 1970s – accounting for about 6 per cent of secondary schools in Britain. Oxford and Cambridge accounted for 20 per cent of UK undergraduates in the late 1930s, 4–5 per cent in the 1960s and 70s and less than 2 per cent after 1992. The following data refer to 1471 holders of elite positions, most of whom held post in 2000/01.

Table 7.1 Elites: education (2000/01) percentages

Schools	Judges 158	MPs (Con) 166	Milit 105	Amb 112	Bish 105	Bus chs 75	Cab 26	MPs (LD) 52	MPs (all) 659	VCs pre-92 81	MPs (L) 412	HCS in 98 155
Public	77.8	65.1	67.7	64.3	50.5	49.0	34.6	32.7	30.0	28.3	16.0	56.2
HMC	75.3	62.1	61.0	58.0	49.5	45.0	26.9	32.7	26.6	23.4	11.4	49.7
Private	2.5	3.0	6.7	6.3	1.0	4.0	7.7	0.0	3.5	4.9	4.6	6.5
State	12.5	27.7	22.9	31.3	29.5	28.0	61.5	65.4	64.6	49.4	81.0	28.4
Overseas	8.2	1.8	4.8	2.7	4.1	17.0	3.8	1.9	1.7	11.1	1.7	3.9
Others	1.7	5.4	5.6	1.7	15.2	5.0	0.0	0.0	3.7	11.1	1.3	11.6
Universities												
Oxbridge	82.9	50.0	14.3	62.5	62.8	22.0	38.5	28.8	27.3	44.5	19.1	68.3
Ox	41.0	27.1	3.8	32.1	29.5	11.0	19.2	19.2	16.4	23.5	12.6	38.1
Cam	42.4	24.0	10.5	30.4	33.3	11.0	19.2	9.6	10.9	21.0	6.6	30.3
Others UK	15.0	39.8	21.9	24.1	41.9	37.0	65.4	63.5	53.3	69.3	59.7	31.0
Overseas	5.7	10.2	2.9	6.3	8.6	22.0	7.7	7.7	7.6	4.0	6.3	9.8
P/S + Oxb	72.2	37.3	13.3	42.9	38.1	22.0	27.0	19.2	15.8	20.0	7.0	45.1

Four elites are notable for the high proportion of their membership who attended public schools (overwhelmingly HMC schools) (see Table 7.1). Over three-quarters of the senior judiciary attended public schools, a figure approached by Tory MPs, the army and navy components of the military elite and ambassadors. Approximately half of bishops, senior civil servants and the chairs of large business corporations were educated in the independent sector, whilst approximately one-third of the Cabinet, Liberal Democrat MPs and MPs in total recorded such an education. Labour MPs were notable among these elites, in that only one-sixth had attended such schools. Put another way, amongst these elites, only vice-chancellors and certain sections of the political elite received their school education predominantly in the state sector.

Turning to university education (the lower half of Table 7.1), approximately four-fifths of senior judges, two-thirds of ambassadors, senior civil servants and bishops, and half of Tory MPs attended Oxford and Cambridge. One-third of the Cabinet and vice-chancellors and a quarter of all MPs gained 'greybrick' degrees, as did one-fifth of business chairs and Labour MPs. Military leaders are trained in their own institutions (Sandhurst, Cranfield and Dartmouth) but were more likely to have attended university than in the past, a seventh attending Oxford or Cambridge. In the case of judges, Tory MPs, bishops, ambassadors and senior civil servants, Oxbridge outweighs the contribution of all other UK universities combined. In contrast, non-Oxbridge universities are more important in the cases of university vice-chancellors, chairs of top companies, the Cabinet, Liberal Democrat MPs, Labour MPs and MPs *in toto*.

It is a truism that the main route to the top in Britain has traditionally been through a public school education followed by an Oxbridge college. In the present era, only in the case of judges is this combination of private schooling and Oxbridge the overwhelming norm, but it remains a substantially more important route than the alternative state/Oxbridge and state/non-Oxbridge paths in the case of judges, Tory MPs, ambassadors, bishops, business leaders and the higher civil service. This illustrates one of the ways social division works in contemporary British society, and can be summarised in four main points:

1. A small percentage of the school population, that attending private schools, has provided the bulk of these elites and continues to do so except for sections of the political elite and vice-chancellors.
2. Oxford and Cambridge universities remain the predominant universities attended en route to the top except for the political elite (with the exception of Tory MPs), vice-chancellors, the military and business leaders (nearly a quarter of the latter attending overseas universities). No other individual university comes close to challenging the importance of Oxford and Cambridge.
3. These figures point to the importance of certain elites in bringing a greater range of educational experience to the higher circles. Among these elites it is only Labour MPs, university vice-chancellors (and chief constables: see Reiner 1991) who have educational origins clearly rooted in the state school sector.

4. The importance of the public school/Oxbridge route is not as important as in the past but remains well represented, especially when one remembers that the state school intake to Oxbridge reached as high as 70 per cent in the 1960s and 70s, when many of these people attended university. (It is now approximately 50 per cent.)

State elites

By way of further illustration, we shall consider several of these elites in greater detail, starting with the formal political system. As the House of Commons entered the new millennium, it did so with the highest proportion of state school-educated MPs in its history. Two-thirds of MPs attended state schools, whilst just under a third attended a public school (the remainder were schooled overseas or their school was unknown (see Table 7.1 above: the numerically minor parties – Scottish Nationalists, Ulster Unionists – are included in total figures but are not accorded separate analysis).

These figures reiterate the often observed contrast in the school experiences of Labour and Conservative MPs. Whereas two-thirds of Tories had attended a public school (nearly all HMC), only just over one-sixth of Labour members had been so educated. Similarly, 50 per cent of Conservatives had taken a degree at Oxbridge compared with 18.6 per cent of New Labour. The combined institutions of the University of London accounted for 86 MPs (13.1 per cent), 34 having taken degrees at the London School of Economics, 26 of whom were Labour MPs. Liberal Democrats sit in the middle, as it were, of the two main parties, with 32.7 per cent having a public school affiliation and 28.8 per cent a degree from one of the two ancient universities. Over a third of Tories combined a private education with Oxbridge, the figures for the other two parties recording much lower figures.

Labour MPs, given their connections to the labour movement throughout the history of the party, have had an educational profile somewhat at odds with most other British elites and closer to that of the whole population. Yet attendance at a school in the private sector (16 per cent in 2000) has always been above the percentage found in the general school population (7–8 per cent). University education has become an increasingly common experience amongst Labour MPs since 1945, when 34.2 per cent recorded a degree: by 2000 it was three-quarters.

Since the Second World War, those attending Oxford or Cambridge have always been a minority of the university graduates in Labour's ranks. Four-fifths of Labour MPs in 2000 who had attended university did so at institutions other than Cambridge or Oxford. However, Oxford could still claim to have educated more Labour MPs in 2000 than any other institution (52), although the LSE (26) almost matched Cambridge (27). Other well-represented universities in Labour's ranks included Edinburgh (16), Manchester (13), York (12), Leeds (12), Hull (12) and Warwick (10). Seventy-five had attended post-1992 universities (but mainly when they were polytechnics) and 54 attended both pre- and post-1992 universities. Naturally, the figures for university education show the general impact of the several expansions of post-war higher education. Notably, gender differences in educational background between the 317 male and 95 female Labour MPs in 2000 were small indeed. Attendance at both public school and Oxbridge is a relatively rare occurrence among Labour MPs, the post-war high being 14.5 per cent, but half this by 2000. In contrast, the 'public school plus Oxbridge' route accounted for about half of Tory MPs between 1945 (50.3 per cent) and 1966 (51.6 per cent), the proportion declining approximately a third in 1979 (37.4 per cent), where it has stabilised (37.3 per cent in 2000).

As has been the pattern throughout the twentieth century, the educational profile of the Cabinet in 2000 differed somewhat from the cohort of governing party MPs from which it is selected. It has always the case that independent schools and Oxbridge have been better represented in the Cabinet than in the ranks of the governing party as a whole. Whereas just over 80 per cent of Labour MPs were educated in the state sector, the figure for the Cabinet is lower at 65.4 per cent. Similarly, more of the Cabinet attended independent schools (34.7 per cent) than did Labour MPs in general (16.0 per cent). The same kinds of regularities are repeated at university level, in that 38.5 per cent (equally divided between the two universities) of the Cabinet attended Oxbridge, whilst the figure for the Labour Party as a whole is 18.6 per cent. Whereas only 7.0 per cent of Labour MPs combined a public school and Oxbridge education, 27 per cent of the Cabinet in 2000 followed this path.

In comparison with Labour Cabinets of previous eras, the percentage of the 2000 Cabinet having a public school education evidences a slight increase on previous eras. Between 1916 and 1955, and 1955 and 1984, 26 per cent and 32 per cent respectively of Labour Cabinet members were educated in private schools, the figure for 2000 being 34.7 per cent. Therefore, just as the percentage of Labour MPs attending public schools recorded a small rise over the figure for the 1980s, so the proportion in the Blair Cabinet privately educated also moved up slightly from the figure covering the Wilson and Callaghan Cabinets of the 1960s and 70s. The pattern is slightly different with respect to Oxbridge representation. In 2000, 38.5 per cent of the Labour Cabinet were graduates of Oxford or Cambridge, a decline from the 1955–84 period (42.8 per cent), but both are above the figure for 1916–55 (27.6 per cent). Whilst under half of Labour Cabinets in the first period (1916–55) had attended university (44.6 per cent), nearly two-thirds (62.5 per cent) of the 1955–84 sample had done so. In 2000, all members of the Cabinet had received a university education, a number as mature students.

Table 7.2 Labour Cabinets: education

	1916–55	1955–84	2000
Public schools	26.1	32.1	34.7
State	74.9	67.9	65.4
Oxbridge	27.6	42.8	38.5
Other UK univs	17.0	19.7	65.4

Source: Data for 1916–84 adapted from Burch and Moran (1985).

The educational backgrounds of elected politicians differ from those of the top civil servants who shape policy and remain in their positions long after the typical minister has been moved on. The highest ranking civil servants have been subject to a number of studies and enquiries investigating their social and educational origins. In the period since the end of the Second World War up to the 1990s, the broad picture is one in which private sector education, particularly the HMC schools, maintain and even increase their contributions to this Whitehall elite: 69.4 per cent between 1945 and 1964; 70.0 per cent between 1965 and 1986; and 77 per cent between 1979 and 1994. However, data for 34 grade 1 civil servants in 1998, a slightly more widely drawn group than permanent secretaries alone but including them, suggests that state sector-educated civil servants are breaking through to the top ranks in greater numbers.

Thus, only half these senior administrators and half the permanent secretaries within the grade 1 group attended HMC schools, with 55.9 per cent of the former being educated in some form of independent school. If this annual sample is consistent with a more general trend, it indicates a gradually declining share for public schools at the highest levels of the civil service. State-educated grade 1 administrators stood at 26.5 per cent in 1998, broadly in line with the figures for permanent secretaries between the late 1940s and the late 1970s, but an increase on the 20 per cent recorded for the 1979–94 cohort. However, the permanent secretaries within this group record a higher state school representation, at 50 per cent.

**Table 7.3 Permanent secretaries (1945–94)
and grade I civil servants (1998)**

	1945–64	1965–86	1960–70	1979–94	1998(G1)
Public School (Ps)	58.7	62.5	40.0	66.0	50.0
Private	10.7	7.5		11.0	5.9
State	24.0	28.8		20.0	26.5
Other	6.7	0.0		3.0	11.8
No information	0.0	1.2	60.0	0.0	5.9
Oxbridge	66.7	75.0	80.0	56.0	70.6
Oxford	40.0	45.0	35.0	30.0	35.3
Cambridge	26.7	30.0	45.0	26.0	35.3
Other University	16.0	17.5	17.5	39.0	41.2
Ps/Oxbridge					44.1

Source: Data for 1945–94 adapted from Theakston and Fry (1989) and Barberis (1996).

With regard to higher education, the position of Oxford and Cambridge remains strong, although subject to some challenge in the last decade of the twentieth century. Theakstone and Fry (1989) recorded a rise in the Oxbridge component of their two post-war samples from 66.7 to 75 per cent. However, Barberis (1996: 101) represents a greybrick figure of 56 per cent for his 1979–95 permanent secretaries and observes that 'the Oxbridge presence among permanent secretaries should decline somewhat in the future'. Data for grade 1 civil servants for 1998 give a figure of 41.2 per cent having received a non-Oxbridge degree, which includes a number of civil servants who have received degrees from both Oxbridge and another UK university. Thus Oxford and Cambridge remain well represented at these levels.

As a final example of state elites, we can briefly consider senior army offi- cers. Otley's work in the 1960s and early 1970s established the social and educational background of the army elite, work extended by von Zugbach (1988) (later with Ishaq (1999)) into the 1980s and 90s, with further findings about the subcultural distinctions between different organisational elements within the army. Between 1965 and 1977, the proportion of major-generals attending HMC schools declined somewhat, as did the contributions of elite public schools, Eton, Harrow and Winchester and Wellington. However, amongst lieutenant generals and generals, elite public schools held their own, Eton, Harrow and Winchester increased their representation, with only Wellington's share continuing to decline. As late as 1977, 53 per cent of generals were drawn from just four public schools (see Whitley's 1974 work demonstrating that approximately 30 per cent of directors of major merchant banks in the early 1970s attended Eton alone, and Bond's (2004) similar finding for business supporters of the Conservative Party).

Von Zugbach's analysis of key post generals demonstrates that 'those who dominate army policy and strategic thinking' were drawn overwhelmingly from a small number of schools. In 1982, 100 per cent of these officers attended HMC schools, 75 per cent attended the elite of these schools and 51 per cent were educated in the four schools mentioned above. The most prestigious units (elite regiments within the fighting arms) were highly selective in terms of educational background, whilst units of lower status (technical and support arms) were of more diverse educational origin.

Writing with Ishaq later in the mid-1990s, von Zugbach detected a shift in the educational origins of the 'Promenente' – those senior officers who control the process of selection to the highest ranks of the army (generals) – and, employing NATO terminology , 'star' ranked generals. In 1996, the highest ranks of the army were still occupied, overwhelmingly, by men educated in the private sector. Only among three- and two-star generals was there substantial state school representation – 30 per cent and 46 per cent respectively. However, since it is from this stratum that the highest ranks are drawn, it is likely that the trend towards increasing state school representation will continue. There was also a reduced Oxbridge share at the very top and amongst two-star generals, but a slight proportionate increase amongst three-star generals. Non-Oxbridge universities show an increasing representation amongst two- and three-star generals.

A similar profile can be detected among Royal Navy admirals (38 in number), with 76 per cent having attended a public school and 21 per cent state schools. In contrast, in the RAF the state sector accounts for nearly half of senior officers (air vice-marshall and above). A higher proportion of the RAF hierarchy have attended university than is the case with the other services.

Overall, the present military elite remains predominantly of private school background with the state slowly gaining ground, but that the balance is likely to swing in favour of state-educated officers unless public-school-educated officers remain, as in the past, quite disproportionately successful in ascending to the highest ranks and securing the most influential posts in the coming decades. And, as MacDonald (2004) has demonstrated, public schools continue to provide the lion's share of recruits to the officer corps of elite infantry regiments, 90 per cent having attended such schools as recently as 1999/2000.

Concluding observations

A fully rounded account of British elites would have to consider issues concerning other dimensions of recruitment as well as matters of structure and power. The disciplines of occupational socialisation and training differ among elites to produce clearly demarcated cultures (for instance judges compared with chief constables, military officers compared with senior civil servants and so on), as well as modes of operation. These procedures induce and encourage coherence within elites and become stronger, as promotion and selection lead to top positions. However, as the structural differentiation of elites proceeds, the commonalities of social origin, gender and education – claimed in the past to be the basis for elite solidarities across institutions – are unlikely to provide the integrative element between elites they once did (if, indeed, they ever did).

It may be that the movement of people between elite positions, what the French call *pantoflage*, may be one means by which fragmentation may be countered. In the past, many judges were drawn from the ranks of practising lawyers sitting as MPs, and there is some evidence of the movement of the higher ranks of the civil service into business in the present era. Perhaps the reformed House of Lords will provide succour for some tired former vice-chancellors, played out Cabinet ministers and fatigued permanent secretaries. But, as of now, there is little systematic evidence on the current state of such inter-elite movements. Past work suggests that, at the level discussed here, it occurred on a rather smaller scale that might be expected and that may continue to be the case.

The other major issue that a more comprehensive study of elites would need to consider is the changing topography of power. For instance, there is general agreement that the House of Commons has declined in influence over the policy-making process and the power of the prime minister has been enhanced even, some argue, to the detriment of the Cabinet. The matter of whether Britain has entered a period of 'presidential' politics has been much debated, as have the role of 'special advisers' and their claimed usurpation of the role of senior civil servants in the policy-making process.

Another matter of central significance is that concerning the impact of economic globalisation. This restricts the capacity of the government to orchestrate the national economy and increases the constraints put on policy choices by the operation of financial markets. Note should also be taken of the declining influence of the Church of England (Chapter 5) and the Trades Union Congress, the changing role of the diplomatic corps and the much reduced size of the military establishment and the forces they lead.

Who gets into elite positions is an index of the distribution of power in British society and, although there has been a restrained move to more demo-graphically representative elites, it has been markedly slow in specific respects. Male elites are the overwhelming norm, although increasing numbers of women can now be found in the 'pools' (MPs, QCs, professors, middle rank civil servants and so on) from which elites emerge. Public school education remains the most common form of education, and affiliation with Oxford and Cambridge universities the predominant form of higher education, in most elites. Whilst the electoral process produces a degree of educational diversity at the top (especially when the Labour Party is well represented), the normal patterns of career advancement in many professions produce elites that have educational profiles marked by the importance of private sector schools and the ancient universities. The extent to which this indicates that these institutions produce talented people best fitted for top positions or reflects deeply ingrained preferences for people of a certain kind remains a matter of continuing debate.

The expansion of the state grammar school system resulting from the 1944 Education Act, billed as the saviour of the bright working-class boy, made a significant impact on routes of career advancement: the vast majority of state-educated men who entered elites in the past 30 years attended such schools. However, it is not clear whether the products of comprehensive and other forms of state school or college will continue to reach elite positions to the same or an increasing extent. In an era of credentialism, when competition for places at the most prestigious universities is intense and unremitting, the independent school sector, for well-documented reasons, continues to dominate the conventional school league tables based on exam results.

It is thus possible that the representation of those with a public school education will be sustained or even increase among holders of elite positions after a period when there were signs that this route of entry was loosening its hold. In this respect, education will remain of critical importance with regard to which sections of the population are drawn on in the composition of future elites. It is certain that educational opportunity and the social structures of ambition, aspiration and opportunity will remain central to both the reproduction and erosion of social divisions and the composition of elites in British society.

Discussion Questions

1. What are the differences between an upper class and an elite?

2. Examine the relationship between elites and other social divisions in British society.

3. Why are the educational origins of MPs so different from those of High Court judges?

4. How does the analysis of elites aid the understanding of the relation-ship between education and social division?

5. Is organisation inevitably hierarchical and divisive?

FURTHER READING

There is no current up-to-date sociological overview of British elites, although there are a number of excellent studies of specific elites, examining not only recruitment but also issues such as the impact of the new managerialism, for instance Dargie, C. and Locke, R. 'The British Senior Civil Service' in Page, E.C. and Wright, V. (eds) *Bureaucratic Elites in Western European States* (Oxford: Oxford University Press, 1999). Reiner, R. *Chief Constables: Bobbies, Bosses or Bureaucrats?* (Oxford: Clarendon, 1991), is the best sociological account of a British elite. Bottomore T. *Elites and Society* (London: Penguin, 1966) is a classic short account of the earlier development of elites theory, whilst Scott J. *Stratification and Power: Structures of Class, Status and Command* (Cambridge: Polity, 1996) represents an integration of the concept of elites with other forms of power. Lasch, C. *The Revolt of the Elites and the Betrayal of Democracy* (New York: Norton, 1995) is an angry and interesting attempt to specify the emergence of a global informational elites. Finally, for useful surveys see Sampson, A. *Who Runs This Place?* (London: John Murray, 2004) and Adonis, A. and Pollard, S. *A Class Act* (London: Hamish Hamilton, 1997).

CHAPTER 8

Age and Old Age

JOHN A. VINCENT

This chapter will provide you with a broad critical understanding of the following issues in age and old age as sources of social division:

- Age as a universal marker of social distinction
- The different ways in which age is institutionalised in different societies
- The social construction of age
- Intergenerational relationships
- The terminology of age, generation and cohort and the contrast of life cycle and life-course
- Patterns of age stratification
- The history of the life-course – pre-modern, modern and post-modern western life-courses
- Life-course and social change; consequences for old age of changing patterns of employment and family relationships
- Population ageing
- The social conditions of older people and the material inequalities in old age
- The generation equity debate
- Ageism and bodily ageing
- The 'double jeopardy' of age and gender
- Age as a distinctive social division

Age has been used in all societies as a way of differentiating people. Anthropological studies suggest that age is one of the few genuinely universal social criteria, forming a significant part of the social structures by which collective life is ordered. However, this fact in itself, although directing us to look towards issues of age, does not take us very far. Understanding age as social division requires us to understand the wide variations in:

- the degree to which age is used as a mechanism for social differentiation
- which age criteria are used
- the significance attached to these criteria.

194

All three factors are extremely varied. Societies range from those in which age is not particularly important, to those in which it is the key structural principle, and from those in which old age is highly valued, to those in which it is of very low status. Further, what is thought to constitute 'old age' varies not only cross-culturally but even within our own society. Our first step needs to be an exploration of the idea of age divisions, and how age has been 'used' in organising human society.

In more egalitarian types of society, the social categories of age and gender do not take on the rigidity and determining quality that these criteria do in many other societies. For example, the Mbuti, as described by Turnball (1984), illustrate the highly flexible character of small-scale societies that live by foraging and have low social differentiation. Many accounts of foraging societies characterise them as living opportunistic lives in the natural environment, gathering and hunting a wide-ranging diet (Lee and De Vore 1968). These people live together in small bands in which, although differences between men and women and old and young are acknowledged, all voices make some contribution to communal decision-making.

On the other hand, in societies in which access to inherited property is crucial for economic well-being, age and gender criteria are frequently quite rigid and strongly sanctioned (Vincent 1995). The idea of the patriarchal extended family, as found for example in parts of rural India, contains the idea of patriarchy as not only the domination by male members of the household over the females (see Chapter 3) but also of the older (particularly the senior generation) over the younger. All household structures have the potential for problems or conflicts. Thus the power and authority of the older over the younger and the duty and obedience owed by the younger to the older may create frustrations in some circumstances. Waiting for the old man to retire so that the younger generation can take control of the land and make their mark on the world is observed in literature (Hardy 1902, 1975; Synge 1911; Naipul 1964) and ethnography (Arensberg and Kimbell 1940, on rural Ireland). From the opposite point of view, the older generation may feel a lack of filial piety on the part of children who have left to work in distant towns.

These frustrations of rural family farmers have parallels in modern Britain, in the emotions of elderly people and their families when making decisions about continued independent living in the face of increasing frailty. What are the right amounts of duty owed and reasonable expectations anticipated from one generation to another? Society's general norms can seldom be applied unambiguously to the complexities of individual circumstance.

The aspect of age that is significant to a society may be the accumulation of years, but in many societies without formal or bureaucratic recording of age, people are not interested in and do not know their chronological age in a precise way. People may measure the passing of the years by reference to personal, social and historical events – when they had their first child, when the pogrom took place or when the great flood happened. In these ways, people know who is older or younger and may be differentiated into age strata even without an exact counting of the years.

In the UK, people's ages are usually described in terms of calendar age – the numbers of years that have elapsed since birth. One may be described as aged '21' between 7665 days and 8030 days (give or take the odd leap year) after one's birth. This is because we use the Gregorian calendar, which has become a worldwide standard. But there are other ways of measuring dates and times – the Jewish and the Islamic to mention but two. Age can be both a verb (to age; to grow older) and a noun (how old one is; the age of consent). Ageing is a process that is continuous. Thus, strictly, age as an attribute requires an additional set of criteria to demarcate people into groups. Society recognises that a group of people, defined by chronological age or through collectively reaching a certain stage in their lives, should occupy certain social roles and be entitled to certain privileges or duties.

In many societies the transitions from one 'age' to another are marked by ritual; ceremonies such as initiation rites, which publicly mark the change from one social role to another. Some age categories may be given or obtain a special significance. In modern society, many legal rights are defined by age. For example, the age at which you can legitimately buy alcohol or tobacco, drive a car, have sex, leave home, marry, join the army, vote, serve as a juror or be expected to retire as a judge are legally defined. Hence the association of 'old age' with those 65 years and over, as historically this has been the pensionable age for men in the UK. Similarly, in the UK, centenarians are regarded as special and were acknowledged by the nation with a telegram from the monarch.

It is important to note that the boundaries of age categories are not fixed by any objective criteria, they are social constructions. The age categories thought up by demographers or legislators for their own convenience are just as much social constructions as any reported sense of common identity among teenagers, pensioners or 'the over forties'. Because of historical social change, the age at which individuals born at different times acquired these age-based rights and duties may have been different. The experience of a generation, or the common experience of those born at a particular time, can form part of developing age-based social structures. People will move in and out of age strata as they add years to their life.

Age and stratification: age groups, chronological age, age classes

Given the wide variation in the way in which age is used as a social criterion, it is important to be clear about the conceptual basis of the categories with which we describe age-based divisions in society. We may first talk of 'age strata' or 'age classes', that is, *groups of people of the same age who, by virtue of this characteristic, have distinct sets of life chances and similar social rights and duties*, much like but not identical to social classes (see Chapter 2). The roles and norms that society allocates to age groups create barriers and opportunities. This can be seen to give people of similar age common interests as against those of people of other chronological ages. A weak view of 'age strata' would be that the people in each stratum simply happened to be in the same chronological age band; a strong view would be that they are people who have conflicting common interests over and against other age strata (see for example the discussion of childhood in Chapter 9).

The idea of age strata is sometimes mixed up with 'generation' and 'cohort'. 'Generation' refers to the fact of *reproduction* and that each family experiences a sequence of people passing through in life. The idea of generations is used to refer to position within the family. Thus, today's children will be tomorrow's parents and will subsequently take their turn as grandparents. The idea of 'generation' can rather more usefully be used to refer to position within the family. Confusion between this and age is easily made when the image of the nation or the society as a family is used, such that those over 60 can be referred to as the 'older generation'. Generation and age are not synonymous – grandparenthood and retirement do not occur together; nephews and nieces may be older than their aunts or uncles. Further, 'the 60's generation' refers to people who were young during a particular period of history, that is, a 'cohort' (or 'historical generation': Edmunds and Turner 2002).

Demographic cohorts (or 'age sets') are *groupings of people born at the same time*. Their members therefore age simultaneously and consequently have many historical experiences in common. Rapid change in society means that people with similar dates of birth may well have distinct sets of experience. The experience of military service differentiates cohorts in Britain and also provides contrasting experiences in different European and North American societies. Those who did national service in Britain or were drafted in the USA carried the mark of this experience throughout their lives. The experiences of the cohort of 'immigrant' minority ethnic groups are quite different from that of the cohort made up of their children (Chapter 4). Common experience may even give rise to a label, such as 'baby-boomers' or 'Thatcher's children'.

Cohorts may also be socially recognised in a more structured way, as when a set of people are given a common identity early in their lives, perhaps by initiation, and carry that common identity through the rest of their days. These groups may be 'age sets', for example all those initiated at a certain time forming a group that earns a reputation and feels a common sense of solidarity throughout the lives of its members. There may even be a special name given to each age set. In contemporary society, and in particular in the USA, a good example would be class groups at school or college ('the class of '91') who keep in touch and hold reunions. Just as age since birth is a continuous variable, so dates of birth can be allocated into cohort categories only by the use of culturally constructed systems of classification. Societies structured around age sets have a static set of age grades into which successive age sets or cohorts pass (Bernadi 1985).

That is, cohorts whose formative years have given them common attitudes, values or perceptions may thus form an identifiable group (Mannheim 1927). These common experiences may lead to a common sense of identity and even common interests. For example, people in Britain who were children in the First World War were starting families in the Great Depression of the 1930s, went through the Second World War in prime middle age and reached retirement when the long postwar economic boom was coming to an end. They developed a distinctive range of political beliefs and behaviours (Vincent 2001, 2003). Similarly, it has been argued that the cohort born in the postwar baby boom, who experienced the changes in social conventions of the 1960s and the collective sense of liberation at that time, has consequently a degree of common identity (Edmunds and Turner 2002). One social repercussion of this differing cohort experience is sometimes misleadingly referred to as a 'generation gap'. However, these cohort differences are not merely cultural: they also fundamentally affect people's chances of social mobility and material success. Chauvel (1999) has shown how the increased social mobility and relative affluence at a young age of those entering the labour market in the 1950s and 60s contrasts with poorer economic prospects, longer dependence on parents for those who set out on their adult life in the 1980s and 90s.

The 'life cycle' is a common-sense term used to describe the typical sequence of age categories in a society. It is most frequently understood in terms of the normative sequence of age statuses which repeat themselves with each generation; a continually turning wheel. Thus, all members of society are thought to age by following typical sequences of roles, for example from child, to adolescent, spouse, parent, grandparent and then ancestor. Sociologists, however, prefer the term 'life-course' because whereas 'life cycle' is a static image of an unchanging society, 'life-course' is an image of a process that reflects the flow of time and the sequencing of cohorts as well as generations. Life-courses happen to people in historical time and in particular places, so they reflect the fact that 'life cycles' change over time and place. Life-courses vary not only between different social groups, for example across genders or ethnic groups, but significantly they also vary historically. Demographic considerations and other changes in family structure will mean that the experience of parenthood, and other inter-generational social relations, will change. The current life-course will now, more typically, include the experience of being grandparents in middle age and a great-grandparent in later life (Bengston 1996).

The life-courses of different cohorts also interact in a complex and dynamic pattern. The cohort born in the years 1920–30 have had opportunities achieved by the struggles, often through trade unions and the Liberal and Labour Parties, of the preceding generations who started the movement down the road to universal retirement pensions. The success of those struggles enabled them to retire with greater security than their parents. Subsequently, they have been affected by the increasing proclivity of their children to separate and divorce. Thus they may find themselves adjusting their previously held expectations of grandparent/grandchild relationships (from loss of contact to quasi-parental responsibilities). In other words, the experiences of that cohort have been determined in part by the action of the immediately preceding and succeeding cohorts.

Age strata and cohorts are two separate bases on which social life is patterned. There are difficult methodological problems when trying to study old age and inequality in working out which phenomena are the result of becoming a certain age and which result from being a member of a particular cohort (Hardy 1997). Thus, for any particular moment in time, those who are old appear to have certain characteristics. However, when viewed critically, these characteristics may not be due to advancing years per se but to cultural conventions that define differences between age strata or cohort experiences of specific historical circumstances. As will be seen in Chapter 14, explaining the health of older people is not just a question of the physiology of ageing, but may well involve looking at particular dietary, housing or occupational experiences earlier in their lives or specific historical circumstances with health consequences.

The changing historical pattern of life-courses

In the centuries leading up to the radical social changes of the eighteenth century, life-courses in Europe and America were structured around certain basic social realities. The most important of these were uncertainties about longevity. Demographic characteristics of the time included high rates of infant mortality, death in childbirth and epidemics of fatal infectious diseases. On the whole, living standards and nutritional levels militated against living in a healthy condition to a ripe old age. There was not the close association between death and old age that exists in contemporary society; death could, and did, strike at any time. The agrarian basis of much of society and the relatively lower levels of geographical and social mobility meant that life-course transitions could be marked by public rituals in the local community, not strictly tied to a bureaucratised, national, legal framework. Baptism, confirmation, marriage, funerals of parents or spouse and the birth of one's children were ritualised transitions that placed people appropriately and publicly into their life-course positions. Old age was not identified with a particular chronological age but implicit in relationships vis-à-vis children and other relatives, control of property and an independent livelihood (Grillis 1987; Cole 1992).

We need to be careful not to exaggerate the position of respect and care provided for elderly people in these earlier extended families in a romanticised image of a traditional past, as a lost golden age. The demographic patterns were different; many people did not live for so long, although some did. Not only were many families larger than today but there were also more celibate/never-married people and childless couples. Historical research has suggested that extended families may well have been an adaptation to urban poverty and housing shortage as much as an inherited rural tradition (Laslett 1968; Laslett and Wall 1972; Phillipson et al. 2001).

Three major changes since the eighteenth century have been industrialisation, urbanisation and the development of the nation-state (Chapter 6), and along with these have come characteristic ways of thinking and behaving. Kohli's (1986) threefold life-course pattern identified pre-work, characterised by education and training and other forms of socialisation; work, as the dominant life-course stage; and postwork, usually characterised by loss of income and status. The key life stage in 'modern' society was that of work. It was through employment that people gained their principal income and achieved status. The pre-work and post-work stages were, as a corollary, of less status and income. In Britain, old people feared the degradation of the 'workhouse', the repository of those who could not maintain themselves, and disliked the loss of status felt when having to accept charity (Townsend 1957, 1979; Phillipson and Walker 1986). These attitudes are still widespread among older British people, many of whom do not claim welfare benefits to which they are entitled, in some cases associating residential care with the workhouse (indeed in many towns there are buildings which have a direct historical continuity from one function to the other).

Only with the development of a well-established urban industrial working class did retirement become an established stage of life, following a long and hard labouring life. Large-scale industrial employment organised and controlled the labour force into set patterns of timekeeping – shiftwork, the six-day/50-hour week, 'wakes week' for holiday – which dominated the lives of the vast majority of people. Set patterns of apprenticeship for craft skills, the introduction of compulsory education and a minimum school leaving age also set a lifetime schedule for work. Following on from 'work', old age in the twentieth century became a recognised part of 'Fordist' mass-production society.

Pensions were previously the prerogatives of the military, professional and administrative classes. In the late nineteenth and early twentieth centuries came the experience of a common mass of retired working people. Although an improvement on a situation where people had to either work or depend on charity or endure the rigours of the workhouse, this retired population generally had a lower standard of living than the working population. Almost universally, a person's rights to a pension still derive from their work history. This is particularly significant for women and those who are disabled or ill and who thus have experienced an interrupted work and pension contribution history (Chapter 3).

The framework of governance for urbanisation and industrialisation was the emerging nation-state (see Chapter 6). In the new nation-states, people were increasingly governed by universalistic criteria that treated all citizens as being equal, rather than on the basis of personal favour or privilege. The development of modern political thought in the eighteenth century elaborated the ideas of constitutions, citizenship and equality before the law. Paradoxically, the achievement of new individual rights was dependent on greater regulation: national systems for birth and death registration were required to administer duties, such as conscription and taxation, and rights such as child benefit and pensions. Legal-rational authority was the basis of bureaucratic allocation of rights and duties by age.

Kohli (1991) argues that the concept of age-specific rights runs against many of the modern state's universalistic, liberal democratic tenets, for example that all individuals should be equal before the law. In practice, of course, some people are not equal because of their age. He cites struggles in America over compulsory retirement ages, which were seen as conflicting with anti-discriminatory legislation. The issues surrounding the Children Act 1989 in Britain, which granted children rights independent of, and potentially in conflict with, those of their parents, are a parallel example of the conflict between universal and age- (or generation-) based rights.

The interconnection of age and social change

Over the past 200 years, life-course patterns in the West do appear to be more regulated by age than in the past, but certain writers have started to suggest that this age-determined life-course is now starting to break down (Grillis 1987; Hareven 1994). Elderly people are now able to choose from a wide diversity of lifestyles. Featherstone and Hepworth (1989), writing from a post-modernist perspective, suggest that the life-course is becoming de-structured. Common social patterns determined by chronological age are becoming less critical to people's life experiences. In many parts of today's world, political instability and forced migration have added to the unpre-dictability of the life-course. Mass expulsions and genocide may be as old as state society but modern society has an unparalleled technical and organisa-tional ability with which to execute them.

Two key areas where this apparent breakdown of established life-course patterns, and therefore a weakening of the social division of age, has been particularly remarked on are in the fields of employment and the family. With regard to the first of these, the former threefold pattern of school, work and retirement that framed employment has been undermined. There have been significant changes in retirement; early retirement has dramatically expanded, depriving the age of 65 (for men) of its watershed character (Kohli et al. 1992). Across most of Europe, the effective retirement age has dropped and Guille-mard (1989, 1990) suggests that not only is the age of retirement declining, but there is a whole loosening of the life-course grid. Early retirement is more popular these days with firms, workers and the state, but this can also be seen as a response to the particular conditions of the labour market, the growth in unemployment and the structure of incentives in particular pension systems. Many state policies are now directed to raising the retirement age and labour force participation amongst people in their fifties in the UK is rising. At the other end of the age range, education has been extended and a comparatively small section of the population leave school at 16 while fewer still start their work careers from such a young age (Chapters 3 and 9).

Decreasing labour market stability and rapidly changing employment patterns introduce increased uncertainty and decreased standardisation of the work career components of the life-course. Patterns of migration, employ-ment and early retirement interact, as do periods of unemployment, retraining and extended periods of education, to create complex life careers. Current welfare structures across Europe (Giarchi 1996) depend substantially on insurance contributions and a work record. High levels of unemployment and disrupted careers will have lasting effects into old age for young, casualised entrants to the labour market (Laczko and Phillipson 1991; Walker 1993; Hugman 1994). Growing dependence in many countries, including the UK, on pensions which depend on the value to stock markets adds a further layer of uncertainty. The 1990s saw the growth of a fragmented society in which some have been able to use market position (earnings-related pensions and property-related windfalls) to secure good (that is, not much reduced) material conditions while others have missed out. Those who miss out are those with poor market opportunities.

The second area of life-course modification lies in the family. Patterns of married life and cohabitation are changing. This is often portrayed as consisting of more living together instead of marriage, and more divorce among those who do marry. It is true that the family of orientation (the family in which we were born) is no longer automatically followed by a single, formalised family of procreation (the family we set up on marriage and in which we raise our own children).

However, whereas it is clear that divorce rates have increased substantially, it would be simplistic to look on this as the sole cause of family dissolution and changes in the form of the family. In 1891, a woman aged 50–54 would have had a 20 per cent chance of being a widow, while a woman of the same age in 1951 would have had a 10 per cent chance and in 1991 a 5 per cent chance of having become a widow, a figure which had already declined to 4 per cent a decade later. Her chances of being divorced in 1891 were so small they were not recorded in the census, while in 1951 her chances were still less than 1 per cent, but in 1991 over 10 per cent of women of this age were divorcees (OPCS 1993) and in 2001 the figure was 15.6 per cent. Although early widowhood has declined, widowhood in old age has become normal and feminised. Women will experience an average of nine years widowhood. On the other hand, male widowers are more likely to remarry.

The problems of adjustment/bereavement after a long marriage are not to be underestimated. Davidson (2001) discusses domestic and caring relationships through the language of the older widows. The widows described themselves as 'selfish'. The gendered nature of selfishness as articulated by widows seemed to express both a desire but some difficulty in distancing themselves from normative lifestyles. Davidson suggests that selfishness to the widows meant doing what they wanted, when they wanted and not having to consider the needs of a partner. Several said the primary reason for not wishing to form a new partnership, particularly marriage, was because they had become so selfish. They had been prepared and, for most of them, happy to look after the man they had married when they were young and lived with for a number of decades, but they were not prepared to 'take on' another man (Davidson 1998: 6–7). One solution to these issues for older women, and also linked to the value of property, is the increasing phenomenon amongst those of late middle age of 'living together apart', that is, an intimate relationship involving frequent companionship, sharing leisure, holidays and lifestyle but each partner retaining their own domicile (Gierveld et al. 2001).

Whereas many policy initiatives and much research are actually oriented towards 'strengthening the family', the dissolution of family units and kinship networks comes from several causes, such as greater geographical mobility and changing life expectancy. Rural-urban migration and the ageing of the countryside are worldwide phenomena (Sen 1994: 10). The social barriers erected by the cultural assimilation of migrants also disrupts intergenerational expectations of old age and the final part of the life-course (Askham et al. 1993; Blakemore and Boneham 1994; Chapter 4).

Changing demography

Changing patterns of longevity mean that spouses live together longer and the majority of married life is no longer spent rearing children. One of the successes of modern society has been to improve the health and increase the life expectancy of people. Thus, in contrast to what 'post-modernist' writers have seen as a decline in stability of family work and lifestyle patterns, a certain demographic standardisation has taken place. People are now more likely to live a full span and die in their eighties. The age of death and length of life is becoming more standard; although more people are living to older ages, the maximum life span does not seem to have increased.

Although recently some demographers have challenged this view and some bio-gerontologists are claiming breakthroughs in scientific knowledge which will extend the life span, the life span for those currently alive has strongly determined biological limits. Further, medical advances mean that there are fewer childless couples due to infertility, while the extent to which more women in the UK are choosing childlessness as a lifestyle is the subject of conflicting evidence. The expanded technical ability to control family size has meant that family size is standardising at one or two children, most typically born to parents in their twenties, and with extended periods of family life in a post-child-rearing stage (Jackson 1998).

The world's population has started to age as a result of the successful diminution of premature mortality and decline in the numbers of babies born on average to each mother. The developed world experienced the earliest decline in fertility, with countries like France, Sweden and the UK leading the way. Late industrialising countries, for example Japan and Italy, have experienced rapid post-war declines in fertility and are amongst the most rapidly ageing populations at the beginning of the twenty-first century. The pace of demographic ageing is increasing fastest in the developing world. It is most noticeable in countries like China where fertility has successfully been checked within a relatively short time span. Projections suggest that by 2025

China alone will contain more over 60-year-olds than the whole of Europe. The median age of the world's population increased from 23.5 years in 1950 to 26.4 years in 1999. By 2050, the median age is projected to reach 37.8 years (UN 2002).

In 2002, life expectancy at birth for females born in the UK was 81 years, compared with 76 years for males. British life expectancy continued to rise in the last decades of the twentieth century and into the new millennium but for different reasons to the large increases achieved in the first half of that century. In 1901, life expectancy stood at 49 for women and 45 for men. It has been the decline in infant mortality which largely drove this increase in life expectancy, particularly associated with control of infectious disease through public health measures. Between 1981 and 2002, life expectancy for those aged 65 increased by three years for men and two years for women. Projections from the government actuaries department suggest that life expectancies for those at retirement age will increase by around a further three years by 2020. Cancer and heart disease remain the major causes of death in old age, but deaths due to smoking-related illnesses are on the wane (Chapter 14).

The social conditions of older people

Demographically, economically and culturally, old age is experienced differently by different people. This difference in life expectancy means that old age is most typically a feminine stage of life and is becoming increasingly feminine (see Table 8.1). Women also tend to marry men older than themselves. These two factors together mean that not only are women more likely to be widowed, they are also more likely to live on their own. More than half of women aged 75 and over live alone, while only slightly over a half of men at that age live alone (also Chapter 3). About twice as many women as men are in residential care. In the 85 and over age group, 15 per cent of men and 27 per cent of women are in residential care (Arber and Ginn 1991, 1995; Ginn and Arber 1996). The 2001 census reports that there are about a third of a million people aged 90 and over in the UK. Interestingly, they also tell us that nearly 4000 of these people are providing 50 or more hours of unpaid care per week to someone else. Caring is frequently thought of as a feminine activity but older partners of either gender are in practice willing to take on caring responsibilities for the other member of a couple. Although only 26.2 per cent of people aged 90 and over living in households are men, they make up just over half the carers in this age bracket.

**Table 8.1 Historical and projected changes in
the age composition of the UK population**

	Age	1950	1975	2000	2025	2050
Age groups	0–14	22.3	23.3	19.0	15.2	15.0
(percentage)	15–59	62.1	57.0	60.4	55.4	51.1
	60+	15.5	19.6	20.6	29.4	34.0
Median age (years)		34.6	33.9	37.7	44.5	47.4
Sex ratio (men per	60+	74.3	69.8	76.4	83.9	83.8
100 women)	65+	71.9	63.4	71.2	79.1	80.0
	80+	56.5	39.3	46.4	58.2	62.6

Source: UN World Population Ageing (2002).

Material deprivation in old age is of central importance. Age helps to explain the distribution of 'poverty' (Chapter 12), and lack of income is the means by which social divisions can be seen to open up. Poverty in old age interacts with former social class and gender: the interplay of social divisions is striking. We therefore need to discuss income and pensions as indicators of poverty and the way these have changed in recent decades. In practice, making such comparisons is not straightforward, because we need to know who are dependent on pensions and whether we are to count people or households.

The United Nations Development Programme has estimated that only 20 per cent of people aged 60 and over in the world can be regarded as having income security. Retirement pensions are available to only a small proportion of the world's older people. Only 30 per cent of people aged 60 and over worldwide are eligible for any form of pension and most of these live in more developed countries. Pensions are most frequently the prerogative of those who work for government or the formal sector of the economy; even in many quite highly developed countries, the rural population has little or no cover (Help Age International 1999).

In the UK, material deprivation in all areas of society is structured by gender, class and ethnicity, but these differences become exaggerated in later life. This is related in particular to the structure of the labour market. As incomes in later life tend to be dependent on pension rights achieved through contributions from salary and saving and investments made from income during working life, those who received the best material rewards in their working lives do best in old age. Those who found difficulty entering the labour market at all and who achieved poor rewards from their labour tend also in their old age to be among the most materially deprived section of the British population.

While the value of the state pension has continued to decline in value relative to average earnings since 1979, in recent years average pensioner income has risen because of improving occupational pensions. Since 1997, there have been increases in means-tested benefits, many of which now form part of what the government calls a 'minimum income guarantee'. For pensioner couples in 2002/03, the average net income per week was £327 compared with £177 for single pensioners.

The General Household Survey (ONS 2003) conducted in 2001 indicated that the median weekly household income was £302. Older people did rather less well, for a single person aged sixty and over it was £118 per week and for a two-person household it was £252. In contrast, single adults aged 16–59 had a median income of £281, while for two-person households in the same age range it was £544. These figures do not show the disparity of income within these types of household. The bottom 20 per cent of all households were getting a weekly income of less that £93, while the bottom 20 per cent of older couples were getting less than £124 and for lone adults aged 60 and over the figure was £79 per week. The contrast with the top 20 per cent is stark. Such households have a weekly income in excess of £684 but even the top 20 per cent of older people have incomes significantly lower, at £475 per week for couples and £210 for old single-person households.

Younger pensioners tend to have higher incomes than older pensioners because they are likely to receive more occupational pension and earnings income than older pensioners. The poorest pensioners tend to be older people who live on their own and who are dependent on state benefits. For those who have worked, exit from employment is typically at 61 for men and 57 for women. This means that men average 17 years and women 25 years of life after leaving paid employment. Women are more likely to work part time and tend not to have the same benefits from occupational pensions as men. The General Household Survey (ONS 2003) suggests that only 26.5 per cent of women aged 45–54 belong to an employers pensions scheme as opposed to 42.5 per cent of men. There is a great deal of ignorance amongst many sections of the population about their pension entitlements. Small occupational pensions tend to bring women only up to the point where they become ineligible for income support so that many do not really gain benefit from paying into such schemes.

It might be argued that it is expenditure which is the better guide to the material standards that older people can achieve. Certainly, expenditure is clearly greatly influenced by age (Table 8.2). Middle age groups spend more than young people and much more than older people. Older people spend substantially less on housing and travel, but spend about as much and a much greater proportion of their income on fuel and power.

Table 8.2 Average weekly household expenditure in pounds by age of head of household (2000–01)

	Under 30	30–49	50–64	65–74	75 and over	All households
Housing (net)	78.70	84.00	56.80	34.80	30.30	63.90
Fuel and power	9.90	12.30	13.00	11.80	10.00	11.90
Food and non-alcoholic drinks	55.00	73.60	67.10	47.00	34.70	61.90
Alcoholic drink	18.70	17.90	17.40	7.90	4.90	15.00
Tobacco	7.50	6.90	7.20	3.90	1.80	6.10
Clothing and footwear	25.00	29.80	21.10	12.20	5.80	22.00
Household goods	28.20	37.30	37.80	28.90	14.40	32.60
Household services	20.80	26.90	21.70	17.60	11.80	22.00
Personal goods and services	16.30	17.00	15.70	11.20	7.50	14.70
Motoring	52.00	67.30	67.60	32.70	15.40	55.10
Fares and other travel costs	12.00	11.80	10.10	5.40	2.50	9.50
Leisure goods	18.80	25.60	19.60	14.20	7.30	19.70
Leisure services	38.30	61.20	60.80	34.90	22.40	50.60
Miscellaneous	0.60	1.20	0.60	0.20	0.10	0.70
All expenditure groups	381.70	472.80	416.40	262.60	169.10	385.70

Source: Family Spending 2000–01, ONS (2002b).

These figures document a growing substantial material inequality (and by implication social division) between older people and the general population and a growing differentiation among older people themselves. However, older people's subjective feeling about their standard of living is influenced by a range of things over and above simply how much they can afford to spend. They have, for example, a variety of reference groups against which to compare their own living standards. Older people's memory of the past includes memories of the conditions in which older people lived in the early part of the last century. They are also aware of the former standard of living they were able to achieve before retirement. They may also compare themselves favourably, or otherwise, with other retirees, as well as with those enjoying the current general living conditions of society as a whole. Thus, just as there is no clear single common experience of material deprivation among contemporary older people, so there is also no common interpretative framework by which older people feel a collective sense of their standard of living.

Social policy issues: everybody needs pensions

The most obvious change shown in Table 8.1 is the increase in people over 75. The extent to which the prolongation of life results in a consequent period of physical frailty, greater dependency and need for new services is controversial (Victor 1991). It is in the interests of certain sections of society, such as the financial elites seeking to expand their profit-making potential in the fields of pensions and insurance or the professional groups whose members provide care for the elderly, that such concerns become widespread (Vincent 1996). What is clear is that the issue has been taken up as a threatening 'social problem', to the extent of warranting reports from the World Bank, the OECD and even the CIA. How will care for these very old people be delivered and how can a society, with relatively fewer of its members being of working age, afford to pay for it? This reaction has the character of a 'moral panic', where a small-scale issue is amplified by the media and those with other agendas into appearing to be a much bigger problem than it really should be.

This is not to deny that there are real problems to do with the social conditions in which many older people live, and the way society needs to provide for them. However, this is a problem of wealth distribution, not demography. Where economic growth is progressively produced by an economy that requires a smaller and smaller labour force, with time to adapt and plan, no country is facing a crisis of elder care. Nor is it true to represent 'older people' as being 'a problem', as if they were a single homogeneous category. There are substantial differences in the way in which pensions systems are organised in different countries. Pensions have become an important political issue in that they form a key point in the debate on the role of the state in the redistribution of wealth, the provision of welfare and managing a framework for economic activity. Should the state provide pensions for all? Should it merely look after the most vulnerable, whether economically or through infirmity? Should the state administer pensions schemes or should that be left to the private sector?

What is at stake here can be called 'generational equity'. It has been argued that the younger age groups are being disadvantaged by paying for the pensions of the current generation of older people, but because of demographic changes, they cannot themselves necessarily expect to receive an equivalent pension from the succeeding generation (Johnson et al. 1989; Johnson 1995). Despite the way it is frequently presented, this problem is not merely, or at all, a demographic issue. The issue is in essence one of redistribution and the role of the state in evening out unacceptable inequalities of wealth and power. In other words, it is a question of how government deals with the factors that generate a significant part of the social division based on age. If we take a wider view of redistribution than who pays and who benefits from various forms of taxation, we can also take into account issues associated with exploitation and non-financial contributions to society's well-being.

In these terms, the debate centres on rights and claims to a share of society's current economic output. After all, nursing care cannot be stored or saved up to bring out when needed later in life. 'Care' exists only at a single moment, so that if there is currently not enough to go round, it has to be rationed (allocated) through some mechanism, whether this happens through a market to the highest bidder, by allocation to the most needy, offered first to those who fought to defend their country or some other process. We need to see age as a division in a wider context, but a balanced one. Why do we hear more about the future cost of state pensions or healthcare than, for example, the long-term cost to future generations of disposing of nuclear waste or in terms of global warming for today's consumption of hydrocarbon fuels?

The extent to which there will be an economic difficulty in meeting the need for satisfactory pensions in the future must be related to the future productivity of the workforce and the extent to which declining rates of economic participation among older people continue. The assumption is frequently made that the older population is economically unproductive. Patterns of work and the reasons for non-participation in the labour market have varied considerably over time, but older people have not always with-drawn from work. In Britain in 1881, according to Johnson (1985), 73 per cent of the male population of 65 and over were in employment, but by 1981 the percentage had shrunk to less than 11 per cent. This major change in the distribution of work is not because the population has become physically less able and therefore less employable. Non-employed does not mean non-productive; it may mean productive potential is being lost or that useful work is not recorded or recognised as such. Most countries across the world have taken steps to increase the official age of retirement, but many social commentators identify the way in which retirement is in practice used by governments and employers as a way to manage the supply of labour.

Ageism and the cultural construction of old age

There is a debate between critical gerontologists who wish to examine the position of old people as part of an unequal society and cultural sociologists who give priority to understanding the diversity of old age phenomena in a post-modern world. Cultural gerontologists draw on themes of post-modernism which emphasise that modern affluence for at least some pensioners creates new cultural agendas based on consumer choice. Examples of such work are Gilleard and Higgs (2000) and Blaikie (1999). These writers are correct in drawing attention to the importance of cultural phenomena in understanding contemporary old age. They are, however, sometimes in danger of neglecting the empirical evidence that older people in Britain remain consistently amongst the poorest in the community and most remain excluded from the benefits of consumer society. Older people not only suffer from increased chances of a materially deprived lifestyle but are also subject to the experience of 'ageism':

> Ageism is about acting on stereotypes about chronological age which prevent (older) people from having control over their lives and participating fully and purposefully in society. (Age Equality Action Group, 1991, quoted in Meade 1995)

Because old age tends to be culturally devalued, getting older is regarded by most people as a kind of inevitable tragedy. People do develop cultural resources with which to resist these ascriptions. The poem of Jenny Joseph quoted in the Introduction has itself become a focus for older women who have taken the image as a symbol around which they can form social groups. These women in the 'Red Hat' Society meet together to expand their own and other people's cultural horizons and wear read hats and purple dresses as a badge of membership. Those who have not yet attained sufficiently mature years but wish to attend are required to wear violet instead. There are even local groups of older adults who chose to label themselves as 'the wrinklies', and political activists who call themselves 'grey panthers' in ways reminiscent of other oppressed groups using the stigmata of their identity as a badge of pride.

The cultural construction of femininity and sexuality has its impact on older people. Sociologists of gender have shown how patriarchy involves male control of female bodies not just for their labour value but also reproductive sexual functions and how it impacts on the aesthetics of femininity. These aspects of patriarchy have been challenged by women's groups and other social movements. Three stages of the feminist movement have been identified, coinciding firstly with campaigns on civic status, property rights and the vote, secondly on work and career opportunities and thirdly on femininity, personal appearance identity and sexuality. It has been argued by de Beauvoir ([1949]1972) and others that there is a 'double jeopardy' of age and gender. For women who are also older, the risks of marginalisation and deprivation are significantly greater. Their experience of multiple divisions is not simply one plus the other. Their experience of being old and being a women needs to be understood as an experience which is unique and has its own problems and possibilities. It does not contrast simply with younger women or older men, but, in de Beauvoir terms, constitutes a 'third sex', meaning that a woman's gender status changes post-menopause and with the loss of reproductive function.

De Beauvoir and others argue that a woman's status derives from presenting a 'desirable' appearance and her perceived reproductive value of her body. The enormous market in anti-ageing products (in excess of three billion pounds sterling annually) is indicative of the anxiety about lack of attractiveness linked with age. Sexuality in old age is suppressed and gender-specific. Large age differences between spouses or lovers attract social unease, but the opprobrium for an overtly sexually active older women is the greater – indeed so much so that she cannot be named. While there are words in various English dialects for an older man (sugar daddy) with a young women (trophy wife), there are none for an older woman with a younger man (toy boy). Positive images of older women are desexualised. They are associated with 'matronly figures' and caring social roles:

> Sexuality in old age is a subject which is enveloped with secrecy and half-knowledge, and referred to in society in general with embarrassment and by joking allusions, that is if it is not dismissed altogether, the old so patently being 'past it'. (Pickard 1995: 268)

The areas of gender, old age and sex indicate vividly the constraints that age imposes on behaviour.

Ageism, like racism or sexism, refers to both prejudice and discrimination; the first being an attitude, the second a behaviour. Comfort (1977, quoted in Meade 1995) suggests that ageism is based on fear, folklore and hang-ups and, like racism, needs to be met by information, contradiction and, when necessary, confrontation. Negative stereotypes of people based on their age may refer to different age groups; both young and old can be stereotyped. The negative image of old age is extremely prevalent and, indeed, getting older often seems to carry no positive connotations at all. A quick browse through any shop selling birthday cards will indicate the disgust with which ageing is widely held.

Discrimination on age grounds is not, at the time of writing, illegal in the same way as sexism or racism, although in practice the legal status of age discrimination, particularly with regard to employment, is changing with incorporation of European employment and human rights legislation into British law. It is common for young job applicants to find themselves passed over for older, supposedly more mature applicants and for older people looking for work to find younger, supposedly more lively, people preferred. It may be feared that training older workers will not be cost-effective, or that they will be more prone to illness and absence. Reverse discrimination also takes place, whereby older workers are offered dead-end jobs in which employers assume that younger people looking to further themselves would not stay.

Bytheway (1995: 1–18) suggests that simple definitions of ageism are inadequate for two reasons. First, they should not be based on parallels with sexism and racism because each is a unique phenomenon. Second, he points out that it should not be presumed that old people exist as a group (older people are as varied as the rest of the population) and that labelling them with this single category is itself part of the problem. Separating out older people for special consideration (even for special study, as in the field of social gerontology or this chapter) implies a 'them' and 'us' situation. It is to take the social division of age as a given.

However, old age can also be a liberation from social constraints. In social terms, this could mean liberation from the constraints of middle age. The social obligations of middle age may become burdensome. In terms of the world of work, this would mean the end of wage slavery with retirement and the opportunities of the third age. However, such liberation also depends on solving issues of poverty that still afflict many older people. In terms of the constraints of family life, the meaning of the empty nest phase of life, despite the negative imagery implicit in the term, might be construed positively. Car stickers proclaiming 'recycled teenager – spending the kids inheritance' suggest at least the potential for liberation in a post-child-rearing period of life.

One of the exciting prospects for the newly developing period of extended retirement associated with the third age is that it offers the prospect of new forms of social relationships. Will the 60's generation now growing old also seek liberation from the cultural constraints of ageism? There are many ideas for new forms of social relationships and institutional arrangements in old age. People do not necessarily get more conservative as they get older, and the young are not automatically the radicals. It may be that in future old age will be a time for rebellion and attempts to change the social order. Some writers, such as Betty Freidan (1993), have suggested that groups of women living in various forms of domestic arrangements perhaps with a man, could provide support, care and physical relationships more effectively than widowhood. For some, these possibilities represent a nightmare, for others a challenge.

Age as a social division

Age is a distinctive social division if for no other reason than we anticipate moving from one side of the division(s) to the other, thus ultimately having direct experience of it in more than one form as we follow our life-courses. As we have seen, life-courses are social because they have general and observable patterns, shaped by norms and values (for example those associated with the life-course), which are part of the structure of society. They are also given characteristic forms by historical patterns of social change. This means that while the life-course is the normatively expected transition of stages in the process of social ageing, those of us currently at different ages will not experience the life-course in the same way. The life-course is both an individual and a social process of ageing.

Life is periodicised through age strata sequences: the teenagers of today will become the pensioners of tomorrow. It is structured by the sequence of generations: today's children are tomorrow's great-grandparents. It is further structured by history, in that the life-course of each succeeding cohort takes its form from the historical events through which it lives. The idea of the life-course, in addition to these social and historical aspects, has a psychological dimension, in that individuals will develop and change personality in response to life experience.

Therefore, when we seek to understand social inequality and stratification, we must consider the life-course as a social process, rather than a static social divide between generation or cohort. The systematic differences in material circumstances and life chances of people of different age do not arise, because when people's hair gets greyer, they slip into a prepared social box labelled 'old, poor and useless'. Rather, in the struggle for a decent standard of living and a modicum of social esteem, the life-courses of some people offer them greater chances of success than others. Some kinds of people collectively reach old age in times and circumstances in which their personal history and changing social circumstances lead to a relative lack of social and economic power; it is this that constitutes the real basis of social division.

Discussion Questions

1. Look at the birthday cards sent to someone 10 years younger and 30 years older than yourself. How do they differ from the ones you got at your last birthday? What kinds of people sent them, what kinds of written messages to do they include, what kinds of images are portrayed? What does this tell you about attitudes to age and getting older?

2. Talk to a relative, neighbour or friend who is over 70 years of age. Ask them (politely and respectfully, without being intrusive) what is the single most important thing that has happened to them in their life.

What would their life be like now if that 'most important' event had not happened? Does this tell us anything about the social significance of the life-course?

3. Make a list of all the things you are allowed to do and those you are not allowed to do when you are 18 years of age. How would this differ for someone who is 85 years of age? What conclusions would you draw from this comparison?

FURTHER READING

A good starting point for the sociology of old age is Estes, C., Biggs, S. and Phillipson, C. *Social Theory, Social Policy and Ageing: a Critical Introduction* (Maidenhead: Open University Press, 2003), while John A. Vincent *Old Age* (London: Routledge, 2003) sets out contemporary conflicts, struggles and issues using a global perspective. Blaikie, A. *Ageing and Popular Culture* (Cambridge, Cambridge University Press, 1999), Gilleard, C. and Higgs, P. *Cultures of Ageing* (New York: Prentice Hall, 2001) and more recently Fairclough, C. (ed.) *Ageing Bodies* (Walnut Creek, CA: AltaMira Press, 2003) offer important cultural insights. Wilson, G. *Understanding Old Age* (London: Sage, 2000) focusing on globalisation, and Grubium, J. and Holstein, J. *Ageing and Everyday Life* (Oxford: Blackwell, 2000) on social constructions also have distinctive useful approaches. An overview of current ways of understanding old age can be found in Phillipson, C. *Reconstructing Old Age* (London: Sage, 1998). An excellent anthropology of the cultural process of ageing, which looks at both children and older people, is Hockey, J. and James, A. *Growing Up and Growing Old* (London: Sage, 1993), while for a thorough empirical examination of the relationship between the two social divisions of age and gender, Arber, S. and Ginn, J. (eds) *Connecting Gender and Ageing* (Buckingham: Open University Press, 1995) is a valuable source.

CHAPTER 9

Childhood

STEVI JACKSON AND SUE SCOTT

This chapter will provide you with a broad critical understanding of the following issues in childhood as a source of social division:

- The social construction of childhood
- Changes in childhood and the conception of the child over time
- Conceptions of the innocent and demonic child
- Child-rearing as a reflexive project
- The tensions between protecting children and allowing them autonomy
- The social division between adults and children
- Social divisions between children
- Risk anxiety surrounding children and childhood
- Differing conceptions of children's rights

Childhood is the only form of social subordination that is still romanticised as a state of freedom. This may seem a startling assertion, given that this is not how childhood is usually thought about in everyday life. Generally, childhood is seen as a natural state, as a stage of biological immaturity during which children are both prepared for and protected from the 'real', adult world. It is supposed to be a carefree time, a time for play rather than work, a time without the burdens of adult worries and responsibilities. Yet childhood is also, and perhaps self-evidently, a social status, one of subordination to adults. Childhood is defined, in part, by exclusion from adult rights of citizenship and also by dependence on adults. Children spend most of their lives either within families or within institutions catering for their supposed 'needs'. In all these settings, they live under adult authority.

Traditionally, social scientists have conceptualised childhood primarily within the socialisation paradigm, in which children were seen as adults-in-waiting, whose experiences were only worth investigating in so far as they shaped adult attributes or life chances (Thorne 1987). Since the 1980s, sociologists have challenged such adult-centred approaches (Thorne 1987, 1993; James and Prout 1990; Leonard 1990; Waskler 1991; Mayall 1994; Wyness

2005), but developmental perspectives remain prominent in everyday thinking and professional and public discourse. It is still taken for granted that the process of maturing from child to adolescent to adult unfolds as a series of naturally occurring stages, that there is a 'right age' at which children should develop certain competences and acquire particular freedoms and responsibilities. These assumptions are so pervasive that it is difficult to think outside them, so widely accepted that they have become unquestioned 'truths'. Childhood is thought of as a linear trajectory towards the future and children as themselves representing the future. It is not only the future of society as a whole that is the issue, but the propensity of parents to live vicariously through their children, to treat them as carriers of their own hopes and dreams (Beck and Beck-Gernsheim 1995).

Contemporary sociological approaches suggest that rather than viewing children as future adults in the making, we should focus on children's own lives and activities. This entails a shift away from the idea of a child as 'becoming' an adult to the 'being child', conceptualised as an active social agent (James et al. 1998). While such perspectives are essential in challenging adult-centred views, we should not forget that children's lives are largely bounded by adult surveillance. There is no free and autonomous realm of childhood outside the social relations in which childhood in general, and particular individual childhoods, are forged. In this chapter, we are concerned with the construction and maintenance of the social division between children and adults and therefore treat childhood and adulthood as social constructs rather than natural, given stages of life.

The lives of children are, of course, shaped by divisions of gender, class, ethnicity, (dis)ability and so on. Since these divisions are discussed in detail in other chapters, here we are concerned with the division between children and adults as a fundamental social division in its own right. We begin by discussing the social construction of childhood, drawing attention to its cultural and historical variability and identifying specific features of late modern childhood. Two issues are explored in some detail: relations of power and dependence between adults and children, and the risk anxiety associated with childhood and children. We conclude by drawing attention to differences among children, locating childhood within wider social divisions.

Childhood as socially constructed

In arguing that childhood is socially constructed rather than being intrinsic to the state of being a child, we suggest that the construction of childhood needs to be understood at a number of different levels: the structural, the discursive and the situated. Childhood is institutionalised through the family, education and the state, resulting in dependence on adults and exclusion from full participation in adult society. At the level of discourse, childhood has been constituted as an object of the scientific gaze through such disciplines as psychology, social work and education, which have claimed expertise in monitoring, categorising and managing childhood and children. These expert knowledges have in turn shaped common-sense thinking, so that we are all assumed to 'know' what a child is and be able to comment on what constitutes a 'proper' childhood. The meaning of childhood is also negotiated through everyday situated interaction, where children themselves enter into the picture as active social agents. However, children's participation in constructing their own everyday world takes place within the constraints set by their subordinate location in relation to adults.

Anthropological and historical evidence suggests that current ideas of childhood and practices of child-rearing are culturally and historically specific. Childhood is not the same the world over. There are vast differences between the cosseted and protected lives of many children in wealthy (post) industrial nations and the harsh realities facing street children in, say, India or Brazil. Yet 'western' ideas about childhood profoundly affect the ways in which children in poorer countries are represented in the global media. They are almost universally depicted as helpless victims deserving of our sympathy and patronage – an image exploited in charity fund-raising campaigns. The autonomy and resilience of these children, their ability to look after themselves, is rarely acknowledged, or where it is noted, it is seen as either a tragedy or a threat, evidence of children deprived of the childhood they should have had. This is not to deny the harsh reality of such children's lives, nor the exploitation and suffering they experience, but rather to point out that our ideas of a 'proper childhood' may be entirely inappropriate to the social, cultural and economic contexts in which such children live (Punch 1998). Some anthropologists have argued that modern western societies are unusual in the sharp distinction they make between childhood and adulthood and in the degree to which children are excluded from adult concerns and activities (Benedict 1938). In societies based on subsistence technologies, children are more fully integrated into adult life, whether or not they play an active part in the economy, and generally develop adult competences earlier than is common in the modern West (Turnbull 1966; Fortes 1970; Draper 1976; Punch 1998 – but see also Chapter 8).

In European societies, ideas about children and childhood have changed markedly over the centuries. In drawing attention to these changes, the historian Ariès (1962) suggested that there was no concept of childhood in medieval Europe, that once past infancy children were treated simply as miniature adults. They were dressed like adults, took an active part in adult work and recreation and were held fully responsible for their actions. Ariès, however, overstated his case. While children in medieval times were treated far more like adults than they are today, it is clear that they were not regarded as exactly the same as adults. In particular, Ariès' own evidence indicates that children were seen as social subordinates within a patriarchal and feudal social order, that they were very much under the authority of the head of the household in which they lived and worked. Moreover, childhood was regarded as a stage that prepared the young for later responsibilities, a period of moral and practical training for later life (Shahar 1990). Yet medieval childhood was not childhood as we know it today. Archard (1993) suggests that while there has probably always been a concept of childhood, the current conception of childhood is a modern invention. The way childhood is actually lived has also changed over time.

In medieval and early modern times (up to the early eighteenth century), infancy, childhood and youth were socially recognised as stages of life preceding adulthood, but these stages did not have the same meaning as they have today (Gillis 1974). Infancy was the period before a child attained the 'age of reason', which for most medieval thinkers was at the age of 7, the age at which they could be betrothed, or, in the case of boys, begin training for the priesthood (Shahar 1990). Even before they reached this age, however, children were expected to work, to make a contribution to household subsistence. Although children could be tried and sometimes executed for crimes, from age 7, the age of full criminal responsibility corresponded with the beginning of youth, at 12 for girls and 14 for boys. These were also the ages at which is was legally permissible to marry, although early marriage was in fact very rare. During youth, it was common for children of all classes to leave the parental home to enter service or apprenticeships in another household, thus becoming more independent of their parents but remaining under the authority of their employer or patron. The end of youth and the beginning of adulthood was ill-defined, but was usually taken to occur on marriage and the establishment of an independent marital household, which for women, who could not hold property once married, meant becoming dependent on their husbands.

In general children were far more integrated into adult working and social life than they are today. For those privileged enough to receive any formal education, there was no notion of age-grading or reading material tailored to children's needs. Boys (and only boys) could go to university at age 11 or 12 and only in the seventeenth century was the age of university entrance raised to 15. By this time, it had become less common for the sons of the bourgeois and landed classes to be sent into service and more usual for them to be formally educated – trends that affected girls of these classes a century later

(Pinchbeck and Hewitt 1969). Age-grading in schools was gradually being introduced, books to educate and entertain children began to be published and children began to be dressed differently from adults.

The inception of modern childhood was, however, apparent only among the privileged classes. The bourgeoisie, in particular, became concerned for the moral welfare of children. It has been argued that the dominant image of the child at this time was that of the 'demonic child' tainted by original sin (Skolnick 1973), whose spiritual well-being was best safeguarded by breaking his or her will. The idea of the 'innocent child' did not appear until the end of the eighteenth century and did not gain wide credence until its Victorian sentimentalisation in the nineteenth century. By this time, modern ideas of childhood were beginning to affect working-class children.

Once industrialisation separated the worlds of work and home, working children became more visible and increasingly offensive to the bourgeois ideal of childhood. As the nineteenth century wore on, children's work was gradually limited, while their lives came under more surveillance from philanthropists, educators and legislators. As older family or craft-based forms of training became obsolete, schools came to be seen as the most efficient context in which to impart knowledge. As children were excluded from work, it was seen as necessary to keep them occupied and contained. Elementary education became compulsory in 1870. Moral welfare, especially that of girls, also became a major issue and the age of heterosexual consent for girls was raised to 16 in 1882. Childhood was thus prolonged and increasingly seen as a stage of life requiring particular forms of regulation, protection and guidance:

> The modern child has become the focus of innumerable projects that purport to safeguard it from physical, sexual and moral danger, to ensure its 'normal development', to actively promote certain capacities or attributes such as intelligence, educability and emotional stability. (Rose 1989: 121)

This trend has continued and is particularly evident in the developmental paradigm and its institutionalisation in school age-grading. The result is that children are held to be incapable of doing what, in fact, they are not permitted to do (Thorne 1987). This learnt incapacity in turn justifies their exclusion from the adult world.

The late modern conception of childhood entails an imputation of 'specialness' to children (as particularly cherished beings) and childhood (as a cherished state of being). There is a strong cultural emphasis on marking the boundary between childhood and adulthood (Jackson 1982), on maintaining childhood as a protected state and children as a protected species. Childhood is now frequently being constructed as a precious realm under siege from those who would rob children of their childhoods, and as being subverted from within by children who refuse to remain childlike. Anything which threatens to destabilise the boundary between childhood and adulthood provokes anxiety about childhood itself:

> To have to stand and wait as the charm, malleability, innocence and curiosity of children are degraded and then transmogrified into the lesser features of pseudo-adulthood is painful and embarrassing and, above all, sad. (Postman 1994: xiii)

Here Postman is expressing a widely aired concern that children are growing up too quickly without experiencing childhood to the full. Childhood is seen as being at risk from pressures towards early maturity, conspicuous consumption and precocious sexuality, highlighting a fundamental contradiction in discourses around children and childhood: childhood is regarded as a natural state and yet also as perpetually at risk. This contradiction and the constant vigilance required in order to protect, preserve and manage childhood should lead us to question whether childhood is as natural as it seems.

The boundaries we construct between childhood and adulthood are clearly products of history and change over time. Modern legal systems institution-alise childhood by setting an age of majority at which a person becomes a legal subject responsible for their own affairs and able to exercise citizenship rights. The UN Convention on the Rights of the Child defines a child as anyone under the age of 18 unless, under the laws of his or her country, the age of majority comes sooner. Even with such legalistic dividing lines, there are still areas of ambiguity. Within any one country there may be various markers of adult status, so that one ceases to be a child for some purposes while remaining one for others. For example, the right to vote and the right to marry without parental consent may be acquired at different times. In both the USA and the UK, a young person can hold a driving licence, marry and fight for his or her country while still being below voting age – in the words of the Barry McGuire song from 1966 'old enough to kill but not for voting'. Indeed in some states of the USA it would be possible to marry (with parental consent) up to nine years before being able legally to purchase alcohol. In the UK, at the time of writing, the age of heterosexual consent is 16 – two years below that for homosexual men (there is still no legislation pertaining to lesbian sex: see Chapter 10).

Despite our cultural emphasis on the distinction between childhood and adulthood, we lack a clear rite of passage marking the boundary. The prolon-gation of childhood and uncertainty about where it ends has created adoles-cence as a peculiarly problematic liminal stage of life. Young people in their teens are excluded from many adult activities while being expected to behave like adults in other respects. However, when they do behave like adults, for example in relation to sexual activity, it can cause an outcry in defence of the need for the retention of childhood innocence. It is hardly surprising that young people are often confused and resentful. Adolescence itself, along with many of the problems associated with it, is a product of a specific, modern, western construction of childhood.

Power and dependence

As we have noted, children in western societies have historically lost their role as economic actors. For children to work is now seen as intrinsically problematic, as antithetical to being a child. Children's exclusion from work has been seen as a mark of social progress, what differentiates us from the exploitative past, in which children laboured in mines and factories, and Third World nations, in which child labour is still common. Yet 'freeing' children from economic exploitation has rendered them economically powerless, increasing their dependence on adults, specifically their parents. Economic dependence is now a defining feature of childhood, one that marks children as subordinates in a society where the capacity to earn – and thus to spend and consume – is central to the construction of identity.

Economic dependence has long been a marker of subordinate social status and power. For women, gaining economic independence, the right to earn and the right to control their own income was seen as a key step towards emancipation (Chapter 3). Yet, as women have gained financial independence, children have lost it (and, ironically, mothers' extra earnings often go into maintaining children's dependence). The gradual raising of the minimum school-leaving age from 12 to 14, to 15 and finally to 16 has prolonged economic dependence. Little over a generation ago, most young people left school and entered the labour market at 15 and and it is only just over 60 years since most did so at the age of 14.

More recently, changes in the benefit structure have meant that those who leave school early have no entitlement until they reach 18. For the more privileged who go on to higher education, the erosion of the value of student grants and their replacement by loans has lengthened the period of dependence on parental support until young people reach their early twenties. At the same time, a higher proportion of young people have been entering higher education. Hence, although the legal age of majority was reduced from 21 to 18 in 1971, for many young people the period of dependency has since increased.

Paradoxically, as economic dependence has increased, so children have come to be targeted as consumers. Indeed, the pressure to consume is often seen as a pressure towards precocious maturity (Postman 1994). While the emphasis on the child as consumer has no doubt intensified in recent years, there has long been a trend in this direction. As soon as children became singled out as a special category of being, this created a market niche for products designed specifically for them, toys, games, books and clothes and wallpaper and furniture for their rooms. Those targeting parents and children have drawn heavily on developmental psychology to fragment the market for children's goods and create categories such as 'the toddler' (Cook 2000a, b). Children's very separateness from the adult world thus serves to include them in the adult economy as consumers.

Children do not, however, consume in quite the same way as adults: children's consumption is dependent, adult-mediated consumption (Leonard 1990). Children have things bought for them and exercise consumer choice only if their parents permit it. Gifts of money and pocket money are given at adults' discretion and adults may seek to influence how these sums are spent. Young children in particular are constrained to consume only what their parents buy for them. They can wheedle, cajole, shout and scream to get what they want, and they may sometimes succeed, but ultimately it is adults who hold the purse strings. Older children may be permitted more latitude in disposing of their own pocket money but only if, in their parents' eyes, they exercise this discretion responsibly. However, despite widespread discussion of and concern about the impact of the market on children, relatively little research has been done on children's own consumption practices in the context of their everyday lives (Martens et al. 2004).

Ability to earn their own money through paper rounds, weekend or holiday jobs can be attractive to children in enabling them to have an income which is not dependent on the goodwill of adults (Morrow 1994). Children may also work, paid or unpaid, in the home (Brannen 1995) or a family business (Song 1996). However, whether or not children are allowed to undertake any paid work or receive payment for tasks in the home will depend on whether parents view this positively as preparation for economic independence. On the other hand, parents may see such economic activity as a slur on their ability to provide adequately for their offspring, or as interfering with more legitimate childhood activities, such as homework or recreation. Giving and withholding money, and indeed permission to earn outside the home, is one means by which parents seek to control their children.

Parents not only exercise power over children through controlling them, but also seek to mould and shape their children. This is a facet of the responsibility placed on parents to raise children 'properly'. This responsibility extends beyond caring and providing for children, because parents are also held responsible for their children's well-being and conduct. Not only are parents expected to govern and regulate their children's current lives, but their futures as well. Child-rearing can thus be seen as a reflexive project:

> A child can no longer be accepted as it is, with physical idiosyncracies, perhaps even flaws. Rather it becomes the target of a diversity of efforts. All possible flaws must be corrected ... all possible talents must be stimulated ... Countless guides to education and upbringing appear on the book and magazine market. As different as each one is, at bottom they all have a similar message: the success of the child is defined as the private duty of the parents/the mother. And the duty reads the same everywhere: the parents must do everything to give the child 'the best start in life'. (Beck-Gernsheim 1996: 143)

Of course, the resources available to parents for this project vary according to not only the income (Chapter 2) but also the knowledge and social networks (what Bourdieu (1984) has termed 'cultural capital') available to them. The ways the project is executed will reflect parents' own priorities for their children, their ideas about what is appropriate according to their children's gender, the neighbourhood in which they live and the cultural milieu they inhabit. Nonetheless, the assumption that children are what their parents make them is widespread. Modern families are often described as child-centred and certainly children's needs may be given a high priority, but these needs are defined for them by adults. Children's own autonomous desires frequently take second place to their parents' view of what is best for them.

It has been suggested that parental power is no longer as absolute as it once was, that child-rearing is now 'policed' by a host of experts and state agencies (Donzelot 1978) and that, with the rise of the 'psy' professions, child development has become subject to increasing surveillance (Rose 1989). 'Expert' advice not only informs parents' practices, but bureaucratises child-rearing and increases anxieties about 'doing it properly'. While this constrains parents, it does not necessarily increase children's autonomy within families. Children are neither citizens nor full legal subjects and thus live, in a very real sense, under their parents' jurisdiction. Any other agencies that deal with them, from schools and clubs to care facilities, are seen as acting *in loco parentis*. Parents themselves retain a great deal of latitude to rear their children as they wish, set acceptable standards of behaviour and decide how they should be educated and disciplined. Think, for example, of the ways in which debate about choice of schooling for children are framed in terms of parents' rights rather than children's rights. If others interfere with parents' practices or choices, it is seen as an infringement of their rights and an assault on family privacy. Public regulation is seen as justifiable only where parents are deemed to have abused their power or not exercised it effectively enough – where children are 'at risk' or 'out of control'.

Holding property in one's bodily person is a fundamental aspect of citizen's rights in modern democratic societies; however, this right is not extended to children. Adults, and parents in particular, exercise an exceptional degree of control over the bodies of children (Hood-Williams 1990). Children's bodies are routinely regulated by adult decisions about what and when they should eat, what clothes they can wear on what occasions, admonitions about bodily movement and deportment, and restrictions on their mobility – all of which would only be experienced by adults under extreme conditions of institutionalisation, in prisons, residential care or the military (Goffman 1961). It is quite acceptable for known adults to pat children's heads, tickle them, throw them in the air, tidy their hair and clothing and even pick them up and move them bodily – behaviour that would only be acceptable between adults in the most intimate of relationships, and then only with consent. It is interesting that one of the greatest anxieties surrounding children today is that they might be molested, and they are taught, in order to protect themselves, that their bodies are sacrosanct, yet those same bodies are routinely interfered with and contained in the name of hygiene, tidiness and discipline, and also, ironically, to ensure their safety.

Children are not always willing to be bounded either by definitions of them as dependent and lacking in adult competences or attempts to curtail their activities. Moreover, the powerlessness of children does not go unchallenged by the wider, adult society. At the same time as we have seen increasing surveillance of children in the name of protection or control, we have also witnessed a growth in the movement for children's rights, enshrined in documents such as the 1989 UN Convention on the Rights of the Child. At first sight, this would seem to signal a shift towards recognising children as autonomous beings, but this is not always the case. Some of the rights conferred by the UN Convention include children into basic internationally recognised human rights such as freedom of association, freedom of expression and the right to privacy. Other provisions of the Convention exclude children from adult activities or responsibilities such as work and armed conflict. Still other rights are specific to children such as the right to education and freedom from abuse and neglect. On the other hand, the rights conferred on parents by the Convention can, in practice, undermine all these rights.

The confusion evident in the different forms of rights enshrined in the UN Convention derives from a widespread ambivalence about the forms of rights children should be granted. Children's rights can be framed from two opposing perspectives: in terms of rights to autonomy, control over their own lives and independent status as citizens or in terms of rights to protection and freedom from adult risks and responsibilities. The former conceptualisation of rights challenges the subordinate status of children, the latter rarely does. The UN Convention attempts to balance these opposing views, to expand children's autonomy without undermining adult authority. Hence children's continued exclusion from citizenship is tacitly reinforced.

However, even rights that offer protection rather than independence can improve children's lives and potentially temper the near absolute authority that parents wield over them. Within the UN Convention, parental rights are not absolute and legislation within Britain and elsewhere can override parental authority in the interests of the child. For example, state agencies can now intervene to protect children against parents who abuse or neglect them. In such cases a higher – adult – authority is called on to decide what is in 'the best interests of the child' (the guiding principle behind the Convention).

Risk, risk anxiety and the construction of childhood

The tension between protecting children from harm and fostering their autonomy also underpins many of the anxieties expressed about children and childhood in late modern society. Social theorists such as Giddens (1990, 1991) and Beck (1992) have suggested that we live in a climate of heightened risk awareness, engendered by an increasing lack of trust in both the project of modernity and expert knowledges. While anxieties about children and childhood – a product of the modern idea of the child as an innocent in need of protection – date back to the nineteenth century, the conditions of late modernity may have exacerbated them. The anxieties specific to childhood are part of a general sense that the social world itself is becoming less stable and predictable, coupled with a nostalgia for an imagined past in which children played safely throughout a carefree innocent childhood.

Risk anxiety helps to construct childhood and maintain its boundaries – the specific risks from which children must be protected serve to define the characteristics of childhood and the 'nature' of children themselves. Threats to children's well-being are seen as coming from all-pervasive, global social 'ills', such as the 'pernicious' consequences of sex and violence in the media, and the unforeseen (but constantly anticipated) danger from a specific 'monstrous' individual – the shadowy figure of the paedophile who haunts the popular imagination. For example, a new film version of *Lolita*, released in 1998, was read as symptomatic of a generalised moral depravity and a potential incitement to individual paedophiles.

Beck (1992, 1998), one of the major theorists of the 'risk society', associates risk anxiety with the individualisation and de-traditionalisation characteristic of modernity. Individualisation entails the almost constant reflexive monitoring of risk that pervades our sense of how to manage ourselves and the world. Risks may be produced by social conditions, but we are expected to assess and manage them as individuals. De-traditionalisation has produced a less predictable world, in which we are faced with many options and no easy solutions (Beck 1998). Where childhood is concerned, de-traditionalisation engenders anxieties about the loss of stable families embedded within secure communities (Chapter 13). The everyday world of childhood no longer seems so safe and predictable. At the same time, individualisation renders each parent uniquely responsible for their children and encourages them to invest in their children's childhood as part of their own life project (Beck and Beck-Gernsheim 1995; Beck-Gernsheim 1996). Parents must not only guard against immediate threats to their children's well-being but must also plan for any event that might disrupt their development towards physically and psychologically healthy adulthood. Hence the developmental paradigm, so central to modern constructions of childhood, may heighten risk anxiety.

It is these individualised parental hopes and fears for their children that are mobilised in wider, publicly aired concerns about children and childhood. Increasing anxiety about risk has been superimposed on an older 'protective discourse' (Thomson and Scott 1991), within which children are located as vulnerable innocents to be shielded from the dangers of the wider social (implicitly adult) world. The fusion of risk anxiety with protectiveness engenders a preoccupation with prevention (Scott and Freeman 1995; Green 1997), a need for constant vigilance in order to anticipate and guard against potential threats to children's well-being. Concern for children's safety is of a different order from concerns about adult safety. Risks to children are represented as inherently more grave than risks to adults. This is most marked in extreme circumstances, as in the media reaction to the shooting of 16 children in the Scottish city of Dunblane in March 1996.

Children most often come under public scrutiny when they are perceived as being in danger (as victims of adult abuse or neglect) or as a danger to others (as delinquents and vandals: Thorne 1987). Often such concerns can be seen to reflect risk anxiety as much as actual danger, for example heightened awareness of sexual and fatal risk from strangers in the UK, despite the lack of evidence that risk to children comes primarily from this quarter. While there has been an increase in recorded crimes of violence against children, three-quarters of the perpetrators are parents and other relatives. The children most at risk of being murdered are infants under the age of one –

hardly those most exposed to 'stranger danger' – while children aged 5–15 are, of all members of society, the least likely to be victims of homicide. It is not until children reach the age of 15 or 16 that danger from strangers becomes more significant than that from intimates (CSO 1994, 1995). Up to February 1996 (prior to the killings in Dunblane), fewer than six children under 14 had been killed by strangers each year since 1984 in the UK. This can be contrasted with approximately 600 per year who die in accidents (CSO 1994). Yet fear of attack by strangers continues to be seen as the single most significant risk to children when they venture outside the home (Hood et al. 1996).

It would, however, be unwise to interpret this apparent gap between parental worries and statistical probabilities as indicative of ignorance or stupidity. We cannot assume, in the absence of reliable research, that parents fail to assess risks 'realistically'. Parents may know the statistical probability of their child being sexually assaulted or murdered by a stranger to be slight, but the fact that it happens at all might be enough to make them fear for their own. This point has been borne out in our own recent research (Jackson and Scott 2001). Parents cannot even be sure that their children are safe from others at home, since electronic media render them open to contact from 'strangers' via the internet and exposure to 'unsuitable' material through television, video and computer games (Buckingham 2000).

Risk anxiety has material effects. Parental fears can limit children's lives and experiences in a range of ways, thus increasing their dependence on adults. For example, whereas 80 per cent of seven- and eight-year-olds in the UK went to school on their own in 1971, only 9 per cent were doing so in 1990 (Hillman et al. 1990). While there are undoubtedly other factors that contribute to this trend, such as increased car ownership, this statistic is nevertheless indicative of decreasing opportunities for children to develop autonomy and self-reliance. This in turn produces yet another set of publicly aired risk anxieties relating to children's health and life experience (see for example *Guardian* 10 March 1999). These concerns, initially focused on fears about unfit overweight children, are increasingly giving way to anxieties about the longer term consequences of overprotecting children. For example, an article in the *Scottish Daily Mail* (20 January 1998) accused parents of 'raising a generation of mollycoddled children who will be incapable of taking responsible decisions as they grow up'. This, we were told, came as a warning from 'experts'.

It is hardly surprising, given the tensions between protecting children and permitting their autonomy, that parents should look to 'experts' for a set of rules which, having external authority, may lend a sense of certainty to the decisions parents take. In Britain, the National Society for the Prevention of

Cruelty to Children offers guidelines on the age at which children are competent to do certain things. For example, eight-year-olds are too young to go to school alone and seven-year-olds are too young for unaccompanied visits to the shops. Such guidelines tend to bureaucratise decisions in relation to children, producing standardised responses without regard to the social context or life experience of individual children. They are couched within a developmental linear model that serves to delineate the boundaries of children's lives, thus creating a self-fulfilling prophecy – children cannot be competent to do things which they have never been allowed to do (Thorne 1987). Thus keeping children 'safe' can entail keeping them child-like and dependent.

The degree of anxiety generated by risks to children is associated with a particular construction of childhood as an age of innocence and vulnerability. Yet the idea of the innocent child has never entirely subsumed an alternative, older view of the child as sinful and unruly (Skolnick 1980; Jackson 1990). Children are often characterised in everyday talk as little devils in one breath and little angels in the next. However, it is common for parents to see their own children primarily as innocent and vulnerable as opposed to other children who are potentially threatening (Valentine 1996). Whereas the dead children of Dunblane, as innocent angels, symbolically became all our children (Scott and Watson-Brown 1997), those children whose actions belie the notion of innocence are characterised as truly demonic. When, in 1993, the British toddler James Bulger was murdered by two older boys, idealised images of childhood were de-stabilised (Jenks 1996): hence the efforts made to distance the boy killers from 'normal' children through depictions of them as evil beyond comprehension. Similarly, a spate of killings at schools in the USA in the late 1990s received global media coverage. One of these involved 15-year-old Kip Kinkel, who murdered his parents and two schoolmates. Kinkel was described as a '"schizoid" kid from a good home'. As in most cases of this kind, it emerges (in retrospect of course) that he was 'dangerously disturbed' but that adults aware of this did nothing about it (*Guardian* 23 May 1998).

The demonisation of child killers parallels the media representation of women such as Myra Hindley and Rosemary West; women and children who kill are deemed monstrous, doubly transgressive – in having murdered, they have also acted against their feminine or childlike 'nature'. In May 1998, considerable controversy was generated in the UK by the publication of a book about Mary Bell who, over 30 years earlier when she was 13, had killed two small children. Bell was retrospectively re-demonised as both a child who killed and a woman profiting from her crime by accepting payment for her story. Her depiction as monstrous was highly gendered. 'Her extraordinarily pretty, heart-shaped face looked out beneath headlines, as it looks out again now: a beautiful icon of evil' (*Observer* 3 May 1998: 3).

Here our attention was drawn to the appearance of feminine, childish innocence and the 'truth' of the evil beneath the surface. We were reminded of the lack of remorse shown by Mary Bell at her trial (and by implication since) in contrast with her co-accused who was acquitted and described as 'normal' in her tearful appearance in court, as 'just a little girl'. Mary Bell, however, was clearly not a proper 'little girl'. Throughout the trial, she was 'tearless and defiant, bandying words with the prosecution' (*Observer* 3 May 1998: 3). Her cleverness and her refusal to be cowed by the full weight of adult power represented by the court underline her exclusion from normal childhood and her status as a monstrosity.

Differences among children

Since our primary focus has been on the institution of childhood and the social division between childhood and adulthood, we have made only passing references to differences of class, gender, ethnicity and age (Chapters 2, 3, 4 and 8). Clearly, children are not socially homogeneous. One aspect of the social construction of childhood and the distinctions drawn between children and adults is that 'the child' becomes an abstraction representing a universal and often idealised childhood. It is this universal child that figures in media representations of tragedies affecting children, such as the Dunblane shooting, and which, as a symbolic representation of all our children, evokes an emotional response (Scott and Watson-Brown 1997). In other contexts, this universalising of childhood serves to conceal or pathologise social divisions among children. If children's differing experiences of childhood are noticed at all, it is within a developmental paradigm that assumes a fixed set of stages that all children pass through, or within a discourse that marks out 'deviant', 'problem' or 'deprived' children from the ideal, 'normal' child. This normal child is, unsurprisingly, defined from a white, middle-class perspective that even in its most liberal, caring variants has the effect of branding working-class or black children as 'other' (Lawler 1999). It is these children who are likely to be seen as not proper children, cast either in the mould of the demonic child or the child deprived of a childhood.

This is not to deny that middle-class children enjoy all manner of privileges that working-class children lack. The point is that setting up middle-class childhood as the norm results in it being viewed uncritically as a more positive version of childhood. It also tends to represent the difference of working-class childhoods as the product of cultural deficit or lack, so diverting attention away from the material inequalities that underpin both working-class and middle-class childhoods. Where ethnic differences are concerned, taking white, middle-class childhood as the norm too easily gives rise to racist stereotypes of dysfunctional black families and neighbourhoods or a glib multiculturalism that celebrates diversity while denying racism.

Arguably the greatest social division affecting children is poverty, both between rich and poor areas of the world and within relatively affluent countries such as the UK. It is important to point out, however, that children are poor because adults are poor and children are, as we have shown, highly dependent on adults economically (Chapter 12). Children are extremely vulnerable to the effects of poverty – malnutrition, disease and so on. Adults with children are generally worse off than equivalent adults without children, because there are economic costs entailed in having children. Children are dependent on parental altruism and while the evidence suggests that mothers generally display such altruism (see the discussion of poverty in Chapters 3, 12 and 14), fathers frequently do not and thus poor households may be financially better off without men (Graham 1987). However, because children are considered to be the personal responsibility, or even the property, of their parents, there is rarely adequate social support for children.

Thus the issue of poverty can be taken as an illustration of children's dependence. While, as a result of their dependence, children are particularly vulnerable to poverty, the ways in which concerns about this are expressed clearly illustrate and reinforce the issues that we have raised in this chapter. More concern is expressed about child poverty than about the situation of women in general or older people (Chapters 3 and 8) – both groups in which poverty levels are high globally. This is, we suggest, because images of 'innocents' are more appealing – quite literally in the context of charity campaigns. Poor children are the antithesis of idealised images of childhood and can easily be appropriated into a story that constructs them as deprived of a 'proper' childhood and thus of particular concern and interest (Lawler 1999).

The central argument of this chapter is that the division between childhood and adulthood, despite not having received as much sociological attention as divisions like class, gender and so on, should, nevertheless, be seen as one of the key lines of stratification along which societies are organised. It follows from this that, for children as for adults, the actualities of their everyday lives are shaped by their location in relation to all the other divisions discussed in this book. It is important therefore that the adult/child division is not simply reproduced by a reading of the other chapters as if they pertained only to adults.

Discussion Questions

1. Look at the UN Convention on the Rights of the Child, available at www.unicef.org/crc/crc.htm and also on the UNHCR website, www.unhcr.org. Which rights are framed in terms of children's autonomy and which in terms of the protection of children? Are there tensions between these differing conceptualisations of rights?

2. Interview someone over 50 about their experiences of being a child and compare this with your own childhood and with discussions in the media about what it is safe for children to do now.

FURTHER READING

A now classic account of how knowledge of children is deeply adult-centred can be found in Thorne, B. 'Re-Visioning Women and Social Change: Where are the Children?' (*Gender and Society*, 1: 85–109, 1987). Jenks, C. *Childhood* (Routledge: London, 1996, 2006) in the Key Ideas series offers an introduction to sociological ways of thinking about childhood from a social constructionist perspective. The collection edited by James, A. and Prout, A. (eds) *Constructing and Reconstructing Childhood* (Basingstoke: Falmer Press, 1990) provides an emphasis on cultural and historical differences. Mayall, B. *Towards a Sociology for Childhood* (Open University Press: Buckingham, 2002) argues that feminist theory and practice are useful for understanding childhood and that we should start from the children's own accounts to show how the organization of social relations provides an explanation for their social position. Mayell's earlier edited collection, *Children's Childhoods Observed and Experienced* (London: Falmer Press, 1994), explores the social status of children in a range of settings and children's rights.

CHAPTER 10

Sexuality

SUE SCOTT AND STEVI JACKSON

This chapter will provide you with a broad critical understanding of the following issues in sexuality as a source of social division:

- What is meant by essentialism and why it is challenged by social theorists
- The idea of the social construction of sexuality
- Definitions of gender, sexuality and institutionalised heterosexuality
- Social divisions of gender in relation to sexuality
- The institutionalisation of heterosexuality
- The privileging of heterosexuality in relation to other sexualities
- Gender differences in heterosexual practices
- The heterosexual and gendered assumptions underpinning sex education
- Psychoanalytical approaches to sexuality
- The interactionist approach to sexuality
- Foucault's approach to sexuality
- Feminist, lesbian, gay and queer contributions to understanding sexuality
- Issues associated with lesbian and gay rights
- The commodification of sexuality

The social ordering of sexuality gives rise to two forms of social division and inequality. On the one hand, within modern western societies, heterosexuality is institutionalised as the 'normal' form of human sexuality and this is reflected at many levels of society from the legal regulation of marriage and the provisions of the social security system to the content of popular culture and everyday social practices. This privileging of heterosexuality serves to marginalise lesbian and gay sexualities, gives rise to both formal and informal discrimination against lesbians and gay men and sometimes to more brutal forms of oppression. On the other hand, heterosexuality is itself, by definition, differentiated by gender. Being heterosexual does not have the same consequences for men and women – indeed historically it has evolved as an institution that is closely bound up with the perpetuation of male dominance and female subordination, as was argued in Chapter 3.

While there are apparently two distinct forms of inequality here – between heterosexuals and non-heterosexuals and between men and women – they are interrelated. A sociological understanding of both forms of inequality requires that we pay critical attention to the taken-for-granted character of the hetero-sexual norm. This chapter will therefore draw on sociological analysis of heterosexuality as institution and practice. We will begin by introducing some basic concepts, defining key terms such as gender, sexuality and institution-alised heterosexuality. We will then explore sociological challenges to biolog-ical determinism, explaining why sociologists see sexuality as socially constructed and how we might conceptualise the sexual as fully social, rather than 'natural' or individual. Having explained the concepts and theories underpinning sociological approaches to sexuality, we will examine some of the research that has accumulated on both heterosexual relations and the forms of social exclusion experienced by lesbians and gay men. We will argue that, despite changes in sexual mores towards less restrictive and more egali-tarian ideals, inequalities associated with sexuality persist.

Sexuality, gender and institutionalised heterosexuality

Sexuality cannot be understood without consistently paying attention to its intersection with gender. The concepts of gender and sexuality both take 'sex', a highly ambiguous term, as a point of reference. In the English language, the word 'sex' can denote either the distinction between male and female (as 'two sexes') or sex as an erotic activity (to 'have sex'). Similarly, 'sexual' can refer to the different activities or attributes of men and women, as in phrases such as 'the sexual division of labour', or it can refer to the erotic sphere of life, for example 'sexual fantasies'. Moreover the term 'sex' can be used – more commonly in French, but sometimes in English – to name sexual organs which are simultaneously erogenous zones and body parts that distinguish male from female.

This linguistic confusion is no mere accident, but tells us something about the male-dominated and heterosexist culture in which we live (Wilton 1996). It is commonly assumed that being born with a particular set of genitals (sex organs) defines one as of a particular sex (female or male), which means that one will normally become 'properly' feminine or masculine (the appropriate gender) and will desire and engage in erotic activity with 'the other sex', with someone possessing a different set of sex organs from one's own. This circular and deterministic reasoning has served to justify women's subordination as a 'natural' outcome of sex differences and define heterosexuality as the only fully 'natural' and legitimate form of sexuality. As sociologists, we should chal-lenge the taken-for-granted assumptions underlying this way of thinking.

A first step is to separate out the three terms 'sex', 'gender' and 'sexuality'. Sociologists and feminists usually distinguish between them, but there is by no means a consensus on how each of these three terms should be used. Hence we need to define the sense in which they are being used in this chapter. The term 'gender' was originally adopted by feminist sociologists to emphasise the social shaping of femininity and masculinity, to challenge the idea that relations between women and men were ordained by nature. In the past, it was common to make a distinction between 'sex' as the biological differences between male and female and 'gender' as the cultural distinction between femininity and masculinity along with the social division between women and men (Oakley 1972). This is no longer acceptable, because it has become increasingly apparent that our understanding of the anatomically sexed body is itself socially constructed, scientific understandings of sex difference have been shaped by cultural ideas about gender and the everyday recognition of others as men and women is a social act requiring us to decode cultural signifiers of gender (see for example Butler 1990; Delphy 1993). This realisation also helps to resolve the ambiguity of the word 'sex', which is still often used – even by some sociologists – to denote both the male–female distinction and intimate erotic activity.

Here we will use the term 'gender' to cover all aspects of what it means to be a woman or a man and refer to the social division and cultural distinction between women and men. The word 'sex' is then reserved to describe erotic activity. The term 'sexuality' is generally broader in meaning, encompassing erotic desires and identities, as well as practices. In this sense, the concept of 'sexuality' remains somewhat fluid, in part because what is deemed erotic, and hence sexual in this sense, is not fixed. What is erotic to one person might be disgusting to a second and immoral to a third. In using this rather slippery term, we wish to convey the idea that sexuality is not limited to 'sex acts', but involves our sexual feelings and relationships, the ways in which we are, or are not, defined as sexual by others, as well as the ways in which we define ourselves.

While gender and sexuality are analytically distinct, they are empirically interrelated. When we label ourselves and others as heterosexual, lesbian, gay or bisexual, we define sexuality by the gender of those we desire. Masculinity and femininity are validated, in part, through conventional heterosexuality, hence the idea that lesbians are not 'real women' and gay men are not 'real men'; conversely, those who flout conventions of femininity and masculinity are often assumed to be lesbian or gay. Sexual desires and practices are also gendered and heterosexual relationships, in particular, are governed by all manner of gendered expectations from the double standard of morality to the sequences of acts that occur within any given sexual encounter. The normative status of heterosexuality is pivotal to the social ordering of both gender and sexuality.

The term 'institutionalised heterosexuality' refers to all social practices and forms of social regulation through which 'normal' sexuality is equated with heterosexuality. Heterosexuality is a social institution; it is definitive of another key social institution – marriage – and is the norm against which other forms of sexuality are judged and policed. Not only does it entail the outlawing of dissident sexualities, but it governs social expectations about relations between women and men in both the private and public spheres of life. Heterosexuality is so taken for granted, even by sociologists, that we often overlook its importance; we think within what has been called 'the hetero-sexual imaginary', which masks the operation of heterosexuality as an institution (Ingraham 1996: 169). Moreover, heterosexuality is legitimated by the concealment of its social character, through its definition as simply 'natural'. This brings us to the most important contribution that sociology has made to the study of sexuality: the demystification of its apparent naturalness.

The critique of essentialism

Since the 1970s, sociologists and feminists have challenged 'essentialist' modes of thinking that view sexuality as an essential, innate, universal fact of human nature. Within western culture there has been a long history of reli-giously based essentialism within which some sexual practices were defined as natural, in the sense of God-given, and others as 'against nature' and hence a transgression of God's law. In modern societies, however, it is biological essentialism that predominates, although the moral categorisation deriving from its older, religious form has by no means disappeared. It is now common to find human sexuality reduced to hormones, genes and the urge to pass on our genetic inheritance to the next generation. This perspective remains popular in lay and scientific circles even though sexual activity is now increas-ingly thought of as recreation rather than procreation.

Sociologists have identified a number of problems with essentialism. In the first place, it rests on something unknowable, a hypothesised 'natural' sexu-ality somehow uncontaminated by cultural influences. Human beings do not exist outside society and culture; we each become sexual within specific social contexts. The forms of sexuality we are familiar with today are the product of a particular society at a particular point in its history. Even within our own society, experiences of both gender and sexuality are highly variable. Since gender and sexuality intersect with other social divisions, such as those based on class, ethnicity, age and community (Chapters 2, 4, 8 and 13), we each live our sexuality from different locations within society and our individual biog-raphies affect our sexual preferences and practices in complex ways. When we turn to historical and anthropological evidence we find even greater diversity.

Erotic conventions change over time and vary from one society to another. We know, for example, that in medieval Western Europe women were regarded as beings possessed by insatiable carnal lust, while in the Victorian era they were seen as almost asexual. This might be explained by differing degrees of repression of some innate female sexuality, but this is not a very satisfactory explanation. The idea of differential repression cannot account for the complexity and variety found in different cultures. In our own society, the 'missionary position' (man on top and woman supine) has, until recently, been considered the most 'normal' and 'natural' way to engage in heterosexual inter-course. Yet people in other societies did not always agree (hence the term 'missionary position'). According to the anthropologist Malinowski (1929: 284), the Trobriand Islanders 'despise the European position and consider it unpractical and improper' – mainly because it restricts women's movements and deprives them of pleasure. Early anthropologists documented a wide variety of sexual practices within different cultures, demonstrating that what counts as erotic varies from one society to another (Ford and Beach 1952). More recent anthropological work has questioned the very definition of the sexual, suggesting that what is sexual is by no means self-evident. Consider, for example, a young man sucking an older man's penis. Is this a sexual act? Is it, more specifically, a homosexual act? In some Highland New Guinea societies, this act is ritualised as part of the passage to manhood; ingesting the semen of an adult man is essential if a boy is to become a man. In this context, it is an act with more immediate significance for gender than sexuality, although it also prepares the initiate for heterosexual adulthood (Herdt 1981; Meigs 1990).

Given that there is no natural, universal human sexuality, we cannot simply peel back the layers of social and cultural influences and find some core, 'natural' sexuality. The idea that there is some essential human sexuality that is then moulded, modified and repressed runs counter to anthropological and historical evidence. It also misleads us into thinking of the social regulation of sexuality as a negative force and hence does not allow for the social construc-tion of sexuality. The social and cultural shaping of sexuality happens not simply through prohibiting, restricting or repressing sexual practices but, more tellingly, through permitting, promoting and organising particular forms of eroticism. In other words, we learn not only what not to do, but what we should be doing sexually, how we should do it and in what order we should perform the actions which make up a sexual encounter. This is why there are so many cross-cultural variations in what is seen as erotic and in the range and form of acts deemed 'normally' sexual.

The essentialist paradigm does not address the social divisions arising from sexuality. It cannot account for differences in masculine and feminine sexu-ality except in terms of 'natural' differences or differential repression. Either women and men are innately different and nothing can change this, or women's sexuality is seen as more repressed than that of men. This latter view takes current definitions of male sexuality as the benchmark of unrepressed sexuality, in other words, what sexuality should be like, and does not allow for any other possibilities for either women or men. It also equates normality with heterosexuality. Since the essentialist paradigm ultimately reduces sexuality to reproduction, only heterosexual sex can be fully 'natural'. Hence its implications are heterosexist as well as sexist.

The social construction of sexuality

In countering essentialism, sociologists have suggested that sexuality is socially constructed. 'Social constructionism' is not a single unified perspective, however, and has been informed by three main strands of theory: psychoanalysis, interactionism and forms of post-structuralist and post-modernist thinking influenced by the work of Foucault (1981) and, especially in recent times, 'queer theory' (see Seidman 1996).

Psychoanalysis originated with the work of Freud in the early twentieth century. Freud saw the human psyche as being shaped by the repression of the libido – an inborn sexual energy. According to Freud, infants are born bisexual (neither male nor female, heterosexual or homosexual), with their sexual desires focused on their mothers. It is only through castration anxiety that, as small children, they become differentiated as boys and girls. The realisation that girls lack a penis leads the boy to fear that his father will castrate him for daring to desire his mother; he represses that desire through identification with his father, but remains sexually oriented to women. The girl, seeing herself as already castrated, blames her mother for this fate, despises her for sharing it and turns her attention to her father. She abandons active clitoral sexuality and later adapts herself to passive, vaginal sexuality directed, in adulthood, towards a father-substitute (see Freud 1977). Read literally, this account remains essentialist, in that it presupposes an innate sexuality and assumes that anatomy is destiny, even if that destiny is mediated through familial relationships. More recent readings of Freud, influenced by the work of Lacan (1977), suggest that it is through entry into language and culture that we become sexed subjects and it is the symbolic phallus, rather than the 'real' penis through which this is ordered. Yet the problematic phallocentricity of Freud persists, as does the assumption of an infantile sexuality later repressed by cultural forces.

The interactionist approach, deriving from the work of Gagnon and Simon (1974), is fundamentally opposed to psychoanalysis. Gagnon and Simon argue that there is no such thing as an innate sexuality that can be repressed. What is sexual depends on what is defined as such. It is through learning 'sexual scripts' (the sexual meanings and conventions circulating through social interaction) that we are able to make sense of acts, emotions and sensations as sexual and locate ourselves within potentially sexual scenarios. Since children in western cultures are denied access to adult sexual knowledge, they acquire a gendered identity before they see themselves as sexual actors. Gender then becomes the lens through which they later make sense of sexual knowledge and practices and construct a sense of themselves as sexual. Here, differences between male and female sexuality have nothing to do with genitals and everything to do with the social construction of gender and the scripting of sexuality in gendered terms (for example assumptions about active male sexuality and passive female sexuality). From this perspective, one's sexuality is not something fixed in childhood but evolves through interaction with others in social settings. Sexual scripts themselves are modified through interaction and subject to historical change (see Simon 1996: Gagnon 2004).

Foucault (1981) also challenges the notion of repression, in this case through historical analysis of shifting sexual discourses – discourses being the language and frameworks of understanding through which we categorise, order and explain the world around us. He contests the idea that the Victorian era was one of repression, arguing that it produced a 'discursive explosion' around sexuality. It was in this period that 'sexuality' as we understand it was brought into being, constituted as an object of discourse, in which diverse sexualities were classified, catalogued and elaborated. These discourses made it possible to distinguish between normal and perverse sexualities, to think of sexuality as an attribute of our inner selves. Acts once considered as carnal sins (to which all were susceptible) came to define the essential character of those who engaged in them. For example, where committing an act of sodomy was once a crime, but one which any sinful man might commit, that act was now seen as definitive of a particular sort of person: it became possible to be a homosexual.

Feminist sociologists have also made major contributions to the study of sexuality. Feminism is not a single theoretical perspective and feminists have drawn on and contributed to all three theoretical traditions outlined above. What feminism has added is a concern with the intersection between sexuality and gender divisions, with the ways in which the current ordering of sexual relations, especially heterosexual relations, is implicated in the maintenance of male domination (see Jackson 1999, 2005). Radical gay and lesbian and, more recently, 'queer' theorists have shared feminists' interest in social constructionism. Queer theory, which has been influential in recent years, sometimes utilises psychoanalytic concepts but is more centrally preoccupied with developing Foucault's ideas on the historical contingency of sexual identities and destabilising the binary distinction between heterosexuality and homosexuality (see Halperin 1995; Seidman 1996, 1997).

These perspectives offer differing ideas about how sexuality is socially constructed and also about what is being socially constructed, whether it be our individual desires, the cultural meanings of the erotic, the distinctions between normative and perverse sexualities or male-dominated sexual practices. Existing theories often concentrate on only some aspects of the social construction of sexuality while ignoring or downplaying others. We would argue that in order to understand sexuality as fully social, we need to understand how it is constituted at four levels (see Jackson 1999):

1. At the level of social structure and social institutions, through the institutionalisation of heterosexuality and through gender hierarchy.
2. At the level of everyday social and sexual practices.
3. At the level of meaning, through the discourses circulating within our culture as well as the meanings emerging from, and negotiated within, everyday interaction.
4. At the level of our individual subjectivities, through the social shaping of our sexual desires, responses and emotions.

A sexualised culture?

Part of the problem we have in thinking about sexuality is the way in which it is singled out as a 'special' area of life, as uniquely personal and private yet frequently provoking heated and disproportionate public controversy (Hawkes 1996): think, for example, of the number of politicians whose careers have been threatened by sexual indiscretions that had little or no bearing on their capacity to perform their public functions. The American sexual radical feminist Rubin (1984: 278–9), has called this 'the fallacy of misplaced scale' whereby sexual acts have come to be 'burdened with an excess of significance'. Rubin associates this with 'sex negativity', with a culture that has long regarded sexuality as a dangerous, socially disruptive force. Certainly, its sex-negative manifestations are dramatic, when we realise that a single act of anal sex carried the death penalty in England until 1861, men could be imprisoned simply for being homosexual until 1967 and in many states of the USA sodomy (whether heterosexual or homosexual) still carries a prison sentence.

Yet the fallacy of misplaced scale is not only evident among moral puritans but also among those espousing the cause of sexual liberation. Sex is not only uniquely tabooed, but also uniquely valorised as a route to personal fulfilment and even social revolution. The writings of sexual radicals popular in the 1960s saw sexual repression as fundamental to the bourgeois social order (Reich 1951; Marcuse 1964, 1972). Hence free sexual expression came to be seen as a means of undermining capitalism. Later libertarian writers do not make such grand claims for the disruptive power of sexuality, but still argue that transgressive sexual practices destabalise the status quo (see Rubin 1984; Halperin 1995). More generally, sexuality is marketed as a means to personal fulfilment in what Stephen Heath (1982: 3) calls 'the sexual fix', which, far from being a form of liberation, represents 'a new mode of conformity'. For example, numerous sex manuals and magazines now tell us that sexual fulfilment is virtually a precondition for a full and happy life (see also Jackson and Scott 1997, 2004).

Sexual mores at the turn of the millennium are confused, contradictory and contested. We inhabit a culture saturated with representations of sexuality yet who may talk about it, where and with whom is still circumscribed. Sexuality has become an ingredient of most forms of entertainment and is used to sell everything from cars to chocolate, yet it is rarely treated simply as a routine aspect of everyday life. Its very specialness as an area of human experience makes sexuality a problematic public issue and a troublesome aspect of our personal relationships. Young people today grow up in a culture in which they are constantly exposed to sexual imagery and innuendo, yet recent research tells us that they still find it difficult to access appropriate information and articulate their sexual wants and desires within intimate relationships (Holland et al. 1998).

That sexuality is still regarded as problematic in many western societies, including Britain, is illustrated by the issue of sex education. Here, the idea of sex as a 'special' area of life meets the conceptualisation of children as a special category of people (see Chapter 9), so that anything which links childhood and sexuality is potentially highly controversial. Sex education has been a topic of public debate for decades. What is at issue is its form, content and timing: when young people should receive it, what they should be allowed to know and how this knowledge should be imparted. It is not, however, simply access to knowledge that causes concern, but what young people do with that knowledge: whether or not it promotes 'promiscuity', whether it might 'cause' or 'prevent' teenage pregnancy (Thomson 1994). The debate is framed by a tension between public health (the desire to promote 'safer' sex and prevent early pregnancy) and public morality (the concern to maintain 'family' values). In this context, there is little concern with sexual pleasure, at best, sexual activity is an inevitability whose ill-effects should be ameliorated. In practice, school sex education remains didactic, focused on imparting biological and practical information, with little emphasis on the complexities of young people's sexual lives (Thomson and Scott 1991; Wight et al. 1998).

The form and content of sex education is one of the means through which male-defined heterosexuality is institutionalised as the only 'normal' form of sexuality. Priority is given to reproductive sexuality, in that the most important 'facts' to be imparted concern the link between sex and conception. In this context, relationships are an issue; rights (to say 'no') and responsibilities may be included, along with the emotional entanglements of sexual relationships. Yet the sex that happens in these relationships is skirted round and skipped over. Sexual pleasure, and in particular women's pleasure, is rarely discussed. Heterosexual penetrative sex is, in the main, taken for granted as defining what sex is, so that activities designed to 'turn women on' – if discussed at all – are defined as 'foreplay'. Where gay or lesbian sex is addressed, it is at best treated with liberal tolerance. Discussions of issues of sexual pleasure and alternative sexualities are hedged around with all manner of anxieties, in particular teachers' worries about imputations of corruption, causing offence to more conservative parents or provoking a media furore. Teachers and pupils also lack a common language with which to talk openly about sexuality. The constraints on those entrusted with imparting sex education result in what has been called 'defensive teaching' (Trudell 1993), with teachers staying on safe ground as far as possible and seeking to control the agenda, to guard against pupils who might raise difficult issues (Buston et al. 2001). By default, if not by design, heterosexuality dominates the sex education curriculum, the underlying assumption being that young people will grow up to be heterosexuals. While it may be possible, in a classroom context, to challenge the most coercive aspects of heterosexuality, it is rarely possible to challenge the conventional sexual script in which foreplay leads on the 'real sex' (vaginal penetration) which ends when he 'comes'.

Heterosexuality as a gendered sexual practice

The prioritisation of male sexual needs has long been challenged by feminist writers. Feminists seized on the sexological work of Masters and Johnson (1966), which demonstrated that all female orgasms, however produced, are clitorally centred, in order to demystify the 'myth of the vaginal orgasm'. This created the possibility of de-centring so-called 'sexual intercourse', of treating it as one sexual act among many possibilities rather than the predictable end point of a sexual encounter. Information on women's sexual response is now widespread in women's magazines and such writings tend to assume that women possess active sexual desires and have a right to sexual pleasure. If one drew on these magazines as the only source of data, it would appear that equality in sexual relations had been achieved. However, sociological research reveals a different picture. The first National Survey of Sexual Attitudes and Lifestyles (Wellings et al. 1994) found that vaginal intercourse was still far more common than any other form of sexual activity and that non-penetrative sex which did not culminate in intercourse was in the main found among the young, who were avoiding 'going all the way'. The consequences of the double standard were also evident in the data, with 24.4 per cent of men reporting 10 or more sexual partners in total, compared with 6.8 per cent of women. Data emerging from the second National Survey suggest that this gap is narrowing, with 34.6 per cent of men and 19.4 per cent of women reporting 10 or more lifetime sexual partners (Johnson et al. 2001).

The most extensive qualitative study of young people's sexuality so far conducted in Britain is the Women Risk and AIDS Project (Holland et al. 1990, 1991, 1998; Thomson and Scott 1991). The research revealed that young heterosexual women found sexual pleasure both difficult to discuss and hard to attain, and that many of them felt pressurised, by men, into having sex. Almost all the young women and men in the study accepted the conventional equation between sex and penetration. They disciplined their own bodies and pleasures to suit men in ways in which their partners were unlikely even to be aware of. In so doing, they conceded to men's definitions of what was pleasurable and acceptable, finding 'fulfilment primarily in the relationship, in giving pleasure' (Holland et al. 1994: 31). The ethic of service to men is, of course, not confined to erotic encounters and underlines the importance of placing heterosexual sex in the wider context of gender relations. This is not to say that young women simply passively accede to unpleasureable sex. Many do develop strategies of resistance, but their success is constrained both by the assumptions of the majority of their sexual partners and the generally unquestioned norms of heterosexuality. More recent studies suggest that young women continue to find it difficult to develop a sense of embodied sexual agency (see for example Tolman 2002).

There is no comparable data on older heterosexuals, but what does emerge from the few studies that have addressed this issue suggest that these patterns are not confined to the young and inexperienced. Research seems to suggest that sex is experienced positively in the early stages of a relationship, that when couples are 'in love', desire masks any lack of care or competence. In longer term relationships, women begin to feel uncared for and experience men's sexual demands as unwelcome, objectifying and coercive (Duncombe and Marsden 1996; Langford 1999). Duncombe and Marsden found that women in long-term heterosexual relationships complained of being pressured into sex that was mechanical and preceded by only perfunctory foreplay. Men in this study were more likely to complain about their partner's lack of interest in sex and of therefore being deprived of their conjugal rights. As one man said (Duncombe and Marsden 1996: 230):

> It would be no skin off her nose ... Sometimes I just want her to let me put it in and do it ... She's broken the contract. Sex is part of marriage.

Langford (1999) also found that women in long-term relationships expressed deep dissatisfaction with routinised sex in which emotional intimacy was lacking. For some, sex appeared to have become simply a chore that was no more enjoyable than housework and in which they had become objects for men's use. The recent use of viagra among older couples has been found to increase pressure on women to provide sex on demand, particularly as men do not always consult their wives before taking the little blue pill and then expect to 'get on with it', often with minimal foreplay. In one study, a 48-year-old woman said of the perceived power of the drug:

> this made sex inevitable. Sometimes there was no discussion about whether ... the sex act was going to take place, so it would be ... 'I've taken the pill, OK, let's go'. (Potts et al. 2003: 709)

A 65-year-old woman tells a similar story:

> Sometimes we go to bed and I think I'll go to sleep and then I realize ... he's sort of trying to get me to want sex, and it'll be a while and then I'll say 'have you taken the pill'? He'll say 'of course I've taken the pill, you know, what did you think'? And I'll say 'well I had no idea ... I've asked you not to take it unless we discuss it'. He said 'well I don't have to get your permission to take it'. (Potts et al. 2003: 707)

Underpinning these accounts is the widespread belief that men are driven by unstoppable sexual urges that must be satisfied – an idea that is also used to explain rape. These data support the feminist claim that sexual violence is an extension of 'normal' heterosexual sexual practice (Kelly 1988), that our culture supports coercive sex and sexual violence. All the evidence available suggests that there is nothing particularly unusual about the rapist – he is a very average man. Scully (1990), in a US study of convicted rapists, characterises rape as a high reward, low risk crime, in that men gain a great deal of pleasure from it and run a very low risk of being convicted for it. In the UK, despite some improvements in the ways in which the police treat rape victims, there has been a dramatic fall in the proportion of rapists brought to justice in recent years (Gregory and Lees 1999). Since an alleged rapist (like any other defendant) is presumed innocent until proven guilty, the courts effectively treat the victim as guilty (of having 'provoked' rape or 'consented' to it) until proven otherwise. Although there has been legislation limiting the intrusive questioning of rape victims, British courts still scrutinise their sexual histories and reputations; defence lawyers still use any evidence of autonomous female sexuality to discredit a woman's testimony, still routinely imply that if she is less than completely chaste, she must have deserved it (see Brown et al. 1993; Lees 1997). These problems have become particularly evident in recent years in the context of date rape. We live in a society that constructs a form of male sexuality which can readily turn predatory and then fails to call the predator to account. This is why feminists have argued that rape is a product and expression of male domination (Jackson 1999). It is the starkest possible illustration of the inequality and oppression scripted into heterosexual practices.

Heterosexuality as institution

The linchpin of institutionalised heterosexuality is marriage – or at least heterosexual coupledom. Some sociologists, notably Giddens (1992), argue that this emphasis is declining, that we are living in the era of the 'pure relationship', which is freely chosen and conditional for its continuation on both partners defining it as successful. While marriages may be less stable and enduring than was once the case, there is little evidence of the population abandoning the ideal of heterosexual monogamy – even if the reality is now more commonly serial monogamy. The vast majority of the population still marry at least once.

As an institution, heterosexuality is not just about sex, it is as much about who washes the sheets as what goes on between them (van Every 1996). As we have seen, women are still expected to service their husbands sexually and this is bound up with the other services they provide such as housework and child care. Historically, men acquired rights in women's bodies, property and labour through marriage. This is why, until 1990, a man could not be accused of raping his wife: if he did so, he was simply exercising his conjugal rights. It was and is sex (the act of consummation) that confirms the existence of marriage. Women still lack some basic rights in relation to their own bodies, for example a married woman cannot be sterilised without her husband's consent but the converse is not the case.

The assumption that everyone is or should be living in a heterosexual union with a male breadwinner has also underpinned the welfare state and structured the labour market. While many of the resultant gender inequalities are slowly being eroded (Chapter 3), the presumption of heterosexuality itself remains firmly in place. Not only is marriage by definition heterosexual, but rights to welfare benefits and pensions for dependants are premised on the normality of heterosexuality (Liberty 1994). Those who are not heterosexual have until recently been implicitly or explicitly excluded from entitlements granted to heterosexuals, such as access to reproductive technologies, rights to adopt or rights in relation to children they have co-parented but to whom they are not biologically related (Liberty 1994; Jackson 1997). Lesbian and gay sexualities have often been seen as 'threats to family values', the best example of which is the infamous clause 28 of the Local Government Act 1988, which barred local authorities from 'promoting' homosexuality and led to the presentation of homosexuality as a 'pretended family relationship' being outlawed in schools (Weeks 1991; Cooper 1995). These policies have begun to change, with the passing of the Civil Partnerships Act 2004 granting some of the rights associated with marriage to lesbian and gay couples, albeit at the price of conforming to conventional standards of monogamous coupledom (Jackson and Scott 2004).

The lesbian feminist writer Rich (1980) first coined the term 'compulsory heterosexuality' to emphasise that heterosexuality is imposed on us rather than freely chosen. Rich was concerned to explain the ways in which women are kept within the boundaries of heterosexuality and kept down within it (Jackson 1999). Some of her arguments apply only to women, for example the idea that lesbianism is a form of resistance to patriarchal domination. In other respects, however, the concept of compulsory heterosexuality can be applied to the ways in which both lesbianism and male homosexuality are socially and culturally marginalised. One of the most pervasive forms this takes is through the everyday assumption that everyone is heterosexual unless we know otherwise. Heterosexuals are rarely named and identified as such. While key aspects of their identity may be related to their heterosexuality (for example as a wife or husband), they rarely adopt the identity 'heterosexual' for themselves. Lesbian and gay sexualities, on the other hand, are routinely named and made visible as 'other'.

While heterosexuality entails a great deal more than sex, homosexuality is always and everywhere sexualised, and lesbians and gays reduced to their sexualities. For example, the rationale behind the exclusion (until the year 2000) of lesbians and gays from the British armed forces was that their sexuality was in some sense threatening to others, somehow ever present and predatory, threatening to undermine morale. Until the recent change in the law, lesbians and gays serving in the British military were, if discovered, immediately discharged, even if they had exemplary records in all other respects: the only thing that counted was their sexuality. Elsewhere, there are signs of greater tolerance even a certain fashionability associated with sexual dissidence, with lesbian and gay characters and images increasingly visible in the media. Yet lesbians and gays are still represented as the exception to the heterosexual norm.

The binary divide between heterosexuality and homosexuality has been deconstructed by what has become known as 'queer theory', a perspective developed by lesbian and gay writers influenced by post-modern theory. The main aim of queer theory is to expose the hetero/homo binary divide as a cultural artifice rather than a natural division, in such a way as to reveal its arbitrariness and instability. Hence, queer theory challenges the idea that there is such a thing as a fixed homosexual identity, rather queerness is constituted by its marginal location in relation to the heterosexual norm (Halperin 1995; Seidman 1997). Conversely, the normativity of heterosexuality depends on the identification of lesbians and gays as 'outsiders'; yet in shoring itself up in relation to its 'outside', it admits a destabilising potential, the possibility that lesbian and gay sexualities might disrupt its claims to be the only legitimate form of sexuality (Fuss 1991). Thus queer theorists tend to focus on the points at which heterosexual normativity can be disrupted. However, while heterosexual normativity might be unstable in theory, in everyday life it is sustained through a range of oppressive and coercive practices.

Physical violence and verbal abuse are still common experiences among lesbians and gay men; young gay men are routinely raped by heterosexual men in prisons. The HIV epidemic provoked widespread concern only when it was seen to be spreading from gay men to the 'general public' – the terminology used illustrates the exclusion of gay men from the 'normal' population (Watney 1987). This exclusion is underpinned by the law. While homosexual behaviour has been decriminalised since 1967, it is legal only within limited circumstances – in private (that is, indoors with no other person present in the house) and between 'consenting adults', and at present the age of consent remains 18, two years later than the age applying to heterosexual women. Sexual consent is a highly gendered concept. Applied to gay sex only after decriminalisation, it arose in a heterosexual context and rests on a construction of sex as something that men do and women consent to (McIntosh 1993; Waites 2005). This is why there has never been an age of consent for lesbians and indeed why lesbianism has never been legally prohibited. Since the definition of the sexual act has been enshrined in law as the penetration of a vagina by a penis, premised on the assumption of an active male and a passive female, women can neither initiate sex with each other nor consent to it. This absurd illogicality, while it might make lesbians safer from prosecution, effectively erases lesbian sexuality, stigmatising it as so 'unnatural' as to be beyond definition. Where lesbianism does come into view, it can provoke punitive responses. For example, until recently, lesbian mothers sometimes lost custody of their children solely on the grounds of their sexuality (Harne 1984). With the increased focus on equal human rights, this is no longer the case and lesbian and gay couples have been permitted to foster and adopt children.

Conclusion: sexual inequality and commodity culture

Hennessy (1998: 1) has drawn attention to the contradictions of a society in which claiming a non-heterosexual identity is, on the one hand, 'a potentially lethal transgression' and, on the other, a sign of radical 'cool'. She cites the case of a young gay man brutally beaten to death in the USA in October 1998, a far from isolated victim of bigotry in a nation where, according to the FBI, lesbians and gays are twice as likely to be physically assaulted as African-Americans. Yet at the same time, lesbians and gays are being marketed as icons of style in advertising, fashion and film. The continued stigmatisation of lesbian and gay sexualities persists in a society in which those same sexualities are increasingly visible, and apparently acceptable, in the cultural mainstream. This is not merely a case of bigotry and tolerance existing side by side, but tells us something about the limits of tolerance and the place of sexuality within the commodity culture of late modernity – a culture in which consumerism is increasingly associated with the maintenance of identity.

'Tolerance' is not, of course, the same thing as equality and even where valorised as 'cool', the radical chic that lesbians and gays embody depends on their marginal location in relation to the straight world. They are still singled out as 'other', whether damned as the perverse other or celebrated as the exciting, exotic other, and still serve to confirm the heterosexual norm in relation to which their 'otherness' is established. Lesbians and gays have made real gains in terms of rights, but their marginality creates a barrier to further progress. As Sinfield (1994: 189) puts it: 'The trick is to have us here but disgraceful'. Non-heterosexual lifestyles can be tolerated, even admired, as long as gays and lesbians know their place and do not attempt to challenge heterosexual privilege. Evans (1993) suggests that the only capacity in which lesbians and gays are regarded as full citizens is as consumers and this may have become a substitute for, and a deterrent to pursuing, more fundamental rights. The visibility of gays and lesbians within our society and culture is in part a result of their political struggles, but it is also a result of late capitalism's relentless search for innovative advertising images and new markets. Here it should be noted that the purchasing power of the 'pink pound' is concentrated in male hands, since lesbians share with all women a disadvantaged position in the labour market relative to men.

The commodification of gay sex is also part of a wider aestheticisation of daily life, evident in the preoccupation with 'lifestyle' in the commercial sense (Hennessy 1995, 2000). In this context, it is not only gay sexuality that has been commodified, but also heterosexual sex. 'Good sex' is itself increasingly associated with other indices of taste and style such as wearing the right jeans or drinking the right coffee (see Jackson and Scott 1997). The concern with sexual proficiency sustains and is sustained by a huge market in books and magazines devoted to sexual self-improvement. Meanwhile, the sociological evidence we have cited suggests that the lived reality of everyday heterosexuality is a long way from the glossy advertising and even the apparently endless 'consumer choice' offered by the new sex manuals entails little more than variations on the conventional sequence of heterosexual sex.

Of course, commercial sex itself is nothing new. Women's sexuality, in particular, has long been commodified through prostitution and pornography. Even when it is male sexuality on sale, it is marketed largely for male consumers. Many feminists have seen pornography and prostitution as an instance of the sexual exploitation, enslavement and objectification of women (see for example Jeffreys 1997). Others, however, see 'sex work' as just another occupation. Here the issue is the economic exploitation of workers and the exacerbation of that exploitation by their social exclusion (Alexander 1988). More careful research on sex workers themselves has illustrated the importance of keeping the gendering of sexuality in view, while avoiding the characterisation of sex workers as inevitable victims (see for example O'Connell Davidson 1998). We would argue that we need to keep both gender and sexual hierarchies in view when considering these issues. That it is largely men who provide the demand for this sort of sexual service should make us think critically about the construction of male sexual desires and ask why it is the prostitutes rather than their clients who are stigmatised. That commercial sex is today being transacted within a society that increasingly commodifies sex itself should also cause us to consider whether the marketing of sex opens up new possibilities for self-realisation, or imposes new constraints on us. We also need to take into account the ways in which the sexual marketplace is becoming increasingly globalised, as exemplified by sex tourism, the trafficking of women and children and the transmission of HIV and other sexually transmitted diseases across national boundaries.

The idea that we are all free consumers able to make whatever 'lifestyle choices' we choose is clearly sociological nonsense in a world still characterised by gross economic inequalities. In the sexual realm, access to choice in our sexual practices is limited by institutionalised heterosexuality and gender hierarchy. The concern with style and aesthetics also diverts attention away from the labour entailed in producing the objects we consume and where heterosexual sex is concerned this includes sexual services performed by women for men. The commodification of sexuality glamorises and mystifies sexuality, concealing the inequality, oppression and human suffering associated with the gender inequalities and heterosexual privilege underlying everyday sexual relations and practices.

Discussion Questions

1. Spend a day collecting examples from the media and conversations which illustrate the ways in which heterosexuality is privileged over other sexual preferences.

2. Look at the Sex Education Forum's website www.ncb.org.uk/sef/ and think about your own experience of sex education. Why do you think it is so difficult for adults to talk to young people about sexuality?

FURTHER READING

Chapters in Richardson, D. (ed.) *Theorising Heterosexuality: Telling it Straight* (Buckingham: Open University Press, 1996) address aspects of contemporary feminist debates on heterosexuality. A more recent collection on heterosexuality is Ingraham, C. *Thinking Straight: The Power, Promise and Paradox of Heterosexuality* (New York: Routledge, 2005). A useful historical account is provided by Weeks, J. *Sex, Politics and Society* (Harlow: Longman, 1989), which has an introductory chapter on theories of sexuality, and deals with social regulation up to and including the so-called 'permissive' era. Seidman, S. *Queer Theory/Sociology* (Oxford: Blackwell, 1996) includes some of the classic pioneering articles on the sociology of sexuality, as well as more recent work. A collection of reading covering feminist debates on sexuality since the 1960s can be found in Jackson, S. and Scott, S. (eds) *Feminism and Sexuality: A Reader* (Edinburgh: Edinburgh University Press, 1996). A more general sociological reader is *Sexualities and Society: A Reader* edited by Weeks, J., Waites, M. and Holland, J. (Cambridge: Polity, 2002).

CHAPTER 11

Disability

MARK HYDE

This chapter will provide you with a broad critical understanding of the following issues in disability as a source of social division:

- The medical model
- Social disadvantage reflects the choices made by individual disabled people: Marsland
- The social model
- The historical development of social disadvantage among disabled people: Abbott and Sapsford, Oliver
- Disadvantage in employment: Labour Force Survey
- Low income and poverty: Berthoud
- Inadequate community care provision: Barnes
- Unsatisfactory education provision: Barnes
- Ineffective employment policy: Hyde
- Negative stereotypes of disabled people: Reiser
- The internalisation of negative experiences by disabled people: Oliver and Barnes
- The distinction between organisations *for* and *of* disabled people: Oliver
- The decline of grassroots disability activism: Finkelstein
- Weberian class analysis and disability: Payne, Payne and Hyde
- Marxist class analysis and disability: Hyde

Without wishing to underestimate the dimensions of inequality reviewed in other parts of this book, which of course are also relevant to the concerns of this chapter, they do not account for the unique and intense forms of deprivation that disabled people experience. Although they represent more than seven million of the working age population, disabled people are largely excluded from satisfactory employment opportunities, experience considerably higher levels of poverty and are often dependent on state social services and benefits. Mainstream sociological approaches to the analysis of social divisions therefore provide a necessary but insufficient basis for understanding disability. Disabled people are disadvantaged because they belong to a social group that is the object of pervasive institutionalised discrimination. Thus disability engenders distinct forms of social inequality and, like gender, age and social class, should be regarded as an organising principle of social inequality in its own right. Disabled people are socially divided from the rest of society.

Disability in modern industrial society needs to be understood as a series of social restrictions that prevent disabled people from taking part in mainstream taken-for-granted activities, leading to profound social disadvantage. Although there is a substantial body of work on the significance of disability in contemporary society, it has largely developed outside mainstream sociology, in the specialist field of disability studies. It follows that the starting point for our analysis is to look at the concepts and perspectives used to (mis)understand disability, not least the recent ideas and arguments developed in official studies of disability, and the pioneering work of disabled writers (Union of Physically Impaired Against Segregation 1976; Barnes 1990; Oliver 1990).

Competing definitions

Debates about the meaning of disability in the social science literature typically centre on two definitions. 'Official' or 'medical' definitions tend to focus on the *functional limitations* of people with impairments, whereas the disabled people's movement has defined disability as the *social restrictions* faced by disabled people in their daily lives. Official and medical definitions of disability are usefully summarised by the International Classification of Impairment, Disability and Handicap (ICIDH), developed for the World Health Organization in 1981 (see Berthoud et al. 1993). The ICIDH distinguishes and links four concepts in a causal sequence; a *complaint* such as a spinal injury may lead to an *impairment* where a person is unable to control his or her legs, which may lead to a *disability* such as the inability to walk resulting in a *handicap* where the individual is unable to take part in normal day-to-day activities. This approach is often referred to as the 'medical model' because of its primary focus on impairment and functional limitation. Ultimately, it treats disability as a property of individuals who, because they are physically or mentally incompetent, are unable to take advantage of the opportunities enjoyed by those without impairments.

The influence of this individualistic medical model (see also Chapter 14) on official policy and government-sponsored research into disability is suggested by the nature of the questions in Table 11.1, taken from one of a series of OPCS surveys of disabled people in the UK (see Martin et al. 1988). The questions clearly suggest that the inability of the individual to take part in social activities can be explained in terms of an underlying impairment. Instead of promoting social rights and opportunities, the welfare state has attempted to compensate disabled people for the limitations allegedly imposed by their impairments, either by segregating them in specialist institutions or exposing them to rehabilitation programmes.

Table 11.1 Selected questions from the 1985 OPCS survey of disabled adults

1. Can you tell me what is wrong with you?
2. What complaint causes your difficulty in holding, gripping or turning things?
3. Does your health problem/disability mean that you need to live with relatives or someone else who can help look after you?
4. Does your health problem/disability make it difficult for you to travel by bus?
5. Does your health problem/disability affect your work in any way at present?

Source: Adapted from Oliver (1990).

In spite of its influence, the medical model has been criticised on a number of grounds. First, it takes the notion of 'normality' for granted and therefore as fixed, when what is and is not normal is socially and culturally relative. For example, the once widespread view of heterosexuality as the norm, backed by the law and sanctioned in mainstream arts, literature and especially popular culture (Chapter 10), is arguably now beginning to give way to a greater acceptance of diverse and legitimate sexual preferences. Second, the medical model fails to recognise the social constraints that prevent social participation and therefore offers only a partial explanation of social disadvantage. For example, while a focus on impairment may highlight some of the difficulties experienced by disabled people at work, it ignores discriminatory barriers such as prejudice among employers that impede their progress in the labour market. Third and following on from this, the medical model endorses policies that at best are likely to be ineffective in promoting social participation and at worst reinforce disadvantage and social exclusion. Employment policy has focused on individual rehabilitation, when an emphasis on the removal of discriminatory barriers may have been more successful (see Hyde 1996 for a fuller discussion).

Recognising these inadequacies, academics associated with the disabled people's movement have proposed a simpler classification scheme, which distinguishes two concepts, impairment and disability:

We define impairment as lacking all or part of a limb, or having a defective limb, organ or mechanism of the body; and disability as the disadvantage or restriction of activity caused by a contemporary social organisation which takes no or little account of people with physical impairments and thus excludes them from participation in the mainstream of social activities. (Union of Physically Impaired Against Segregation 1976: 14)

Frequently referred to as the 'social model', this approach to defining disability also makes causal assumptions about the factors underlying social disadvantage. It argues that people with impairments are excluded by a social environment that is inaccessible and discriminatory. For example, disabled people are often prevented from travelling to work, not by their inability to use the buses, but because public transport has been designed for the exclusive use of people without impairments. If the social model of defining disability had been used to frame the OPCS disability survey questions, they could have been reformulated to resemble those in Table 11.2. Clearly, these questions suggest that inability to take part in social activities can be explained primarily if not exclusively in terms of a discriminatory and inaccessible social environment.

Table 11.2 Survey questions informed by the social model

1. Can you tell me what is wrong with society?
2. What defects in the design of everyday equipment like jars, bottles and tins causes you difficulty in holding, gripping or turning them?
3. Are community services so poor that you need to rely on relatives or someone else to provide you with the right level of personal assistance?
4. Do poorly designed buses make it difficult for someone with your health problem/disability to use them?
5. Do you have problems at work because of the physical environment or the attitudes of others?

Source: Adapted from Oliver (1990).

Although the social model provides a definition that may be preferable to many disabled people, it is weakened by its apparent lack of reference to the role of impairment in restricting social participation. It is possible to imagine circumstances in which impairment is a considerable influence on a person's inability to perform social activities, for example people with profoundly debilitating mental impairments may find it difficult to take part in social activities, irrespective of how these activities are defined and organised. Although the limiting effects of impairment are not always this clear-cut, they should not be dismissed lightly.

The two definitions reviewed here provide radically different interpretations of disability, each of which is endorsed by particular social constituencies. The view of disability as the inability of the individual to perform normal social activities is not only widely held by the public but has been the main influence on government-sponsored disability research and policy. In contrast, the definition of disability as social restriction is endorsed by the disabled people's movement, by definition a much smaller and less influential minority group. Both definitions have distinct implications for the nature of social policies for disabled people.

Individualism

Any account of social inequalities would be incomplete if it did not consider the possibility that those who are socially disadvantaged are, by their own actions, responsible for their circumstances. Economic liberals, in particular, have advanced explanations of social disadvantage that focus on causation at the level of the 'individual'. This theme that has two variations, one focusing on labour market inequalities, the second on welfare dependency. Economic liberals reject the claim that occupational success reflects unfair social advantages accruing to privileged socio-economic groups, insisting that the market provides the foundation for a meritocracy where economic opportunities are open to all. Although middle-class children have a higher statistical probability of occupational success as adults (Chapter 2), Saunders (2000) argues that this largely reflects an unequal distribution of abilities, particularly 'intelligence', but also motivation However, occupational selection is sufficiently fluid to favour those from working-class backgrounds with demonstrable abilities, ensuring that, overall, individuals arrive at social class destinations to which they are entitled, by merit, irrespective of where they start from. But if low cognitive ability leads to occupational failure, it also increases the probability of long-term, work-limiting health problems, or so we are told. Those who perform poorly on ability tests have a significantly higher probability of unemployment due to physical disability, prompting Herrnstein and Murray (1994: 162) to speculate that 'smarter workers are typically more productive workers, and we can presume that some portion of what makes a worker productive is that he avoids needless accidents'. The authors acknowledge, however, that health problems may be cited as an 'excuse' for worklessness by a large number of non-disabled people who are merely unemployed, a notion that fits comfortably with the idea of 'welfare dependency'.

For economic liberals, welfare dependency results from a distinctive feature of contemporary society, the widespread availability of social security benefits.

A particularly influential variant of this argument is reflected in the work of Charles Murray on the underclass, which argues that a 'permissive' statutory commitment to welfare has progressively removed the structure of 'natural' incentives which encourage individual responsibility, in particular, the fear of destitution (Murray 1990, 1994). The availability and generosity of social security benefits have encouraged voluntary unemployment, which sets a bad example for young people, who are thus socialised into a culture of dependence. Increasingly, society is characterised by polarisation between a majority of 'motivated' households whose members are in employment and an underclass, an expanding segment of society which is geographically isolated, workless and morally impoverished.

Because they have remarkably high levels of economic inactivity, disabled people of working age are identified as being an integral part of this underclass. Economic liberals distinguish between a negligible number of those who are in receipt of disability benefits who are genuinely disabled – the 'deserving poor' – and the vast majority who are capable of working and, in effect, are fraudulently claiming benefits – the 'undeserving poor' (Marsland 1996). The problem of moral hazard has been particularly evident in the disability benefit system, where the possibility of collusion between medical practitioners and their patients has made it easier to qualify for benefits. There has been a proliferation of new official disability categories (as we shall see later in Table 11.4), expanding the size of the population that is, potentially, eligible for benefits. Most disability benefits have been provided on a long-term basis without sufficient assessments of work capacity. In short:

> The uptake of invalidity benefit and the prevalence of sickness absence from work is a function of the accessibility and generosity of benefits, entirely regardless of the objective condition of the population. (Marsland 1996: 124)

Welfare dependency, then, reflects the failure of the state to maintain economic conditions that promote individual responsibility.

This understanding of the causation of social disadvantage and its attendant welfare reform agenda were a clear influence on Conservative government social policies during the 1980s and early 1990s. In this view, because the overwhelming majority of those of working age who are in receipt of social security benefits, including disabled people, belong to the undeserving poor, they should be forced into self-reliance through rigorously applied means and ability tests. For this group, the route out of welfare dependency is, quite simply, the denial of social assistance (Murray 1990, 1994; Marsland 1996). For the deserving poor – those who are temporarily incapable of self-help – eligibility for social assistance should be based on needs rather than rights in order to ensure that provision goes only to those who are genuinely unable to support themselves, and it should be temporary (Marsland 1996). Time limits on benefit eligibility encourage the expectation of independence whilst obligations, of the kind inherent in workfare schemes, reinforce the principle that economic reward should be attached to personal effort. Ultimately, this exclusive focus on the promotion of self-reliance can be traced back to the 1834 Poor Law, which, through the incarceration of disabled people in the workhouse, sought to deter pauperism. Harsh as this may seem, however, economic liberals remind us that its modern equivalent, an efficiently administered programme of social assistance, is essential to the abolition of welfare dependency.

While the argument that perverse incentives in the social security benefit system discourage independence may have a degree of validity (Deacon 2002), the focus on causation at the level of the individual entirely ignores the social barriers that prevent disabled people from playing a full role in society. It is to these barriers that I now turn.

The social construction of disability

Although impairment, individual motivation and the social environment all play a role in preventing disabled people from participating in mainstream social activities, the latter must have primary importance in any sociological explanation of social disadvantage. In western societies, from Greek civilisation to the present day, disabled people have been socially marginalised, discriminated against and oppressed. However, social disadvantage among disabled people takes a distinct form in western capitalist societies, involving exclusion from economic activity and dependence on statutory social services.

In an influential contribution, Oliver (1990) relates the experiences of disabled people in contemporary society to the distinctiveness of capitalist economic relations. Before the Industrial Revolution, many disabled people were able to take part in economic activities that were largely based in scattered rural communities involving agriculture and small-scale industry. The development of industrial economic organisation during the eighteenth century had profound implications for disabled people:

> The speed of factory work, the enforced discipline, the time-keeping and production norms – all these were a highly unfavourable change from the slower, more self-determined and flexible methods of work into which many handicapped people had been integrated. (Ryan and Thomas 1980: 101)

The subsequent development of heavy industry based on coal, iron and shipping in the nineteenth century reinforced the exclusion of disabled people from employment. Moreover, the worth of individuals came to be assessed according to their economic value, particularly the extent and nature of their participation in paid employment. Thus the prevailing ideology of industrial capitalism, individualism, ensured that those among the working class who were not in employment were assigned an inferior social status.

This economic marginality was reinforced by the distinct form taken by many state welfare interventions during the nineteenth century. With the rise of capitalism, the 'total institution' was adopted as the main official response to the needs of the non-working poor. At first, people with impairments were treated less harshly than able-bodied paupers but, in practice, official concern about work incentives led to many being incarcerated in the workhouse. In distinguishing between able-bodied paupers and the long-term sick, the 1834 Poor Law represented a significant milestone in the treatment of disabled people. From the early 1800s onwards, disabled people were increasingly admitted to long-stay hospitals and asylums, indicating a shift in official responsibility away from the Poor Law authorities to the expanding medical profession (Abbott and Sapsford 1988). Medical practitioners assumed growing responsibility for the assessment, treatment and care of people with impairments – a legacy that continues to this day.

Institutionalisation continued to be the main official response to the needs of people with impairments up to the 1930s. Since then, there has been a significant shift in the location of care back to the community, but disabled people continue to experience isolation, social disadvantage and dependence. Oliver describes how these problems are constructed around three organising principles. First, disabled people continue to be excluded from employment, resulting in higher levels of deprivation and social exclusion:

> Work is central to industrial societies not simply because it produces the goods to sustain life but also because it creates particular forms of social relations. Thus anyone unable to work for whatever reason is likely to experience difficulties both in acquiring the necessities to sustain life physically, and also in establishing a set of satisfactory social relationships. (Oliver 1990: 85)

Second, disabled people are largely excluded from the formal political process, meaning that they are unable to take part in public debates about the development of rights, provisions and services to meet their needs. Policy for disabled people is framed by able-bodied public servants who have a poor understanding of the needs and aspirations of disabled people, resulting in the provision of inappropriate services. Third, services for disabled people are largely delivered by able-bodied professionals who often fail to take account of the felt needs and preferences of those who use them. Taken together, these experiences result in profound levels of social disadvantage among disabled people in Britain today.

Experiencing disability: economic disadvantage

The most striking levels of social disadvantage are experienced by disabled people of working age. Work is central to personal welfare and life chances in industrial society, but many disabled people are excluded from satisfactory employment opportunities. This can be illustrated by the findings of three main studies. The first is the Labour Force Survey (LFS) for spring 2003, which provides, inter alia, data on the labour market circumstances of disabled people in the UK (see Hibbett 2003). Second is a study of data combined from other UK official surveys, an OPCS survey of disabled people and the Family Expenditure Survey (FES), both conducted in 1985 (Berthoud et al. 1993). Although the data in this study are becoming slightly dated, it continues to be the most detailed quantitative analysis of labour market and social disadvantage among disabled people in the UK. Our third source is the 1994 European Community Household Panel (ECHP) survey, which provides the best source of comparable data on the labour market circumstances of disabled people in the member states of the EU (European Commission 1998).

Perhaps the most significant form of labour market disadvantage among disabled people is that they experience higher unemployment. Recent figures show disabled people have an official unemployment rate of 4.2 per cent, compared to only 3.7 per cent for non-disabled people (see Table 11.3). During times of high unemployment, this difference is greater: under the last Conservative government, disabled people had unemployment rates around 20 per cent compared with 7.5 per cent for non-disabled people (Hyde 2000).

These data show disabled people as only 1.1 times more likely to be unemployed, but this official figure underestimates the full scale of the problem because it excludes those who have been classified as 'economically inactive', that is, not in paid employment nor actively seeking it at that point; 51 per cent of disabled people were economically inactive compared to only 19.3 per cent of non-disabled people. The LFS study also provides an estimate of the proportion of those who are economically inactive who would nonetheless like to work; 14.1 per cent for disabled people and 2.7 per cent for non-disabled people. For convenience, this group can be referred to as the 'hidden unemployed'.

Table 11.3 The employment circumstances of people of working age in the UK (spring 2003 – not seasonally adjusted)

	Disabled		Not disabled	
	Millions	*Per cent*	*Millions*	*Per cent*
Population of working age	7.1	100.0	30.1	100.0
Economically inactive	3.6	51.0	5.8	19.3
Officially unemployed	0.3	4.2	1.1	3.7
Hidden unemployment				
Economically inactive but wants work	1.0	14.1	0.8	2.7
True unemployment[1]	1.3	18.3	1.9	6.4

Note
1 Official unemployment plus hidden unemployment.

Source: Labour Force Survey, spring 2003.

Table 11.3 shows that when the hidden unemployed are taken into account, the true unemployment rate for disabled people is 18.3 per cent compared to 6.4 per cent for non-disabled people. In other words, in 2003, disabled people were actually 2.9 times more likely to be unemployed, rather than the official figure of 1.1. This pattern of exclusion from work is evident in all EU member states, although unemployment levels among disabled people vary according to overall levels of unemployment. Thus in countries where general unemployment is higher, unemployment among disabled people is more significant; in countries where general unemployment is lower, unemployment among disabled people is less significant.

A second area of labour market disadvantage is suggested by the number of hours worked by disabled people in paid employment. Again, it is widely acknowledged that part-time work is not as highly regarded or rewarded as full-time work; part-time workers tend to be concentrated in low-status occupations, they have lower hourly earnings, fewer employment rights and little job security. On average, disabled workers are more likely to be found in part-time jobs. According to the LFS study, 28 per cent of disabled workers are in part-time work compared to only 22 per cent of non-disabled workers. The ECHP study suggests that disabled workers are more likely to be in part-time employment in all member states of the EU.

Disabled workers are also more likely to be employed in low-status occupations. The LFS study shows that 14 per cent of disabled workers are in 'elementary' occupations compared to only 11 per cent of non-disabled workers; 13 per cent of disabled workers are in managerial posts compared to

15 per cent of non-disabled workers; and 10 per cent are in professional occupations, compared to 12 per cent on non-disabled workers. The ECHP survey confirms that disabled people are disproportionately employed in low-status occupations throughout the member states of the EU.

The social division of age (Chapter 8) also interacts with disability in the employment field. Reflecting the 'ageist' values of the wider society (see Fennell et al. 1988), disabled workers tend to experience higher levels of labour market disadvantage when they reach 'middle age'. Berthoud et al. (1993) show that the chances of finding employment for disabled workers aged 45 and over are considerably less than for younger disabled workers. For the former, 'disability' and 'age' foster significant disadvantage in employment, resulting in higher levels of poverty. However, economic disadvantage is less significant among disabled pensioners who, as a group, are less likely than non-pensioners to be living on incomes that are below the state benefit poverty threshold. The overall impact of chronological age on the welfare of disabled people is therefore ambivalent. Labour market disadvantage has implications not just for the welfare of disabled people of working age but also for disabled people in retirement. Because their employment circumstances are unfavourable, disabled people are in a weaker position to accumulate savings and adequate pension entitlements. Their economic and social well-being is thus reduced throughout the life-course.

Evidence on the income of disabled people from employment is not as extensive as the areas that have been looked at so far, but it suggests that disabled workers are particularly disadvantaged in terms of their earnings. According to the LFS, disabled workers earn on average £1.02 per hour less than non-disabled workers. Similar earnings differentials are found elsewhere in the EU (European Commission 1998).

In view of these experiences, it is hardly surprising that disabled people have a higher risk of poverty. The OPCS/FES study (Berthoud et al. 1993) estimates that 45 per cent of disabled adults are living in poverty, while only 13 per cent could be classified as 'prosperous'. The poverty standard used is the long-term rate of means-tested social assistance, combined with an estimate of the additional costs that are often incurred by disabled people. Prosperity is defined as an income that is at least 200 per cent of this standard. Not surprisingly, poverty rates are higher among those not in employment (59 per cent), the long-term unemployed (42 per cent) and those on unemployment benefits (33 per cent). Prosperity rates are higher among those in employment (48 per cent) and those on a war pension or industrial injuries benefit (36 per cent). More recently, this picture of greater poverty has been reinforced by the findings of the LFS, which show that 37 per cent of working age disabled people are dependent on social security benefits, compared to a mere 5 per cent of the non-disabled working age population. Overall, the weight of evidence suggests that disabled people in the UK today experience profound economic disadvantage.

Experiencing disability: discriminatory social barriers

Social disadvantage among disabled people in modern industrial society reflects their experiences of discriminatory social barriers. This section explores the nature of some of these barriers, drawing on the findings of a number of studies of disabled people in the UK (Barnes 1990; Oliver and Barnes 1998; Barnes et al. 1999). The analysis below focuses on three areas of social policy; community care, education and employment practices.

While they represent a vast improvement on the institutional provision of previous decades, current arrangements for delivering community care are often unsatisfactory (see also Chapter 14). Although ostensibly designed to move away from a reliance on specialist institutions, institutional care continues to be a significant component of state support for disabled people. A large proportion of health and local authority spending on community care is directed towards residential and hospital-based services and many disabled people are confined to segregated residential homes.

The response of health and local authorities to the needs of disabled people who are living in the community at large is also widely regarded as being unsatisfactory (Chapter 14). For example, although local authorities are required by the 1986 Disabled Persons Act to provide disabled people with information that is relevant to their needs, few do so. According to OPCS surveys, many disabled people fail to receive the technical aids and equipment that they need; this limits their participation in mainstream social and economic activities and reinforces their dependence on others. Where assistance from local authorities is provided, it is largely directed towards informal carers rather than disabled people. Because they fail to receive the support they require to live independently, 'disabled people are denied the right to organise their daily lives in the same way as the rest of the population' (Barnes 1990: 144).

It is widely acknowledged that there is a strong association between educational attainment and employment outcomes (see Chapter 3), but disabled people are particularly disadvantaged in the education system. In principle, education policy in the UK has endorsed 'integrated' provision but in practice, a large number of children and young people with impairments continue to be educated in segregated special schools. If the perpetuation of special schools is the most obvious form of discrimination in the education system, children with impairments are also disadvantaged in mainstream schools.

Many receive their education in separate special educational needs (SEN) classes, while others are placed in classes with younger non-disabled children, even though their impairments may be physical. The low priority assigned to SEN within mainstream schools often leads to inadequate provision for children and young people with impairments (few teachers are trained to work with students with special needs). Not surprisingly, this results in lower levels of educational attainment.

Disabled people also experience considerable discrimination in tertiary education. Increasingly, young people with impairments are taking up places in further education, but the nature of the opportunities provided reflects those that are available in compulsory education and is therefore subject to the same criticisms. Disabled students are frequently segregated in special programmes in which they are invited to study courses in 'life skills' rather than academic or vocational areas. This further education experience does little to compensate for the lower levels of educational attainment from secondary education. Not surprisingly, very few disabled people become qualified for higher education. Because the education system is failing to enable disabled people to acquire the qualifications and credentials required for access to satisfactory employment, it is directly contributing to subsequent economic disadvantage among the disabled when they go on to seek paid employment (see Payne 2006).

However, the primary responsibility for the unsatisfactory employment circumstances of disabled people lies with employers; disabled applicants for jobs are six times more likely to be refused an interview than non-disabled applicants, even when they have suitable skills and qualifications. Employers are reluctant to adapt premises and equipment to the needs of disabled workers. Statutory employment policy and provision, despite any intention to counteract this, have in fact also played an important role in reinforcing labour market disadvantage among disabled people. The 1944 Disabled Persons (Employment) Act introduced the quota scheme, a measure which required employers to hire a 3 per cent quota of disabled workers. However, there were only ten prosecutions over a 50-year period for a failure to comply, even though a majority of employers have been 'under quota'. In 1996, the quota scheme was replaced by the employment provisions of the Disability Discrimination Act, providing disabled people with a right not to be discriminated against, but this legislation is widely regarded as being inadequate.

In practice, the government continues to rely on a policy of voluntary compliance and persuasion, even though a considerable volume of research has shown that a large majority of employers are prejudiced against, and in some cases actually hostile to, disabled people. The failure of the voluntary approach has resulted in many disabled people taking jobs in segregated sheltered workshops or subsidised placements in mainstream industry. For these reasons, employment policy has failed to provide an adequate response to the vocational needs of disabled people.

Given what is happening in other social institutions, perhaps it is not surprising that employment policy has been such a failure. Research has shown that discriminatory practices also pervade the political process, social security, transport systems, the mass media and the leisure industry (Oliver and Barnes 1998; Barnes et al. 1999). Many disabled people are therefore excluded from taking part in mainstream social activities. In a variety of ways, disabled people experience pervasive discrimination resulting in profound social disadvantage.

Structure, identity and action

If the experience of disadvantage and discrimination is a certainty for many disabled people, their responses to these problems is variable. A number of sociological studies of social divisions in contemporary society have posited a causal relationship between structure, identity and action (for example Crompton 1998); the assumption is that social conditions such as structured economic inequalities are strongly associated with individual psychology and behaviour and group identity (see Chapter 1). In the context of disability, 'structure' can be defined in terms of the discrimination and social disadvantage reported in the previous section; 'identity' is defined as the psychological responses of disabled people to these experiences, particularly the persona they adopt in relation to the social world; 'action' refers to their behavioural response to social marginality and, in particular, to patterns of acquiescence and resistance.

In addition to the forms of discrimination and social disadvantage already discussed in this chapter, disabled people are frequently the object of negative stereotypes in popular media such as books, movies, theatre, magazines and national and local newspapers. In a review of research on popular disability imagery, Reiser (1995) identifies a number of negative stereotypes that are perpetuated by the mass media. One powerful image is that disabled people are pitiable and pathetic. This stereotype is particularly evident in the publicity campaigns of the disability charities which aim to maximise income from public donations.

An alternative common stereotype is that disabled people are sinister and evil. For example, people with mental health problems are often presented as frightening and dangerous when in reality they are likely to be confused and withdrawn. A third stereotype is that disabled people are incapable of taking part in everyday life. This is mainly perpetuated by the absence of images of disabled people as members of the workforce, schools and families. Other negative media stereotypes about disabled people are that they are self-pitying and non-sexual. In the absence of positive images, it is hardly surprising that the general public regards disabled people in a negative light. The preponderance of these images perpetuates and compounds economic and social disadvantage.

Oliver and Barnes (1998) identify four mechanisms through which disabled people internalise these negative experiences and images. The first concerns those who are born with impairments who grow up as members of communities in which there are few disabled people to provide positive role models. Because they experience a range of discriminatory barriers from day one, children in this situation are socialised into an early acceptance of an inferior social status. We can contrast this position of early acceptance with the experiences of those with congenital impairments who are shielded from the wider community until they reach adolescence. Children in this category may not be fully aware of the existence of discriminatory barriers until they attempt to access mainstream social activities such as leisure and work. The acquisition of a negative personal identity for this group tends to occur during their late teenage years and early twenties.

A third mechanism of internalisation of negative experience concerns those who are forced to reconsider their personal identity as a result of acquiring an impairment. The sudden realisation that disability implies discrimination and exclusion often leads to negative feelings of hopelessness and despair. Oliver and Barnes' fourth mechanism relates the experiences of those who refuse to accept their impairment and attempt to pass themselves off as 'normal'. This is easier for those with a hidden disability such as diabetes but still requires diligence at managing information and social interaction. For those with an obvious impairment, denial is perpetually self-defeating. Many disabled people respond to their circumstances by adopting a negative self-image and, ultimately, a passive acceptance of discrimination and social marginality.

This suggests that the link between structure, identity and action is one-directional for a majority of disabled people. In spite of this, a growing number of disabled people have challenged conventional negative stereotyping, a process that has developed in the context of political self-organisation. The disabled people's movement provides a collective framework in which a minority of disabled people have been able to re-evaluate their negative experiences in the light of the social model, developing what might be described as a 'positive disabled identity'.

The disabled people's movement can best be defined by distinguishing between organisations *for* and organisations *of* disabled people. Organisations for disabled people are concerned with disability issues but are largely staffed by able-bodied people, working in partnership with national and local government agencies. Examples of such organisations include SCOPE, the Royal National Institute for the Blind (RNIB) and the Royal Association for Disability and Rehabilitation (RADAR). Organisations for disabled people have been criticised for adopting conventional official and medical approaches to the needs of disabled people. In contrast, organisations of disabled people are run exclusively by and on behalf of people with impairments and are informed by the social model.

Oliver (1990) develops a threefold typology of these organisations. 'Consumerist/self-help' organisations are those that provide services to meet the self-defined needs of members. A good example is the Centres for Independent Living, which aim to provide appropriate support for disabled people living in the community. 'Populist/activist' organisations typically focus on consciousness-raising and political action. During the 1970s, the Union of Physically Impaired Against Segregation was established to promote political organisation among disabled people living in residential institutions. More recently, the Direct Action Network has achieved national publicity through its involvement in a campaign of civil disobedience. 'Umbrella/coordinating' organisations are those with a membership of disabled people's groups. In 1981, the British Council of Organisations of Disabled People was established to provide a national focus for the activities of its constituent organisations. Now the British Council of Disabled People, this organisation has been at the forefront of the campaign against discrimination in the UK, and is itself a member of another umbrella organisation, the Disabled People's International. In addition to the three types of organisation, 'disability arts' has emerged as a form of cultural self-expression for disabled people.

The existence of these collective political and cultural activities may have a considerable impact on the psychological responses of disabled people to discrimination. The active propagation of the social model provides an alternative framework through which they are able to reinterpret their negative experiences, one that focuses on discriminatory barriers rather than personal inadequacies. The disabled people's movement also provides a focus for disabled people to become actively involved in challenging dominant negative stereotyping and discriminatory practices, an experience that can be profoundly empowering:

> Direct action is in your face. Disabled people are supposed to be invisible; they are not supposed to go out and be seen. Direct action has changed this. We are noticed! (Liz Carr, disabled activist, cited in Varo-Watson 1998: 13)

Significantly, collective organisation among disabled people can have a broader positive impact on society, as suggested by shifts towards minority programming on British television. Arguably, the Disability Discrimination Act 1995 was introduced in response to the growing public profile of discrimination, engendered by the activities of the disabled people's movement. If collective self-organisation provides an ideological and experiential framework within which disabled people develop a positive identity, it also has the potential to transform official responses to their needs, suggesting a multi-directional link between structure, identity and action.

Although the achievements of the disabled people's movement appear to be significant, it has recently been criticised by dissenting voices from within its ranks. It has been suggested, for example, that the movement is not representative of disabled people as a whole. A recent study by Barnes et al. (1999) observes that people with physical and sensory impairments are disproportionately involved in disability politics. While this seems to sit comfortably with popular stereotypes of disabled people, it may exclude a substantial number of people such as those with 'intellectual' impairments, in addition to those not registered as disabled but who have extensive literacy deficiencies (Payne 2006). Table 11.4 shows that 33 per cent of those who are defined as disabled by the Disability Discrimination Act have learning and understanding-related impairments. Similarly, Shakespeare et al. (1996) argue that disabled women, gays and lesbians are not adequately represented at an executive level within the disabled people's movement. This suggests that the 'positive disabled identity' associated with collective political action is a privilege that is enjoyed disproportionately by heterosexual disabled men with physical and sensory impairments.

Table 11.4 Type of reported functional problem by sex

Reported functional problem	Men	Women	All
Lifting and carrying	50	68	60
Mobility	52	50	51
Physical coordination	51	47	48
Learning and understanding	40	28	33
Seeing and hearing	26	17	21
Manual dexterity	21	19	20
Continence	15	13	14
Perceptions of risk	7	5	6
Unweighted base	500	763	1263

Note
Columns total more than 100 per cent as people could report having more than one functional problem. Base is all people covered by the Disability Discrimination Act.

Source: Adapted from Whitfield (1987).

Taking a different approach, Finkelstein (1996), a leading UK disability activist, identifies two recent developments which he believes have reduced the effectiveness of the disabled people's movement. First, he notes that there has been a shift away from 'grassroots' activity to parliamentary lobbying, resulting in fewer disabled people being actively involved in disability politics. Second, and perhaps more contentiously, he argues that the disabled people's movement has been 'hijacked' by disabled academics who have replaced the 'active' vision of disability rights as political action with the 'passive abstraction' of intellectual enquiry. For these reasons, Finkelstein believes the disabled people's movement has 'run out of steam'.

Disability and social divisions

These accounts of contemporary disability incidentally show how much of the source material has been only marginally 'sociological'. The basic framework for the analysis has, however, been sociological. The core idea has been a society characterised by social divisions, suggesting that social exclusion may have a variety of causes that need to be seen in terms of social processes shared with other social divisions. Nonetheless, it remains true that while in the late 1990s sociology has begun to provide some welcome descriptions of the social processes of disablement, it has largely failed to develop explicit and systematic theories to account for the unique and particularly intense deprivation experiences among disabled people.

Payne et al. (1996) provide a useful summary of three mainstream sociological approaches to understanding the relationship between social divisions and deprivation. Drawing on the work of Max Weber, one approach sees deprivation as resulting from people's (in)capacity to sell their labour to employers. A person's life chances including their income, health and housing are strongly associated with their type of employment, manifested in social divisions based on occupational status or class (see Chapter 2). In this view, deprivation is a consequence of sharply constrained ability to sell one's labour in a socially defined market, leading to unemployment or low occupational status. This approach has particular relevance for the circumstances of disabled people who, as reported above, experience considerable difficulties in selling their labour to employers. It identifies the interaction in the labour market between the sellers (both abled and disabled) and the buyers (employers). However, it does not entirely explain the processes that produce the disproportionate representation of disabled people among the ranks of the semi-skilled and the unemployed, suggesting the need for a more specific and clearly defined focus on disability.

Perhaps a more fruitful approach within the Weberian sociological tradition is provided by 'consumption sector' theory, which argues that social divisions need to be understood in terms of differential access to public and private welfare. Encouraged by privatisation policies during the 1980s and 90s, growing numbers of working-class households have opted out of the welfare state, leaving behind a minority who are entirely dependent on public sector provision, providing the basis for a new social division based on consumption sector. However, although disabled people are disproportionately dependent on the state, their consumption experiences are not identical to those of other groups of the poor. As reported previously, many disabled people are excluded from areas of state welfare provision such as local authority housing and mainstream education and instead are segregated in special disability programmes. While it seems to articulate the exclusion of disabled people from private welfare, consumption sector theory fails to specify their unique experiences of state welfare.

Post-Marxist formulations of the 'non-working poor' seems to be particularly relevant to understanding the experiences of disabled people in industrial society. For Wright (1993), the key to understanding this 'underclass' lies in the exclusion of the poor from satisfactory education and training, leading to long-term unemployment. Paradoxically, although the non-working poor are largely surplus to the requirements of the industrial system, they are sometimes deployed as a 'reserve army' to accommodate fluctuations in the demand for labour.

Using this approach, Hyde (1996, 1998) describes how disabled people were actively encouraged to take up paid employment during the Second World War to substitute for able-bodied men who had been conscripted into the armed forces; after the war, they were promptly expelled from the labour market and segregated into special employment programmes. During the 1980s, out-of-work disability benefits were expanded, and the disabled were reclassified as being entitled to non-work-related benefits as part of the Conservative government's massaging of the official unemployment count. Currently, disabled people of working age are, once again, being encouraged to enter the labour market, 'assisted' in no small measure by the welfare reforms of the 'New Labour' government (see Hyde et al. 1999 for a fuller discussion). This government wishes to reverse Conservative policies, believing that a combination of vocational training and reductions in eligibility for welfare benefits will encourage disabled people to take up employment opportunities in the flexible labour market. While a focus on labour market regulation seems to account for changes in employment policy for disabled people, it fails to explain fully the disproportionate representation of the disabled among the ranks of the non-working poor, which, as we have seen, has much more to it than state policies alone.

The three approaches reviewed so far have little to say about the particular experiences of disabled women even though they often have higher levels of social disadvantage than disabled men. For example, the LFS reported earlier shows that the higher incidence of low-paid, low-status and part-time work among disabled women mirrors similar trends among non-disabled women, highlighting the importance of underlying gender inequalities. While feminist theories have been instrumental in promoting a growing profile for gender divisions in sociology (Chapter 3), they have neglected deprivation experiences that are specific to disabled women. For example, the latter's failure to conform to popular cultural body images leads many physically disabled women to be stereotyped as unattractive and non-sexual. Thus, in addition to the discrimination and disadvantage they experience because of their gender, disabled women are often prevented from taking up traditional female roles such as those of wife and mother.

It has also been argued that 'ethnicity' is a powerful source of social division among disabled people, although there is much less published empirical evidence on this. For Vernon (1998), black disabled people experience the 'double disadvantage' of racial discrimination (Chapter 4) and discrimination on the grounds of disability. When combined, both result in qualitatively distinct and intense forms of social disadvantage.

The interplay that we have seen between disability and other social divisions – ethnicity, gender, age and occupational class – means that there is a general framework of analysis with which to explore the isolation of disabled people. However, contemporary sociology on its own can provide a necessary but as yet insufficient basis for understanding disability in present-day society. Disabled people have unique and particularly intense experiences of deprivation, suggesting that there is something distinctive about their circumstances. It has been argued throughout this chapter that disabled people:

- experience profound levels of economic disadvantage, resulting in intense deprivation and, ultimately, a poor quality of life
- are particularly dependent on state social services and benefits, which means they are frequently regarded as objects of charity
- are often segregated by state welfare programmes, reinforcing the belief that they are unable to take part in mainstream social activities
- experience a significant level of state regulation, a problem that may undermine individual freedom and autonomy
- experience considerable discrimination throughout society, resulting in exclusion from a range of mainstream social activities
- are the object of negative stereotyping in popular media. Negative attitudes towards disabled people are deeply entrenched in popular culture.

The distinctiveness of these experiences suggests that disabled people are divided and separated from the able-bodied in the rest of society: disability provides the foundation for a social division in its own right. Like other disadvantaged groups in society, disabled people experience pervasive institutionalised discrimination. At the same time, their experiences of disadvantage may also be shaped by broader social divisions based on social class, consumption and gender. Ultimately, a flexible approach is required that recognises the specificity of disability as distinct from other social divisions but which is sufficiently sensitive to recognise differences between disabled people.

Discussion Questions

1. Can social disadvantage among disabled people be explained in terms of individual characteristics, such as impairment or work motivation?

2. Does class analysis provide an adequate foundation on which to develop an explanation of social disadvantage among disabled people?

3. How useful is the distinction between 'structure', 'identity' and 'action' in identifying the possibilities for creating a fairer and more equal society?

FURTHER READING

Barnes, C., Mercer, G. and Shakespeare, T. *Exploring Disability* (Cambridge: Polity Press, 1999) provides an up-to-date and comprehensive introduction to disability, while a 'classic' statement of the social model can be found in Oliver, M. *The Politics of Disablement* (London: Macmillan – now Palgrave Macmillan, 1990). Barton, L. (ed.) *Disability and Society: Emerging Issues and Insights* (Harlow: Longman, 1996) is a collection of articles from the journal *Disability & Society*, which looks particularly at how sociological theories may be applied to disability research and the experiences of disabled people. The findings of the first comprehensive audit of discriminatory social barriers in the UK, Barnes, C. *Disabled People in Britain and Discrimination* (London: Hurst Calgary, 1990), still contain many relevant insights.

The Interplay of Social Divisions

CHAPTER 12

Poverty

LUCINDA PLATT

This chapter will provide you with a broad critical understanding of the following issues in poverty as a source of social division:

- Why poverty is a social division
- Poverty definitions: lack of income
- Lack of necessities
- Deprivation
- Inability to participate in social life
- Lack of capability for not being deprived
- Relative versus absolute poverty
- Poverty as a fixed amount of income or goods
- Poverty conceived relative to socially endorsed standard
- Poverty relative to changing incomes or income at a fixed point in time
- Changes in poverty over time
- Experience of long-term versus short-term poverty
- Poverty as a social division: ethnicity, gender, age or stage of life

At first glance, poverty may seem like a self-evident concept synonymous with lack of income. Lack of income, however, implies other 'lacks': it is often felt that poverty can only be understood explicitly through its consequences. Poverty can therefore be defined as *a level of income* which renders it impossible or unlikely that certain material goods can be obtained or certain activities can be engaged in, or, alternatively, as *the direct lack of those goods and activities*. It can sometimes also be defined (a little problematically) as *the poorer outcomes themselves* in terms of health, educational achievement and so on that are more likely for those on a low income. For example, the UN Report of the World Summit (1995) talks about poverty's

> various manifestations, including lack of income and productive resources to ensure sustainable livelihoods; hunger and malnutrition; ill-health; limited or lack of access to education and other basic services; increased morbidity and

mortality from illness; homelessness and inadequate housing; unsafe environments and social discrimination and exclusion. It is also characterised by lack of
participation in decision making and in civil, social and cultural life. It occurs in
all countries: as mass poverty in many developing countries, pockets of poverty
amid wealth in developed countries, loss of livelihood as a result of economic
recession, sudden poverty as a result of disaster or conflict, the poverty of low-
wage workers, and the utter destitution of people who fall outside family
support systems, institutions and safety nets. (quoted in Howard et al. 2001: 21)

This wider perspective shows that poverty is also closely associated with other
social divisions – such as class, ethnicity and gender – being both produced by
those divisions and contributing to their character. For example, certain ethnic
minorities are over-represented among the poor, leading to poorer outcomes for
them. Equally, their over-representation is in part a consequence of differential
treatment by wider society (Chapter 4). In addition, it is often argued that there
is a cyclical aspect to poverty, such that poverty results in poorer outcomes
which lead to a greater risk of subsequent poverty. The relationship between
poverty and health, whereby poverty leads to poorer health outcomes, but those
who are ill are also more likely to be poor, is one illustration of the intertwined
nature of cause and effect in relation to poverty (Chapter 14). In order to understand these connections, we need as a first step to give further consideration to
the different definitions of poverty that have been used.

What is poverty?

Poverty can be defined as a state in which lack of resources leads to an unac-
ceptably low standard of living. However, what is meant by 'resources' and
what is deemed acceptable is clearly open to debate, resulting in a plethora of
approaches and measurements, from living on less than a dollar a day, to specifying a particular 'basket of goods and services' which people need in order to
avoid poverty.

In Britain, much of the debate has focused around distinguishing a supposedly *absolute* level of poverty from a *relative* standard. According to this
distinction, 'absolute poverty' is regarded as being concerned with minimum
human needs for survival, such as implied in the following quotation:

a condition characterised by severe deprivation of basic human needs,
including food, safe drinking water, sanitation facilities, health, shelter, education and information. It depends not only on income but also on access to services. (UN 1995, quoted in Gordon et al. 2000: 9)

The levels of deprivation that existed in nineteenth-century Britain or currently exist in other parts of the world (Townsend and Gordon 2002) do not encompass the experience of the British population today. This recognition has on occasions led people to deny that poverty is an issue in Britain at all. For example, the former senior Conservative minister Sir Keith Joseph said in 1976 that: 'A family is poor if it cannot afford to eat ... By any absolute standards there is very little poverty in Britain today' (quoted in Oppenheim and Harker 1996: 8).

In contrast, 'relative poverty' is concerned with specifying people's lack of welfare relative to acceptable standards within the society in which they live. For example, this is the understanding in the following EU definition:

> the poor shall be taken to mean persons, families and groups of persons whose resources (material, cultural and social) are so limited as to exclude them from the minimum acceptable way of life in the Member State in which they live. (European Commission 1984, quoted in Gordon et al. 2000: 12)

This latter approach, with its emphasis on exclusion, fits more comfortably with the idea of 'social division'.

The focus on relative poverty is intended to challenge the denial of poverty that in more recent times has sometimes gone with an absolute poverty perspective, although, in making the distinction, it can reinforce the misleading impression that there is a more fundamental alternative definition that can be employed. The definition of poverty as a relative concept owes much to the work of Peter Townsend, who, with colleagues including Brian Abel-Smith, was responsible for the 'rediscovery of poverty' in the late 1950s and 60s. Their investigations demonstrated that the post-war welfare state had not succeeded in eliminating poverty, as had previously been assumed (Abel-Smith and Townsend 1965).

Townsend, in developing his understanding of poverty (most comprehensively put forward in his major study *Poverty in the United Kingdom* in 1979), set his approach in opposition to what he saw as the absolute definition of poverty originally propounded by Rowntree, and first established with the latter's primary poverty line in his 1899 study of poverty in York (Rowntree 1902). This approach to poverty was repeated and re-used by both Rowntree and other social investigators subsequently (Rowntree 1918, 1937, 1942; Rowntree and Lavers 1951). In fact, however, as Veit-Wilson (1986) has pointed out, Townsend's conception of Rowntree's primary poverty line as an absolute definition of poverty against which to contrast his own approach derived from a misreading of Rowntree (see also Hennock 1991).

Townsend was, then, effectively establishing a 'straw man' of absolute poverty to emphasise those aspects of his own conception of 'relative poverty' that stressed the importance of the ability to participate in everyday life according to contemporary standards:

> Poverty can be defined objectively and applied consistently only in terms of the concept of relative deprivation ... The term is understood objectively rather than subjectively. Individuals, families and groups in the population can be said to be in poverty when they lack the resources to obtain the types of diet, participate in the activities and have the living conditions and amenities which are customary, or are at least widely encouraged or approved, in the societies to which they belong. Their resources are so seriously below those commanded by the average individual or family that they are, in effect, excluded from ordinary living patterns, customs and activities. (Townsend 1979: 31)

'Luxuries' and the bare 'necessities' of life

The absolute/relative dichotomy was also pursued in the work of Amartya Sen, who returned to the work of Adam Smith, the eighteenth-century social philosopher and economist. Sen argued that while the understanding of what constitutes deprivation or excludes people from participation may be contextually specific, there are underlying elements or capabilities which everyone requires, although they may be differentially interpreted or mean different things in different circumstances. Adam Smith, as long ago as 1776, had argued that undergarments were essential for acceptability within contemporary society, even if they may not have been in Roman times. In a much cited passage, Smith said that:

> By necessaries I understand, not only the commodities which are indispensably necessary for the support of life, but whatever the custom of the country renders it indecent for creditable people, even of the lowest order, to be without. A linen shirt, for example, is, strictly speaking, not a necessary of life. The Greeks and Romans lived, I suppose, very comfortably, though they had not linen. But in the present times, through the greater part of Europe, a creditable day-labourer would be ashamed to appear in public without a linen shirt, the want of which would be supposed to denote that disgraceful degree of poverty, which, it is presumed, nobody can well fall into without extreme bad conduct. (Smith 1976: 399)

Sen (1983) took off from this position to argue that freedom from shame constitutes a capability or essential which is necessary for someone not to be deprived. What goods or attributes will allow such freedom are contextually specific – in Smith's day a linen shirt, in other times and contexts something else. Sen thus maintained that it was important to retain the absoluteness of needs in the conception of poverty. He argued for seeing needs in terms of needs for absolute minimum capabilities, which:

> translates into a relative approach in the space of commodities, resources and incomes in dealing with some important capabilities such as avoiding shame from failure to meet social conventions, participating in social activities, and retaining self-respect'. (Sen 1983: 167–8)

Or, as he expressed it in a lecture given in 1985:

> Some capabilities, such as being well nourished, may have more or less similar demands on commodities (such as food and health services) irrespective of the average opulence of the community in which the person lives. Other capabilities, such as the ones with which Adam Smith was particularly concerned, have commodity demands that vary a good deal with average opulence. To lead a life without shame, to be able to visit and entertain one's friends, to keep track of what is going on and what others are talking about, and so on, requires a more expensive bundle of goods and services in a society that is generally richer, and in which most people have, say, means of transport, affluent clothing, radios or television sets, and so on. Thus, some of the same capabilities (relevant for a 'minimum' level of living) require more real income and opulence in the form of commodity possession in a richer society than in poorer ones. The same absolute levels of capabilities may thus have a greater relative need for incomes (and commodities). There is thus no mystery in the necessity of having a 'relativist' view on the space of incomes even when poverty is defined in terms of the same absolute levels of basic capabilities. (Sen 1987: 18)

Sen's attachment to retaining an absolute element in defining poverty resulted in a somewhat unedifying print disagreement between himself and Peter Townsend. The latter rejected the idea that any 'absolute' understandings of poverty should have a role in its definition, while the former objected to being misrepresented (Sen 1985; Townsend 1985). Nevertheless, substantively, the distance between them does not seem to be that wide. In fact, despite Townsend's major contribution to ways of thinking about poverty that incorporate understandings of participation and social activity rather than simply material needs, the absolute/relative distinction, even as it retains wide currency is a somewhat spurious one, as Ringen (1988) has noted.

This soon becomes apparent at the level of measurement. As soon as researchers are faced with the business of attempting to identify what constitutes poverty in order to count those in poverty or distinguish the poor from the non-poor, it is impossible to escape consideration of what is normative practice and what is local convention. Adam Smith had recognised this in the eighteenth century, not only in his famous discussion of the linen shirt, which recognised the relevance of temporal context, but also in his discussion of shoes, which, he observed, could vary geographically and with gender at the same point in time:

> Custom, in the same manner, has rendered leather shoes a necessary of life in England. The poorest creditable person of either sex would be ashamed to appear in public without them. In Scotland, custom has rendered them a necessary of life to the lowest order of men; but not to the same order of women, who may, without any discredit, walk about bare-footed. In France, they are necessaries neither to men nor to women; the lowest rank of both sexes appearing there publicly, without any discredit, sometimes in wooden shoes, and sometimes bare-footed. Under necessaries therefore, I comprehend, not only those things which nature, but those things which the established rules of decency have rendered necessary to the lowest rank of people. (Smith 1976: 399–400)

Moreover, when trying to consider what normatively defined practices or goods could actually be seen as necessary, he was found to waver in his consideration of beer from one edition of *The Wealth of Nations* to the next. Such indeterminacy illustrates both the salience of the researcher's judgement (on the relevance of explicit judgements in poverty measurement, see Atkinson 1987) and the recognition of the significance of actual behaviour patterns, regardless of what is formally recognised as important. Smith states categorically:

> All other things I call luxuries; without meaning by this appellation, to throw the smallest degree of reproach upon the temperate use of them. Beer and ale, for example, in Great Britain, and wine, even in the wine countries, I call luxuries. A man of any rank may, without any reproach, abstain totally from tasting such liquors. Nature does not render them necessary for the support of life; and custom nowhere renders it indecent to live without them. (Smith 1976: vol II, 400)

Yet the 1976 editor points out that in the original version of the list of necessities in volume I, malt beer was listed first, before 'soap, salt, leather, candles etc.' (Smith 1976: vol I, 488).

A similar difficulty with separating custom or habit from even socially defined needs can be found in Rowntree's development of his supposedly 'absolute' poverty measure. First, Rowntree took pains to show that his 'primary poverty' line was actually an inconceivable measure in terms of people's actual or expected behaviour:

> And let us clearly understand what 'merely physical efficiency' means. A family living upon the scale allowed for in this estimate must never spend a penny on railway fare or omnibus. They must never go into the country unless they walk. They must never purchase a halfpenny newspaper or spend a penny to buy a ticket for a popular concert. They must write no letters to absent children, for they cannot afford to pay the postage. They must never contribute anything to their church or chapel, or give any help to a neighbour which costs them money. They cannot save, nor can they join sick club or Trade Union, because they cannot pay the necessary subscriptions. The children must have no pocket money for dolls, marbles, or sweets. The father must smoke no tobacco, and must drink no beer. The mother must never buy any pretty clothes for herself or for her children, the character of the family wardrobe as for the family diet being governed by the regulation, 'Nothing must be bought but that which is absolutely necessary for the maintenance of physical health, and what is bought must be of the plainest and most economical description.' Should a child fall ill, it must be attended by the parish doctor; should it die, it must be buried by the parish. Finally, the wage-earner must never be absent from his work for a single day. (Rowntree 1902: 134)

In addition, even his 'primary poverty' line used relative elements: it took the actual cost of housing, and involved a discussion with his subjects over the minimum cost of adequate and respectable dress. In Rowntree's attempt to develop his poverty line into a more realistic measure of poverty (*Human Needs of Labour*, 1918), he engaged in deliberations comparable to those of Adam Smith over beer when considering whether meat and tea – and even alcohol – should be included in a basic diet:

> In this country almost everyone takes a mixed diet – even the poorest try to get a certain amount of meat; and though undoubtedly health can be maintained without it, we cannot, in selecting our dietary, ignore the fact that meat-eating is an almost universal custom. So is the drinking of tea and coffee, and though these do not actually supply any nutriment, a certain amount must be included in the dietary … I think we may reasonably exclude alcoholic beverages, but should bear in mind possible expenditure upon them when considering the amount to be allowed for personal sundries. (Rowntree 1937: 78–9)

The measurement of 'absolute' poverty was always a lot more relative than the proponents of a relative line have made out. And the suggestion that specifying a minimum set of goods *in itself* presupposes an absolute approach to poverty is similarly misleading. Baskets of goods (and services) representing the selection of goods necessary to avoid poverty do not in themselves constitute absolute measures, and are not necessarily open to the criticism that they do not reflect normative standards and expectations. Indeed, Townsend's own poverty measure in his major (1979) study (discussed further below) was constituted from a selection of goods and activities deemed to represent an appropriate standard of living at the time. It is the failure to adjust such baskets of goods to changing circumstances that leads to their appearing inappropriate or inadequate.

Thus, despite its currency and use as a reference point, the absolute/relative dichotomy tends to dissolve as soon as we move to operationalisation and measurement. Whatever the chosen operationalisation, it will occur along a continuum rather than involving a dichotomous distinction. And, in all measurement, both judgement (about what actually constitutes necessities or a poverty line) and context (a relationship to what occurs and/or is acceptable in the surrounding society) continue to have a bearing, regardless of the claimed approach.

Before moving on to consider the measurement of poverty, however, it is important to mention another context in which the absolute/relative contrast is used. This is in relation to the common practice of measuring poverty or low income by means of proportions of average income. The numbers or population proportions of those below a proportion of average income, such as 50 per cent of the mean or 60 per cent of the median, can be compared over time. In such comparisons, the proportion in poverty can be measured in relation to contemporary average income allowed to vary year by year (the 'relative line'). Alternatively, the value of the proportion at a particular point in time can be held constant, and the proportions below that fixed value can be compared over time (the 'absolute line': we shall come to examples of these two lines over a comparable period in Figure 12.2 later). While it is appropriate to make a distinction between these two approaches to an income line, the terminology in terms of absolute versus relative has very little connection with the debate on *defining* low income in absolute or relative terms. This is because the choice of year at which to set the absolute line and hold it fixed is an arbitrary choice which is not supposed to represent a fixed set of necessities (indeed, it is relative to the population in the year in which it is set). Representing the distinction as one between relative and absolute low income, while a widespread practice, can thus potentially lead to confusion. For this reason, I prefer to use the formulation of 'proportion of contemporary income' and 'proportion of income of x year held constant'.

Measuring poverty

There are two primary ways in which to measure poverty among the population or among sub-populations. The first of these is by *income*, representing the resources available to achieve a particular standard of living. The basis for setting the income level is the moot question. The alternative is to attempt to measure *standard of living* directly. Again, what indicators should be used for measures of standard of living, and at what point to designate an individual or household in poverty or suffering material deprivation, are vexed questions.

Using *income* as a means of measuring poverty has a number of advantages. It is transparent and easy to understand and is available as a measurement in a wide range of sources from which we might wish to estimate poverty. While assumptions about necessities and reasonable expenditure might go into setting the amount of income that constitutes the poverty line, it also does not require that people actually spend their money in particular ways, and therefore allows for people getting welfare out of a set income in a diverse manner of ways. It also enables direct comparison with incomes provided by subsistence benefits intended to meet minimum needs. Moreover, income lines allow comparison over time much more straightforwardly than measures of consumption, which may either become out of date or, if adjusted over time, result in difficulties in claiming that they are strictly comparable.

On the other hand, a number of criticisms can be made of income as a poverty measure. It is only a proxy for standard of living (Ringen 1988), that is, it does not necessarily measure standard of living or consumption. These may be related to future expectations and ability to incur debt, the length of time that poverty has been experienced or the differential costs of goods and services for those in different circumstances (for example disabled as opposed to able-bodied: Chapter 11) or living in different areas (for example the wide variations in housing costs by area: Chapter 13). In fact the development of longitudinal measures of income poverty, as well as extra costs measures and different adjustments for households of different composition have made some of these criticisms less salient, while excluding housing costs in certain circumstances avoids one of the most problematic aspects of defining a consistent poverty level (see below).

When setting an income poverty line, there have been two main approaches. The 'basket of goods' or 'budget standards' approach is based on estimating the cost of a set of goods necessary to avoid poverty (or ensure participation). The more arbitrary but simpler approach is to select a fixed proportion of average income. Additional approaches have been to use the actual value of subsistence benefits or some multiple of them (for example Abel-Smith and Townsend 1965), or select some essential components of standard of living (such as food) and increase these by a factor deemed to take account of expenditure on other essentials (for example Orshansky 1965).

The first main method, the budget standards approach, was developed by Rowntree in setting his 'primary poverty line' in his first study of York (Rowntree 1902) and was subsequently adopted in a range of poverty surveys, as well as in Rowntree's own *Human Needs of Labour* (1918). More recently, there have been a number of studies which have adopted this approach. Piachaud (1979) estimated an income line for children, to enable direct comparison with allowances in supplementary benefit allowances; Bradshaw and colleagues developed a set of budgets for a selection of families of different sizes and compositions (Bradshaw 1993); and Parker with others developed income levels for both families with children and older people (Parker 1998, 2000). In each of these instances, the lines could be explicitly compared with subsistence benefit rates for families with the same composition as those estimated, thus illustrating the adequacy (or inadequacy) of state benefits which have never explicitly used estimates of needs in their rates, even though implicitly such benefits constitute a poverty line (Veit-Wilson 1992, 1994; Platt 2003b). Bradshaw explained this potential:

> Policy makers who have responsibility for making decisions about the level of benefits can be faced through budget standards with the consequence of those decisions. If the low cost budget is more than the income support scales then they can indicate which items in the budget claimants should expect to go without. (Bradshaw 1993: 238)

Early proponents of the budget standards approach used it to set a poverty line for the whole population, by attempting estimates of additional adults and children as well as for families, so that the proportion of a population in poverty could be counted by comparison of incomes with this line. However, the more recent studies do not easily allow for this: geographical specificity in the Bradshaw project and the lack of disaggregated costs in the Parker project militate against such uses. Moreover, while illuminating at the time, the extent to which they can be effectively uprated over time is questionable.

Although budget standards are not intended to be prescriptive, but instead to act as reference points, they at least *imply* that if incomes based on them are not spent roughly as indicated, the family will suffer hardship.

Piachaud, on the other hand, has argued that it might be more appropriate to take as an income measure the level of income at which the vast majority of the population (he suggests 95 per cent, leaving 5 per cent who would perhaps never allocate income to identified necessities) can be guaranteed to spend the prescribed amounts on the different necessities, even if their priorities are not those specified by the 'ideal' budget (Piachaud 1987: 159–60).

Given the difficulties that budget standards measures have in providing methods of estimating poverty in the population, it is perhaps unsurprising to find that the income poverty measures which have gained the greatest currency among both researchers and governments are those which enable a straightforward estimation of proportions and composition of those in poverty at a point in time and over time. The establishment of the *Households Below Average Income* (HBAI) series in the mid-1980s has provided an annual series of measures of low income in relation to various proportions of household income adjusted for household size and composition. It also demonstrates the relative risks of different forms of household of falling below the relative proportions, and the proportion of different household types across fifths of the income distribution. Currently, the preferred cut-off for low income is 60 per cent of median income by 'equivalised household' (see below). Trends over time and differential risks of different family types using the 60 per cent of median cut-off are illustrated below.

These relative income lines of poverty have been criticised on the grounds that they are informative about inequality but not about poverty per se (Sen 1983). Others would argue that inequality is in itself significant: and this was the approach adopted in the Joseph Rowntree Foundation *Inquiry into Income and Wealth* (Hills 1995b; see also the discussion of this point in Atkinson 1987). In fact, a highly unequal distribution of resources is likely to exclude those near the bottom, as the discussion above has shown (see also Goodman et al. 1997). Wilkinson (1996) has repeatedly argued that as far as health is concerned, in developed countries it is inequality as such rather than income which results in health divides and that greater equality of income, even at lower average level (once a certain minimum has been achieved), results in better average health.

While the poverty or low income lines used in this approach are, in a sense, arbitrary, they represent an acceptance of the notion that poverty is related to general living standards and, in so far as average income is a proxy for them, participation in or attainment of normative standards of living are hard to achieve at incomes that fall far short of the average. It has also been recommended that to verify the picture of poverty and who it affects, particularly for comparative purposes, a range of lines can (and should) be used (Atkinson

1987, 1998). Relative poverty lines, by being comparable over time and over populations, also enable evaluation of the extent to which policy is influencing the extent of poverty in a population. For example, the current government's aim of eliminating child poverty within a generation can be (and is) evaluated against the proportions of children in child poverty according to such a measure, although other measures of child poverty are also employed (DWP 2002, 2003).

The extent to which poverty lines are appropriate for measuring risks of low income across individuals living in different sizes of household will depend to a certain extent on the way that household incomes are adjusted to take account of the number (and ages) of the people living in them. HBAI uses an adjustment scale known as the McClement's scale. This adjusts incomes of households to make them comparable to a household containing two adults. Thus, single-person households with the same real income are accorded a higher 'equivalised' income and households with two adults and children are accorded a lower 'equivalised' income. The McClement's scale tends to estimate the proportion of income absorbed by children rather parsimoniously, which may downwardly bias estimates of children in poverty. On the other hand, individuals' consumption or standard of living may not be fully represented by the household income adjusted for size, as distributions may not be equitable within the household. In so far as children are prioritised for expenditure by their parents, they may be better off than their household income implies. There may also be variations in the experienced standard of living according to sex, to the extent that actual distributions of household income are gendered, an issue taken up in the discussion of differential risks of poverty below.

As well as giving proportions of the population below different fractions of average income, HBAI also provides two estimates of the distributions of equivalent incomes: those before and those after housing costs have been deducted (BHC and AHC). Housing costs have always been a problematic element of measuring poverty because of their geographic variability and the fact that people are not necessarily able to choose cheaper accommodation than that which they occupy. Thus, in order to engage with the fact that greater spending on housing may not necessarily represent greater amenity and a higher standard of living, disposable incomes after housing expenses are also measured. Poverty rates AHC tend to be higher than those BHC and thus this procedure may give an inflated account of poverty relative to overall equivalised incomes. Nevertheless, it may be useful to use AHC when comparing groups which are likely to be differentially geographically concentrated. For example, in illustrating the extent of poverty in Britain today (below), I give the estimates of poverty for the whole population BHC, but when comparing ethnic groups I give the estimates AHC to account for the facts that the different ethnic groups have distinct patterns of regional distribution and several minority groups have high concentrations in London, which is an area of extremely high housing costs.

Temporal issues in poverty measurement

Income-based poverty lines, then, represent the most appropriate measure of poverty, even more so when they are able to take the issue of time into account (Platt 2004a). There are two aspects of time that are important in the measurement of poverty – life-course and poverty duration. Life-course issues refer to the fact that there are times when people are more vulnerable to poverty, which also might have knock-on effects on their subsequent experiences. One example might be students, who may have very low incomes – and high levels of debt – but whose future income is likely to be above average, and their current consumption patterns may in part reflect their anticipated income. Another example would be lone parents, who are on average more vulnerable to poverty, even though some will move out of poverty faster than others. Those who become poor, for example through divorce or separation, may also be at greater risk of poverty later in life through missed pensions contributions (Ginn et al. 2001; Bardasi and Jenkins 2002; Ginn 2003). Being able to recognise poverty risks and their implications at different points in the life-course is obviously important for understanding well-being in the population and appropriate policy intervention. Given the changing relationships between income and consumption throughout the life-course, expenditure rather than income provides a better and more direct measure of well-being and poverty, although it brings its own issues of complexity of measurement and reliability.

The second issue is that of duration of poverty. Poverty for ten years is more serious in terms of its impact on both standards of living and life chances than poverty for one month. While this aspect of poverty duration has been recognised as significant for a long time – and has been one of the criticisms of the appropriateness of cross-sectional income measures as representations of poverty risks – it is only relatively recently that it has been possible to measure durations of poverty in Britain. The measurement of poverty as a temporal phenomenon and a state that people can enter and leave (and return to) has also tended to emphasise the conceptualisation of poverty as a general risk rather than an inherent characteristic of certain individuals (Jarvis and Jenkins 1998; Noble et al. 1998). The inception of the British Household

Panel Survey (BHPS) in 1991, where members of a representative sample of households are re-interviewed annually and their experience over time charted, has been a core element in the ability to track poverty over time (Taylor 2003).

Material disadvantage and consumption

Consideration of poverty duration has also illustrated that there is a connection between the duration of income and the inability to participate or have particular consumer goods, which is the alternative way of measuring poverty. The two types of current poverty research thus tend to come together here. Nevertheless, there is ongoing development of measures of material disadvantage and commitment to them as direct rather than proxy measures of poverty.

In his 1979 survey, Townsend measured poverty using a range of indicators, without which people were deemed to be disadvantaged. Nevertheless, he attempted to use these to identify a point of income at which a steep decline in participation in everyday life occurred. Despite criticism of his method and his indicators (Piachaud 1981), a number of other studies building on his work have tried to use direct measures of poverty to ascertain the levels of disadvantage in this country (see Payne et al. 1996). Some, which argued that they were producing a consensual measure of poverty (Mack and Lansley 1985; Gordon and Pantazis 1997; Gordon et al. 2000), used a sample of respondents to validate which of the listed items and activities were necessities. Those items which were regarded as necessities by 50 per cent of the population were considered to reflect a consensus about what represented an adequate standard of living. Deprivation or poverty was deemed to be present among those who did not have – and did not have because they could not afford – two or more of the necessities.

There was much subsequent discussion of the desirability and practicality of a consensual measurement of poverty (Walker 1987; Veit-Wilson 1986; Piachaud 1987), including criticism of deeming a bare majority to represent consensus. Re-examination of the survey on these lines has shown that there is substantial heterogeneity in the rating of necessities by different subgroups of the population (McKay 2004). The fact that necessities measured this way might be inappropriate for measuring deprivation among subgroups of the population has also been pointed out (Platt 2002, 2004b). Moreover, the combination of deprivation measures with a confirmatory low income measure is clearly problematic for the claims of a direct measurement of poverty through deprivation indicators, as is the arbitrary choice of a cut-off of deprivation at two or more items.

Another focus on the measurement of material deprivation that has been influential in developing the role of deprivation measures in poverty research and measurement was carried out with Irish data (Callan et al. 1993; Nolan and Whelan 1996), but has more recently been expanded to incorporate European comparisons as well (Whelan et al. 2001; Layte et al. 2001). In these studies, part of the point has been to show that deprivation and low income do not necessarily correlate, although again the combination of material deprivation and low income is held to represent a truer understanding of poverty. There has also been criticism here of the meaningfulness – and the susceptibility to policy intervention – of an index of deprivation that is supposed, through indicators, to represent an underlying continuum of poverty. In addition, it could be pointed out that the measures of deprivation are market-based and can be therefore be removed through expenditure – thus a conceptualisation in relation to income levels is already implicit. Moreover, in the Nolan and Whelan study (1996), it transpires perhaps unsurprisingly, that it is the element of time which explains the difference between those suffering deprivation as a result of current low income and those not. Those who were not suffering deprivation had only been on a low income short term, and the longer the duration of low income, the greater the levels of deprivation.

Despite some of the problems around the use of measurements of material deprivation to represent poverty, they have nevertheless been incorporated into the government's assessment of progress on its child poverty targets by the Department of Work and Pensions (DWP 2003). Moreover, a set of questions on participation and necessities, which check both for their lack and their lack through unaffordability (to avoid conflation with lifestyle choices) is regularly asked in many national surveys.

To summarise some of these different issues around conceptions, definitions and measures of poverty, Figure 12.1 illustrates the different ways that poverty has been conceived and measured and the intersections between them. Three general approaches are identified, which then lead via the solid lines to different measures and definitions. These illustrate the multiple ways in which poverty has been realised. However, as the dotted lines make clear, there are points of correspondence across the measures stemming from the different approaches (even if their proponents would dispute them). What is taken to be poverty becomes more a matter of emphasis than approaches being inherently contradictory.

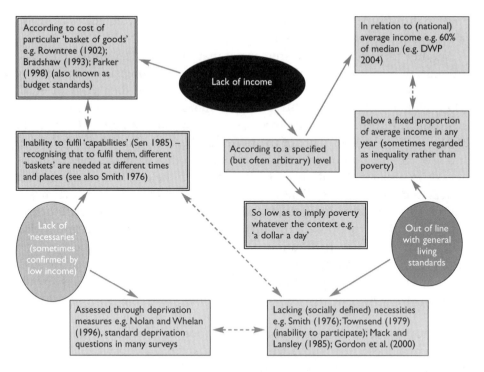

According to cost of particular 'basket of goods' e.g. Rowntree (1902); Bradshaw (1993); Parker (1998) (also known as budget standards)

Lack of income

In relation to (national) average income e.g. 60% of median (e.g. DWP 2004)

Below a fixed proportion of average income in any year (sometimes regarded as inequality rather than poverty)

Inability to fulfil 'capabilities' (Sen 1985) – recognising that to fulfil them, different 'baskets' are needed at different times and places (see also Smith 1976)

According to a specified (but often arbitrary) level

Lack of 'necessaries' (sometimes confirmed by low income)

So low as to imply poverty whatever the context e.g. 'a dollar a day'

Out of line with general living standards

Assessed through deprivation measures e.g. Nolan and Whelan (1996), standard deprivation questions in many surveys

Lacking (socially defined) necessities e.g. Smith (1976); Townsend (1979) (inability to participate); Mack and Lansley (1985); Gordon et al. (2000)

Figure 12.1 What is poverty?

Poverty in Britain today

We can start by looking at the trends in the proportions in poverty going back to 1979. Figure 12.2 shows a poverty line held constant at 60 per cent of the 1996/7 median as well as the proportions below 60 per cent of contemporary income. This enables us to see the shape of what happened to the real incomes of those in the lower part of the income distribution over the period, as well as how the proportions in poverty relative to the contemporary income rose, with the rapid increase in inequality over the 1980s, and has only recently declined (and even then not back to 1979 levels).

Figure 12.3 illustrates the trends over a shorter period and broken down by person type, that is, between men, women and children. It shows the higher risks of poverty among women and children both when the poverty line is held constant at 1996/7 values and when it varies with contemporary income. It also shows that the while the differences remain they have tended to narrow over time.

Figure 12.2 Proportions of the population in poverty (1979–2002/3)

Source: Derived from DWP (2004a), Tables H1 and H5.

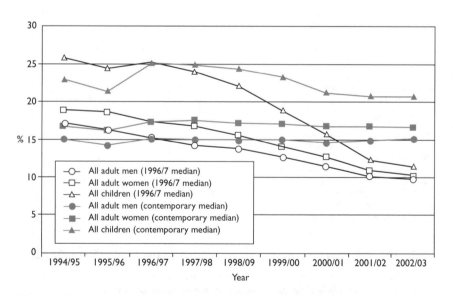

Figure 12.3 Proportions of population below fixed and contemporary poverty lines according to person type (1994/5–2002/3)

Source: Derived from DWP (2004a), Tables D5.1 and D9.1.

Moving on to look at trends measured in terms of material deprivation, Figure 12.4 compares those deprived of certain activities/necessities because of their unaffordability. The indication is that over the six-year period measured, there was a substantial decline in deprivation across households on all measures. Given the assumption about the relative and contextual nature of poverty, it might be possible to ask whether the questions asked in 1996 are still pertinent in 2002; however, the relatively short period between the two time points would suggest that they should still be reasonably salient in 2002 if they were in 1996.

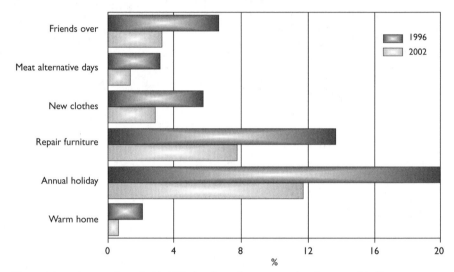

The set of questions was first asked in 1996, therefore a longer comparison is not possible. The actual form of the questions used to derive these measures is as follows: Here is a list of things which people might have or do. Please look at this card and tell me which things you (and your household) have or do?

    Keep your home adequately warm.
    Pay for a week's annual holiday away from home.
    Replace worn-out furniture.
    Buy new, rather than second-hand, clothes.
    Eat meat, chicken, fish every second day.
    Have friends or family for a drink or meal at least once a month.
And for each item they do not have:
Would you like to be able to [item], but must do without because you cannot afford it?

Figure 12.4 Material deprivation among households (1996–2002)

Source: British Household Panel Survey, main sample households (n=4978 in 1996, n=4574 in 2002) with cross-sectional weights, author's analysis.

Similarly, looking at the number of indicators on which households are deprived (Figure 12.5), we see that a reduction at all levels of deprivation would appear to hold across the seven-year period.

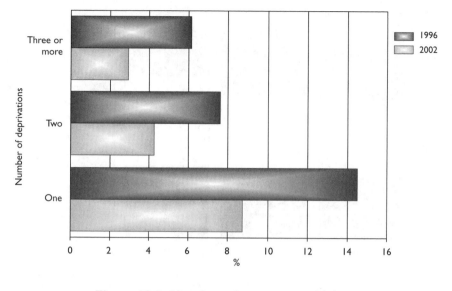

**Figure 12.5 Number of counts on which
households are deprived (1996–2002)**

Source: British Household Panel Survey, main sample households (n=4978 in 1996,
n=4574 in 2002) with cross-sectional weights, author's analysis.

Another way to consider how well people are doing is to consider their own subjective views of their situation. The results of asking people their perspective on how well they are managing financially and the change in that over time is shown in Figure 12.6. Here 1991 and 2002 are compared. 1996 is also included for comparability with Figures 12.4 and 12.5. It shows a declining number of respondents finding it quite or very difficult to get by and an increasing number 'doing alright'.

The trends give some indication of declining poverty but with a share of the population still excluded from the normal activities of everyday life. Turning now to look in more detail at the composition of the poor, we can consider either the differential risks of people according to their household characteristics or, alternatively, the profile of all those in poverty. Table 12.1 provides the distribution across fifths of the income distribution for those living in households with different economic profiles. It shows the way those in households where all adults are earning are concentrated towards the top of the distribution while those in households with economically inactive and unemployed adults are concentrated overwhelmingly in the bottom 40 per cent of the income distribution.

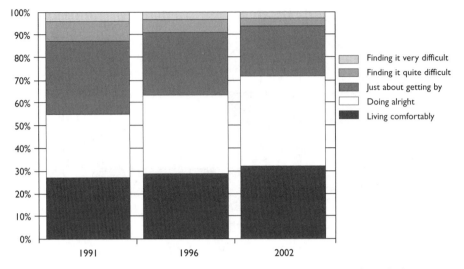

The form of the question is 'How well would you say you yourself are managing financially these days? Would you say you are: Living comfortably; Doing alright; Just about getting by; Finding it quite difficult; Finding it very difficult'.

Figure 12.6 Subjective views of poverty (1991–2002)

Source: British Household Panel Survey, Main sample respondents
with cross-sectional weights, author's analysis.

Table 12.1 Percentages of individuals across fifths of the income distribution according to household economic status (2002/3)

	Bottom fifth	Second fifth	Middle fifth	Fourth fifth	Top fifth
One or more full-time self-employed	19	15	16	20	31
Single/couple in full-time work	4	8	20	31	37
Couple, one full-time, one part-time work	4	16	28	29	22
Couple, one full-time work, one not working	17	25	21	19	17
No full-time, one or more part-time work	27	28	20	14	11
Workless, head or spouse aged 60 or over	29	31	21	12	7
Workless, head or spouse unemployed	70	16	9	3	3
Workless, other inactive	51	28	12	6	3
All individuals	**20**	**20**	**20**	**20**	**20**

Source: DWP (2004a), Table 3.1 (BHC).

Table 12.2 shows the risks of falling below the 60 per cent of the median threshold for those in households with a range of characteristics that are associated with higher risks of poverty. It shows the poverty risk, (that is, the proportion of the group in poverty), measured before and after housing costs.

Table 12.2 Percentage of individuals in poverty by characteristics of household/household head (2002/3)

Characteristics of household/household head	Below 60% median BHC	Below 60% median AHC
Workless, head or spouse aged 60 or over	24	25
Workless, head or spouse unemployed	64	75
Workless, other inactive	43	64
White	16	20
Mixed	18	31
Indian	20	22
Pakistani/Bangladeshi	59	69
Black Caribbean	24	32
Black non-Caribbean	30	46
Chinese or other ethnic group	23	32
1 or more disabled adults	22	27
1 or more disabled children	23	29
Disabled adult(s) and disabled child(ren)	30	38
All individuals	17	22

Note
Household characteristics are not mutually exclusive – risks on one characteristic may be associated with risks in another (for example high rates of worklessness among certain minority groups; higher risks of disability among those who are retired), or may be compounded (for example the risks of poverty among those from particular ethnic groups who are also living with a disabled adult may be particularly high).

Source: DWP (2004a), Tables 3.5 and 3.6.

By contrast, Table 12.3 shows the share these high-risk groups make up of those who fall below the 60 per cent median line, revealing the way that poverty rates and numerical representation in the population intersect, so that most of the poor are not from the highest risk groups. Both approaches are important from a policy point of view, as impacting on the high-risk groups will do most to meet the demands of social justice and avoid the exclusion from society of certain groups, while focusing on those who make up the biggest share of the poor is likely to do more to bring down overall poverty rates.

Table 12.3 Contribution of individuals in households at risk of poverty to all those below 60 per cent of median income (2002/3)

Characteristics of household/household head	Proportion of all those below 60% median BHC	Proportion of all those below 60% median AHC
Workless, head or spouse aged 60 or over	24	19
Workless, head or spouse unemployed	11	10
Workless, other inactive	28	32
Mixed	1	1
Indian	2	2
Pakistani/Bangladeshi	6	5
Black Caribbean	2	2
Black non-Caribbean	2	2
Chinese or other ethnic group	2	2
1 or more disabled adults	35	33
1 or more disabled children	6	6
Disabled adult(s) and disabled child(ren)	3	3

Note
Proportions are not additive as they neither include those without high risks of poverty (for example non-disabled adults) nor are they mutually exclusive (many of those living with a disabled adult may also be living in a workless household).

Source: DWP (2004a), Tables 3.3. and 3.4.

As has been mentioned, income poverty over a period could offer a preferable way of considering people's resulting levels of deprivation. On the other hand, understanding the factors associated with risks of moving into or chances of moving out of poverty can be important for policy purposes. Jenkins and Rigg (2001) explored both the persistence of poverty among individuals, and how they differed by individual and family characteristics, as well as identifying moves into and out of poverty and 'trigger' events associated with them. Using four-year and nine-year windows of observation, they found that while in any given year, around 20 per cent of the population were poor, 35 per cent were poor for at least one year in four, and 14 per cent were poor for three or four of the four years. Eight per cent of the population were poor for at least seven out of nine years, representing a group who are likely to be highly deprived and marginalised.

However, chances of being continuously in poverty varied with the characteristics of the individual: children were more likely to be persistently poor than adults and women were more likely to be persistently poor than men. Of those in one-parent families, 35 per cent were persistently poor, compared to 13 per cent of couples with children; and 25 per cent of single pensioners experienced persistent poverty compared with 17 per cent of pensioner couples. Poverty persistence in workless households with an unemployed head reached 47 per cent. Changes in labour earnings accounted for the largest share of both moves into and moves out of poverty, but demographic events (for example the birth of a child) were also important in accounting for moves into poverty.

Cappellari and Jenkins (2002) used multivariate methods to explore the risks of persistent poverty and becoming poor. This meant that they could look at the risks associated with individual or household characteristics, measuring their effect net of other characteristics. They found that, controlling for the other factors, having a household head who was young, a lone parent, Pakistani or Bangladeshi, or lacking educational qualifications increased the probability of both moving into poverty and remaining there. Being poor itself was also shown to increase the risks of poverty per se, thus contributing to the idea that poverty can lead to reduced opportunities and a vicious cycle of increasing deprivation and exclusion.

Differential risks of poverty: ethnicity; gender; children

There is extensive evidence that minority group members have both higher risks of poverty than the majority and also that there are great differences between different minority groups in relation to the proportions in poverty: this is particularly true of minority ethnic groups (Berthoud 1997, 1998; Platt 2002, 2003a). While all minorities appear to experience excess poverty, that is, higher rates than those for the population as a whole, for some, in particular Bangladeshis and Pakistanis, the levels of poverty are extremely high. And even here, although these two groups are commonly aggregated in available statistics, there are differences between the groups, with Bangladeshis having substantially higher rates of poverty than Pakistanis. Figure 12.7 shows the differences in poverty rates between the different groups (using 60 per cent of the median AHC as the threshold). The striking rates of poverty among Bangladeshis and Pakistanis and the excess rates of poverty for both adults and children from all minority groups are clearly evident. While factors such as concentration in deprived areas, demographic profile and differential rates of educational achievement play some part in explaining the differences in poverty between different minorities and the majority, all the evidence suggests that there remains an 'ethnic penalty' in incomes, as in earnings and employment, which cannot be accounted for by the characteristics of group members (see for example Heath and McMahon 1997; Blackaby et al. 2002; Platt 2002).

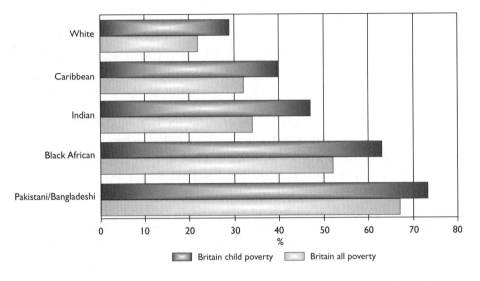

Figure 12.7 Proportions of all individuals and children below 60 per cent of the median (AHC) by ethnic group (2001/2)

Source: Adapted from Platt (2003c), Figure 4.4.

As Figure 12.3 illustrated, women have a higher risk of poverty than men. Yet the relatively small gap in the proportions in poverty disguises the fact that certain groups in which women are over-represented have much higher risks of poverty (Rake 2000). The two most striking such groups are lone parents (of whom 90 per cent are women) and older single people, among whom women are over-represented (Chapter 8), and for whom poverty risks are much greater than for male single pensioners (Chapter 3). The poverty of older women and lone parents has been extensively discussed (for example Rowlingson and Mackay 1998; Ginn 2003). Here I give the risks for these two groups as found in the most recent HBAI. Figure 12.8 shows the increased risks for single female pensioners and how those risks increase with age. It also indicates the scale of the issue, with a substantial proportion of pensioners falling into this particularly vulnerable group.

Moving on to look at lone parents, the poverty risks of a lone parent are 29 per cent, compared to risks of 14 per cent for an adult living as part of a couple with dependent children. However, only 5 per cent of working age adults are lone parents, with the result that lone parents make up only 11 per cent of those living below 60 per cent of median income, while couple parents (who form 30 per cent of working age adults) make up 29 per cent of the poverty among such adults.

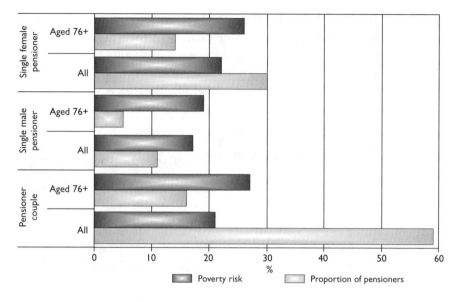

Figure 12.8 Poverty risks and proportions in risk groups among older people (2002/3)

Source: Derived from DWP (2004a), Tables B9 and G3.1.

Marriage or living in a partnership would appear to protect women against poverty to a degree. However, the situation is not as clear-cut as that, since the way these poverty proportions are calculated assumes both certain economies of scale within households and that the aggregate income of all household members will result in the same standards of living for all household members. To a certain extent this is a valid assumption, in that housing, amenities and common goods such as refrigerators are likely to benefit all household members in a fairly similar fashion. However, the assumption that net household income is equally shared has long been problematised, particularly in relation to women's command over resources (Glendinning and Millar 1992).

Thus there may be hidden poverty among women within partnerships that apparently take them above the poverty line and the poverty of women living on their own may not be, after all, such a striking contrast with the experience of some of their partnered counterparts. On the other hand, there is evidence from some studies (Middleton et al. 1997) that parents, and particularly mothers on a limited income, will sacrifice their standard of living to ensure that their children are not deprived. However, in their study of child poverty over an extended period of time, Gregg et al. (1999: 210) used the expenditure data in the Family Expenditure Survey to extrapolate whether the spending on children reflected increasing poverty of their families and found that it did. The authors concluded that 'increasing inequality in expenditure is having a direct impact on the living standards of children, and excluding the poorest from the rising material well-being of the majority'.

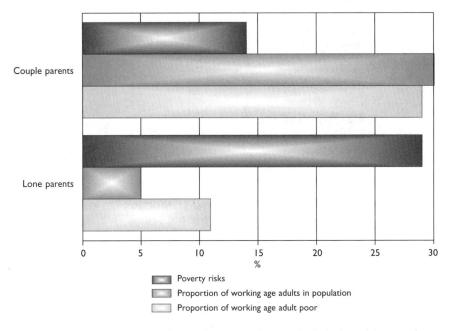

Figure 12.9 Poverty risks and proportions of adult (working age) poor among couple parents and lone parents (2002/3)

Source: Derived from DWP (2004a), Tables B6, F3.1, F5.1.

Children as a group have tended to suffer higher rates of poverty in Britain than the population as a whole, as Figures 12.3 and 12.7 indicated. They have historically borne much of the burden of total poverty, which has been shown to have the potential to have lasting impacts into their later lives. Nevertheless, despite strong campaigning interest over an extended period, it is only with the current administration that their poverty has been acknowledged as a priority within government (Walker 1999; Platt 2005). In a lecture in 1999, Tony Blair famously announced that:

> Poverty should not be a birthright. Being poor should not be a life sentence ...
> Our historic aim will be for ours to be the first generation to end child poverty,
> and it will take a generation. It is a 20-year mission but I believe it can be done.
> (Blair, 1999: 17)

Children are recognised as being a particular concern because of their perceived vulnerability (Chapter 9), the fact that they are the future of the nation and fears that disadvantage can repeat itself across generations in a cyclical form. Moreover, international comparisons have shown that not only did rates of child poverty earlier in the decade cause Britain to rank near the top of the league table of industrial nations, but that the excess poverty experienced by children relative to their adult compatriots (as illustrated in Figure 12.3) – a persistent feature of poverty in Britain – is not a universal phenomenon (Bradbury and Jäntti 1999).

Table 12.4 Children's poverty risks

Risk characteristic	Proportion in poverty	Proportion of all children	Share of children in poverty
Lone parent	52	25	45
At least one adult in work, but not all	32	26	29
Workless households	79	18	48
Three children	32	22	25
Four or more children	48	10	18
I or more disabled adults	39	17	24
Indian head	22	2	2
Pakistani/Bangladeshi head	75	4	10
Black Caribbean head	39	2	2
Black non-Caribbean head	53	1	3
Chinese or other ethnic group head	35	2	2
All children	**28**	**100**	**100**

Source: DWP (2004a), Tables 4.4 and 4.7.

Children's individual risks of poverty are not just a function of their status as children but also vary with other household characteristics, such as ethnicity, disability and economic activity. As we saw earlier (Figure 12.7), the increased risk of poverty by ethnicity is not just a consequence of certain groups having more children than others but even within groups, children tend to have a higher risk of poverty than adults. Conversely, children from different ethnic groups have widely varying poverty risks. Table 12.4 illustrates the poverty risks for children according to household characteristics associated with higher than average poverty. It also shows the prevalence of such characteristics within the child populations, with, in the third column, the consequent contribution of such households to total child poverty. Again we see that the highest risks are not necessarily associated with major contributions to total child poverty, given their relatively low prevalence. The exceptions are workless households and lone-parent households, where very high risks combine with substantial prevalence to result in either of them (and there will be substantial overlap between the two) contributing almost half of child poverty.

In addition, the development of longitudinal assessments of child poverty have illustrated the importance of considering the duration of poverty in attempting to explain and understand the impact of poverty on life chances (Ashworth et al. 1992; Duncan et al. 1998). Work on specifically British children's poverty durations using the BHPS has shown not only the higher risks of poverty persistence among children (Jenkins and Rigg 2001) but also how vulnerable children can be to extended periods of poverty at particular stages in their upbringing (Hill and Jenkins 2001).

Conclusion

This chapter has shown that while poverty and what it means to be poor is intuitively straightforward, the concept can prove complex in terms of both definition and measurement and has been much contested. Nevertheless, it has been argued that there are clear points of contact between the various approaches and that the reality of poverty – a state of disadvantage which impacts on life chances, divorces people from connections with the surrounding society, finds expression in a lack of the basic goods with which normal life can be pursued and is cumulative in effect – is a characteristic of modern Britain.

Moreover, poverty disproportionately affects particular groups in the population: it is both an illustration and a consequence of social divisions. Thus, the recognition of the different poverty rates – between different ethnic groups, between different age groups, between disabled and able bodied, between men and women – serves to give such distinctions continuing salience. While the reasons for these different poverty rates may not rest in the characteristics themselves (why should disability per se increase the risks of poverty?), it reveals the ways in which society is structured so that it impacts disproportionately on those from particular groups or with particular characteristics. Thus an analysis of poverty and poverty rates is a crucial element to understanding the operation of social divisions within society.

This chapter has stressed the importance of a temporal understanding of poverty. Poverty needs to be located within a specific temporal context and measured over time to be fully meaningful. A further temporal issue is the patterns over time and whether we should be optimistic or pessimistic in relation to the future. Tony Blair's commitment in 1999 to abolish poverty – or at least child poverty – within a generation was a highly significant moment, as it marked both an explicit recognition at government level of the existence of poverty and made a commitment towards doing something about it.

This statement was reinforced by both the words and policies of the Chancellor, Gordon Brown. At the beginning of 2005, he reiterated in print that 'our aim is the freedom of every child and every adult to fulfil their potential' (Brown 2005). While a time of increasing prosperity may mark a good point at which to redistribute wealth in order to ensure that there are no groups left behind in poverty, if a time of recession came, it might test the commitment to such redistribution and the long-term perspective on poverty elimination (Fimister 2001).

The widening inequality in incomes that has accompanied general increases in prosperity risks cutting off a few from the rising living standards of the many. While inequality, however measured, has appeared to stabilise since 2000, it remains near a 40-year high, despite the substantial redistributive measures undertaken by the Labour administration (Goodman and Oldfield 2004). To the extent that those who are left behind to form a residualised, impoverished group have particular characteristics, social divisions – or particular social divisions – may be enhanced. The current stress on social exclusion as a complement to or substitute for discussions of poverty and a focus for policy intervention can be regarded as acknowledging this point, although what precisely constitutes social exclusion or how you measure it are far from clear (Gordon and Townsend 2000; Hills et al. 2002; Lister 2004). Instead, it is important to retain the concept and use of the term 'poverty', and continue to take stock of trends in poverty measured in different ways – as indeed the *Opportunity for All* series aims to do (DWP 2004b). It is essential that, subject to the elimination of poverty, policy and research continue to consider the ongoing reality of poverty and assess whether poverty reduction policy is succeeding in breaking down the divisions that poverty tends to sustain. Without differences in poverty risks to sustain them, social divisions lose salience as indicators of structures determining life chances and shift towards focusing on the fluid aspects of culture and identity as the main elements of differences between groups.

Discussion Questions

1. Why does it not make sense to contrast relative and absolute definitions of poverty? Think of the different ways in which relative and absolute are used and those writers associated with the different uses.

2. Why is it important to take account of time when measuring poverty? You can think here of time as a point in time/history, time as duration or time as change over time.

3. Who is poorer: a person with a high income who doesn't spend it and lacks 'essentials'; a person who lives well but spends more than their income and lives in debt; or a person who has a low income but lives within it and spends only on essentials? Perhaps you can think of examples of these from your own experience, as well as thinking who would be shown to be poor on different measures.

4. How and why does poverty intersect with other social divisions – including those not covered in this chapter? You can think about cause and effect, that is, is it the other division which results in the poverty or is it differences in poverty which cause us to notice the other divisions?

FURTHER READING

The two books giving the most accessible and up-to-date treatment of poverty are Alcock, P. *Understanding Poverty* (Basingstoke: Macmillan – now Palgrave Macmillan, 1997, 2nd edn) and Flaherty, J., Veit-Wilson, J. and Dornan, P. *Poverty: The Facts* (London: CPAG, 2004, 5th edn). Ruth Lister's *Poverty* (Cambridge: Polity Press, 2004) adds thoughtful depth and a contemporary context, while Platt, L. (2002) *Parallel Lives? Poverty among Ethnic Minority Groups in Britain* (London: CPAG) provides more details of the ethnic dimension.

CHAPTER 13

Community

GRAHAM CROW AND CATHERINE MACLEAN

This chapter will provide you with a broad critical understanding of the following aspects of community as a source of social division:

■ The relevance of community to the analysis of social divisions
■ The distinction between communities of place, interest and identity
■ The bases of distinctions between community insiders and outsiders
■ The dynamic nature of community relationships and solidarities
■ The tradition of regarding community as being in decline: Ferdinand Tönnies
■ The impact of geographical and social mobility on community relationships
■ The importance of kinship networks in community ties and support
■ The potential of new means of communication to facilitate alternative community links
■ The mechanisms by which control is exercised in informal social life
■ Community as an arena in which rival groups compete to secure access to scarce resources
■ The dangers of idealising community as a sphere of harmonious social relationships
■ The potential of community to be defined in a variety of ways
■ The challenges that face researchers who seek to gain access to communities
■ The rhetorical appeal of community as a sphere in which diverse individuals can come together

The inclusion of a chapter on 'community' in a book about social divisions is not as odd as it might appear at first sight. There is nothing automatic about people coming together as communities, even though the most effective community bonds may be those that members believe to be 'natural'. The unity of any community is always vulnerable to disputes among the individuals and social groups who make it up, and the achievement of community

305

solidarity requires members to be mindful of the collective good alongside their own more immediate agendas. Communities frequently encompass divisive social identities: in many villages, for example, a distinction is made between those who 'belong' and those viewed as 'outsiders', while in urban areas, neighbourhoods often have distinctive population profiles and reputations into which some people fit more readily than others. In addition, community is often the arena in which the social divisions discussed in preceding chapters are played out. It is here that the various dimensions of social division manifest themselves and come together in making up people's everyday lives, rather than existing as separate ideas, principles or variables in the realm of sociological 'macro' analysis.

Sociological interest in community matters has revived in recent years. In both theoretical and methodological terms, sociologists working in the field have become more sophisticated than earlier generations of researchers, whose work frequently suffered from uncritical conceptions of 'community' and unreflexive techniques of investigation. This chapter examines the nature of 'community' and the ways in which social divisions figure in community life. In so doing, it raises the issue of social cohesion: if we are all so divided from one another, how do we collaborate in social life? In particular it discusses the various bases of community, the factors influencing the ease with which an individual can join or leave a community and the question of the desirability of community as an ideal. The analysis first outlines the development of sociological analysis in this field, then considers recent conceptual trends.

The nature of community

Communities place a requirement on members to limit their individualism and acknowledge their dependence on a wider network of relationships. The same sort of point can be made about community solidarity as Durkheim ([1893]1984) famously made about social solidarity more generally, namely that people who have only narrow self-interest to motivate them constitute an insufficient basis for sustainable social relationships. Just as sociologists from Durkheim onwards have sought to answer the fundamental question of what makes 'society' possible, so too has the issue of the basis of 'community' been the subject of extensive discussion. If communities are defined as groups of people who have something in common, then the thing that they share may be identified as *geographical* location, position in the wider *social structure* or sense of *identity*. On this basis, Willmott (1986) makes the useful analytical distinction between 'place community', 'interest community' and 'community of attachment', although he is careful to note that in practice particular communities probably will have more than one of these elements in common.

The fact that they are constructed around members having something in common makes it appropriate to treat communities as phenomena of social cohesion rather than social division. However, even if potential social divisions between community members can be overcome, communities will still have associations with rivalry and conflict, because communities are exclusive as well as inclusive. People who do not share the common characteristic(s) by which a community is defined are necessarily 'outsiders'. Individuals who do not 'belong' to a community pose a threat because affiliations to other places, interests and/or identities make them potential rivals for the scarce material resources and social status to which communities lay claim. The sense of solidarity among community members may even be strengthened where divisions between 'insiders' and 'outsiders' are highlighted. Often it turns out to be harder to specify who we are than who we are not, and in this way a strong and positive sense of 'us' will be enhanced by a clear and correspondingly negative sense of 'them', the 'other' against which we define ourselves (Bauman 1990). Putnam's (2000: 350) reference to intolerance as the 'dark side' of community is relevant here.

This is perhaps most obvious in 'place communities', but also applies to 'imagined communities' (see Chapters 4, 5 and 6). In Chapter 1, the discussion of separateness and identity stressed that being *different* is not just an isolated state of distinctive existence but involves beliefs, feelings and attitudes to others. What appears to be a sense of community is often a way of expressing other underlying social divisions, which are perceived to mark off *our community* from the rest of the world, and *our part* of the community from their part of the community. The distinction between us and them that arises from this is an important one.

A common way this has been expressed has been through concerns about respectability. Traditional working-class communities frequently operated with a distinction between 'respectable' and 'rough' groupings (see Chapter 2), the difference being defined in terms of standards of appearance, type of employment, patterns of money management, religious observance, leisure activities and sexual behaviour. The judgmental language in which the respectable/rough distinction is framed could be contested by the alternative portrayal of people as either 'stuck up' or 'ordinary', but the underlying social division could not be denied. Similar distinctions operate in contemporary communities, as the continued use of vocabulary such as 'good neighbourhoods' and 'rough areas' demonstrates. Friction and rivalry between parts of communities identified in this way have also persisted, so that, in so far as community is a social division, it could be said to operate in a fragmented, localised way. Nonetheless, it is one that is nationally replicated, and which has been well established over a long period of time (Chapter 15).

On the other hand, the dynamic nature of relations within communities and the competitive nature of links between communities mean that people's sense of the communities to which they belong is not fixed. Despite the appeal of the common-sense notion that communities have enduring qualities, with a fixed character that is so desirable that we should all aspire to attain it, change is inherent in communities because of the inevitability that community membership is altered with the passage of time (Crow et al. 2001). Geographical mobility, social mobility and individuals' progression through the life-course all necessitate adjustment in community relationships (see Chapter 8). In consequence, the continuity of community phenomena is just as difficult to explain sociologically as the process of change in community attachments.

The main focus of sociological writing on community has been on change. From Tönnies' classic *Community and Association* ([1887]1955) onwards, a powerful body of literature has argued that the Industrial Revolution, the development of capitalism and, more generally, 'modernity' brought with them loss of community. Although it remains influential, this conclusion can be challenged. Many writers have identified important continuities in community relationships, thereby casting doubt on the claim that community is a declining phenomenon (Crow and Allan 1994; Payne 1996). Others have argued that vigorous new forms of community are emerging in response to major social trends such as globalisation and the rise of internet communities (Castells 1997). Globalisation may have the effect of generating new solidarities, some of which are constructed defensively around places or values that are felt to be threatened, while others involve people taking advantage of opportunities to communicate in the different ways that developments in information technology have made possible. Both perspectives suggest that the significance of community relationships in societies like contemporary Britain extends well beyond bemoaning the passing of how things used to be.

It has been noted already that communities are diverse phenomena that may be based on people having *place*, *interests* and/or *identities* in common. The association of community with place is an established tradition within the sociology of community, epitomised by community studies being given place names as their titles (sometimes substituting pseudonyms in order to protect anonymity). Whalsay, one of the smaller Shetland Isles, (Cohen 1987) provides one example of how easily community can be read into place. However, community is not just a sense of division between 'us in this locality' and the rest of the world.

People who share common interests are less readily identified in everyday language as 'communities'. One example would be certain kinds of elite group (Chapter 7). Another common example is people with the same employer, who may constitute 'occupational communities'. Most studies of occupational communities have been of male-dominated heavy industries, such as Warwick and Littlejohn's (1992) study of coal miners, but other groups of workers besides these (such as police officers) are also usefully regarded as occupational communities (Salaman 1986). Of course, where occupational communities live in a single, physically identifiable location, the two senses of community reinforce each other, giving an even stronger sense of separate identity.

Communities of the third type, 'communities of attachment' are built around common identities and are more free-floating than either place or interest communities, because they are not tightly bounded by geography or social structural features such as social class. People in these communities come together through their shared culture, uniting around symbols that emphasise, for instance, common ethnicity (Baumann 1996; Chapter 4), shared difference from able-bodied norms (Gregory and Hartley 1991; Chapter 11), shared political visions (Lichterman 1996) or aspects of lifestyle such as taste in music (Finnegan 1989).

Willmott's point that, in practice, communities do not always fall neatly into one of the three analytical types that he distinguishes is evident in the above examples. The people of Cohen's (1987) Whalsay are less a place community than a community of attachment, in which place is drawn on in the symbolic construction of boundaries around 'insiders' and 'outsiders'. Likewise, Roberts (1993) notes that the occupational community of Wearside shipbuilders has been weakened by their dispersal through patterns of residential migration, while Baumann's (1996) analysis of ethnic communities in Southall locates them in relation to common interests as well as shared cultural affinities.

As several of the chapters in this book show, particular social divisions can be demonstrated to operate across society as a whole, that is, at the macro-level. In practice, where individuals find that they share a position with other people on the same side of a social divide, those others are likely in the first place to be found close to hand. If we can see and talk to others 'in the same boat' as ourselves in respect of social divisions, namely those who live and work nearby, our interaction has the potential to grow into a sense of shared social identity with regard to that division. Where residential areas are largely homogeneous, for example in terms of the social class or ethnicity of the residents, the social divisions discussed earlier in the book take on a sharp new focus. Middle-class suburbs and inner-city areas in which poorer ethnic minority populations are concentrated are exclusive in a way that more mixed areas are not. Proximity does not necessarily entail common identity but community of place in practice often overlaps with community of interest.

The less concrete community of attachment also depends on mechanisms for sharing symbolic meanings, a cultural sharing, and such non-located attachments cut across the simplistic idea of homogeneous, unified 'communities' without social divisions.

Communities and change

It is also important to consider the temporal dimension of community relationships (Crow and Allan 1995). By constantly moving into and out of communities, people's arrival or departure highlights the fundamental question of what it is that community members share. Place communities may be constructed to include former residents who have migrated elsewhere but retain some attachment to the location (so-called 'diaspora communities'), while excluding those local residents whose recent arrival or temporary residence disqualifies them from being considered 'real locals' (Cohen 1982). Mewett (1982: 230) has reported how people who have left the Scottish island of Lewis are referred to as 'exiles', a term which implies that 'though physically absent, the migrant retains a social presence'. Conversely, physical presence does not grant a person 'local' status, although the distinction between 'old incomers' and 'new incomers' that Phillips (1986) found in a Yorkshire parish indicates that the exclusion of inmigrants (those coming in from another area of the same country) can diminish over time. Similarly, new recruits are frequently accepted as full members of interest communities and attachment communities only once they have been appropriately socialised and established the trust of existing members by demonstrating their loyalty to the group (Salaman 1986).

The question of how community relationships are affected by changing membership has particular significance in contemporary societies that are characterised by high rates of geographical and social mobility. Inmigrants have to start from scratch when they enter a new community: their learning process and initial absence or lower levels of personal relationship will be complicated if the incomers are socially different, for example in class or attitudes to the locality (Payne 1973). Inward geographical mobility can be disruptive of existing arrangements where newcomers enter into competition with established community members for scarce resources such as housing. It is certainly the case that conflicts have been associated with much geographical relocation, including the migration of middle-class ex-urbanites into the countryside (Newby 1980), ethnic minority populations in urban areas (Rex and Moore 1967), and, more recently, middle-class gentrifiers into favoured inner-city locations (Butler and Robson 2003).

There are well-known problems associated with the arrival of more affluent newcomers. These new middle classes (with their easier access to mortgages and loans) can afford to pay much larger sums for the kinds of properties local (often working-class) young couples would otherwise rent, buy or inherit. This process prices existing local people out of the local housing market, producing social antagonisms far removed from the idealised notions of community that attracted the inmigrants in the first place.

In more extreme cases, the new middle-class residents own other houses elsewhere and have less need of a local school, shop, library, public transport or other welfare or commercial services. Such part-time presence does not offer much to community life. Having contributed to the displacement of the next generation by buying up the available houses, their lack of involvement tends to weaken what is left. Even in localities in which this tendency is less pronounced, the potential for conflict between inmigrants' ways and those of the locals, often expressed through competition for control of policy in clubs, committees and councils, remains high (Frankenberg 1957; Maclean 2003).

However, there is no simple causal connection between inmigration and conflict, since many of these patterns of inmigration were preceded by population exoduses. In such cases, as one local resident put it:

> You can't blame them (incomers) for wanting their own place to live. If they get a house then it's our own fault for selling it to them or letting them build it in the first place. Once they're in there's nothing you can do about it, so there's no point complaining. (Macleod 1992: 198)

Rural areas often have a history of migration to the towns that long pre-dates the more recent pattern of middle-class settlement – which is connected to the expansion of the middle classes (Chapter 2) – and a similar point can be made about 'white flight' from inner-city areas preceding the settlement there of much of Britain's black population. Inner-city areas were losing population for most of the twentieth century, and it was only once this process was underway that they became major centres for settlement by ethnic minorities who are better understood as a 'replacement population' (Sarre 1989: 139) than as a group whose arrival displaced others.

Migration, then, affects social divisions in two contradictory ways. It may weaken the common sense of identity among the 'original' members of a category, by the loss of some of their number who gain new identities through migration. Alternatively, migration may strengthen division through new encounters with non-members across categories and the conflicts that frequently arise as a result between locals and incomers. One particularly interesting case study of migration and community is O'Reilly's (2000) analysis *The British on the Costa Del Sol*, a group who constitute a trans-national community whose members' identities are neither straightforwardly British nor Spanish, but something in between.

The conventional view of inmigration as a cause of social problems has had to be modified further in the light of the recognition that newcomers may well generate additional resources for the benefit of established residents, not least by stimulating economic activity. In Gilligan's (1990) study of Padstow, for example, local people were often dependent on newcomers for employment, making it difficult to analyse conflicts there as straightforward contests between 'insiders' and 'outsiders'. Without the development of new industries to replace declining ones that had previously been major employers (such as the development of tourism to replace fishing in the case of Padstow), communities are likely to shrink as people move elsewhere in search of work. Despite extravagant claims by its proponents, individual 'teleworkers' can contribute little to shore up collapsing local economies. This story is currently being played out in the former coal-mining areas of Britain. Even in the context of economic decline, however, Wight's (1993) study of the Scottish village of 'Cauldmoss' found people reluctant to move away permanently, and those who did move were careful to keep open the possibility of return migration.

Less research has been undertaken into the impact of outmigration and return migration than has been conducted into the effects of inmigration, but what studies there are tend to emphasise the loss of community vitality (and ultimately viability) that follows from people moving elsewhere. Outmigration can result in residual communities being highly unbalanced in terms of several of the social divisions dealt with in earlier chapters – age, gender, ethnicity and social class. Outmigrants tend to be younger, more affluent and better linked into non-local networks than are their less mobile counterparts, and their relocation can contribute to the social isolation of older relatives who have stayed put (Phillipson et al. 2001). In the extreme, sustained out-migration can lead to the 'death' of communities (Porteus 1989), but it is more common for migration patterns to be made up of a mixture of outmigration, inmigration and return migration.

The common assumption that the dynamism of contemporary communities contrasts with static communities in the past does not bear closer examination, as Maclean (2003) found in her research into the changing population composition of the parish of 'Beulach' in the Scottish Highlands. The recent trend for people from the south of Scotland and beyond to make their homes in 'Beulach' is merely one more twist in a long and complicated story, in which population losses and gains have contributed to a situation of constant flux. Maclean found that many of the elderly 'real locals' had forebears from outside the parish. Macleod and Payne (1994) similarly found that of 105 locally born residents, only 60 had one locally born parent, and less than one in ten could boast that both parents had been born locally.

The dynamics of community living

People's sense of 'belonging' is indisputably important to understanding the attachment that underlies their reluctance to leave and desire to return to place communities. It would be wrong to attach too much significance to place in this context, however, since the attraction is to the social networks of kin and friends that are centred on these places as well as to the familiar geographical location. The association of community with social support reflects the repeated finding that many people live in close proximity to relatives (beyond those in their immediate household). The 'traditional' working-class communities that have entered folklore for their mutual supportiveness frequently revolved around extensive kinship networks.

While this type of arrangement has generally been superseded by decades of social change, the geographical link with kin has not disappeared. Rather it is the case that people's migration strategies often maintain closeness to relatives because of the social support that they provide. Kin ties had been re-established to a significant degree even among the affluent workers of Luton when they were restudied by Devine (1992a) some two decades after Goldthorpe et al. (1969) had identified them as pioneers of more 'privatised' lifestyles.

In communities characterised by geographical immobility, kinship can be a particularly prominent feature, as Wight (1993) reports regarding 'Cauld-moss', where as many as two-thirds of the population were linked together by kin networks and strong kinship loyalties persisted. However, it should also be acknowledged that the other side of the coin of a kinship system linking people together is that it also defines who are not kin and thereby divided off from the category of people who are entitled to support. An offence against one person becomes a potential offence against all other members of the kin group. In some cultures, this is institutionalised into the inter-group conflict involving the prolonged 'settling of scores', namely the 'feud'. Kinship in Britain is, for many people, a much weaker principle of division and attachment, which is why it has not been treated as a full-scale social division in this book. Nonetheless, identity with both immediate family and the wider kinship group is not uniform across the country, having significant social class, gender, age and ethnic variations, as earlier chapters have shown.

The reinforcement of people's attachment to communities by ties of kinship is supplemented by other associations such as those with neighbours, friends and co-workers. Of course, kin, friends and colleagues are not limited to persons living in close proximity, and social network analysts like Wellman et al. (1988) argue that 'personal communities' have the capacity to develop well beyond the confines of an individual's neighbourhood. The extent to which communities have been 'de-territorialised' has been a topic of considerable interest in recent years since, on the face of it, powerful social trends have given individuals greater freedom of choice over those with whom they interact socially. Improvements in transport and communications technology allow people to be more mobile geographically and maintain contact with others over an expanded area. Rising living standards make it possible to take up opportunities to socialise beyond the locality and also make unnecessary the interdependence with neighbours that was forced on members of traditional working-class communities by their shared poverty. In the extreme, Beck (1992) sees participation in community relationships as increasingly a matter of individual choice. Post-modern theorists have argued that personal identities can now be changed and manipulated, because they are no longer class-based. While there is undoubtedly more individual choice in contemporary society (and this must weaken place community identity), place communities can still exert strong influences, and choosing a 'new' social identity may in fact be only to exchange membership of a local community for membership of an 'imagined community'.

It is, of course, important not to exaggerate the impact of broad trends towards geographical mobility and rising affluence. In societies characterised by widening inequalities, the easy mobility enjoyed by those in more advantaged situations is closed off to marginal groups (such as lone parents), whose poverty and social exclusion effectively deny them the same opportunities to overcome the constraints of place (Duncan and Edwards 1997: also Chapter 12). In a society increasingly dependent on the car as the means of transport that gives access to all aspects of life outside the home, we should also recognise that car use is uneven both across the population and within households, with the result that women and children may be more closely tied to place communities (see Chapter 9).

Additionally, it is necessary to keep in mind the peculiar character of face-to-face interaction to which theorists such as Goffman (1972) have drawn our attention. Communities are not confined to people who have face-to-face contact, as the extensive usage of Anderson's (1991) concept of 'imagined communities' demonstrates, but at some level community relationships need to be sustained by people coming together to reaffirm their shared membership (Weeks 1995). Family gatherings, conferences, political meetings and local carnivals all serve to bring people together in one place periodically for face-to-face interaction, which revitalises their sense of community in a way that impersonal contacts maintained at a distance cannot. On the more mundane level of everyday life, the significance of routine encounters and conversations for reproducing social solidarity among community members also deserves to be acknowledged. The young Punjabis living in Southall in Gillespie's (1995) research were aware of the relevance of such everyday inter-actions, even though they were acknowledged to be more prosaic than the community scenarios portrayed in the television soap operas with which they compared them. These processes help to forge the strength of category membership on either side of any social division.

Researchers in this area have examined the ways in which gossip operated in traditional working-class communities not just to reinforce what by today's standards appear to be highly restrictive and oppressive codes of behaviour but also to promote social support. Gossip helps to build and maintain collective identities. Information passed on through gossip has often been vital to the well-being of poor households where it has concerned employment and benefit opportunities (Allatt and Yeandle 1992). While people now are generally less constrained financially and socially than their ancestors were, gossip networks continue to thrive and be effective in a variety of settings (Dempsey 1990; Gill and Maclean 2002). Analyses framed in terms of economic necessity are clearly inadequate to account for people's acquiescence to such social control, so explanations of gossip's continuing effectiveness within communities have to be sought elsewhere. What accounts of gossip emphasise is the role it plays in maintaining people's sense of place in and belonging to communities alongside the influence over the behaviour of others that it gives.

One feature of community life that the analysis of gossip highlights is the persistently unequal nature of community relationships. Patterns of gossip reveal that established community members, affluent groups and men are more powerful than newcomers, poorer people and women and children. What is revealed, in other words, is that while gossip may serve to reinforce existing norms of behaviour by negative assessments of acts that transgress those norms, it also reinforces hierarchies and divisions whose existence is written into the heart of community arrangements. The very language in which everyday conversations are conducted reproduces the marginality of certain groups, such as when inmigrants are referred to pejoratively as 'emmets', 'blow-ins', 'bongleys', 'white settlers', 'outsiders' and 'foreigners', or when poorer people are labelled 'rough' and 'no-hopers'. In addition, the exchange of information that is a vital part of gossip is conducted selectively within communities, and exclusion from such exchanges reinforces the powerlessness of groups which are negatively labelled.

Against this background, it is unsurprising to find that 'leadership' of communities is generally monopolised by more 'respectable' figures, although the processes determining precisely who becomes a community leader are often convoluted. Baumann's (1996) Southall study and Eade's (1989) study of Tower Hamlets both found political processes underlain by competition between the different ethnic groups living in the two areas of London, and Farrar's (2002) research in the Chapeltown area of Leeds comes to similar conclusions. Among these groups, there were widely divergent views about which individuals would be best placed to represent the community within formal political structures that define 'community' in territorial terms as the local ward or constituency population. Disputes over who should act as leaders to represent communities in turn reveal the contested nature of community definition.

Baumann (1996), Eade (1989) and Farrar (2002) all show that notions of place community sit uneasily alongside conceptions of ethnic community rooted in the common culture of a linguistic or religious group (Chapters 4 and 5), and the same could be said about tensions existing with conceptions of 'community' that are constructed around common interests. Competing community leaders operate with different understandings of community, with boundaries drawn more or less inclusively or exclusively, and with different conceptions of how actively community members can be mobilised. When faced with powerful challenges, such as the redevelopment of the Isle of Dogs into part of 'Docklands', the competition between leaders, local council organisations and between the two can incapacitate local involvement or resistance to change even among strongly based communities (Foster 1999). Having said that, 'community' does have the potential to be used as a basis for different groups to come together to exert an influence on local regeneration (Mumford and Power 2003).

In the context of the long-term decline in allegiance to traditional (class-based) party politics and the growing heterogeneity of the population (not least in terms of changing class structures (Chapter 2), community politics has increased dramatically in recent decades. The growth of community action is one of the most striking features of the contemporary political scene, and legitimation through appeals to 'community' has become a vital part of mainstream political discourses. This is partly a reflection of the flexibility with which such appeals can be deployed, although this flexibility is double-edged. The proliferation of phenomena treated as communities carries with it the danger that the effectiveness of appeals to community will be undermined by the meaning of the concept becoming ever more imprecise and contested. There are signs that 'community' is no longer automatically assumed to have only positive connotations. For some critics of discourses built around community, the problem is that they serve to mask particular sectional interests, while others detect in them the agenda of state agencies attempting to withdraw from publicly funded service provision (Craig and Mayo 1995). One result of these unfolding debates is that the meaning of 'community' is becoming further politicised.

Recent conceptual developments and trends

The general tendency to associate community with supportiveness and social cohesion has been widely noted, but the word 'community' may be used negatively as well as positively. Recognition has grown that community relationships have the potential to constrain individuals as well as empower them and be exclusive as well as inclusive. Social divisions are as much based on *unifying* the membership of each particular category as in *mutual opposition* across social divides. This reassessment has been prompted by policy initiatives in which community has figured prominently (such as 'community care' policies) as well as being the outcome of more theoretically and methodologically informed analyses. The assumptions made by policy makers about the caring capacities of communities have been confronted by some fairly harsh realities. Numerous research projects have shown that there are definite limits to the extent to which community members are able and willing to provide informal care for dependent people and the bulk of the caring that is provided informally is performed by female relatives (Dalley 1996).

The dangers of operating with idealised conceptions of 'community' have also been revealed in other areas of social policy such as housing. Manipulation of the 'built environment', with the aim of creating 'balanced communities' in the New Towns experiment, was a notably ambitious venture in this respect (Crow and Allan 1994). Its history reveals the disjunction that exists between the image of communities as social phenomena that supposedly have a natural capacity to unite diverse individuals and the tendency in practice for communities to be less than universally inclusive. The persistence of community exclusivity is a common theme in the literature on geographical segregation. A principal lesson of the New Towns experiment is that considerable resistance exists to plans that mix people from different social classes in the same residential area.

The expectation that people from different ethnic backgrounds would become progressively less spatially segregated with the passage of time (Chapter 4) has also not been fulfilled in practice, and there is evidence of spatial segregation along other lines of social cleavage such as those of occupation and age (Crow and Allan 1994; Chapters 2 and 8). Of course, there are limits to how far residential areas can be monopolised by particular groups, but the emergence of the phenomenon of 'gated communities', with definite boundaries and restricted access, is a sign of the times in which we live. Understood alternatively as 'fortress communities', such settlements illustrate the general point that the boundaries of communities will be jealously guarded by members who feel themselves to be under threat from outsiders. Sometimes these boundaries will have the physical expression of fences, walls, 'keep out' notices or surveillance cameras, as in the early example of the Cutteslowe Walls built between two housing estates reported by Collison (1963). On the other hand, exclusion of outsiders can be effected by more informal social means, for example by requiring that members express their commitment or loyalty to some symbol of the community (Cohen 1985).

Such exclusion or residential segregation necessarily limits the opportunities that people have to gain direct experience of 'how the other half lives'. Indeed, this may be one important reason why there is not more enthusiasm for the 'mixed communities' that planners aspire to create. One of the ways that we can tolerate differences in other people's lives – the ways of people on the opposite side of social divisions – is that we may not have to mix with them. If we do not meet, if they remain invisible, we can ignore them: we need not feel upset by encountering their differences. How can we feel human concern for other people's poverty, loneliness or disadvantage if we never engage with them except in the most superficial ways? This may be considered a powerful impetus behind people's frequently expressed desire to live among 'people like us' (Butler and Robson 2003).

This is not to say that if we somehow all lived in neat communities, everything would be fine. The assumptions embodied in inherited notions of community have led to extensive theoretical reflection about the desirability of community. Feminists have been prominent among those who have questioned the meaning of community, prompted in part by the need to re-examine the gender orders written into traditional conceptions of community relationships. As has been noted already, policy makers' views about the caring capacity of communities turn out to assume women's availability and preparedness to undertake care work, and such ideas reflect broader, male-dominated, taken-for-granted understandings of the allotted places of men and women in public and private spheres (Chapter 3). It is for these reasons that feminists and others have been wary of the communitarian agenda, developed by writers like Etzioni (1993), in which the value of community is promoted as an alternative to both unbridled individualism and excessive state involvement in welfare provision. Young (1986), for example, regards as problematic the way in which community is constructed to deny scope for difference and heterogeneity. In like fashion, Dalley (1996) has challenged the way in which the language of community is used as a cover for policies that shift the responsibility for care from state agencies to families (and, within families, to women).

The pursuit of community is open to criticism for introducing a conservative bias into the political agenda, because of its associations with idealised social arrangements in which people of different classes, genders and ages come together in pre-set, traditional ways where everyone 'knows their place'. In addition, critics point to the parochialism of community's negative evaluation not only of change but of all things different, captured in a mistrust of 'strangers' or 'outsiders'. It is undoubtedly true that there are established sociological understandings of community which are conservative, in that they look backwards to supposedly golden ages of authentic communal relationships that have subsequently been lost (Nisbet 1970). Arensberg and Kimball's (1940) classic account of rural Ireland, with its overtones of permanence, integration, cosy neighbouring and the slow turn of the seasons, contrasts sharply with Brody's (1973) later focus on famine, poverty, social dysfunction and clinical depression. Scheper-Hughes's (2001) more recent study of another Irish village further confirms the dangers of romantic images of community.

As was remarked above, however, the notion of a loss of community perspective does not stand up to scrutiny once it is recognised that various forms of community relationships are present in contemporary societies, some of which are modified versions of what went before while others are more innovative. Put another way, the concept of community is most useful sociologically when it is treated as having the potential to capture the essence of a variety of different social arrangements rather than being tied to one particular type, such as village communities of the pre-industrial era (Crow and Allan 1995). There is no compelling theoretical reason to restrict the definition of community to people who have place in common, a point established in Hillery's celebrated review of the many sociological definitions of the term 'community' (Bell and Newby 1971). Once this is acknowledged, then the charge that the concept of community has a built-in conservative bias loses much of its force.

Broadening out the definition of community to include groups of people who have something other than place in common is important if many of the more innovative forms of collective endeavour are to be acknowledged. New social movements such as the groups of environmentalists that have grown in prominence in recent decades may be understood as radical and alternative communities, built as they are around cultural ideas at odds with the dominant ideology of consumer capitalism. A similar point can be made about the emergence of community identities among groups whose shared disability, sexual orientation or ethnicity (Chapters 11, 10 and 4, respectively) marks them as distinct from the 'normal' culture of the majority population (Weeks 1995). At the same time, it should be noted that place continues to figure in the operation of many such alternative communities, even if their members are held together principally by common political, religious or other cultural values. As Castells (1997) notes, most of these new community movements are essentially defensive in character, forged in the attempt to limit the impact of global forces on their lives. The defence of place is a powerful element in the construction of what he calls the 'communal havens' that offer to provide anchor points for an individual's identity in an uncertain world. In similar fashion, Bauman (2001) portrays community as offering safety to people who feel insecure in the modern world.

The 'threat' to community life of the new uncertainty of a global economy can be dramatic. Communities based on single occupations – or, more precisely, on a few employers – are potentially vulnerable to the effects of international competition. Agriculture, fishing, coal mining, shipbuilding, dock work and metal manufacture, industries that tended to have specific, relatively isolated, geographical locations in Britain, have already experienced major decline with the growth of alternative suppliers in other parts of the world. Decisions about people's lives become even more removed from their own hands.

Similarly, the rise of international media, largely funded by advertising, has spread knowledge of consumer behaviour and alternative lifestyles. To the extent that local community cultures depend on a sense of *valued* collective difference, this new awareness can be seen as undermining traditional ways of life. Nevertheless, it would be wrong to place too much emphasis on these broad statements of general tendencies. In practice, life 'on the ground' is far more complex, with people and organisations engaging in a variety of strategies to sustain and change their social and physical environments. Even Foster's (1999: 344) account of major social innovation, which stresses the power of external and global forces to change the local community, notes that connecting macro-economics 'with the alarming predictions about globalisation, and an individual development programme and its impact on local residents is very problematic'.

The growth of different sorts of communities is understandable as the expression of people's dissatisfaction with individualism and their consequent desire to feel part of a collectivity. Where conventional community organisations are exclusive of newcomers and other 'outsider' groups, alternative communities provide rival bases for community identities, quite possibly within the same spatial reference points. P. Wright's (1985) study of how Stoke Newington is home to middle-class, white working-class and various ethnic minority communities provides an excellent illustration of competing claims to place among groups who live alongside each other but do not constitute an integrated whole. Ethnic minority inmigrants and middle-class gentrifiers occupy the same space as the members of the white working class who have lived there for longer, but they live in different social worlds, leading Wright to conclude that they constitute more than one community. There is no necessary contradiction in noting how the definition of community has been broadened, while recognising that place continues to matter to how interest communities and communities of attachment are constructed.

The need to broaden the definition of community beyond people having place in common has been highlighted by the debate over the difference between 'community' and 'locality'. According to Day and Murdoch (1993), the latter term fails to capture the subjective dimension of how place is experienced, and people's frequent use of the language of community to convey their sense of identity, belonging and common endeavour indicates that what is being referred to here is more than just locality. Yet if a broad definition of community has the potential to capture a wider spectrum of social phenomena than do more restrictive definitions, at the same time it compounds the methodological difficulties of studying communities empirically. The problem confronting researchers of how to gain access to a study population is obviously easier if people's location is known than it is when the people being investigated are 'hidden' by their not being fixed to particular places, as was the case with Finnegan's (1989) amateur musicians.

Of course, even place communities are not straightforwardly open to inspection. Frankenberg (1957) famously found himself physically present in the village in which his research was being conducted but excluded from many aspects of the social life of the place until he found his point of entry through involvement in the football team. The problem of research findings being influenced by the researcher's point of access to the social phenomena being studied is common in investigations of community relationships. Indeed, Payne (1996) has suggested that selectivity in terms of the community members consulted by researchers has led to a systematic distortion in which communities are typically represented as being full of nice people and devoid of undesirable characters. When combined with romanticised notions of 'community', research methods that screen out people with whom the researcher has little sympathy produce community studies that are seriously one-sided and incomplete. Recognition of the fact that having something in common does not entail community members being alike in all respects has sharpened awareness that research in the field of community needs to be methodologically sound if it is to be credible, and community researchers have responded to this challenge in careful but imaginative ways (Brunt 2001).

Conclusion

The unity of 'community' cannot be taken for granted once the contested nature of communities is recognised (Hoggett 1997). Central importance is now attached to studying the processes by which unity is created and maintained over time. Equally important is the analysis of how community conflicts are generated and work themselves out. Sociologists of community have shown how appeals to community have the potential to transcend particular social divisions along the lines of gender, social class and ethnicity, through (for example) community relationships being likened to family relationships (Crow and Maclean 2004). An illustration of this point is provided by Dempsey's (1990: Ch. 4) Australian 'Smalltown' study in which he records how the community is represented by many of its members as 'one big happy family'. Such appeals are effective in securing the unity of community members to the extent that ensuing loyalty to the wider group overrides narrower sectional interests and perspectives. We can contrast this with the social situation in Northern Ireland (Chapters 5 and 6).

Where identification with and loyalties to a community are secondary to narrower and more particular interests and perspectives, community solidarity will be correspondingly unstable. Just as contemporary societies are subject to disunity as the power of dominant groups is challenged from a range of other positions, so too are contemporary communities vulnerable to fragmentation. The challenge mounted by women to their subordination within conventional understandings of community has already been mentioned. Neutral-sounding social policies constructed around notions of community can in practice have gender-biased outcomes, and feminists have been prominent among those asking of community discourses, 'who is this "we"?' (Godway and Finn 1994).

In the same way that challenges to conventional conceptions of 'community' have problematised women's allocation to inferior positions, so too has the place of other subordinate groups been problematised by developments in community politics. Parry et al.'s (1987) research in inner-city Manchester found extensive consciousness of ethnic minority groups constituting a black community distinct from the white population and also subject to division into various 'sub-communities'. Taylor et al.'s (1996) comparison of Manchester and Sheffield identifies further cleavages besides gender and ethnicity, along the lines of social class, sexuality and age, which also problematise speaking of local people as if they constitute a community in the singular.

The conventional understanding of community as a sphere of harmonious social relationships does not stand up to scrutiny, and in many ways it is more appropriate to regard community as an 'arena' in which social divisions are given expression. Social divisions are encountered and expressed in specific concrete social situations: the place community in particular acts as a locus for personal life experiences. 'Community' is often in fact an expression of one or more social divisions of the kind explored in this book. This is not to say that the idea of community is reducible to one or more of the other social divisions. The appeal to community is a powerful rhetorical device by which groups can seek to reinforce their solidarity (Crow 2002), although as we have seen, this is often achievable only by the exclusion of others. It follows that the more 'community' is interpreted differently according to people's social class, gender, ethnicity, sexuality, age and health status, the greater the potential for it to be the focus of social conflicts.

Paraphrasing Marx's formulation in the 1859 Preface, community can be treated as one of the ideological battlegrounds onto which people, who have become conscious of conflicts of interest, venture in order to 'fight it out' (Marx and Engels [1859]1969: 504). This ties in with Barnes's (1995) point that people are often motivated to act as members of communities rather than as members of more abstract entities such as social classes. Especially in place communities, there can be real and often visible splits, not least between newcomers and longer term residents, as we have seen earlier in this chapter. These patterns are repeated up and down the country, each conflict independent and localised, but echoing those going on elsewhere. Thus, while the idea of community identity may not offer the same purchase on social division as, say, class or ethnicity, that is, as a macro-principle of categorisation, it does however show how such things may appear 'on the ground'. The interconnection between social divisions means that we cannot think of any one division in isolation: it is only seemingly a paradox that bonds of attachment are part of social division. Attachments to more than one category blur our perception of the sharpness of social divisions.

Currently, fashionable analytical moves to deconstruct communities into their various component parts correspond to broader post-modernist concerns in sociology. People's consciousness of being members of communities is of growing significance in the context of the rise of identity politics, which has seen the rejection of overarching theories of what it is that determines who we are and an emphasis instead on the multifaceted nature of individuals and the communities of which they are a part. Yet the operation of forces that fragment communities is only part of the story, since alongside them there are opposite forces that bring people together. Homans (1951) refers to these as 'centrifugal' and 'centripetal forces', and this idea of social forces pushing people to either the margins or the centre of community relationships has been employed by Warwick and Littlejohn (1992) in their analysis of change in Yorkshire mining villages.

The notion is interesting for several reasons. First of all, it suggests that people may be thrown together or pushed apart despite their personal wishes; a person's position within a community is governed by more than simply individual choice. Second, the notion of centrifugal and centripetal forces directs our attention to the dynamic nature of community relationships and the importance of 'community time' (Crow and Allan 1995). Third, the imagery focuses attention on the question of what constitutes the 'centre' of 'community'. Shared place, shared interests and shared identities are all possible answers to this question, as is some combination of these. Whether such communities can come together on a larger scale as coherent and united societies, in the face of so many powerful social divisions, is one of the most pressing issues of our time.

Discussion Questions

1. What is community?

2. Peter Willmott (1986) distinguishes between 'place community', 'interest community' and 'community of attachment', arguing that people's community relationships connect them to others with whom they share common residence (for example a neighbourhood), common interests (for example an occupation), and common identities (for example a religion). How important is each of these types of community in the modern world?

FURTHER READING

A useful introduction to the sociology of British communities is Crow, G. and Allan G. *Community Life* (London: Harvester Wheatsheaf, 1994). The potential of community studies to capture the complexity of local social life is well illustrated by Foster, J. *Docklands* (London: UCL Press, 1999). Methodological issues relating to community research are considered thoughtfully in Payne, G. 'Imagining the Community' in Lyon, E.S. and. Busfield, J. (eds) *Methodological Imaginations* (London: Macmillan – now Palgrave Macmillan, 1996), while an interesting collection of papers on the policy-relevance of community research can be found in Hoggett, P. (ed.) *Contested Communities* (London: Policy Press, 1997). Baumans, Z. *Community: Seeking Safety in an Insecure World*, London: Polity (2001) is a very readable introduction to contemporary meanings of community.

CHAPTER 14

Health

Judy Payne, Geoff Payne and Matthew Bond

This chapter will provide you with a broad critical understanding of the following issues in social class as a source of social division:

■ Health as a social division: distinct but connected to other divisions
■ Definitions of health and illness
■ Patients' own views of being 'ill'
■ Causes of illness: genetics, biology, responsible behaviour, social factors
■ Health inequalities: material and cultural features
■ Health and other social divisions
■ Social class and illnesses
■ Gender, age and health
■ Ethnic differences
■ Geographical variations in public health

Health is a different kind of social division from the 12 others discussed in this book. In some of its manifestations, it does not even fully meet all the defining criteria as set out in the Introduction or the start of Chapter 15. For example, people can often move quickly from one side of the divide to the other, from the category of being healthy to that of being ill (and indeed back again). Health is also the only social division in which one category, being 'well', is universally seen as desirable, whereas its opposite, being 'ill', has its own major institutions – like Britain's NHS – dedicated to its eradication.

Despite these peculiarities, there is still a strong case for treating health and illness as a social division. At its most basic, the sense of difference that comes from even small losses of health (minor changes that would otherwise hardly warrant calling a social division) is arguably among the more intense of all divisions. The misery and social isolation caused by catching the common cold, let alone being disabled (Chapter 11) or having a serious illness, can feel overwhelming, while in turn serious illness can lead to death, arguably the most absolute of all 'social divisions'. But whereas we all must come in the end to death, the risks of an early death or being ill are not the same for everybody in society. These variations in health, illness and death are strongly related to other social divisions, so health cannot be treated separately from them.

It follows that we need to approach health in a somewhat different way from that used in the earlier chapters in this book. These each took one social division and explored its meaning and significance in contemporary life, analytically separate from all the others. While we shall look at the categories of 'healthy' and 'ill' as comprising a division, this chapter (like those on community and poverty) will also reflect on the ways other social divisions can be seen to interact with and, indeed, produce this particular one. Health can be thought of as an 'arena' in which various social divisions compete to influence a particular outcome. Gender and age are self-evidently related to certain kinds of physical conditions, and therefore the ways that gender and age are socially constructed (Chapters 3 and 8) are relevant to the social construction of what we think of as being 'healthy' or 'ill'. Class and ethnicity have also routinely been shown to have statistical associations with variations in health. It follows that in incorporating the divisions that have already been discussed, and in emphasising social construction rather than a 'biomedical model' (challenged in each of the earlier chapters on childhood, sexuality and disability), this chapter is a natural development of our original approach.

Although the consequences of lack of health are fundamental to our feelings, opportunities to lead a full life and our sense of identity, this chapter is more concerned with the social explanations of health and illness. This focus involves an exploration of how a range of social divisions interconnect to produce health (or interact more generally, as we saw in the last chapter, in the context of producing a sense of community). The starting point for this is to consider what is really meant by the terms 'health' and 'illness'.

Defining health and illness

'Health', 'illness', 'well', 'unwell', 'fit' and 'unfit' are all terms that we use to describe our perceptions of bodily states. Because contemporary society is characterised, inter alia, by having specialist medical services and personnel operating in permanent organisations, there is an administrative system to measure and record illness, but no comparable social apparatus to record health systematically. The existence of social institutions to combat illness – being 'ill' is an undesirable problem whereas being 'fit' is not – means that there is a strong normative tendency to talk more about illness, leaving health to be a residual category implicitly defined as a lack of illness. One notable exception is the positive view of health as well-being, which was central to the definition put forward in the Constitution of the World Health Organization in 1946, and still prominent on its web pages. Here, health is defined as 'a state of complete physical, mental and social well being and not merely the absence of disease or infirmity' (WHO 1999). In contrast, medical definitions are primarily based on the process of diagnosis of the biomedical pathology that constitutes 'disease' (or its absence).

But even a disease-based approach can lead to quite different ways of identifying ill health. What counts as disease is not a given biological fact, but in part socially constructed. When does mental illness become, or cease to be, an illness? Do the symptoms and medical treatment of pregnancy render it an illness? When we say someone is ill, that categorisation arises out of a social process, in which human beings decide what is going to be called sickness or health. A detailed study of the social construction of these medical definitions by clinicians is reported by Brown (1995).

Social construction means not only that our general perceptions of what is health arise out of social processes, but also that some things are counted as lack of health while others are not, and this in turn feeds back into our perceptions. To take the most obvious example, we could define 'illness' as cases recorded by GPs and hospitals. Such morbidity records are used to describe social and geographical variations in health within and between countries. Morbidity data (together with death rates) have played an important part in influencing the development of welfare policies. Information about rates of illnesses has been collected in most countries as they industrialised and so encountered the need for welfare programmes to deal with the public health problems of overcrowding and lack of sanitation (Strong, 1990). However, morbidity measures depend first on what people report as 'illnesses' to doctors, and how that comes about (Dingwall 1976; Blaxter and Paterson 1982); then on how doctors and paramedical professions perceive, process and medically diagnose them and finally on how administrators register them as cases of particular diseases in the population.

Thus on the one hand, there are apparent 'facts' about illness, such as cancer registrations, outbreaks of communicable diseases (for example various types of food poisoning, measles, hepatitis, tuberculosis and meningitis) and cases of congenital malformations such as spina bifida and Down's syndrome. Similarly, the medical process produces data on low birth weight, teenage pregnancies and obesity, which then become the 'truths' around which public policy is debated. On the other hand, even in the examples of serious illness, 'cases' only occur if first the 'patients' see themselves as sufficiently 'ill' to consult a doctor, and second, when doctors decide on medical diagnoses. As we shall see below, attendance at surgeries and self-descriptions of being ill vary between men and women, old and young, and middle and working classes. The ways in which doctors react to and treat their patients are similarly socially patterned and socially produced (Cartwright and O'Brien 1976; Bloor 1976; Doyal 1994, 1995; Bury 2004). This suggests that the 'facts' about illness are more dependent on processes of social construction than is commonly recognised.

A clearer and less disputable measurement is death (certification of death is one of the more complete administrative records), but mortality rates imply a somewhat extreme level of illness, shifting the focus from the living to the dead. Despite this, the Black Report (Townsend et al. 1992) – 'which remains one of the most influential documents on health inequalities' (Bury 1997: 48) – chose mortality rates and causes of death as its key measurements. These convey the powerful notion of life chances, fairness of expectations and the penalty some groups pay through early death. Death rates also are well documented over a long period and do not suffer from short-term fluctuations, so that comparisons between periods, locations and groups are relatively secure.

It has been long recognised that rates of death vary, for example higher mortality rates are found among older age groups and, within this, men tend to die at an earlier age than women. Obviously, populations with high proportions of older people (and men) would be expected to have higher mortality rates than those with lower proportions. To control for this, mortality rates can be statistically standardised to allow for variations in age and gender distributions between sub-populations. The most widely used standardised mortality measure is known as the Standard Mortality Ratio (SMR). However, even when age and gender distributions between specific populations are controlled for, differences in mortality still remain. Other commonly used mortality rates include infant mortality rates and deaths from specific causes (for example different types of cancer, heart disease, asthma and suicide).

These individual rates have normally been used as separate variables. However, they can also be combined to produce composite indices of health status, such as that developed by Townsend et al. (1986) to study the relationship between health and poverty. Administrative health data for census wards, consisting of premature SMRs (deaths below the age of 65), long-term sick and disabled persons (aged over 16 years) and low birth weight rates (under 2500 grams) were used to calculate a single health status score for each ward. The rationale for choosing these particular variables was that they reflected different aspects of health status: past health experience (premature deaths); future child development and past maternal health (low birth weight); and past and current health status (long-term sick and disabled). These index scores were then used with other variables and indices to investigate the association between health status and other socio-economic factors. High correlations were found between poor health status and material deprivation in urban areas, but less clearly so in rural areas.

The example of mortality rates shows that, while medical records and official statistics need to be treated with caution because they are socially constructed, they should not be dismissed out of hand. Often they are the only available data and, as the Black and Townsend studies demonstrate, can still be used effectively to explore social aspects of health. If anything, there is too much data on specific illnesses, so that researchers have to select which items to explore, so opening the door to further confusion.

Asking the 'patient'

The only realistic alternative to starting from the use of medical records, collected for purposes other than social research, is to ask ordinary people directly how well they feel and how they define health. This approach has been forcibly advocated as a corrective to the medical standpoint and a way of increasing information about health among sub-populations such as ethnic minorities and local communities (Williams and Popay 1994; Popay et al. 1998; Payne 1999). Studies that have examined such lay definitions have found that people think about health in several different ways, according to who they are. One of the most influential of these studies identified three different elements of health:

- health as absence of illness or vacuum
- health as reserve or capital (for example a 'strong constitution' that is resistant to illness)
- health as equilibrium or well-being. (Herzlich 1973)

Despite differences in the terminology used, later studies found similar distinctions (Blaxter and Paterson 1982; Pill and Stott 1982; Williams 1983; d'Houtard and Field 1984; Calnan 1987; Blaxter 1990). A fourth element, functional capacity (the ability to do things) is also identified by Blaxter.

These elements are not discrete, and individual accounts are often found to contain aspects of each. This is clear from our comments added to the following extract:

> I feel alert [well-being] and can always think of lots of things to do. No aches and pains – nothing wrong with me – [absence of illness] and I can go out and jog [functional capacity]. I suppose I have more energy [reserve], I can get up and do such a lot. (Blaxter 1990: 19)

Although the different elements are found in combination, accounts are socially patterned. Many studies have found that 'health as well-being' was more likely to be expressed by the middle class or those with higher levels of education, with working-class respondents and those with lower educational levels expressing health as 'absence of illness' (for example d'Houtard and Field 1984). However, this pattern was not repeated in the Health and Lifestyles Survey (Blaxter 1990). Here the greatest distinction was found between those of different age groups, with the young more likely to see health as well-being and older respondents drawing on ideas of functional capacity. Gender differences were found among the younger age group: young men often expressing ideas of physical fitness, while young women emphasised health as vitality. Howlett et al. (1992) also report differences in health beliefs between ethnic groups.

Health status questionnaires have also been designed to quantify health in general populations, those with specific diseases and disabilities, and measure 'quality of life'. These questionnaires attempt to measure the multidimensional aspects (social, psychological and physical) of health and illness through self-rating scales. Thus, the Nottingham Health Profile (Hunt et al. 1986) includes the following 'yes/no' statements, to which we have added comments:

- I'm in pain when I walk [physical]
- I lose my temper easily these days [psychological]
- I feel there is nobody I am close to [social]

The widely used Short Forms-36 and -12 (Ware 1993) concentrate on the self-assessment of physical and psychological health alone, while others focus on behavioural/lifestyle factors (for example Berkman and Breslow 1983; Pill et al. 1993). Although not often employed by sociologists, these approaches have been important in health policy, such as the 'Health of the Nation' programmes. A full discussion of these and other health status scaling techniques can be found in Bowling (1997).

Explaining patterns of health

The previous section showed that the study of health variations involves dealing with a complex phenomenon. They can be studied from the perspectives of several disciplines, not least sociology, social policy and epidemiology (the branch of medicine concerned with the distribution of disease in human populations) and, indeed, from alternative positions within disciplines. Differences between these approaches are made all the more acute by the political nature of health policies: each particular conception of health and illness implies that one kind of intervention would be more effective than others.

In other words, there are variations both in how health is defined and in the kinds of explanations that are sought for them; of course, definitions also imply certain types of explanation. If ill health is thought of mainly as symptoms, viruses or genetics, this points towards solutions in medical technology, whereas if ill health is defined in terms of loss of well-being, then intervention might mean tackling pollution, poverty, unemployment, loneliness or institutionalised racism. Those accounts that have drawn on lay definitions and focused on health status have been associated mainly with identifying inequalities in health and have sought explanations of them based in social processes. But even here there are disagreements about what are the most important causes of differences in health. These disagreement have sometimes been intense (Macintyre 1997).

Dahlgren and Whitehead (1991) have suggested that the complex picture of factors affecting inequalities in health can be mapped into five related clusters:

1. biological models of illness
2. lifestyles
3. social and community influences
4. living and working conditions
5. general socio-economic, cultural and environmental conditions

Their starting point is the cluster of studies using physical or straightforward *biological models of illness*. These take age, sex, genetic inheritance and *in utero* (pre-birth) experiences, which predispose to being at risk of certain illnesses later in life, as producing differences in health. Individuals have no control over these factors.

In contrast, a second cluster of factors are sometimes seen (not least by health educators, moralisers and right-wing politicians) as things that people can and should control as matters of personal responsibility. These are the individual *lifestyles* of diet, consumption of alcohol, nicotine and other drugs, and exercise that differentially predispose to health. The 1999 White Paper's 'Popular Summary' (DoH 1999), with its '10 Tips for Healthy Living', is a good example of this kind of well-intentioned advice.

Any objection that unhealthy lifestyles are mainly associated with people living in poverty, and therefore that intervention should be addressed to the alleviation of poverty, found little favour with government in the 1980s and 90s. The 'official line' was reflected in the Conservative minister of health's 1986 observations about the connection between health and poverty:

> I honestly don't think that it has anything to do with poverty. The problem very often for many people is just ignorance ... and failing to realise that they do have some control over their own lives. (quoted in Bury 1997: 64)

Dahlgren and Whitehead's next two clusters are more sociological: *social and community influences*, and *living and working conditions*. Although these might be considered by some as individual features, in practice most refer to life experiences that no single person can control. For instance, social circumstances involving a lack of supportive personal relationships, community processes such as risk of crime and the occupational experiences of stress or accidents at work are not simply there for individuals to experience or avoid at will.

In this sense, the distinction between the two categories, social/community and living/working, is not particularly helpful, nor should they be regarded as equally important: for example, the 'Whitehall studies' have demonstrated how working conditions have a major impact on health (see below). There is also overlap with Dahlgren and Whitehead's final category, *general socio-economic, cultural and environmental conditions*, which is meant to identify factors even more susceptible to international market forces and therefore even less within individual control. In practice, this category is similar to the previous two – are poor housing, low income, and unemployment 'general socio-economic' or 'living and working' conditions?

While the Dahlgren and Whitehead typology is less than perfect (Syme 1996; Shy 1997), it has been widely adopted: if nothing else it offers a way of identifying where particular research contributions stand. Developments of the model have been influential in the Acheson Report (DoH 1998a) and the subsequent public health Green and White Papers (DoH 1998b, 1999). These government documents placed greater emphasis on the social nature and interactions of the clusters and the need for improvements in access to services.

In the most recent public health White Paper, significantly titled Choosing Health (DoH 2004), greater emphasis has been laid on 'individual responsibility'. Reflecting New Labour's attempts to use 'choice mechanisms' in the delivery of health and social policy, the White Paper lays out plans to facilitate healthy lifestyle choices. While displaying some similarities to policy solutions usually advocated by previous Conservative governments, the White Paper also stresses that it is harder for disadvantaged sections of the population to make healthy choices.

It would be wrong to think that this change in government policy reflects unanimity among those who have studied health inequalities. A number of writers have identified four major points of disagreement about the explanations of inequalities (see Armstrong 1994; Benzeval et al. 1995; Bury 1997; Macintyre 1997; Scambler 1997; Taylor and Field 1997; and, with a more medical emphasis, BMA 1995). On the one hand, there are two arguments why health inequalities are not a product of socio-economic processes, and in particular, social class. The first of these argues that it is poor health that leads to social disadvantage, rather than the other way round, thus standing the conventional sociological wisdom on its head. The second view proposes that the apparent connection does not even actually exist, being no more than an artificial product of unreliable statistics and incorrect reasoning. Against these two positions are those who do argue that there are health/deprivation connections, but this camp is split into two. One group attributes unequal health outcomes to socially structured differences in people's financial and resource circumstances, while the other sees the key issue as being what people know, believe and think (their 'culture') and how this makes them act. Each of these four positions is given fuller consideration in the next section.

Health inequalities and their explanations

The last-mentioned of these schools of thought – 'cultural' or 'behavioural' theory – is the basis for the 'lifestyle' approach already discussed, in terms of the Dahlgren/Whitehead typology and Conservative reactions to the Black Report. It focuses on what people believe, suggesting that because groups perceive health and its causes in different ways, their health-related behaviours are going to vary. As well as being specifically concerned with 'good practice' in healthy living behaviour, this approach also takes account of basic orientations to life. For instance, compared with less advantaged groups, well-educated people in jobs where they have personal autonomy, and can control others, are more likely to be knowledgeable about good health practice, have higher expectations of the effectiveness of taking action against illness and expect faster and better medical treatment to protect their health. This cultural 'mindset' can be seen as contributing to their lower levels of illness, translating any material advantage into attitudes conducive to good health: it is not the material resources available to them per se that counts but the way they think and act.

As well as offering this general mode of explanation, the cultural perspective has particular resonance in respect of ethnic group variations in health. While it is true that variation within each ethnic group tends to be greater than between groups (Nazroo 1997: 240), there are substantial differences in folkways (traditional and customary ways of living) and traditional remedies, ideas about health, religious beliefs and morally and socially acceptable ways of life. For example, Howlett et al. (1992) report that Indians tend to see health as a matter of luck and regard smoking and alcohol as major causes of illness, whereas the white group see ill health as the 'fault of the individual' and more often caused by stress. Thorogood's (1990) description of the home remedies used by women of Caribbean origin raises the question of when and why African-Caribbean families use medical services and so become part of medical statistics. American research has suggested that psychiatric misdiagnosis of African-Caribbeans may be attributable to cultural misunderstandings, such as the way language is used and social behaviour is sanctioned. These cultural and behavioural factors are not easily reducible to the material circumstances of class or employment.

Critics of this view argue that mindsets come from social locations such as class position and rather than intervening to try to change ideas, it is the structural systems that must first be tackled. The freedom of choice, which is otherwise open to the better off, is constrained among the poor by unsatisfactory housing, physical environments, working conditions and income. This argument from a 'materialist perspective', the second of the four points of contention (and exemplified by the discussion of class differences in Chapter 2) tends to treat cultural variations as a product of social class or wider socio-economic systems. Emphasis may be placed either on the constraints and workings of the economic system, or on the actual poverty that it produces.

The Black Report and Townsend's work on deprivation argued that poverty is a significant cause of ill health. Living in poverty brings direct problems (Chapter 12) as well as the stress of dealing with them. In a 1991 survey of low-income families, a fifth of parents and a tenth of children had gone without food at least once in the previous month (National Children's Home 1991). Low-income interviewees had to do without proper food and heating:

> I don't cut down, as I say, with the kids. I try to make sure they get, but like I cook a meal and as long as there's enough for them, I make do with a piece of toast ... Many a Sunday afternoon our electric has gone. We've just waited 'til Monday. (Kempson et al. 1994)

It is hardly surprising if people exposed to these low levels of living tend to suffer ill health. Among families living on income support, over two-thirds report ill health, with asthma, bronchitis and eczema the commonest complaints (Cohen et al. 1992). They had no 'spare' money to meet the extra costs of illness or pay for the heating needed to relieve symptoms. Not only do poor housing conditions contribute to poor child health, but their parents suffer from depression and stress-related disorders as a result of their financial difficulties (Morris and Ritchie 1994). However, this view of health inequalities as the product of deprivation is rejected by the third of our four schools of thought. While not denying an association between ill health and disadvantaged economic positions in society, it has been claimed that people are 'socially selected' by their health to occupy distinctive social locations (Illsley

1955, 1986; Klein 1988). The healthy get better jobs, the unhealthy descend into unemployment or low-paid jobs. Illness causes their poverty, rather than the other way round.

While at the margins (extreme physical or mental disability), bodily conditions may limit occupational achievement (although the research base to support this is limited), extensive social mobility research has shown that by far the biggest factors in movements up and down the class scale have been the changing availability of types of occupation, and class differences in access to qualifications and desirable jobs (Payne 1987a). Those advocating 'social selection' have not properly understood the dynamics of social mobility. Nor is their underlying logic clear. If we take the case of infant mortality rates (deaths within one year of birth, per 1000 live births, we need to explain why very young children die and why infant mortality rates are worse the lower down the class scale one goes – a pattern that holds even as rates improve over the years (Table 14.1).

Table 14.1 Infant mortality[1] by social class:[2] UK

NS-SEC	1994–96	2000–02
Managerial and professional	4.4	3.6
Intermediate	6.1	5.5
Small employers and own account workers	4.9	4.8
Lower supervisory and technical	5.3	4.3
Semi-routine and routine	7.5	6.9
Sole registration	7.9	7.3

Notes
1 Deaths within one year of birth per 1000 live births.
2 Classified by occupation of father – births 'inside marriage'.

Source: adapted from Figure 6.4. ONS (2004e).

This child health problem, coming after the parents became members of a lower class, could not directly have caused the parents' social class location. The social selection argument actually implies either a three-part logical chain: parents' previous poor health leads to low social class, which leads to poor infant health (that is, class does have a direct effect in the middle of the chain) or that parents' previous poor health directly causes poor infant health (which misses out the class element, but then does not explain the observed class differentials). Similarly, if we examine class differentials in the use of dental services, we see sharp contrasts, as in Table 14.2. Propensity to take up medical services, or prevalence of tooth decay, is an implausible explanation of why people are in their particular occupations or classes, whereas class differences (either as knowledge and good health practice or having the resources to gain access to treatment) are a more convincing explanation of propensity to visit the dentist.

Table 14.2 Adults who visit dentists for regular check-ups (UK, 2003)

Socio-economic group	%
Large employers and higher managerial	71
Higher professional	71
Lower managerial and professional	66
Intermediate	63
Small employers and own account	63
Lower supervisory and technical	58
Semi-routine	54
Routine	50
Never worked and long-term unemployed	45
All	61

Source: adapted from ONS (2003a), Table 7.35.

The last of the four arguments, that class and health are not actually connected in the way the Black Report suggests, is largely based on the argument that 'class' is not a real phenomenon, but rather an intellectual construct. Two things follow from this: first, 'class', because it is only an idea represented by categories of occupations, cannot cause poor 'health', and second, the way in which class is constructed becomes crucial. In connection with health inequalities, Illsley (1986, 1990), Klein (1988) and Carr-Hill (1990) have argued that classes have changed in definition and size (see Chapter 2), so that comparison over time is invalid. As they are large aggregates of people in a range of occupations, there must also inevitably be a range of variation within each class (not least because social mobility moves people between classes). A parallel debate in mainstream sociology has been stimulated by Pahl's doubts about using occupation to define class categories (Pahl 1993).

The case that class is an artefact and its association with health is 'artefactual' is in part correct. It is true that definitions and classification schemes have evolved over time, while the classes they identify have shown major changes – the manual classes decreasing, the middle classes expanding (Chapter 2). This does make time-based comparisons more difficult, and the replacement of the old Registrar General's Social Class schema (extensively used in medical records) for the 2001 census is a long overdue recognition of the need to change. It is also the case that the present members of a class may well have been mobile into it and so bring previous health-related characteristics from their former class.

However, some of the difficulties that Illsley identifies are due precisely to the limitations of the old Registrar General's classification; other schema offer more flexible alternatives. If there is 'excessive' variation within classes, the answer lies in devising better representations of the class structure, not in abandoning class as a variable. It is insufficient to claim that the nature of social classes has changed or that people are socially mobile: that does not render all association between class and health irrelevant.

The main problem with the artefactual critique is that it misrepresents what research based on social class is actually trying to do. The purpose of a class schema is to provide a framework for analysis, not a complete answer. As Chapter 2 showed, class is the connection between the fundamental economic and power structures of society and the lives people lead. Except for a few, unrepresentative purists, most researchers implicitly assume that class is not directly associated with every outcome, but works through a complex of other 'intervening variables' to shape the social patterns under investigation. Class is associated, for instance, with work conditions, education, income, housing and beliefs; each of these factors interacts and is in turn associated with health and illness. Class is only the starting point for the construction of a 'narrative' that explores how the end point of health or illness can be traced back to the deep structures of the social order. To complain that any one class schema does not explain everything perfectly is to miss the point entirely. Tables 14.1 and 14.2 showed clear 'class gradients' in two aspects of health: the challenge is how to explain them, not to try to explain them away.

Health inequalities and other social divisions

Infant mortality and visits to the dentist are only two examples from a strikingly large range of class/health associations. Figure 14.1 from the 1999 White Paper offers another illustration, comparing the death rate of professional male workers with those in the other classes. For the unskilled, the rate is nearly three times greater. The same source (DoH 1999) also shows that this differential, far from decreasing, was not only much smaller in the early 1930s than it is today, but seems to be currently growing at a faster rate. Rather than seeing this as an artefact or social selection at work, the differential can be linked to the 'Whitehall studies', which show how civil servants at different grades, carefully studied over a number of years, developed illnesses in a pattern that reflected their hierarchical positions in employment. Those in controlling positions systematically enjoyed better health and survival rates than those with little control over their working lives (see for example Marmot et al. 1984, 1991; Bosma et al. 1997; Marmot 2004). The 'narrative' linking class to health seems to indicate work conditions and stress levels as key intervening variables.

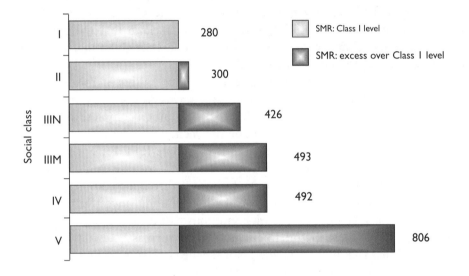

Figure 14.1 European Standard Mortality Ratio per 100,000 population for men aged 20–64 (England and Wales, 1991–93)

Source: adapted from Department of Health (1999), Figure 4.1.

It would be possible to present a series of class-based tables here, but this would be to misrepresent what researchers actually do (it could also create the impression that class is the only important social division). A more typical product is Table 14.3, which shows visits to GP surgeries by gender (here, strictly speaking, 'sex') and age, as well as household head's class (and the unemployed). GP consultations are important because, as we saw earlier, cases of 'illness' cannot become part of the health record without them.

Table 14.3 GP consultations[1] for age, sex and occupational group[2] (GB, 2003)

	Male %				Female %			
	_16–44_	_45–64_	_65+_	_Total_	_16–44_	_45–64_	_65+_	_Total_
Working	7	10	9	8	14	14	13	14
Unemployed	9	21[3]	0[3]	11	13	17	66	15
Economically inactive	14	19	20	18	19	22	22	21
All	8	12	19	11	15	17	21	17

Notes
1 Consultations in previous 14 days.
2 Based on occupation of household head.
3 The values for unemployed men aged 45–64 and 65 and over are 'deemed unreliable'.

Source: adapted from ONS (2003a), Table 7.22.

A broadly similar picture applies to self-reported illness. Unemployed people generally report worse health than working people, and this tends to be greater for people later in their working careers (see particularly the columns for 45–64-year-old men). Table 14.4 suggests that each of the three social divisions – class (indirectly indicated by employment/unemployment), age and gender – have independent effects on health.

Table 14.4 Incidence of self-reported acute and chronic illness for gender, age and occupational groups (GB, 2003, percentages)

	_16–44_		_45–64_		_65 and over_		_Total_	
	Chronic	_Acute_	_Chronic_	_Acute_	_Chronic_	_Acute_	_Chronic_	_Acute_
Male								
Working	7	8	14	9	12	4	10	9
Unemployed	14	7	24	10	0	0	16	7
Economically inactive	27	18	56	33	41	20	41	22
Total	10	9	24	15	39	19	20	13
Female								
Working	8	11	14	13	17	13	10	12
Unemployed	16	14	27	13	0	0	19	24
Economically inactive	20	15	45	29	43	24	37	23
Total	11	12	25	19	41	24	22	17

Note
Chronic – limiting longstanding illness as indicator of chronic illness; Acute – illness in previous 14 days.

Source: adapted from ONS (2003a), Tables 7.17 and 7.19.

Although age and gender are separate social divisions, they also interact, for example women live longer and young men are more prone to die from injuries and poisoning (ONS 1998a). Men are more liable to die of circulatory disease in late working life and cancer in old age. Gender differences alone do not bring this out: it requires the inclusion of age to obtain a fuller picture. Attitudes towards illness, in terms of propensity to say in interview that one has health problems, are also gendered. Table 14.5 shows that men are less likely to define themselves as having health problems, again, most notably among the very old.

As Chapter 8 showed, these data are likely to be subject to change, as 'early old age' is progressively socially redefined as a life stage of greater activity and vitality, and 'late old age' expands with more people living longer.

Table 14.5 EuroQol[1] assessment for age and gender groups (GB, 1996, percentages)

	16–44		45–64		65–74		75 and +		Total	
	M	*F*	*M*	*F*	*M*	*F*	*M*	*F*	*M*	*F*
No problems	74	70	54	50	38	38	30	21	60	55
Mild problems	15	16	18	20	23	19	19	19	17	18
Moderate problems	5	6	9	11	16	16	21	16	9	10
Substantial problems	6	8	18	18	23	27	30	44	14	17

Note
1 A self-assessed health status questionnaire.

Source: ONS (1998b), Table 8.38.

The differences between men and women in these health data are particularly interesting in light of debates about gender. Feminist writers have drawn attention to the distinctive features of women's health (for example Arber 1990; Doyal 1994). On the one hand, medical records indicate that women suffer more from acute and chronic illnesses, are more likely to be treated for mental illness and obviously have distinctive health needs concerning pregnancy and childbirth. On the other hand, they are less likely to work in hazardous occupations, or engage in 'high-risk', macho lifestyle behaviour such as excessive consumption of alcohol, dangerous sports or violence. Women are more likely to consult their doctors and admit to illness, although their willingness to adopt the 'sick role' seems to be related in a complex way to child care and their continuing role in domestic labour (Chapter 3). The prevalence of male doctors (and female nurses) is seen as gendering healthcare. The modern tendency to define social issues as medical problems has resulted in a 'medicalisation' of women's bodies.

This perspective has more recently been questioned in two ways. Cameron and Bernardes (1998: 115) have argued that it is time to consider 'men's health for a change'. Men die younger, do not use health services properly and engage in more life-threatening activities. These basic social facts will not be properly investigated if women are seen as the only category having 'interesting' health research problems. Second, work by Macintyre et al. (1996) has questioned whether women actually are more ill than men. In a study in which men and women were carefully matched for the grade of their jobs and perceived working conditions, there were no gender differences in health. Overall, women reported more colds, eye strain, aches, nerves and sleeping problems, but no more than men in the equivalent jobs. The higher female totals were a product of their concentration into certain jobs. Men as well as women were also found to encounter difficulties balancing domestic and employment commitments. These findings suggest that the relationship between gender, health and other social divisions is a more complex one than hitherto recognised.

The complexity of interacting factors can also be seen in health and illness patterns among ethnic groups. While overall there are relatively few health differences between ethnic groups, some do exist. For example, African-Caribbeans tend to be more prone to strokes, as well as the more commonly mentioned sickle cell anaemia. Several Asian groups suffer more from eye problems, high blood pressure and diabetes.

As well as cultural variations (language difficulties are a particular barrier to communicating about illness), ethnic groups also differ in the kinds of occupations they pursue, the proportions of men and women in paid employment and their demographic profiles (see Chapter 4). Although health data including these factors are not readily available, it is reasonable to suggest that gender and age, in addition to class, play a part in explaining inequalities. In Table 14.6, differences between ethnic groups in standard mortality rates persist even after taking social class into account. Even greater specific group variation exists within the categories used here, as the footnote to this table shows.

Class, gender and age by no means constitute a complete list of explanatory factors in ethnic health inequalities. The range of factors and competing explanations discussed earlier in this chapter should not be forgotten. If we consider the psycho-social stress of being subjected to racism, the fact that some illnesses such as sickle cell anaemia have a genetic component and many ethnic groups live in inner-city locations with poorer health services, we must not only anticipate ethnic health differences but expect to use a variety of explanations for this (see Senior and Viveash 1998: 158–86).

Table 14.6 Standard Mortality Ratio by social class and country of birth, men aged 20–64, all causes: England and Wales (1991–93)

R.G. Social Class	All	Caribbean countries	Indian subcontinent	Scotland	Ireland (all parts)
I/II	71	83	96	82	95
IIIN	100	84	112	121	127
IIIM	117	105	120	169	166
IV/V	135	99	158	186	173
Non-manual	77	83	100	89	102
Manual	124	102	140	176	169
Adjusted for class	100	82	117[1]	132	129

Note
1 India, 114; Pakistan, 110; Bangaladesh, 159.

Source: Drever and Whitehead (1997), Tables 9.4, 9.5.

Table 14.6 also included data for people born in Scotland and Ireland but now living in England and Wales. Particularly among the manual classes, these white migrants share higher SMRs. When we put those data alongside national figures, as in Table 14.7, further differences emerge.

England has the lowest SMRs, and the difference between nations is greater than between men and women. Scotland in particular has poorer health, which, taken together with the political and cultural characteristics discussed in Chapter 6, might suggest that a characteristic way of life exists in Scotland. Some caution is, however, needed in making statements about large aggregates of data like countries: this chapter's earlier analysis suggests that a number of social divisions could be explored in order to account for national patterns. There are nonetheless substantial geographical differences in health, as Table 14.8 shows.

Table 14.7 Standard Mortality Ratio for UK countries and gender (2000)

Country	Male SMR	Female SMR	Region SMR
England	98	98	98
Wales	102	102	102
Scotland	117	117	118
Northern Ireland	105	105	107

Source: ONS; General Register Office for Scotland; Northern Ireland Statistics and Research Agency.

Table 14.8 Self-reported health status indicators for the ONS classification of English areas, 1994–96 (average percentage standardised for age)

Area	Health: poor/bad	Longstanding illness	Acute sickness	Prescribed medication
England	22.6	39.6	15.0	40.3
Mining & industrial	28.0	42.7	16.7	42.7
Inner London	27.9	42.2	18.2	40.7
Urban	25.7	40.3	15.4	40.0
Rural	21.6	38.5	14.4	39.7
Mature	21.5	39.7	14.7	40.2
Prosperous	18.7	38.2	14.2	39.6

Source: adapted from Social and Community Planning Research (1999).

The demographics, occupational opportunities, physical environment and health services of inner London, and areas marked by the run-down of heavy industry, are clearly reflected in these figures (see also Joshi et al. 2000; MacIntyre et al. 2002). Residents of mature areas (long-established towns) are relatively advantaged, while prosperous areas – dormitory suburbs for the prosperous middle classes, mainly in the southeast – show quite different health patterns from those in urban or rural areas (and indeed in other aspects of social life, as we saw in the last chapter on communities). Rural areas contain a wider range of lifestyles, and a distinctive problem of service delivery for remote locations.

Conclusion

We would want to balance two broad views of health. Despite advocating here a sociological rather than an individual or biological approach, we would wish to maintain that no single perspective offers a complete answer. Indeed, while it is easy to show that health is associated with social divisions, there is more work to be done on why there are such associations. What precisely are the causal connections between social factors and health?

We therefore welcome more recent developments that recognise how the various elements (not least the major social divisions) interact, such as Macintyre's (1997: 740) speculation that the combined processes operating at the top of the social scale are not just the mirror image of what is happening at the bottom. Similarly, there seems much promise in new work based on three perspectives: a life-course approach (Chapter 8) that looks at the cumulation of effects and risks (for example Power et al. 1996); the connections being explored between social environment – low income and employment context – and psycho-social factors like stress (for example Marmot and Wilkinson 1999); and the recognition that broadbrush analyses that work for some purposes can also be elaborated into finer-grained and more sophisticated models based on explanations from several levels (for example Popay et al. 1998).

Health does have a social as well as a physical basis. Risk of illness and premature death are socially patterned: health inequalities divide people in a range of ways. Consideration of social divisions – in particular class, gender, ethnicity and age – help at one level of analysis to explain health inequalities. In return, other social divisions, like national differences, childhood, sexuality, disability and community life, are affected by health and access to health services. Health and illness are not simply products of one or other of these other divisions: being sick, particularly chronically sick, is a deeply divisive experience which makes health a social division in its own right, as well as one whose interactions with other social divisions provide a key to unlock the complexity of contemporary society.

Discussion Questions

1. Is health a distinct social division?

2. What factors do Dahlgren and Whitehead identify as causes of illness?

3. What is the relationship between health and social class?

4. Which is the more important for understanding and preventing illness: biological or social factors?

FURTHER READING

An introductory but clear account of this field can be found in Senior, M. and Viveash, B. *Health and Illness* (London: Macmillan – now Palgrave Macmillan, 1998). Among a number of very good textbooks, Bury, M. *Health and Illness in a Changing Society* (London: Routledge, 1997) is particularly well written, while Taylor, S. and Field, D. *Sociology of Health and Health Care*, 3rd edn (Oxford: Blackwell, 2003) gives systematic coverage. Bury, M. provides a 'short introduction' which emphasises the dynamics of health and illness *Health and Illness* (Cambridge: Polity Press, 2005). Townsend, P., Davidson, N. and Whitehead, M. (eds) *Inequalities in Health: The Black Report and The Health Divide*, rev. edn (Harmondsworth: Penguin, 1992) remains a classic on health and poverty.

SECTION V

Conclusions

CHAPTER 15

Social Divisions as a Sociological Perspective

GEOFF PAYNE

This chapter will provide you with a broad critical understanding of the following issues in social division:

- The definition of a social division
- Social divisions are socially embedded forms of social inequality
- Social difference, social inequality and social division
- Although universal and persistent, social divisions are not immutable or 'natural'
- Social division and social cohesion: overlapping memberships, cross-cutting ties and social conformity
- The complexity of multiple memberships and identities
- Social division and sociological theory: structural-functionalism, Marxism and post-modernism
- Are there only a few social divisions or many? Alternative perspectives
- Hierarchy and inequality versus 'others' and personal identity

We have deliberately written each of the chapters so far in a way that 'defines' social divisions indirectly by talking about key examples. This approach gives a good feel of what social division is all about through an exploration of cases and details. An alternative approach would have been to start with a formal definition expressed as a set of abstract principles. A full definition, of course, needs both examples and a precise statement of principles. This final chapter provides the other part of the definition and will also enable us to reflect on what social divisions in the plural might mean as a way of 'seeing' society.

While division can result in two, three or more categories, these form an interrelated whole that includes all members of a society: paradoxically the *distinction* between the categories expresses the logical *connection* between them. These distinctions are marked by clear-cut – rather than minimal – differences in material circumstances or cultural advantages (although 'clear-cut' and 'minimal' are terms which at the margin involve subjective judgements). The differences between categories are maintained by a normative order that supports those who accept the division and constrains those who seek to alter it.

A definition of 'social divisions'

A 'social division' of the kind explored in the preceding chapters conforms to nine core characteristics:

● A social division is a principle of social organisation resulting in a society-wide distinction between two or more logically interrelated categories of people, which are socially sanctioned as substantially different from one another in material and cultural ways.

● Although not permanently established in a given form, a social division tends to be long-lasting and is sustained by dominant cultural beliefs, the organisation of social institutions and the situational interaction of individuals.

● Membership of a category in a social division confers unequal opportunities of access to desirable 'resources' of all kinds and therefore different life chances and lifestyles from membership of other categories.

● A social division is socially constructed, in the sense that it is not a simple manifestation of 'natural' or 'inevitable' laws of existence, but this does not mean that it can be ignored or revised by the moment-to-moment social interactions, interpretations, decisions or social acts of individuals.

● The extent of differentiation between categories varies from social division to social division, but movement across a divide is either rare or relatively slow to be achieved.

● Being socially divided tends to produce shared social identities for people in the same category, often expressed by reference to their perceived difference from those in an alternative category of the same division.

● However much specific social divisions are opposed by those disadvantaged by them, the principle of social divisions is a universal systematic feature of human society.

● Each social division encompasses all members of society in one or other of its categories, but individuals seldom have matching profiles of category membership across the range of social divisions.

● An examination of life chances and lifestyles is an empirical method of identifying social divisions and categories.

This definition means that rather than concentrating on just one or two social divisions, we need to include at least a dozen in our sociological perspective (Payne 2004).

As we saw in Chapter 1, the idea of social division entails both extensive differences and a continuity of existence over time, which stems from its integration in the social order through values, institutions and day-by-day interactions. On the one hand, there is a sense, if not of permanence, then massive inertia: it is not easy to challenge and change the boundaries. On the other hand, all the contributors have shown how things have changed over time and stressed that social divisions are not immutable. The key to understanding this is the embedded nature of the social practices that sustain each division. It follows that, while not 'natural' laws, divisions are typically encountered as constraining (particularly so for those in the less advantaged categories) or sustaining (more so for the advantaged).

It might be tempting – and indeed not unfair – to read this emphasis on constraint, disadvantage and differential life chances as meaning that to some extent each of the contributors perceives social division as inherently undesirable. Some commentators, like Marsland and Saunders, have commented on the general tendency of sociologists to side with the underdog, or indeed to be ideologically biased. While it will be apparent from the style and content of the chapters that the authors have varying degrees of personal commitment to their topics, they are also all concerned with its sociological analysis. The fact that the divisions can reasonably be identified as social injustice, a potential source of unhappiness and even civil strife should lend purpose, rather than bias, to the analysis. All social arrangements entail settlements that bring relative advantage: those who gain most from present circumstances are likely to wish them to continue, not to have them challenged and to present the current outcome as a consensus supported by all parties, rather than one that yields advantages for some, to the disadvantage of others. One task of sociology is to question things that would otherwise be taken for granted, even if there are those who would rather not have such questions raised.

Because a social analyst is unhappy with the current patterns of a particular social division does not automatically lead to bias or a simplistic belief that all social divisions can somehow be removed. One may take comfort that this division or that takes a different form in some society described by anthropologists or historians, but there is no evidence of societies – even the simplest hunter-gatherer societies – operating without divisions. However, the universality of division is no justification for the continuation of all divisions in exactly their current form, or of extremes of differentiation.

Nonetheless, it is a feature of social divisions that they persist. As has been seen, one class system may give way to another, or the role of women may be enhanced through emancipation or entry into the workplace, but the core division survives. It may be possible to be socially mobile between classes, for cracks in the glass ceiling to be exploited or for us all to move through the life-course, but these are opportunities for individuals who need to devote many years of their lives to achieving the transition from one category to the other or moving the boundaries. Divisions are not absolute or invariable, but they do a pretty good job of seeming so to be.

In part, this appearance of substance comes from the nature of the categories. These are 'oppositional' both in the sense of opposing interests of different categories (advantaged/disadvantaged), but also in terms of defining one category in terms of another, as its mirror image. Although it is possible to make more of these notions of difference and comparison (for example see Hetherington and Munro 1997), there is little to be gained from straying into the arcane world of much post-structuralism and post-modernism. Contrary to any impression given by the often wordy elaborations of such writings, the core issue is fairly straightforward. Identity is not only shared with others, but expressed as not sharing or belonging with others. The identification of a more advantaged group, to which the disadvantaged do not belong and which is socially demarcated, makes the probability of change seem less likely. The characteristic lifestyles and life chances that go with category membership and identity mark off the boundaries between them, helping the sociologist to locate social division but reinforcing the maintenance of the differences.

This methodological point also relates to the observation that individuals hold dual (or multi-) memberships in a range of social divisions. As the Introduction stressed, people take their identities from a mixture of categories and therefore have some choice of identity. The 'profile of membership' differs from person to person, and is one of the reasons why simple explanations of social behaviour being 'caused' by membership of a single category do not work. All social life is not determined by social class, whatever may have seemed to be the case with sociological analysis in former times.

Definitions as differentiation

The advantage of formalising and elaborating a definition in this way is that it provides a means of marking off a boundary between social divisions and other similar, but significantly different, ideas. This is a source of potential confusion, as the lack of a clear distinction in some of the literature (for example Braham and Janes 2002) shows. Not all separations of people into opposing categories are of a scale to merit inclusion as social divisions. For example, the many 'rages' and 'hells' popular in contemporary media representations ('road rage', 'trolley rage', 'neighbours from hell', 'holidays from hell' and so on) may involve disagreements and conflicts, but they hardly constitute a social division. They certainly are not society-wide, not all-inclusive divisions, not permanent, nor socially sanctioned as 'natural'. To be counted as a social division requires that all the criteria should be in place. This latter requirement also helps to distinguish between the idea of a social division and other concepts such as social inequality and social differentiation.

'Social inequality' is a condition of disproportionate access to 'resources', that is, not just financial resources but any human or cultural resources. Statements about social inequalities tend to deal, at their most simple, with 'facts'. Thus one can talk about specific social inequalities in, say, housing, educational qualifications, risk of being a victim of crime or access to political influence. It is certainly interesting to learn that 7 per cent of the population own 84 per cent of the land in Scotland, that 1 per cent of adults own over 40 per cent of personal net capital in England and Wales, or that the worst off one-fifth of our society have incomes lower than half the national average. But what is 'interesting' lies in discovering why and how such patterns of inequality come about, are maintained and what the consequences are for those experiencing them.

Patterns of inequality may result from social divisions or be the visible markers of divisions. They are closely associated with divisions. However, as Roberts (2001: 4) has suggested, social division is an all-embracing term: even when it is used to refer only to class, gender and ethnicity, it does not presuppose a simple hierarchy or set of social strata, and places the interaction of the divisions at the centre of research and debate. The idea of social divisions brings greater meaning and structure to the simple patterns of differences. It attempts to include the way in which some core features cover the whole population, contributing to their various senses of identity and working as an interrelated set, without prioritising one division above all others. The discussion of health (Chapter 14) illustrates this point very clearly.

'Social differentiation', on the other hand, is a more specific term often used to deal with a key difference between 'simple' tribal or agrarian societies and more complex, industrial and contemporary societies. In the latter societies, with their more complex social division of labour, the greater specialisation and range of tasks, in particular around production and occupations, demarcates people from each other and groups from other groups. This formulation, drawing on Durkheim's concerns with social cohesion and his ideas of mechanical and organic solidarity, was particularly attractive among those sociologists who were attempting to deal with evident and extensive social inequalities without recourse to class analysis, for example in a US context where 'class' carried the politically charged association of Marxism and anti-American ways.

Social divisions and social cohesion

The account of social life presented in this volume is characterised on the one hand by division, disadvantage, hierarchy, inequality and resistance, and on the other by group or category identity as the basic unit, shaped by a sense of difference from others. The question this poses, and which was noted in passing in the Introduction, is that if social life is so fragmented, does it make much sense to think in terms of such a vast conglomeration as 'society', or even the extensive divisions like class, gender or ethnicity that create the categories on which identity is based. If people lead their lives in terms of divisions and categories, each remarkably different from the next, how is collective life possible (Crow 2002)? Why does everything not fly apart and collapse in chaos? On the whole, despite divisions, things do hold together (as the discussion of community in Chapter 13 showed). The simple answer to understanding this lies in seeing how social divisions interconnect and institutional processes constrain.

In the first place, while human behaviour is not totally constrained by structures of relationships and normative assumptions, individuals conduct their unique lives within frameworks of accepted actions. Social divisions are 'sustained by dominant cultural beliefs', so that they are carried in our heads. Social divisions also operate through complex, powerful and extensive institutions, that is, through systems of ways of acting in recognised, appropriate ways backed by positive and negative social sanctions.

Our capacity to modify this through situational interactions is constrained not just by what is in our heads, or the promise/threat of sanctions, but the willingness of others to engage on their part in that modification. If they are members of the same category, they are also part of a constraining system that encourages group identification and solidarity, not non-conformity. If they are members of a more advantaged oppositional category, they have a vested interest in preventing the individual from modifying relationships that give them advantages. The scope for adapting meanings and beliefs, innovatory action and creating change is limited by the willingness of other actors to tolerate and support non-conforming behaviour.

In that sense, social structuration is essentially a *social* process and one that never starts with a clean sheet of uncommitted other actors. The normative order that is inherited and recreated is certainly not monolithic or uniform, but its component elements and segments are indeed powerful. It is usually easier to go on doing the same thing, easier not to 'rock the boat'; acceptance of one's lot in a given category is usually the easiest solution.

This does not provide a complete answer, however, because if people are all in fragmented categories, how do the cultural/institutional/interactional processes hold the disparate categories together? Social cohesion is more common than social disorder or disintegration and, indeed, lower level conflicts of interest are largely kept within bounds, mainly because individuals have multiple memberships of categories. It follows that unless memberships (or boundary lines) coincide, social divisions do not reinforce one another. For instance, being working class may offer one source of identity and motivation for action, but the members of the working class are also variously black or white, male or female, fit or ill, old or young. These other identities fragment the class identity and in turn are fragmented by class and all the others.

It is also the case that divisions are not equally 'socially visible'. They may be embodied to varying degrees in physical differences (age, ethnicity, gender or disability). They may manifest themselves in more or less dramatic forms: a dichotomy is likely to be more obvious than a division into a mulitplicity of categories. Small minorities may be excluded from public consciousness by media selectivity or physical isolation (Payne 2004). These differences feed back into our senses of identity.

If we think of the 13 main divisions in this book (Chapters 2–14), and treat each of them as consisting of a dichotomy, that alone would offer 26 categories to which individuals could belong. Those categories can logically be combined, in the sense of a profile that an individual might manifest as a result of her or his 13 memberships, in over 8,000 different possible profiles. Of course, some profiles may be unlikely: to a considerable extent, disadvantage on one division tends to be associated with disadvantage on others, as Anthias (1998: 531) argues with reference to gender, ethnicity and class. However, this is numerically balanced by the fact that most of the social divisions exist with more than two categories in each (see for example the number of classes in Chapter 2).

Complex multiple memberships blur differences in two ways. First, their complexity intervenes to reduce the chances of a 'single issue' identity or cause for action emerging. Even when individuals consciously define themselves in specific terms – feminist, black, class warrior, grey panther – their own other memberships still have a part to play. The same is true of those who attempt a dual identity, for example black feminist. The multiplicity of memberships of people in a group mitigates against them all 'moving in the same direction' at once; whatever the individual may intend, the views of others have to be taken into account and their membership-based agendas contribute to a confusion of perspectives. Complex profiles disguise the underlying divisions.

Multiple memberships bring together individuals in one social context who are disparate in other contexts. Employees may define themselves in class terms, but share national identity with their employers. Conversely, they may use gender or ethnicity as grounds for not acting in class terms, by seeking to exclude or discriminate against women or the minority ethnic groups despite their shared membership of the working class. Employers and managers are then able to exploit such differences for their own ends. Only when social divisions coincide are major 'fault lines' in society likely to develop.

These 'overlapping ties' were sharply demonstrated in Gluckman's (1960) classic account of feuding between clans among the Nuer and other African peoples. Drawing on several anthropological studies, he shows first that even in open conflict, what today we would call 'rules of engagement' apply. Fighting with sticks was allowed among close kin, but not with spears or knives. The ultimate weapon of burning the granaries and killing the livestock of other tribes was acceptable, but never practised within one's own people. By extension, the capacity for society to fall apart is always reduced by constraints on how conflict is to be managed, constraints that protect social cohesion by virtue of still recognising that other shared memberships remain valid even when relationships concerning one division do break down.

Second, Gluckman argues that in practice, this is not a simple matter of cultural norms but an outcome of situational processes. Because people belong to several groups, they have a vested interest in constraining and resolving conflict in any one group. In a simple society based largely on kinship, marriage partners may be chosen from outside the immediate kin group: clans intermarry. If there is a feud between two clans, both those who have 'married in', and their immediate marriage partners have a strong interest in achieving a resolution. This is worked out, in part, in the relationships between partners and the interpersonal pressures that can be brought into play. In this sense, the multiple memberships bind. Individuals become the glue that helps to hold the institutions together, rather than the untidy and uncooperative components that threaten to break them apart.

Even the process of challenging division is in itself a means of releasing tensions. A number of other safety valves (humour, symbolic public events, role-reversal festivals and so on) operate to promote accommodation. At another level, institutional frameworks, such as citizens' rights in law, can offer a means of limiting the full impact of division, exploitation and discrimination. This is not to say that conflict is always contained. Societies do sometimes collapse into open warfare: Northern Ireland, the Balkans and post-invasion Iraq are painful reminders of what happens when the urge to compromise is weaker that the pressure to dispute.

Social divisions as a distinctive theoretical perspective

It was earlier suggested that a social divisions approach represents a distinctive perspective on society. In part this is evident in its systematic concern with division, inequality and social injustice. However, to appreciate the extent to which this does constitute a particular perspective, it is necessary to reflect briefly on alternative theoretical stances.

Without wishing to engage in a detailed analysis, it can be claimed that sociological theories operate with underlying domain assumptions about the nature of the social world. This point can be illustrated by contrasting the core metaphors that seem to operate in three well-known theoretical perspectives. In the first, that of structural-functionalism (and in particular in the earlier work of Parsons), the image of society is one of coherence, order and integration: humans operate willingly within institutions, whose forms follow naturally from the socially sustaining functions fulfilled by those institutions. Any apparent inequalities or divisions (for example occupational classes or gender) are seen as positively contributing in some way to social cohesion and maintenance. Only those who are psychologically disturbed will disrupt this precise system. The metaphor is Newtonian clockwork, its cogwheels accurately machined and neatly interlocking: a place for each part and each part in its place in a tidy, integrated system.

In contrast, the conception advocated by Marx and Marxian accounts of society presents conflict as endemic, periodically breaking out as revolutionary change. The parts of the system are held in place by the power of the ruling classes, who are able to enforce their wishes on the working class by virtue of their ownership of the means of production and promoting their own ideological interpretations to create false consciousness among the other classes. The routine experience is exploitation, and the 'social' is essentially the 'economic'. Social order, indeed, all social forms can be derived from the economic 'base' of production, and in that sense are a superficial 'superstructure'. The one essential social division of class renders other social divisions mere superstructural irrelevancies. The image that can stand for this view of society is a heavy weight, balanced precariously on a coiled spring, or two animals fighting inside a large but frail paper bag. Both images convey the idea of two forces in mutual opposition.

We can compare the clock and the struggling bag with the view from the wilder shores of post-modernism. Here the emphasis is on individuals, reflectively selecting a personal identity from a host of possible choices and reconstituting the world through the thoughts and words used to understand experience. The idea of large-scale social processes or structures is an illusion, a product of social science's fevered imagination, of no more value than any other person's opinion. There is no need for 'logical consistency' or 'evidence', since these, too, are artificial constructions. Our social image might be taken either from a New Wave film, with the self-absorbed inmates of an upmarket asylum drifting past each other on a sunlit lawn, or alternatively, particles of dust floating in a beam of light.

A social divisions perspective does not start from the assumption that society depends on neatly integrated and accepted social practices. Rather it seeks to question the assumptions and normative beliefs that veil division, in contrast to structural-functionalism's acceptance of the status quo. 'Social divisions' emphasise the multiplicity of social divisions, in contrast to the narrow Marxian focus on class. In displaying systematic undesirable social inequalities and injustices, the constraining power of institutions and the ordered way in which identities are socially created, social division rejects the hyper-individualism and relativism of post-structuralism and post-modernism.

One advantage of this perspective is that the components (or subsystems of division) of 'society' do not need to be neatly or tightly connected, or held in some specific relationship to each other. Social order is achieved through the operation of one or more social divisions, rather than through all of them, all of the time, in a fixed relationship to each other (called 'society'). This fluidity is one reason for not adopting the otherwise helpful metaphor of the 'vertical mosaic', so tellingly employed in Porter's (1965) analysis of Canadian society. In taking a more fluid or flexible view of society, the point is that flexibility operates through divisions rather than just individuals and makes up a series of constraining practices that do not apply equally or consistently in every context. Not all aspects of multiple divisions impinge directly on our day-to-day interactions at the same time. Social division as the social injustice suffered by others is easier to accept when much of its multifaceted visibility is largely hidden from us. The metaphor might be a young child's very inexpert attempt to construct a complex multicoloured assemblage of Lego blocks.

Furthermore, as the chapters show, there is a tension within each division between its capacity to constrain social action and the mutability of its assumptions and forms. In terms of how institutions operate at any given point, their constituent roles are not rigid blueprints that precisely, minutely and exactly define social action, but rather rough sketches that can be altered. There is a great deal of 'play', in the engineering sense, in role play. In social situations, we exploit the room to manoeuvre that this 'play' allows us. Social divisions, however well defined each may seem to be at one level, are part of a conception of society as more messy, untidy and hard to see than in most other accounts. It is *normal* for there to be a conflict of expectations between social divisions.

Social divisions and sociology

Sociologists, like other people, bring to their work their own intellectual and personal baggage. The variety of stances this creates does not however make it impossible to work within a social divisions framework, because there is no need to commit to a single narrow perspective. For example, Reid (1998: 238) operates 'on the assumption that social class is the most fundamental form of social stratification':

> Put as boldly as possible, being Black, female or elderly and middle class is different from being Black, female or elderly and working class ... This is not to deny the importance of gender, ethnicity and age either objectively or subjectively, or to suggest that changes in class would necessarily end the differences between them.

A similar view can be found in Carling (1991), who acknowledges other divisions but concentrates on class. Conversely, Anthias's (2001) treatment of social division prioritises gender and ethnicity, but nonetheless lists class as the third division.

The highlighting of class, gender and ethnicity does reflect a basic prioritisation, but the inclusion of the other divisions indicates the importance of taking a broad view. It is not the intention of this book to claim that one or other division is the most important (although each of the contributors might well wish to make such a case).

Whichever division(s) is accorded priority, the question remains as to how, given a multiplicity of divisions, they intersect. Reid argues that class takes precedence, while Anthias (1998: 531–2) suggests two possible outcomes: cross-cutting systems of domination may articulate by being 'mutually reinforcing' – 'social divisions articulate to produce a coherent set of practices of subordination' – or may give rise to 'contradictory locations', where individuals dominate within one division but are subordinate in another. Ifekwunigwe (1999) also focuses on this capacity of divisions to offer alternative statuses and identities, but concentrates on gender, nationality and sexuality. In contrast, our own position as outlined above has tended to stress a lack of articulation in a larger complex of social divisions.

This is not the only approach to social divisions. Drawing heavily on the work of Foucault, Best (2005) stresses the sense of 'other' in divisions, and argues that social divisions are not material or social realities but exist only as defined by the ideas of the time – the cultural discourses by which we make sense of them. This leads to a rather confused and all-inclusive treatment of a great many social differences as social divisions. A less extreme version of the emphasis on difference can be found in the work of O'Brien and Howard (1998: xiii), who argue that the call for inclusion of race, class, gender and other 'differences':

> has served to point out the weaknesses in attempts to compare sexism with racism or classism (and other 'isms'). Additive approaches to incorporating

race, class and gender fail to comprehend how experiences are qualitatively different from others rather than being simply an additional component.

As ethnographers, they favour the study of how social inequalities and difference are 'performed' in everyday life or, in our terms, how systems of social division are manifested on the ground. This places sociological research into situational interactions, rather than at the more macro-level adopted by most of the contributors here. While O'Brien and Howard start from this different methodological stance, much of their basic view of divisions, as about hierarchy, has a lot in common with our own.

Their approach has a quite separate origin in concerns with affirmative action and the 'celebration of difference'; the attempt to promote acceptance of cultural differences between (mainly) ethnic groups. They find a simplistic reliance on difference unhelpful, as it leaves the 'what' from which things differ, that is, the normative structures of white middle-class male America, unproblematised. Gender, for example, is not just a statement of difference, but one of hierarchy. The celebration of difference, which resonates so directly and strongly in the lives of American students, nonetheless makes those who have 'difference' carry the responsibility for it; this is like blaming the victim for the crime.

The study of divisions is therefore not simply a means of examining a random selection of segments of society. Its coherence lies in the notions of hierarchy, social inequality and social injustice that such a study entails. The way the divisions come together is a difficult sociological problem that we may not have entirely resolved, but we have tried to show that worse errors are likely if one takes the crude perspective that prioritises a single social division. This latter approach may help to simplify but it is unlikely to generate an adequate analysis. If we want an adequate analysis of specific social situations, it is the range of social divisions which provides perspective and structure: for example, Gibbon (2000) explores health by examining gender, class, ethnicity and place community; Callaghan (1998) illuminates women's experiences by showing how gender, class and neighbourhood interact; and Marcus and Manicom (2000) combine class, ethnicity and gender with wealth and location in researching children's experiences in a new education system.

These examples also serve to make the point that social divisions are not just about the intellectual problems of how sociology conceives of society, but also about how we research and make sense of more concrete events and small-scale processes. Equally, because they share the idea of social inequality, they connect academic considerations with our ordinary concerns as citizens about the way the world we live in operates. Because divisions are persistent, the social injustices they entail are a constant source of frustration and anger for ordinary people. Division is not itself pathological; divisions are the normal state of society. It is the *persistence* of their associated disadvantages that is the problem, with extremely unequal access to the desirable things in life continually impinging on the same categories of people. Only by the integrated analysis of social divisions can we understand, let alone change, the nature of contemporary society and the lives of its citizens.

Discussion Questions

1. Are some social divisions more important than others?

2. Locate your own position on each of the social divisions described in this book: are there any other divisions that you think might be usefully included?

3. Contrast the meanings of 'social inequality', 'social differentiation' and 'social division'.

4. Are social divisions 'pathological'?

5. What is the importance of cross-cutting ties and overlapping memberships?

6. Is social division just another term for what post-modernists call 'difference' and 'other'?

7. Can social divisions be changed?

Bibliography

Abbott, P. and Ackers, L. (1997) 'Women and employment'. In Spybey, T. (ed.) *Britain in Europe*. London: Routledge.

Abbott, P. and Sapsford, R. (1987) *Women and Social Class*. London: Tavistock.

Abbott, P. and Sapsford, R. (1988) *Community Care for Mentally Handicapped Children*. Milton Keynes: Open University Press.

Abbott, P. and Tyler, M. (1995) 'Ethnic variations in the female labour force: a research note'. *British Journal of Sociology*, **46**(3): 339–53.

Abbott, P. and Wallace, C. (1992) *The Family and the New Right*. London: Pluto.

Abbott, P. and Wallace, C. (2005) *An Introduction to Sociology: Feminist Perspectives* (2nd edn). London: Routledge.

Abbott, P., Wallace, C. and Tyler, M. (2005) *An Introduction to Sociology: Feminist Perspectives*. London: Routledge.

Abel-Smith, B. and Townsend, P. (1965) *The Poor and the Poorest*, Occasional Papers on Social Administration, 17. London: G. Bell & Sons.

Albrow, M. (1993) 'Skills and capacities in the sociology curriculum'. In Payne, G. and Cross, M. (eds) *Sociology in Action*. London: Macmillan – now Palgrave Macmillan.

Aldridge, A. (2000) *Religion in the Contemporary World: A Sociological Introduction*. Cambridge: Polity Press.

Alexander, P. (1988) 'Prostitution: a difficult issue for feminists'. In Delacoste, F. and Alexander, P. (eds) *Sex Work*. London: Virago.

Allatt, P. and Yeandle, S. (1992) *Youth Unemployment and the Family*. London: Routledge.

Allen, C. and Nielsen, J. S. (2002) *Summary Report on Islamophobia in the EU after 11 September 2001*. Vienna: European Monitoring Centre on Racism and Xenophobia. http://eumc.eu.int.

Anderson, B. (1996) 'Introduction'. In Balakrishnan, G. (ed.) *Mapping the Nation*. London: Verso Books.

Anderson, G. (1976) *Victorian Clerks*. Manchester: Manchester University Press.

Anderson, P. (1991) *Imagined Communities*. London: Verso.

Ansari, H. (2004) *'The Infidel Within': Muslims in Britain Since 1800*. London: Hurst.

Anthias, F. (1998) 'Rethinking social divisions'. *Sociological Review*, **46**(3): 505–35.

Anthias, F. (2001) 'The concept of "social divisions" and theorising social stratification'. *Sociology*, **35**(4): 835–54.

Anthias, F. and Yuval-Davis, N. (1992) *Racialized Boundaries: Race, Nation, Gender, Colour and Class and the Anti-racist Struggle*. London: Routledge.

Arber, S. (1990) 'Opening the 'black box': Inequalities in women's health'. In Abbott, P. and Payne, G. (eds) *New Directions in the Sociology of Health*. London: Falmer Press.

Arber, S. and Ginn, J. (1991) *Gender and Later Life: A Sociological Analysis of Resources and Constraints*. London: Sage.

Arber, S. and Ginn, J. (1995) *Connecting Gender and Ageing*. Buckingham: Open University Press.

Archard, D. (1993) *Children, Rights and Childhood*. London: Routledge.

Arensberg, C. and Kimball, S. (1940) *Family and Community in Ireland*. Gloucester, MA: Peter Smith.

Ariès, P. (1962) *Centuries of Childhood*. London: Jonathan Cape.

Armstrong, D. (1994) *Outline of Sociology as Applied to Medicine*. London: Butterworth-Heinemann.

Ashworth, K., Hill, M. and Walker, R. (1992) A New Approach to Poverty Dynamics. Working Papers of the European Scientific Network on Household Panel Studies. Paper 52. Colchester: University of Essex.

Askham, J., Henshaw, L. and Tarpey, M. (1993) 'Policies and perceptions of identity: Service needs of elderly people from black and minority ethnic backgrounds'. In Arber, S.and Evandrou, M. (eds) *Ageing, Independence and the Life Course*. London: Jessica Kingsley.

Atkinson, A. (1987) 'On the measurement of poverty'. *Econometrica*, **55**(4): 749–64.

Atkinson, A. (1998) *Poverty in Europe*. Oxford: Blackwell.

Bailey, J. (1998) 'In front of the arras: some new introductions'. *Sociology*, **31**(1): 203–9.

Banton, M. (1967) *Race Relations*. London: Tavistock.

Banton, M. (1977) *The Idea of Race*. London: Tavistock.

Banton, M. (1987) *Racial Theories*. Cambridge: Cambridge University Press.

Banton, M. (1988) *Racial Consciousness*. London: Longman.

Banton, M. and Harwood, J. (1975) *The Race Concept*. Newton Abbot: David and Charles.

Barberis, P. (1996) *The Elite of the Elite: Permanent Secretaries in the British Higher Civil Service*. Aldershot: Dartmouth.

Bardasi, E. and Jenkins, S. (2002) *Income in Later Life: Work History Matters*. Bristol: Policy Press.

Barnes, B. (1995) *The Elements of Social Theory*. London: UCL Press.

Barnes, C. (1990) *Disabled People in Britain and Discrimination: A Case for Anti-Discrimination Legislation*. London: Hurst & Company.

Barnes, C., Mercer, G. and Shakespeare, T. (1999) *Exploring Disability: A Sociological Introduction*. Cambridge: Polity Press.

Barnett, A. (1997) *This Time: Our Constitutional Revolution*. London: Vintage.

Barrett, M. and Phillips, A. (1992) *Destabilising Theory: Contemporary Feminist Debates*. Cambridge: Polity.

Barth, F. (ed.) (1969) *Ethnic Groups and Boundaries*. Bergen: Universitetsforlaget.

Bartkey, S. L. (1990) *Femininity and Domination: Studies in the Phenomenology of Oppression*. London: Routledge.

Bauman, Z. (1990) *Thinking Sociologically*. Oxford: Basil Blackwell.

Baumann, G. (1996) *Contesting Culture*. Cambridge: Cambridge University Press.

Beck, U. (1992) *Risk Society: Towards a New Modernity*. London: Sage.

Beck, U. (1998) 'Politics of risk society'. In Franklin, J. (ed.) *The Politics of Risk Society*. Cambridge: Polity Press.

Beck, U. and Beck-Gernsheim, E. (1995) *The Normal Chaos of Love*. Cambridge: Polity Press.

Beckford, J. A. (1989) *Religion and Advanced Industrial Society*. London: Unwin Hyman.

Beckford, J. A. (1999) 'The management of religious diversity in England and Wales with special reference to prison chaplaincy', *MOST Journal on Multicultural Societies*, 1(2), http://www.unesco.org./most/vlln2bec.htm.

Beckford, J. A. and Gilliat, S. (1998) *Religion in Prison: Equal Rites in a Multi-Faith Society*. Cambridge: Cambridge University Press.

Beck-Gernsheim, E. (1996) 'Life as a planning project'. In Lash, S., Szerszynski, B. and Wynne, B. (eds) *Risk, Environment and Modernity: Towards a New Ecology*. London: Sage.

Beechy, V. and Perkins, T. (1986) *A Matter of House: An Investigation of Women's Part-time Employment*. Cambridge: Polity Press.

Bell, C. and Newby, H. (1971) *Community Studies*. London: Allen & Unwin.

Benedict, R. (1938) 'Continuities and discontinuities in cultural conditioning'. *Psychiatry*, 1(1): 161–7.

Bengston, V. (1996) 'Continuities and discontinuities in intergenerational relationships over time'. In Bengston, V. (ed.) *Adulthood and Aging: Research on Continuities and Discontinuities*. New York: Springer.

Benzeval, M., Judge, K. and Whitehead, M. (eds) (1995) *Tackling Inequalities in Health*. London: King's Fund.

Berger, P. L. (1967) *The Sacred Canopy: Elements of a Sociological Theory of Religion*. New York: Doubleday.

Berkman, L. and Breslow, L. (1983) *Health and Ways of Living: The Almeda County Study*. Oxford: Oxford University Press.

Bernardi, B. (1985) *Age Class Systems: Social Institutions and Polities Based on Age*. Cambridge: Cambridge University Press.

Berthoud, R. (1997) 'Income and living standards'. In Modood, T. and Berthoud, R. (eds) *Ethnic Minorities in Britain*. London: Policy Studies Institute.

Berthoud, R. (1998) *The Incomes of Ethnic Minorities*. ISER Report 98-1, Colchester: University of Essex, Institute for Social and Economic Research.

Berthoud, R. (2000) 'Ethnic employment penalties in Britain'. *Journal of Ethnic and Migration Studies*, 26(3): 389–416.

Berthoud, R., Lakey, J. and McKay, S. (1993) *The Economic Problems of Disabled People*. London: Policy Studies Institute.

Best, S. (2005) *Understanding Social Divisions*. London: Sage.

Blackaby, D., Leslie, D., Murphy, P. and O'Leary, N. (2002) 'White/ethnic minority earnings and employment differentials in Britain: Evidence from the LFS'. *Oxford Economic Papers*, **54**.

Blackburn, R. (1997) 'The reproduction of social inequality'. *Sociology*, **31**(3): 491–509.

Blaikie, A. (1999) *Ageing and Popular Culture*. Cambridge: Cambridge University Press.

Blair, T. (1999) 'Beveridge revisited: A welfare state for the 21st century'. In Walker. R. (ed.) *Ending Child Poverty: Popular Welfare for the 21st Century?*. Bristol: Policy Press.

Blakemore, K. and Boneham, M. (1994) *Age, Race and Ethnicity*. Oxford: Oxford University Press.

Blaxter, M. (1990) *Health and Lifestyles*. London: Routledge.

Blaxter, M. and Paterson, E. (1982) *Mothers and Daughters*. London: Heinemann.

Bloor, M. (1976) 'Professional autonomy and client exclusion'. In Wadsworth, M. and Robinson, D. (eds) *Studies in Everyday Medical Life*. London: Martin Robertson.

Boal, F., Keane, M. and Livingstone, D. (1997) *Them and Us: Attitudinal Variation among Churchgoers in Belfast*. Belfast: Institute of Irish Studies.

Bond, M. (2004) 'Social influences on corporate political donations in Britain'. *British Journal of Sociology*, **55**(1): 33–78.

Booth, C. (1901–2) *Life and Labour of the People of London*, 17 volumes. London: Macmillan – now Palgrave Macmillan.

Bosma, H., Marmot, M., Hemingway, H., Nicholson, A., Brunner, E. and Stansfeld, S. (1997) 'Low job control and risk of coronary heart disease in the Whitehall II (prospective cohort) study'. *British Medical Journal*, **314**: 558–65.

Bourdieu, P. (1984) *Distinction: A Social Critique of the Judgment of Taste*. London: Routledge & Kegan Paul.

Bowling, A. (1997) *Measuring Health* (2nd edn). Buckingham: Open University Press.

Bradbury, B. and Jäntti, M. (1999) 'Child poverty across industrialized nations'. *Innocenti Occasional Papers, Economic and Social Policy Series*. Paper 71. UNICEF.

Bradley, H. (1996) *Fractured Identities: Changing Patterns of Inequality*. Cambridge: Polity Press.

Bradley, H. (1999) *Gender and Power in the Workplace*. Basingstoke: Macmillan – now Palgrave Macmillan.

Bradshaw, J. (ed.) (1993) *Budget Standards for the United Kingdom*. Aldershot: Avebury.

Braham, P. and Janes, L. (2002) *Social Differences and Divisions*. Oxford: Blackwell.

Brannen, J. (1995) 'Young people and their contribution to household work'. *Sociology*, **29**(2): 317–38.

Braverman, H. (1974) *Labor and Monopoly Capitalism*. New York: Monthly Review Press.

Breen, R. (1998) Self Interest, Group Interest and Ethnic Identity. Florence: Department of Political and Social Sciences, European University Institute (unpublished paper).

Brewer, J. and Higgins, G. I. (1999) 'Understanding anti-Catholicism in Northern Ireland'. *Sociology,* **33**(2): 235–55.

British Attitudes Survey (1997) http://www.natcen.ac.uk/natcen/pages/or_socialattitudes. htm.

British Attitudes Survey (2001) http://www.natcen.ac.uk/natcen/pages/or_socialattitudes. htm.

British Household Panel Survey http://www.iser.essex.ac.uk/ulsc/bhps/.

BMA (British Medical Association) (1995) *Inequalities in Health.* BMA Occasional Paper. London: BMA.

Brody, H. (1973) *Inishkillane.* London: Allen Lane.

Brown, B., Burman, M. and Jamieson, L. (1993) *Sex Crimes on Trial: The Use of Sexual Evidence in Scottish Courts.* Edinburgh: Edinburgh University Press.

Brown, C. (1984) *Black and White Britain: The Third PSI Survey.* Aldershot: Gower.

Brown, C. and Gay, P. (1985) *Racial Discrimination: 17 Years After the Act.* London: Policy Studies Institute.

Brown, G. (2005) 'Make this a manifesto for children', *Guardian,* 5 January 2005.

Brown, M. (1995) 'Naming and framing: the social construction of diagnosis and illness'. *Journal of Health and Social Behaviour,* **36** (extra issue): 34–52.

Brubaker, R. (1992) *Citizenship and Nationhood in France and German.* Cambridge, MA: Harvard University Press.

Bruce, S. (1986) *God Save Ulster: The Religion and Politics of Paisleyism.* Oxford: Clarendon Press.

Bruce, S. (1996) *Religion in the Modern World: From Cathedrals to Cults.* Oxford: Oxford University Press.

Bruce, S. (2002) *God is Dead: Secularization in the West.* Oxford: Blackwell.

Brunt, L. (2001) 'Into the community'. In Atkinson, P., Coffey, A., Delamont, S., Lofland, J. and Lofland, L. (eds) *Handbook of Ethnography.* London: Sage.

Buckingham, D. (2000) *After the Death of Childhood: Growing up in the Age of Electronic Media.* Cambridge: Polity Press.

Bulmer, M. (ed.) (1975) *Working Class Images of Society.* London: Routledge & Kegan Paul.

Burch, M. and Moran, M. (1985) 'The changing British political elite, 1945–83: MPs and Cabinet ministers'. *Parliamentary Affairs,* Winter: 1–15.

Burgess, A. (1990) 'Co-education – the disadvantage for schoolgirls'. *Gender and Education,* **2**: 91–6.

Burnham, J. (1941) *The Managerial Revolution: What is Happening in the World.* New York: John Day.

Burnham, J. (1944) *The New Machiavellians: Defenders of Freedom.* Chicago: Gateway.

Bury, M. (1997) *Health and Illness in a Changing Society.* London: Routledge.

Bury, M. (2004) 'Researching patient/professional interactions'. *Journal of Health Services Research and Policy,* **9**(1): 48–54.

Buston, K., Wight, D. and Scott, S. (2001) 'Difficulty and diversity: the context and practice of sex education'. *British Journal of Sociology of Education*, **22**(3): 353–68.

Butler, J. (1990) *Gender Trouble: Feminism and the Subversion of Identity*. New York: Routledge.

Butler, T. and Robson, G. (2003) *London Calling: The Middle Classes and the Re-Making of Inner London*. Oxford: Berg.

Bytheway, W. (1995) *Ageism*. Buckingham: Open University Press.

Callaghan, G. (1998) 'The interaction of gender, class and place in women's experience'. *Sociological Research Online*, **3**(3): http://www.socresonline.org.uk/3/3/8.html.

Callan, T., Nolan, B. and Whelan, C. (1993) 'Resources, deprivation and the measurement of poverty'. *Journal of Social Policy*, **22**: 141–72.

Calnan, M. (1987) *Health and Illness: The Lay Perspective*. London: Tavistock.

Cameron, E. and Bernades, J. (1998) 'Gender and disadvantage in health: men's health for a change'. In Bartley, M., Blane, D. and Davey Smith, G. (eds) *The Sociology of Health Inequalities*. Oxford: Blackwell.

Cannadine, D. (1998) *Class in Britain*. New Haven, CT: Yale University Press.

Cappellari, L. and Jenkins, S. (2002) 'Who stays poor? Who becomes poor? Evidence from the British Household Panel Survey'. *The Economic Journal*, **112**: 478: C60–7.

Carling, A. (1991) *Social Division*. London: Verso.

Carr-Hill, R. (1990) 'The measurement of inequalities in health'. *Social Science and Medicine*, **31**(3): 393–404.

Cartwright, A. and O'Brien, J. (1976) 'Social class, variations in health care and the nature of general practitioner consultations'. In Stacey, M. (ed.) *The Sociology of the NHS*. Sociological Review Monograph No. 22. Keele: University of Keele.

Castells, M. (1997) *The Power of Identity*. Oxford: Blackwell.

CSO (Central Statistical Office) (1994) *Social Focus on Children*. London: HMSO.

CSO (Central Statistical Office) (1995) *Social Trends*, 25. London: HMSO.

Chaney, J. (1981) Social Networks and Job Information: The Situation of Women who Return to Work. Report presented to the Equal Opportunities Commission. London: Equal Opportunities Commission.

Chauvel, L. (1999) 'Classes et générations: l'insuffisance des hypothèses de la théorie de la fin des classes sociales', *Actuel Marx*, **26**: 37–52.

Clark, C. (1940) *The Conditions of Economic Progress*. London: Macmillan – now Palgrave Macmillan.

Clift, D. and Fielding, D. (1991) *A Survey of Management Morale in the 90s*. London: Institute of Management.

Cobban, A. (1994) National Self-Determination (extract reprinted). In Hutchinson, J. and Smith, A. D. (eds) *Nationalism*. Oxford: Oxford University Press.

Cockburn, C. (1990) *In the Way of Women: Men's Resistance to Sex Equality in Organisations*. London: Macmillan – now Palgrave Macmillan.

Cohen, A. (ed.) (1982) *Belonging*. Manchester: Manchester University Press.

Cohen, A. (1985) *The Symbolic Construction of Community*. London: Tavistock.

Cohen, A. (1987) *Whalsay*. Manchester: Manchester University Press.

Cohen, M. (1998) 'A habit of healthy idleness: boys underachievement in histori-cal perception?'. In Epstein, D., Elwood, J., Hey, V. and Maw, J. (eds) *Failing Boys: Issues in Gender and Achievement*. Milton Keynes: Open University Press.

Cohen, R. (1994) *Frontiers of Identity: The British and Others*. London: Longman.

Cohen, R., Coxall, J., Craig, G. and Sadiq-Sangster, A. (1992) *Hardship Britain*. London: CPAG/FSU.

Cole, T. (1992) *The Journey of Life: A Cultural History of Ageing in America*. Cambridge: Cambridge University Press.

Colley, L. (1992) *Britons: Forging the Nation, 1707–1837*. New Haven, CT: Yale University Press.

Collison, P. (1963) *The Cutteslowe Walls*. London: Faber & Faber.

Comfort, A. (1977) *A Good Age*. London: Mitchell Beazley.

Connor, W. (1994) *Ethnonationalism: The Quest for Understanding*. New Jersey: Princeton University Press.

Cook, D. T. (2000a) 'The rise of "the toddler" as subject and as merchandising cat-egory in the 1930s'. In Gottdiener, M. (ed.) *New Forms of Consumption: Consumers, Culture and Commodification*. Oxford: Rowman & Littlefield.

Cook, D. T. (2000b) 'The other "child study": figuring children as consumers in market research 1910s–1990s'. *Sociological Quarterly*, **41**(3): 487–507.

Cooper, D. (1995) *Power in Struggle: Feminism, Sexuality and the State*. Buckingham: Open University Press.

Craig, G. and Mayo, M. (eds) (1995) *Community Empowerment*. London: Zed Books.

Crompton, R. (1998) *Class and Stratification: An Introduction to Current Debates* (2nd edn). Cambridge: Polity Press.

Crompton, R. and Le Feuvre, N. (1996) 'Paid employment and the changing sys-tem of gender relations: a cross national comparison'. *Sociology*, **50**(3): 427–45.

Crompton, R. and Mann, M. (1986) *Gender and Stratification*. Cambridge: Polity Press.

Crossick, G. (1977) 'The emergence of the lower middle class in Britain'. In Crossick, G. (ed.) *The Lower Middle Class in Britain, 1870–1914*. London: Croom Helm.

Crow, G. (ed.) (1996) *The Sociology of Rural Communities*. London: Edward Elgar.

Crow, G. (2002) *Social Solidarities: Theories, Identities and Social Change*. Buckingham: Open University Press.

Crow, G. and Allan, G. (1994) *Community Life*. Hemel Hempstead: Harvester Wheatsheaf.

Crow, G. and Allan, G. (1995) 'Community types, community typologies and community time'. *Time and Society*, **4**(2): 147–66.

Crow, G. and Maclean, C. (2004) 'Families and local communities'. In Scott, J., Treas, J. and Richards, M. (eds) *The Blackwell Companion to the Sociology of Families*. Oxford: Blackwell.

Crow, G., Allan, G. and Summers, M. (2001) 'Changing perspectives on the insider/outsider distinction in community sociology'. *Community, Work and Family*, 4: 29–48.

Curtice, J. (1990) 'The Northern Irish dimension'. In Jowell, R., Witherspoon, S., Brook, L. and Taylor, B. (eds) *British Social Attitudes: The 7th Report*. Aldershot: Gower.

d'Houtard, A. and Field, M. (1984) 'The image of health: variations in perceptions by social class in a French population'. *Sociology of Health and Illness*, 6: 30–60.

Dahlgren, G. and Whitehead, M. (1991) *Policies and Strategies to Promote Social Equity in Health*. Stockholm: Institute for Future Studies.

Dalley, G. (1996) *Ideologies of Caring* (2nd edn). Basingstoke: Macmillan – now Palgrave Macmillan.

Daniel, W. W. (1968) *Racial Discrimination in England*. Harmondsworth: Penguin.

Davidson, K. (1998) Doing Good Offices. Sheffield: Paper presented to the British Society of Gerontology Conference on 'Ageing: All Our Tomorrows', September.

Davidson, K. (2001) 'Late life widowhood, selfishness and new partnership choices: a gendered perspective'. *Ageing and Society*, 21(3): 297–317.

Davie, G. (1994) *Religion in Britain since 1945: Believing Without Belonging*. Oxford: Blackwell.

Davis, D. (1984) *Slavery and Human Progress*. New York: Oxford University Press.

Day, G. and Murdoch, J. (1993) 'Locality and community'. *Sociological Review*, 41(1): 82–111.

de Beauvoir, S. ([1949]1972) *The Second Sex* (trans Purskley, H.). Harmondsworth: Penguin.

Deacon, A. (2002) *Perspectives on Welfare: Ideas, Ideologies and Policy Debates*. Buckingham: Open University Press.

Delphy, C. (1984) *Close to Home: A Materialist Analysis of Women's Oppression*. London: Hutchinson.

Delphy, C. (1993) 'Rethinking sex and gender'. *Women's Studies International Forum*, 16(1): 1–9.

Delphy, C. and Leonard, D. (1992) *Familiar Exploitation: A New Analysis of Marriage in Contemporary Western Societies*. Cambridge: Polity Press in association with Blackwell.

Dempsey, K. (1990) *Smalltown*. Melbourne: Oxford University Press.

Dennis, N., Henriques, F. and Slaughter, C. (1956) *Coal is our Life*. London: Eyre and Spottiswoode.

DETR (Department of the Environment, Transport and the Regions) (1998) *Index of Local Deprivation*. London: DETR.

Devine, F. (1992a) *Affluent Workers Revisited*. Edinburgh: Edinburgh University Press.

Devine, F. (1992b) 'Gender segregation in the engineering and science professions: a case of continuity and change'. *Work, Employment and Society*, 6(4): 557–95.

Dingwall, R. (1976) *Aspects of Illness*. London: Martin Robertson.

Dixon, C. (1996) 'Having a laugh, having a fight. Masculinity and the conflicting needs of the self in design and technology'. *International Studies in Sociology of Education,* **6**(2).

Djilas M. (1957) *The New Class: An Analysis of the Communist System.* London: Thames & Hudson.

DoE (Department of Employment) (1978) *Family Expenditure Survey 1977.* London: HMSO.

DoE (Department of Employment) (1988) *Family Expenditure Survey 1987.* London: HMSO.

DoE (Department of Employment) (1998) *Family Expenditure Survey 1997.* London: HMSO.

DoH (Department of Health) (1998a) *Independent Inquiry into Inequalities in Health* (Acheson Report) London: Stationery Office.

DoH (Department of Health) (1998b) *Our Healthier Nation.* London: Stationery Office, Cmd 3852.

DoH (Department of Health) (1999) *Saving Lives: Our Healthier Nation.* London: Stationery Office, Cmd 4386.

DoH (Department of Health) (2004) *Choosing Health.* London: Stationery Office.

Donzelot, J. (1978) *The Policing of Families: Welfare versus the State.* London: Hutchinson.

Dowds, L. and Young, K. (1996) 'National identity'. In *British Social Attitudes: the 13th Report.* Aldershot: Dartmouth.

Doyal, L. (1994) 'Changing medicine? Gender and the politics of health care'. In Gabe, J., Kelleher, D. and Williams, G. (eds) *Challenging Medicine.* London: Routledge.

Doyle, L. (1995) *What Makes Women Sick.* London: Macmillan – now Palgrave Macmillan.

Draper, P. (1976) 'Social and economic constraints on childlife among the !Kung'. In Lee, R. and DeVore, I. (eds) *Kalahari hunter-gatherers.* Cambridge, MA: Harvard University Press.

Drever, F. and Whitehead, M. (eds) (1997) *Health Inequalities.* Decennial Supplement. DS Series no. 15. London: Stationery Office.

Dryler, H. (1998) 'Parental role model: gender and education choice'. *British Journal of Education,* **49**(3): 377–98.

Duffield, M. (1985) 'Rationalization and the politics of segregation: Indian workers in Britain's foundry industry, 1945–62'. In Lunn, K. (ed.) *Race and Labour in Twentieth Century Britain.* London: Frank Cass.

Duncan, G., Brooks-Gunn, J., Yeung, W. and Smith, J. (1998) 'How much does childhood poverty affect the life chances of children?' *American Sociological Review,* **63**: 406–23.

Duncan, S. and Edwards, R. (eds) (1997) *Single Mothers in an International Context.* London: UCL Press.

Duncombe, J. and Marsden, D. (1996) 'Whose orgasm is this anyway? "Sex work" in long-term heterosexual couple relationships'. In Weeks, J. and Holland, J. (eds) *Sexual Cultures.* Basingstoke: Macmillan – now Palgrave Macmillan.

Dunleavy, P. (1980) *Urban Political Analysis*. London: Macmillan – now Palgrave Macmillan.

Durkheim, E. ([1893]1984) *The Division of Labour in Society*. Basingstoke: Macmillan – now Palgrave Macmillan.

DWP (Department for Work and Pensions) (2002) *Opportunity for All: Fourth Annual Report*. London: Stationery Office.

DWP (Department for Work and Pensions) (2003) *Measuring Child Poverty Consultation: Preliminary Conclusions*. London: Department for Work and Pensions.

DWP (Department for Work and Pensions) (2004a) *Households Below Average Income 2002/03*. London: Department for Work and Pensions.

DWP (Department for Work and Pensions) (2004b) *Opportunity for All, Sixth Annual Report*, London: Stationery Office.

Eade, J. (1989) *The Politics of Community*. Aldershot: Avebury.

Edmunds, J. and Turner, B. (2002) *Generations, Culture and Society*. Buckingham: Open University Press.

EOC (Equal Opportunities Commission) (2003) *Pay and Income*. Manchester: EOC.

EOC (Equal Opportunities Commission) (2004) *Facts about Women and Men in Great Britain*. Manchester: EOC.

Erikson, R. and Goldthorpe, J. (1993) *The Constant Flux*. Oxford: Clarendon Press.

Etzioni, A. (1993) *The Spirit of Community*. New York: Touchstone.

Euro-barometer (1997) 'Women and Men in Europe: equality of opportunity Summary Report'. *Equal Opportunities Magazine*, 2 July 1997.

European Commission (1998) *Employment in Europe 1997*. Luxembourg: Office for Official Publications of the European Communities.

Evans, D. (1993) *Sexual Citizenship: The Material Construction of Sexualities*. London: Routledge.

Evetts, J. (1994) *Women and Careers*. Harlow: Longmans.

Farrar, M. (2002) *The Struggle for 'Community' in a British Multi-Ethnic Inner-city Area: Paradise in the Making*. Lampeter: Edwin Mellen.

Featherstone, M. and Hepworth, M. (1989) 'Ageing and old age: reflections on the postmodern life course'. In Bytheway, W. (ed.) *Becoming and Being Old: Sociological Approaches to Later Life*. London: Sage.

Fennell, G., Phillipson, C. and Evers, H. (1988) *The Sociology of Old Age*. Buckingham: Open University Press.

Fenton, S. (2003) *Ethnicity*. Cambridge: Polity Press.

Fevre, R. (1984) *Cheap Labour and Racial Discrimination*. Aldershot: Gower.

Field, S. (1987) 'The changing nature of racial discrimination'. *New Community*, 14(1/2): 118–22.

Fieldhouse, E. and Gould, M. (1998) 'Ethnic minority unemployment and local labour market conditions in Great Britain'. *Environment and Planning A*, 30(5): 833–53.

Fimister, G. (ed.) (2001) *An End in Sight?* London: Child Poverty Action Group.

Finkelstein, V. (1996) 'The disability movement has run out of steam'. *Disability NOW*. February: 11.

Finnegan, R. (1989) *The Hidden Musicians*. Cambridge: Cambridge University Press.

Firestone, S. (1974) *The Dialectic of Sex: The Case for Feminist Revolution*. New York, Morrow.

Ford, C. and Beach, F. (1952) *Patterns of Sexual Behaviour*. London: Eyre & Spottiswoode.

Fortes, M. (1970) 'Social and psychological aspects of education in Taleland'. In Middleton, J. (ed.) *From Child to Adult: Studies in the Anthropology of Education*. Austin: University of Texas Press.

Foster, J. (1974) *Class Struggle and the Industrial Revolution*. London: Methuen.

Foster, J. (1999) *Docklands*. London: UCL Press.

Foucault, M. (1981) *The History of Sexuality*, vol. I. London: Allen Lane.

Frankenberg, R. (1957) *Village on the Border*. London: Cohen & West.

Freud, S. (1977) *The Penguin Freud Library*, vol. 7: *Sexuality*. Harmondsworth: Penguin.

Friedan, D. (1993) *The Fountain of Age*. London: Simon & Schuster.

Fulcher, J. and Scott, J. (1999) *Sociology*. Oxford: Oxford University Press.

Fuss, D. (1991) *Inside/Out: Lesbian Theories, Gay Theories*. New York: Routledge.

Gabriel, J. (1998) *Whitewash: Racialized Politics and the Media*. London: Routledge.

Gagnon, J. (2004) *An Interpretation of Desire*. Chicago: University of Chicago Press.

Gagnon, J. and Simon, W. (1974) *Sexual Conduct*. London: Hutchinson.

Giarchi, G. (1996) *Caring for Older Europeans*. Aldershot: Ashgate.

Gibbon, M. (2000) 'The health analysis and action cycle: an empowering approach to women's health'. *Sociological Research Online*, 4(4) http://www.socresonline. org.uk/4/4/gibbon.html.

Giddens, A. (1974) 'Elites in the British class structure'. In Stanworth, P. and Giddens, A. (eds) *Elites and Power in British Society*. Cambridge: Cambridge University Press.

Giddens, A. (1981) *A Contemporary Critique of Historical Materialism*, vol. I: *Power, Property and the State*. London: Macmillan – now Palgrave Macmillan.

Giddens, A. (1985) *A Contemporary Critique of Historical Materialism*, vol. II: *The Nation-State and Violence*. London: Polity Press.

Giddens, A. (1990) *The Consequences of Modernity*. Cambridge: Polity Press.

Giddens, A. (1991) *Modernity and Self-Identity: Self and Society in the Late Modern Age*. Cambridge: Polity Press.

Giddens, A. (1992) *The Transformation of Intimacy: Sexuality, Love and Eroticism in Modern Societies*. Cambridge: Polity Press.

Gierveld, J., de Valk, H. and Blommesteijn, M. (2001) 'Living arrangements of older persons and family support in more developed countries'. In *Population Ageing and Living Arrangements of Older Persons: Critical Issues and Policy Response*. United Nations Population Bulletin, Special Issue Nos. 42/43.

Gill, F. and Maclean, C. (2002) 'Knowing your place: gender and reflexivity in two ethnographies', *Sociological Research Online* 7(2). http://www.Socresonline.Org.Uk/7/2/Gill.Html.

Gilleard, C. and Higgs, P. (2001) *Cultures of Ageing*. New York: Prentice Hall.

Gillespie, M. (1995) *Television, Ethnicity and Cultural Change*. London: Routledge.

Gilligan, H. (1990) 'Padstow'. In Harris, C. (ed.) *Family, Economy and Community*. Cardiff: University of Wales Press.

Gillis, J. R. (1974) *Youth in History*. London: Academic Press.

Ginn, J. (2003) *Gender, Pensions and the Lifecourse: How Pensions Need to Adapt to Changing Family Forms*. Bristol: Policy Press.

Ginn, J. and Arber, S. (1996) 'Gender, age and attitudes to retirement in mid-life'. *Ageing and Society*, 16(1): 27–55.

Ginn, J., Street, D. and Arber, S. (eds) (2001) *Women, Work, and Pensions: International Issues and Prospects*. Buckingham: Open University Press.

Glendinning, C. and Millar, T. (1992) *Women and Poverty in Britain in the 1990s* (2nd edn). Hemel Hempstead: Harvester/Wheatsheaf.

Gluckman, M. (1960) *Custom and Conflict in Africa*. Oxford: Blackwell.

Glucksmann, M. (1995) 'Why Work?' *Gender, Work and Organisation*, 2: 67–9.

Godway, E. and Finn, G. (eds) (1994) *Who is This 'We'?* Montreal: Black Rose Books.

Goffman, E. (1961) *Asylums*. New York: Anchor.

Goffman, E. (1972) *Encounters*. Harmondsworth: Penguin.

Goldthorpe, J. (1964) 'Social stratification in industrial society'. In Halmos, P. (ed.) *The Development of Industrial Societies*. Sociological Review Monograph, 8. Keele: University of Keele.

Goldthorpe, J. (1980) *Social Mobility and Class Structure*. Oxford: Clarendon Press.

Goldthorpe, J. (1983) 'Women and class analysis: in defence of the conventional view'. *Sociology*, 17(4): 465–88.

Goldthorpe, J. and Lockwood, D. (1963) 'Affluence and the British class structure'. *Sociological Review*, 11(1): 133–63.

Goldthorpe, J., Lockwood, D., Bechhofer, F. and Platt, J. (1969) *The Affluent Worker in the Class Structure*. Cambridge: Cambridge University Press.

Goodman, A., Johnson, P. and Webb, S. (1997) *Inequality in the UK*. Oxford: Oxford University Press.

Goodman, A. and Oldfield, Z. (2004) *Permanent Differences? Income and Expenditure Inequality in the 1990s and 2000s*. London: Institute for Fiscal Studies.

Gordon, D. and Pantazis, C. (1997) *Breadline Britain in the 1990s*. Aldershot: Ashgate.

Gordon, D. and Townsend, P. (eds) (2000) *Breadline Europe: The Measurement of Poverty*. Bristol: Policy Press.

Gordon, D., Adelman, L., Ashworth, K., Bradshaw, J., Levitas, R., Middleton, S., Pantazis, C., Patsios, D., Payne, S., Townsend, P. and Williams, J. (2000) *Poverty and Social Exclusion in Britain*. York: Joseph Rowntree Foundation.

Goulbourne, H. (1991) *Ethnicity and Nationalism in Post-imperial Britain*. Cambridge: Polity Press.

Graham, H. (1987) 'Women's poverty in caring'. In Glendenning, C. and Miller, J. (eds) *Women and Poverty*. Hemel Hempstead: Harvester/Wheatsheaf.

Gray, P., Elgar, J. and Bally, S. (1993) Access to training and employment for Asian women in Coventry. Coventry: Coventry City Council, Economic Development Unit, Research Paper.

Gray, R. (1981) *The Aristocracy of Labour in Nineteenth Century Britain*. London: Macmillan – now Palgrave Macmillan.

Green, J. (1997) *Risk and Misfortune: the Social Construction of Accidents*. London: University College London Press.

Gregg, P., Harkness, S. and Machin, S. (1999) *Child Development and Family Incomes*. York: York Publishing Services.

Gregory, J. and Lees, S. (1999) *Policing Sexual Assault*. London: Routledge.

Gregory, S. and Hartley, G. (eds) (1991) *Constructing Deafness*. London: Pinter.

Grillis, J. (1987) 'The case against chronologization; changes in the Anglo-American life cycle 1600 to the present'. *Ethnologia Europaea*, **17**(2): 97–106.

Guardian (1998) 'Now I am old ...' interview with John Ezard, G2 Arts: 9, 14 April.

Guardian (2004a) 12 October, 2004, accessed March 6, 2005 http://www.guardian.co.uk/religion/Story/0,2763,1325094,00.html.

Guardian (2004b) 22 November, 2004, accessed March 6, 2005 http://www.guardian.co.uk/religion/Story/0,2763,1356581,00.html.

Guillaumin, C. (1995) *Racism, Sexism, Power and Ideology*. London: Routledge.

Guillemard, A. (1989) 'The trend towards early labour force withdrawal and reorganisation of the life course: a cross-national analysis'. In Johnson, P., Conrad, C. and Thomson, D. (eds) *Workers versus Pensioners*. Manchester: Manchester University Press.

Guillemard, A. (1990) 'Re-organising the transition from work to retirement in an international perspective: Is chronological age still the major criterion determining the definitive exit?' Madrid: paper presented to the International Sociological Association Conference.

Guttsman, W. (1963) *The British Political Elite*. London: MacGibbon & Kee.

Hakim, C. (1991) 'Grateful slaves and self-made women: fact and fantasy in women's work orientations'. *European Sociological Review*, 7: 101–21.

Hakim, C. (1995) 'Five feminist myths about women's employment'. *British Journal of Sociology*, **46**(4): 424–55.

Hakim, C. (2003) 'Public morality versus personal choice'. *British Journal of Sociology*, **54**(3): 339–45.

Hall, S., Held, D. and McLennan, G. (eds) (1992) *Modernity and its Futures*. Cambridge: Polity Press.

Halliday, F. (1999) '"Islamophobia" reconsidered'. *Ethnic and Racial Studies*, **22**(5): 892–902.

Halperin, D. M. (1995) *Saint Foucault: Towards a Gay Hagiography*. Oxford: Oxford University Press.

Halson, J. (1991) 'Young women: sexual harassment and mixed-sex schooling'. In Abbott, P. and Wallace, C. (eds) *Gender, Power and Sexuality*. London: Macmillan – now Palgrave Macmillan.

Hardy, M. (ed.) (1997) *Studying Ageing and Social Change: Conceptual and Methodological Issues*. London: Sage.

Hardy, T. (1902) *The Mayor of Casterbridge*. London: Macmillan – now Palgrave Macmillan.

Hardy, T. (1975) *Jude the Obscure*. London: Macmillan – now Palgrave Macmillan.

Hareven, T. (1994) 'Ageing and generational relations – a historical and life-course perspective'. *Annual Review of Sociology*, **20**: 437–61.

Harne, L. (1984) 'Lesbian custody and the new myth of the father'. *Trouble and Strife*, 3: 12–14.

Hartman, H. (1978) 'The unhappy marriage of Marxism and Feminism: towards a more progressive union'. *Capital and Class*, 8: 1–33.

Hawkes, G. (1996) *A Sociology of Sex and Sexuality*. Buckingham: Open University Press.

Health Statistics Quarterly 23 (2004): Autumn. London: HMSO.

Heath, A. and McMahon, D. (1997) 'Education and occupational attainments: the impact of ethnic origins'. In Karn, V. (ed.) *Ethnicity in the 1991 Census: volume Four: Employment, Education and Housing Among the Ethnic Minority Populations of Britain*. London: Office for National Statistics.

Heath, A., McMahon, D. and Roberts, J. (2000) 'Ethnic differences in the labour market'. *Journal of the Royal Statistical Society Series A*, **163**(3): 303–39.

Heath, S. (1982) *The Sexual Fix*. London: Macmillan – now Palgrave Macmillan.

Held, D. (1992) 'The development of the modern state'. In Hall, S. and Gieben, B. (eds) *Formations of Modernity*. London: Polity Press.

Help Age International (1999) *The Ageing and Development Report: Poverty, Independence and the World's Older People*. London: Earthscan.

Hennessy, R. (1995) 'Queer visibility and commodity culture'. In Nicholson, L. and Seidman, S. (eds) *Social Postmodernism*. Cambridge: Cambridge University Press.

Hennessy, R. (1998) 'Disappearing capital: the queer material of sexual identity'. Paper presented at the Centre for Interdisciplinary Gender Studies, Leeds.

Hennessy, R. (2000) *Profit and Pleasure*. London: Routledge.

Hennock, E. (1991) 'Concepts of poverty in the British social surveys from Charles Booth to Arthur Bowley'. In Bulmer, M., Bales, K. and Kish Sklar, K. (eds) *The Social Survey in Historical Perspective*. Cambridge: Cambridge University Press.

Herdt, G. (1981) *Guardians of the Flutes*. New York: McGraw-Hill.

Herzlich, C. (1973) *Health and Illness: A Social Psychological Analysis*. London: Academic Press.

Herrnstein, R. and Murray, C. (1994) *The Bell Curve: Intelligence and Class Structure in American Life*. New York: The Free Press.

Hetherington, K. and Munro, R. (1997) *Ideas of Difference*. Oxford: Blackwell.

Hibbett, A. (2003) *Disability and Gender Briefing*. London: Women and Equality Unit.

Hill, M. and Jenkins, S. (2001) 'Poverty amongst British children: chronic or transitory?'. In Bradbury, B., Jenkins, S. and Micklewright, J. (eds) *The Dynamics of Child Poverty in Industrialised Countries*. Cambridge: Cambridge University Press.

Hillman, M., Adams, J. and Whitlegg, J. (1990) *One False Move: A Study of Children's Independent Mobility*. London: Policy Studies Institute.

Hills, J. (ed.) (1995a) *New Inequalities*. Cambridge: Cambridge University Press.

Hills, J. (1995b) Income and Wealth: A Summary of the Evidence. Joseph Rowntree Foundation Inquiry into Income and Wealth, vol. 2. York: Joseph Rowntree Foundation.

Hills, J., Le Grand, J. and Piachaud, D. (eds) (2002) *Understanding Social Exclusion*. Oxford: Oxford University Press.

Hills, J. and Stewart, K. (eds) (2005) *A More Equal Society? New Labour, Poverty, Inequality and Exclusion*. Bristol: Polity Press.

Hoggett, P. (ed.) (1997) *Contested Communities*. Bristol: Policy Press.

Holcombe, L. (1973) *Victorian Ladies at Work*. Newton Abbott: David and Charles.

Holland, J., Ramazanoglu, C., Sharpe, S. and Thomson, R. (1990) *Don't Die of Ignorance – I Nearly Died of Embarrassment: Condoms in Context*. London: Tufnell Press.

Holland, J., Ramazanoglu, C., Sharpe, S. and Thomson, R. (1991) *Pressure, Resistance, Empowerment: Young Women and the Negotiation of Safer Sex*. London: Tufnell Press.

Holland, J., Ramazanoglu, C., Sharpe, S. and Thomson, R. (1994) 'Power and desire: the embodiment of female sexuality'. *Feminist Review*, **46**: 21–38.

Holland, J., Ramazanoglu, C., Sharpe, S. and Thomson, R. (1998) *The Male in the Head: Young People, Heterosexuality and Power*. London: Tufnell Press.

Homans, G. (1951) *The Human Group*. London: Routledge & Kegan Paul.

Home Office (1998) *Statistics on Race and the Criminal Justice*. London: Stationery Office.

Hood, S., Kelley, P., Mayall, B. and Oakley, A. (1996) *Children, Parents and Risk*. London: Social Science Research Unit, Institute of Education.

Hood-Williams, J. (1990) 'Patriarchy for children: on the stability of power relations in children's lives'. In Chisholm, L., Büchner, P., Krüger, H. H. and Brown, P. (eds) *Children, Youth and Social Change: A Comparative Perspective*. London: Falmer.

Hornsby-Smith, M. P. (2004) 'The changing identity of Catholics in England'. In Coleman, S. and Collins, P. (eds) *Religious Identity and Change: Perspectives on Global Transformations*. London: Ashgate.

Howard, M., Garnham, A., Fimister, G. and Veit-Wilson, J. (2001) *Poverty: The Facts* (4th edn). London: CPAG.

Howlett, B., Ahmad, W. and Murray, R. (1992) 'An exploration of white, Asian and Afro Caribbean peoples' concepts of health and illness causation'. *New Community*, **18**: 281–92.

Hubbock, J. and Carter, S. (1980) *Half a Chance? A Report on Job Discrimination Against Young Blacks in Nottingham*. London: CRE.

Hugman, R. (1994) *Ageing and the Care of Older People in Europe*. Basingstoke: Macmillan – now Palgrave Macmillan.

Hunt, S. McEwen, J. and McKenna, S. (1986) *Measuring Health Status*. London: Croom Helm.

Hyde, M. (1996) 'Fifty years of failure: Employment services for disabled people in the UK'. *Work, Employment and Society*, 10(4): 683–700.

Hyde, M. (1998) 'Sheltered and supported employment in the 1990s: the experiences of disabled workers in the UK'. *Disability and Society*, 13(2): 199–215.

Hyde, M. (2000) 'Disability'. In Payne, G. (ed.) *Social Divisions*. Basingstoke: Macmillan – now Palgrave Macmillan.

Hyde, M., Dixon, J. and Joyner, M. (1999) 'Work for those that can, security for those that cannot: The new United Kingdom social security reform agenda'. *International Social Security Review*, 52(4): 69–86.

Ifekwunigwe, J. (1999) *Scattered Be-Longings*. London: Routledge.

Iganski, P. and Payne, G. (1996) 'Declining racial disadvantage in the British labour market'. *Ethnic and Racial Studies*, 19(1): 113–34.

Iganski, P. and Payne, G. (1999) 'Socio-economic re-structuring and employment: the case of minority ethnic groups'. *British Journal of Sociology*, 50(2): 195–216.

Iganski, P., Payne, G. and Roberts, J. (2001) 'Inclusion or exclusion? Reflections on the evidence of declining racial disadvantage in the British labour market'. *International Journal of Sociology and Social Policy*, 21(4–6): 184–211.

Illsley, R. (1955) 'Social class selection and class differences in relation to still births and infant deaths'. *British Medical Journal*, 2: 1520–4.

Illsley, R. (1986) 'Occupational class, selection and the production of inequalities in health'. *Quarterly Journal of Social Affairs*, 2: 151–65.

Illsley, R. (1990) 'Comparative review of sources, methodology and knowledge'. *Social Science and Medicine*, 31(3): 229–36.

Ingraham, C. (1996) 'The heterosexual imaginary'. In Seidman, S. (ed.) *Queer Theory/Sociology*. Oxford: Blackwell.

Isin, E. and Wood, P. (1999) *Citizenship and Identity*. London: Sage.

Jackson, B. (1968) *Working Class Community*. London: Routledge & Kegan Paul.

Jackson, P. and Salisbury, J. (1996) 'Why should secondary schools take working with boys seriously?' *Gender and Education*, 8: 103–16.

Jackson, S. (1982) *Childhood and Sexuality*. Oxford: Blackwell.

Jackson, S. (1990) 'Demons and innocents: western ideas on children's sexuality in historical perspective'. In Money, J. and Musaph, H. (eds) *Handbook of Sociology*, vol. VII. Amsterdam: Elsevier.

Jackson, S. (1997) 'Women, marriage and family relationships'. In Richardson, D. and Robinson, V. (eds) *Introducing Women's Studies* (2nd edn). Basingstoke: Macmillan – now Palgrave Macmillan.

Jackson, S. (1998) *Britain's Population: Demographic Issues in Contemporary Society*. London: Routledge.

Jackson, S. (1999) *Heterosexuality in Question*. London: Sage.

Jackson, S. (2005) 'Gender, sexuality and heterosexuality: Re-thinking the inter-sections'. In Casey, M., McLaughlin, J. and Richardson, D. (eds) *Queer Intersection*. London: Palgrave Macmillan.

Jackson, S. and Scott, S. (1997) 'Gut reactions to matters of the heart: reflections on rationality, irrationality and sexuality'. *Sociological Review*, 45(4): 551–75.

Jackson, S. and Scott, S. (2001) *Gender: A Sociological Reader*. London: Routledge.

Jackson, S. and Scott, S. (2004) 'Sexual antinomies in late modernity'. *Sexualities*, 7(2): 233–48.

James, A. and Prout, A. (1990) *Constructing and Reconstructing Childhood*. London: Falmer.

James, A., Jenks, C. and Prout, A. (1998) *Theorizing Childhood*. Cambridge: Polity Press.

Jarvis, S. and Jenkins, S. (1998) 'How much income mobility is there in Britain?' *The Economic Journal*, 108: 428–43.

Jeffreys, S. (1997) *The Idea of Prostitution*. Melbourne: Spiniflex.

Jenkins, R. (1986a) 'Social anthropological models in inter-ethnic relations'. In Rex, J. and Mason, D. (eds) *Theories of Race and Ethnic Relations*. Cambridge: Cambridge University Press.

Jenkins, R. (1986b) *Racism and Recruitment*. Cambridge: Cambridge University Press.

Jenkins, R. (1997) *Rethinking Ethnicity*. London: Sage.

Jenkins, R. (2004) *Social Identity* (2nd edn). London: Routledge.

Jenkins, S. and Rigg, J. A. (2001) *The Dynamics of Poverty in Britain*. Department for Work and Pensions, research report 157. London: DWP.

Jenks, C. (1996) *Childhood*. London: Routledge.

Jewson, N., Mason, D., Waters, S. and Harvey, J. (1990) *Ethnic Minorities and Employment Practice, a Study of Six Employers*. London: Department of Employment, research paper, No. 76.

Johnson, A., Mercer, C., Erens, B. et al. (2001) 'Sexual behaviour in Britain'. *Lancet*, 358(9296): 1835–42.

Johnson, M. (1995) 'Interdependency and the Generational Compact'. *Ageing and Society*, 15: 234–65.

Johnson, P. (1985) *The Economics of Old Age in Britain: A Long-run View 1881–1981*. London: Discussion paper no. 47. Centre for Economic Policy Research.

Johnson, P., Conrad, C. and Thomson, D. (eds) (1989) *Workers Versus Pensioners*. Manchester: Manchester University Press.

Johnson, T. (1972) *Professions and Power*. London: Macmillan – now Palgrave Macmillan.

Jones, T. (1993) *Britain's Ethnic Minorities*. London: PSI.

Joseph, J. (1992) 'Warning, when I am an old woman'. In Jenny Joseph, *Selected Poems*. Tarset: Bloodaxe Books.

Joshi, H. (1990) 'The cash opportunity costs of child bearing: an approach to esti-mation using British data'. *Population Studies*, 44: 52–3.

Joshi, H., Wiggins, D., Bartley, M., Mitchell, R., Gleave, S. and Lynch, K. (2000) 'Putting health inequalities on the map'. In Graham, H. (ed.) *Understanding Health Inequalities*. Buckingham: Open University Press.

Kelly, L. (1988) *Surviving Sexual Violence*. Cambridge: Polity Press.

Kempson, E., Bryson, A. and Rowlingson, K. (1994) *Hard Times*. London: Policy Studies Institute.

Kingston, P. (2000) *The Classless Society*. Stanford: Stanford University Press.

Klein, J. (1965) *Samples From English Culture*. London: Routledge & Kegan Paul.

Klein, R. (1988) 'Acceptable Inequalities'. In Green, D. (ed.) *Acceptable Inequalities? Essays on the Pursuit of Equality*. London: Institute of Economic Affairs.

Kohli, M. (1986) 'The world we forgot: a historical review of the life course'. In Marshall, W. (ed.) *Later Life: The Social Psychology of Ageing*. London: Sage.

Kohli, M. (1991) 'Retirement and the moral economy: an historical interpretation of the German case'. In Minkler, M. and Estes, C. (eds) *Critical Perspectives on Ageing: The Political and Moral Economy of Growing Old*. Amityville, New York: Baywood.

Kohli, M., Rein, M., Guillemard, A. and Van Gunstern, H. (eds) (1992) *Time for Retirement: Comparative Studies on Early Exit for the Labour Force*. Cambridge: Cambridge University Press.

Kuhn, T. (1970) *The Structure of Scientific Revolutions* (2nd edn). Chicago: Chicago University Press.

Kumar, K. (1978) *Prophecy and Progress*. Harmondsworth: Penguin.

Lacan, J. (1977) *Écrits*. London: Tavistock.

Laczko, F. and Phillipson, C. (1991) *Changing Work and Retirement*. Milton Keynes: Open University Press.

Langford, W. (1999) *Revolutions of the Heart: Gender, Power and the Delusions of Love*. London: Routledge.

Laslett, P. (1968) *The World We Have Lost*. London: Methuen.

Laslett, P. and Wall, R. (1972) *Household and Family in Past Times*. Cambridge: Cambridge University Press.

Lawler, S. (1999) 'Why difference (still) makes a difference: sociology's obligations'. Paper presented to the British Sociological Association Annual Conference, Glasgow.

Layte, R., Whelan, C. T., Maître, B. and Nolan B. (2001) 'Explaining levels of deprivation in the European Union'. *Acta Sociologica*, 44: 105–21.

Layton-Henry, Z. (1992) *The Politics of Immigration: Immigration, 'Race' and 'Race' Relations in Post-war Britain*. Oxford: Blackwell.

Lee, R. and De Vore, I. (1968) *Man the Hunter*. Chicago: Aldine.

Lees, S. (1993) *Sugar and Spice: Sexuality and Adolescent Girls*. Harmondsworth, Penguin.

Lees, S. (1997) *Carnal Knowledge*. London: Penguin.

Lengermann, P. M. and Niebragge-Brantly, J. (1998) *The Women Founders: Sociology and Social Theory 1830–1930*. Boston and London: McGraw Hill.

Leonard, D. (1990) 'In their own right: children and sociology in the UK'. In Chisholm, L., Büchner, P., Krüger, H. H. and Brown, P. (eds) *Children, Youth and Social Change: A Comparative Perspective*. London: Falmer.

Leslie, D., Drinkwater, S. and O'Leary, N. (1998) 'Unemployment and earnings among Britain's ethinic minorities'. *Journal of Ethnic and Migration Studies*, 24(4): 489–506.

Levitas, R. (1998) *The Inclusive Society?* Basingstoke: Macmillan – now Palgrave Macmillan.

Liberty (1994) *Sexuality and the State: Human Rights Violations Against Lesbians, Gays, Bisexuals and Transgendered People*. London: National Council for Civil Liberties.

Lichterman, P. (1996) *The Search for Political Community*. Cambridge: Cambridge University Press.

Lister, R. (2004) *Poverty*. Cambridge: Polity Press.

Locke, J. ([1693]1989) 'Some Thoughts Concerning Education'. In Yolton, J. and Yolton, J. S. (eds) *The Clarendon Edition of the Works of John Locke*. Oxford: Clarendon Press.

Lockwood, D. ([1958]/1993) *The Black-coated Worker*. Oxford: Oxford University Press, 1993.

Lockwood, D. (1960) 'The new working class'. *European Journal of Sociology*, 1(3): 248–59.

Lockwood, D. (1975) 'Sources of variation in working class images of society'. In Bulmer, M. (ed.) *Working Class Images of Society*. London: Routledge & Kegan Paul.

McCrone, D. (1992) *Understanding Scotland: The Sociology of a Stateless Nation*. London: Routledge.

McCrone, D. (1998) *The Sociology of Nationalism: Tomorrow's Ancestors*. London: Routledge.

McCrone, D. and Kiely, R. (2000) 'Nationalism and citizenship'. *Sociology*, 34,(1): 19–34.

McCrone, D. and Surridge, P. (1998) 'National identity and national pride'. In McCrone, D., Brown, A. and Paterson, L. (eds) *Politics and Society in Scotland*. Basingstoke: Macmillan – now Palgrave Macmillan.

MacDonald, K. (2004) 'Black Mafia, loggies and going for the stars: the military elite revisited'. *The Sociological Review*, 52(1) 106–28.

McIntosh, M. (1993) 'Queer theory and the war of the sexes'. In Bristow, J. and Wilson, A. R. (eds) *Activating Theory*. London: Lawrence & Wishart.

Macintyre, S. (1997) 'The Black Report and beyond: what are the issues?' *Social Science and Medicine*, 44(6): 723–45.

Macintyre, S., Ellaway, A. and Cumins, S. (2002) 'Place effects on health'. *Social Science and Medicine*, 55: 125–39.

Macintyre, S., Hunt, K. and Sweeting, H. (1996) 'Gender differences in health'. *Social Science and Medicine*, 42(5): 617–42.

Mack, J. and Lansley, S. (1985) *Poor Britain*. London: Allen & Unwin.

McKay, S. (2004) 'Poverty or preference? What do "consensual deprivation indicators" really measure?' *Fiscal Studies*, 25(2): 201–23.

McKibbin, R. (1998) *Class and Cultures: England, 1918–1951*. Oxford: Oxford University Press.

McKnight, A., Elias, P. and Wilson, R. (1998) *Low Pay and the National Insurance System: A Statistical Picture*. Manchester: Equal Opportunities Commission.

Maclean, C. (2003) '"Making it their home": in-migration, time, social change and belonging in a rural community'. In Allan, G. and Jones, G. (eds) *Social Relations and the Life Course*. Basingstoke: Palgrave Macmillan.

Macleod, A. (1992) Social Identity, Social Change and the Construction of Symbolic Boundaries in a West Highland Settlement. PhD thesis, Plymouth: University of Plymouth.

Macleod, A. and Payne, G. (1994) 'Locals and incomers'. In Baldwin, J. (ed.) *Peoples and Settlements*. Edinburgh: SSNS.

McRae, S. (2003a) 'Constraints and choices on mothers' employment'. *British Journal of Sociology*, 54(3): 317–38.

McRae, S. (2003b) 'Constraints and choices on mothers' employment: McRae replies to Hakim'. *British Journal of Sociology*, 54(4): 585–92.

Malinowski, B. (1929) *The Sexual Life of Savages in North-Western Melanesia*. London: Routledge & Kegan Paul.

Mannheim, K. (1927) 'The problem of generations'. In Hardy, M. (ed.) *Studying Aging and Social Change: Conceptual and Methodological Issues*. London: Sage.

Marcus, T. and Manicom, D. (2000) 'Consciousness in transition'. *Sociological Research Online*, 4(4): http://www.socresonline.org.uk/4/4/marcus.html.

Marcuse, H. (1964) *One Dimensional Man*. London: Routledge & Kegan Paul.

Marcuse, H. (1972) *Eros and Civilization*. London: Abacus.

Marmot, H. (2004) *Status Syndrome: How Your Social Standing Directly Affects your Health and Life Expectancy*. London: Bloomsbury.

Marmot, M. and Wilkinson, R. (1999) *Social Determinants of Health*. Oxford: Oxford University Press.

Marmot, M., Davey Smith, G., Stansfeld, S., Patel, C. et al. (1991) 'Health inequalities among British civil servants: the Whitehall II study'. *Lancet*, 337: 1387–93.

Marmot, M., Shipley, M. and Rose, G. (1984) 'Do socioeconomic differences in mortality persist after retirement?' *British Medical Journal*, 313: 1177–80.

Marquand, D. (1988) *The Unprincipled Society*. London: Fontana.

Marshall, G., Rose, D., Vogler, C. and Newby, H. (1988) *Social Class in Modern Britain*. London: Hutchinson.

Marsland, D. (1996) *Welfare or Welfare State? Contradictions and Dilemmas in Social Policy*. London: Macmillan – now Palgrave Macmillan.

Martens, L., Southerton, D. and Scott, S. (2004) 'Bringing children and parents into the sociology of consumption: towards a theoretical and empirical agenda'. *Journal of Consumer Culture*, 4(2): 155–92.

Martin, J. and Roberts, C. (1984) *Women and Employment: A Life Time Perspective*. London: HMSO.

Martin, J., Meltzer, H. and Elliot, D. (1988) *The Prevalence of Disability among Adults*. London: HMSO.

Marx, K. and Engels, F. ([1859]1969) *Selected Works*, vol. 1. Moscow: Progress Publishers.

Mason, D. (1986) 'Controversies and continuities in race and ethnic relations theory'. In Rex, J. and Mason, D. (eds) *Theories of Race and Ethnic Relations*. Cambridge: Cambridge University Press.

Mason, D. (1994) 'On the dangers of disconnecting race and racism'. *Sociology*, 28(4): 845–58.

Mason, D. (1996) 'Themes and issues in the teaching of race and ethnicity in sociology'. *Ethnic and Racial Studies*, 19(4): 789–806.

Mason, D. (2000) *Race and Ethnicity in Modern Britain* (2nd edn). Oxford: Oxford University Press.

Mason, D. (ed.) (2003a) *Explaining Ethnic Differences: Changing Patterns of Disadvantage in Britain*. Bristol: Policy Press.

Mason, D. (2003b) 'Changing ethnic disadvantage: an overview'. In Mason, D. (ed.) *Explaining Ethnic Differences: Changing Patterns of Disadvantage in Britain*. Bristol: Policy Press.

Mason, D. (2003c) 'Changing patterns of ethnic disadvantage in employment'. In Mason, D. (ed.) *Explaining Ethnic Differences: Changing Patterns of Disadvantage in Britain*. Bristol: Policy Press.

Masters, W. and Johnson, V. (1966) *Human Sexual Response*. Boston, MA: Little, Brown.

Mayall, B. (ed.) (1994) *Children's Childhoods: Observed and Experienced*. London: Falmer.

Meade, K. (1995) 'Promoting age equality'. *Generations Review*, 5(3): 7–10.

Meigs, A. (1990) 'Multiple gender ideologies and statuses'. In Sanday, P. and Goodenough, C. (eds) *Beyond the Second Sex: New Directions in the Anthropology of Gender*. Philadelphia: University of Pennsylvania Press.

Mewett, P. (1982) 'Exiles, nicknames, social identities and the production of local consciousness in a Lewis crofting community'. In Cohen, A. (ed.) *Belonging*. Manchester: Manchester University Press.

Michels, R. ([1911]1962) *Political Parties: A Sociological Study of the Oligarchical Tendencies of Modern Democracy*. New York: Free Press (first published as *Zur Soziologie der Partiewesens in der Modernen Demokratie*).

Middleton, S., Ashworth, K. and Braithwaite, I. (1997) *Small Fortunes: Spending on Children, Childhood Poverty and Parental Sacrifice*. York: Joseph Rowntree Foundation.

Miles, R. (1982) *Racism and Migrant Labour*. London: Routledge & Kegan Paul.

Miles, R. (1993) *Racism after Race Relations*. London: Routledge.

Miliband, R. (1969) *The State in Capitalist Society: An Analysis of the Western System of Power*. London: Quartet.

Mills, C. W. (1956) *The Power Elite*. New York: Oxford University Press.

Mills, C. W. ([1959]1970) *The Sociological Imagination*. London: Oxford University Press.

Mirza, H. (1992) *Young, Female and Black*. London: Routledge.

Mitchell, C. (2004) 'Is Northern Ireland abnormal? An extension of the sociological debate on religion in modern Britain'. *Sociology*, 38(2): 237–54.

Modood, T. (1988) 'Black, racial equality and Asian identity'. *New Community*, 14(3): 397–404.

Modood, T. (1990) 'Catching up with Jesse Jackson: on being oppressed and on being somebody'. *New Community*, 17(1): 85–96.

Modood, T. (1992) *Not Easy Being British*. Stoke-on-Trent: Trentham Books.

Modood, T. (1997a) '"Difference", cultural racism and anti-Racism'. In Werbner, P. and Modood, T. (eds) *Debating Cultural Hybridity*. London: Zed Books.

Modood, T. (1997b) 'Employment'. In Modood, T., Berthoud, R., Lakey, J., Nazroo, J. et al. (eds) (1997) *Ethnic Minorities in Britain*. London: Policy Studies Institute.

Modood, T. (1997c) 'Culture and identity'. In Modood, T. and Berthoud, R., Lakey, J., Nazroo, J. et al. (eds) (1997) *Ethnic Minorities in Britain*. London: Policy Studies Institute.

Modood, T., Berthoud, R., Lakey, J., Nazroo, J. et al. (eds) (1997) *Ethnic Minorities in Britain*. London: Policy Studies Institute.

Modood, T. (2003) 'Ethnic differentials in educational performance'. In Mason, D. (ed.) *Explaining Ethnic Differences: Changing Patterns of Disadvantage in Britain*. Bristol: Policy Press.

Montague, A. (1964) *The Concept of Race*. New York: Free Press.

Montague, A. (1974) *Man's Most Dangerous Myth: The Fallacy of Race*. New York: Oxford University Press.

Morris, J. (1974) *Conundrum*. Oxford: Oxford University Press.

Morris, L. (1995) *Social Divisions*. London: UCL Press.

Morris, L. and Ritchie, J. (1994) *Income Maintenance and Living Standards*. York: Joseph Rowntree Foundation/SCPR.

Morris, L. and Scott, J. (1996) 'The Attenuation of Class Analysis'. *British Journal of Sociology*, 47(1): 45–55.

Morris, R. (1990) *Class, Sect and Party: The Making of the British Middle Class, Leeds 1820–1850*. Manchester: Manchester University Press.

Morrow, V. (1994) 'Responsible children? Aspects of children's work and employment outside school in contemporary UK'. In Mayall, B. (ed.) *Children's Childhoods: Observed and Experienced*. London: Falmer.

Mosca, G. (1896) 'Elementi di Scienza Politica'. In Mosca, G. (ed.) (1939) *The Ruling Class*. New York: McGraw-Hill.

Mosca, G. (1923) 'Elementi di Scienza Politica' (2nd edn). In. Mosca, G. (ed.) (1932) *The Ruling Class*. New York: McGraw-Hill.

Mumford, K. and Power, A. (2003) *East Enders: Familyand Community In East London*. Bristol: Policy Press.

Murgatroyd, L. and Neuburger, H. (1997) 'A household satellite account for the UK'. *Economic Trends*, 527, October: 63–71.

Murray, C. (1984) *Losing Ground: American Social Policy 1950–1980*. New York: Basic Books.

Murray, C. (1990) *The Emerging British Underclass*. London: Institute of Economic Affairs.

Murray, C. (1994) *Underclass: The Crisis Deepens*. London: Institute of Economic Affairs.

Naipul, V. S. (1964) *A House for Mr Biswas*. London: Deutsch.

Nairn, T. (1981) *The Break-Up of Britain* (2nd edn). London: New Left Books.

National Association of Citizens Advice Bureaux (1984) *Unequal Opportunities: CAB Evidence on Racial Discrimination*. London: NACAB.

National Children's Home (1991) *Poverty and Nutrition Survey*. London: National Children's Home.

Nazroo, J. (1997) 'Health and health services'. In Modood, T., Berthoud, R., Lakey, J., Nazroo, J. et al. (eds) (1997) *Ethnic Minorities in Britain*. London: Policy Studies Institute.

Newby, H. (1977) *The Deferential Worker*. Harmondsworth: Penguin.

Newby, H. (1980) *Green and Pleasant Land?* Harmondsworth: Penguin.

Nisbet, R. (1970) *The Sociological Tradition*. London: Heinemann.

Noble, M., Cheung, S. and Smith, G. (1998) 'Origins and destinations: social security claimant dynamics'. *Journal of Social Policy*, 27(3): 351–69.

Nolan, B. and Whelan, C. (1996) *Resources, Deprivation and Poverty*. Oxford: Clarendon Press.

Noon, M. (1993) 'Racial discrimination in speculative applications: evidence from the UK's top one hundred firms'. *Human Resource Management Journal*, 3(4): 35–47.

Northern Ireland Life at Times Survey. 2001: http://www.esds.ac.uk/government/nilts/

O'Brien, J. and Howard, J. (eds) (1998) *Everyday Inequalities*. Oxford: Blackwell.

O'Connell Davidson, J. (1998) *Prostitution, Power and Freedom*. Cambridge: Polity.

O'Reilly, K. (2000) *The British on the Costa Del Sol: Transnational Identities and Local Communities*. London: Routledge.

Oakley, A. (1972) *Sex, Gender and Society*. Oxford: Martin Robertson.

Oliver, M. (1990) *The Politics of Disablement*. London: Macmillan – now Palgrave Macmillan.

Oliver, M. and Barnes, C. (1998) *Disabled People and Social Policy: From Exclusion to Inclusion*. Harlow: Longman.

ONS (Office for National Statistics) (1997) *Social Trends 27*. London: Stationery Office.

ONS (Office for National Statistics) (1998a) *Social Trends 28*. London: Stationery Office.

ONS (Office for National Statistics) (1998b) *General Household Survey 1996*. London: Stationery Office.

ONS (Office for National Statistics) (1999) *Annual Abstract of Statistics 1999*, No. 135. London: Stationery Office.

ONS (Office for National Statistics) (2001–2) General Household Survey 2001–2002 London: Stationery Office/(computer file) (2nd edn). Colchester: UK Data Archive (distributor) 14 July 2003 SN: 4646.

ONS (Office for National Statistics) (2002a) *Living in Britain*. London: Stationery Office.

ONS (Office for National Statistics) (2002b) *Family Spending: a Report on the 2001 Family Expenditure Survey*. London: Stationery Office, www.statistics.gov.uk.

ONS (Office for National Statistics) (2003) *Social Trends 33*. London: Stationery Office.

ONS (Office for National Statistics) (2003a) *General Household Survey 2003*. London: Stationery Office.

ONS (Office for National Statistics) (2004a) *Social Trends 34*. London: Stationery Office.

ONS (Office for National Statistics) (2004b) *Focus on Ethnicity: Employment Patterns*. Office for National Statistics, National Statistics Online. January 8, 2004, http://www.statistics.gov.uk, accessed March 1, 2005.

ONS (Office for National Statistics) (2004c) *Focus on People and Migration: Overseas Born*. Office for National Statistics, National Statistics Online, 24 June 2004, http://www.statistics.gov.uk, accessed March 1, 2005.

ONS (Office for National Statistics) (2004d) *Focus on Religion*. London: Stationery Office, http://www.statistics.gov.uk/focuson/religion/.

ONS (Office for National Statistics) (2004e) *Focus on Social Inequalities*. London: Stationery Office.

OPCS (Office of Population Censuses and Surveys) (1993) *Census 1991: Historical Tables*, Great Britain. London: HMSO.

OPCS (Office of Population Censuses and Surveys) (2003) *Census 2001 Great Britain*. London: ONS.

Oppenheim, C. and Harker, L. (1996) *Poverty: the Facts* (3rd edn). London: CPAG.

Orshansky, M. (1965) 'Counting the poor: another look at the poverty profile'. *Social Security Bulletin*, 28(1): 3–29.

Owen, D. (1992) *Ethnic Minorities in Britain: Settlement Patterns*. Coventry: University of Warwick, Centre for Research in Ethnic Relations, National Ethnic Minority Data Archive, 1991 Census Statistical Paper No. 1.

Owen, D. (1993) *Ethnic Minorities in Britain: Economic Characteristics*. Coventry: University of Warwick, Centre for Research in Ethnic Relations, National Ethnic Minority Data Archive, 1991 Census Statistical Paper No. 3.

Owen, D. (2003) 'The demographic characteristics of people from minority ethnic groups in Great Britain'. In Mason, D. (ed.) *Explaining Ethnic Differences: Changing Patterns of Disadvantage in Britain*. Bristol: Policy Press.

Pahl, J. (1983) 'The allocation of money and the structuring of inequality within marriage'. *Work, Employment and Society*, 31(2): 237–62.

Pahl, J. (ed.) (1985) *Private Violence and Public Policy*. London: Routledge & Kegan Paul.

Pahl, R. (1993) 'Does class analysis without class theory have a promising future?' Sociology, 27(2): 253–8.

Pareto, V. (1902) Les Systems Socialistes. Paris: Giard et Briere.

Pareto, V. ([1916]1963) A Treatise on General Sociology. In Livingstone, A. (ed.) The Mind and Society. New York: Dover (four volumes bound as two).

Park, A., Curtice, J., Tomson, K., Jarvis, L. and Bromley, C. (eds) (2002) British Social Attitudes: the 19th Report. London: Sage.

Park, A., Curtice, J., Thomson, K., Bromley, C. and Phillip, M. (eds) (2004) British Social Attitudes; the 21st Report. London: Sage.

Parker, H. (1998) Low Cost but Acceptable: A Minimum Income Standard for the UK. Bristol: Policy Press.

Parker H. (ed.) (2000) Low Cost but Acceptable Incomes for Older People: A Minimum Income Standard for Households Aged 65–74 Years in the UK. Bristol: Policy Press.

Parkin, F. (1971) Class Inequality and Political Order. London: McGibbon & Kee.

Parry, G., Moyser, G. and Wagstaffe, M. (1987) 'The crowd and the community'. In Gaskell, G. and Benewick, R. (eds) The Crowd in Contemporary Britain. London: Sage.

Paxman, J. (1999) The English: A Portrait of a People. London: Penguin.

Payne, G. (1973) 'Typologies of middle class mobility'. Sociology, 7(3): 417–28.

Payne, G. (1987a) Mobility and Change in Modern Society. London: Macmillan – now Palgrave Macmillan.

Payne, G. (1987b) Employment and Opportunity. London: Macmillan – now Palgrave Macmillan.

Payne, G. (1989) 'Social mobility'. In Burgess, R. (ed.) Investigating Society. London: Longmans.

Payne, G. (1992) 'Competing views of contemporary social mobility and social divisions'. In Burrows, R. and Marsh, C. (eds) Consumption and Class. London: Macmillan – now Palgrave Macmillan.

Payne, G. (1996) 'Imagining the community'. In Lyon, S. and Busfield, J. (eds) Methodological Imaginations. Basingstoke: Macmillan – now Palgrave Macmillan.

Payne, G. (2004) 'Social Dividing'. Paper presented to the British Sociological Association Annual Conference, York.

Payne, G. (2006) 'Recounting illiteracy: literacy skills in the sociology of social inequality'. British Journal of Sociology, 57(2) (in press).

Payne, G. and Abbott, P. (1990) The Social Mobility of Women. Basingstoke: Falmer Press.

Payne, G. and Roberts, J. (2002) 'Opening and closing the gates: recent developments in male social mobility in Britain', Sociological Review Online, 6(4): www.socresonline. org.wks/6/4/payne.html.

Payne, G., Payne, J. and Hyde, M. (1996) 'Refuse of all classes? Social indicators and social deprivation'. Sociological Research Online, 1(1): www.socresonline. org.uk/socresonline/1/1/3.html.

Payne, J. (1999) Researching Health Needs: A Community-based Approach. London: Sage.

Phillips, A. and Taylor, B. (1980) 'Sex and skill: moves towards a feminist economics'. *Feminist Review*, 6: 79–88.

Phillips, S. (1986) 'Natives and incomers: the symbolism of belonging in Muker parish, North Yorkshire'. In Cohen, A. (ed.) *Symbolising Boundaries*. Manchester: Manchester University Press.

Phillipson, C. and Walker, A. (eds) (1986) *Ageing and Social Policy: A Critical Assessment*. Aldershot: Gower.

Phillipson, C., Bernard, M., Phillips, J. and Ogg, J. (2001) *The Family and Community Life of Older People*. London:Routledge.

Phizacklea, A. (1983) *One Way Ticket: Migration and Female Labour*. London: Routledge.

Piachaud, D. (1979) *The Cost of a Child*. London: Child Poverty Action Group.

Piachaud, D. (1981) 'Peter Townsend and the holy grail'. *New Society*, 57: 419–21.

Piachaud, D. (1987) 'Problems in the definition and measurement of poverty'. *Journal of Social Policy*, 16(2): 147–64.

Pickard, S. (1995) *Living on the Front Line*. Aldershot: Avebury.

Pill, R. and Stott, N. (1982) 'Concepts of illness causation and responsibility: some preliminary data from a sample of working class mothers'. *Social Science and Medicine*, 16(1): 43–52.

Pill, R., Peters, T. and Robling, M. (1993) 'Factors associated with health behaviour among mothers of lower socio-economic status: a British example'. *Social Science and Medicine*, 36(9): 1137–44.

Pinchbeck, I. and Hewett, M. (1969) *Children in English Society*, vol. I. London: Routledge & Kegan Paul.

Platt, L. (2002) *Parallel Lives? Poverty among Ethnic Minority Groups in Britain*. London: CPAG.

Platt, L. (2003a) The Intergenerational Social Mobility of Minority Ethnic Groups. Working Paper of the Institute for Social and Economic Research Paper 2033-04. Colchester: University of Essex.

Platt, L. (2003b) 'Ethnicity and inequality: British children's experience of means-tested benefits'. *Journal of Comparative Family Studies*, 34(3): 357–77.

Platt, L. (2003c) 'Newham Household Panel Survey: Poverty and Deprivation in Newham'. A report prepared by ISER, University of Essex for the London Borough of Newham. London: London Borough of Newham.

Platt, L. (2004a) Evidence given to the Department for Work and Pensions Committee, Child Poverty in the UK: vol. III (oral evidence). London: House of Commons.

Platt, L. (2004b) 'Memorandum' submitted to the House of Commons Work and Pensions Committee (2004) *Child Poverty in the UK: First Report of Session 2003–04*, vol. II (written evidence). London: House of Commons.

Platt, L. (2005) *Discovering Child Poverty: The Creation of a Policy Agenda from 1800 to the Present*. Bristol: Policy Press.

Pocock, P. (1975) 'British history: a plea for a new subject'. *Journal of Modern History*, 4: 601–21.

Popay, J., Williams, G. Thomas, C. and Gatrell, A. (1998) 'Theorising inequalities in health: the place of lay knowledge'. In Bartley, M., Blane, D. and Davey Smith, G. (eds) *The Sociology of Health Inequalities*. Oxford: Blackwell.

Porter, J. (1965) *The Vertical Mosaic*. Toronto: University of Toronto Press.

Porteus, J. (1989) *Planned to Death*. Manchester: Manchester University Press.

Postman, N. (1994) *The Disappearance of Childhood*. New York: Vintage Books.

Potts, A., Gavey, N., Grace, V. and Vares, T. (2003) 'The downside of viagra: women's experiences and concerns'. *Sociology of Health and Illness*, **25**(7): 697–719.

Poulantzas, N. (1969) 'The problem of the capitalist state'. *New Left Review*, **59**: 67–78.

Power, C., Bartley, M., Davey Smith, G. and Blane, D. (1996) 'Transmission of social and biological risk across the life course'. In Blane, D., Brunner, E. and Wilkinson, R. (eds) *Health and Social Organisation*. London: Routledge.

Power, S., Whitty, C. and Edwards, T. (1998) 'School boys and school work: gender, identification and academic achievement'. In Epstein, D., Maw, J., Elwood, J. and Hey, V. (eds) *International Journal of Inclusive Education* (special edition on boys' under-achievement) **2**: 135–53.

Prandy, K. (1991) 'The revised Cambridge scale of occupations'. *Sociology*, **24**(4): 629–56.

Pringle, R. (1988) *Secretaries Talk: Sexuality, Power and Work*. London: Verso.

Punch, S. (1998) 'Negotiating independence: children and young people growing up in rural Bolivia'. Unpublished paper, School of Geography, University of Leeds.

Putnam, R. (2000) *Bowling Alone: The Collapse and Revival of American Community*. New York: Simon & Schuster.

Rake, K. (2000) *Women's Incomes over the Lifetime*. London: Stationery Office.

Rattansi, A. and Westwood, S. (1994) *Racism, Modernity and Identity on the Western Front*. Oxford: Polity Press.

Rees, T. (1992) *Women and the Labour Market*. London: Routledge.

Reich, W. (1951) *The Sexual Revolution*. London: Vision Books.

Reid, I. (1998) *Class in Britain*. London: Polity Press.

Reiner R. (1991) *Chief Constables: Bobbies, Bosses or Bureaucrats?* Oxford: Clarendon.

Reiser, R. (1995) 'Stereotypes of disabled people'. In Reiser, R. (ed.) *Invisible Children*. London: Save the Children.

Rex, J. and Moore, R. (1967) *Race, Community and Conflict*. London: Oxford University Press.

Rich, A. (1980) 'Compulsory heterosexuality and lesbian existence'. *Signs*, **5**(4): 630–60.

Ringen, S. (1988) 'Direct and indirect measures of poverty', *Journal of Social Policy*, **17**(3): 351–65.

Roberts, I. (1993) *Craft, Class and Control*. Edinburgh: Edinburgh University Press.

Roberts, K. (2001) *Class in Modern Britain*. London: Palgrave – now Palgrave Macmillan.

Rose, D. and O' Reilly, K. (1998) *The ESRC Review of Government Social Classifications*. London: Office of National Statistics and ESRC.

Rose, N. (1989) *Governing the Soul: The Shaping of the Private Self*. London: Routledge.

Rowlingson, K. and McKay, S. (1998) *The Growth of Lone Parenthood: Diversity and Dynamics*. London: Policy Studies Institute.

Rowntree, B. (1901) *Poverty: A Study of Town Life*. London: Longmans Green.

Rowntree, B. (1902) *Poverty: A Study of Town Life* (2nd edn). London: Macmillan – now Palgrave Macmillan.

Rowntree, B. (1918) *The Human Needs of Labour*. London: Thomas Nelson and Sons.

Rowntree, B. (1937) *The Human Needs of Labour* (2nd edn). London: Longmans Green.

Rowntree, B. (1942) *Poverty and Progress: A Second Social Survey of York*. London: Longmans Green.

Rowntree, B. and Lavers, G. (1951) *Poverty and the Welfare State: A Third Social Survey of York Dealing only with Economic Questions*. London: Longmans Green.

Rubin, G. (1984) 'Thinking sex: notes for a radical theory of the politics of sexuality'. In Vance, C. (ed.) *Pleasure and Danger: Exploring Female Sexuality*. London: Routledge & Kegan Paul.

Rubinstein, W. (1981) *Men of Property*. London: Croom Helm.

Rubinstein W. (1993) *Capitalism, Culture and Decline in Britain 1750–1990*. London: Routledge.

Runnymede Trust (1997) *Islamophobia: A Challenge for Us All*. London: Runnymede Trust.

Ruthven, M. (1991) *A Satanic Affair: Salman Rushdie and the Wrath of Islam*. London: Hogarth Press.

Ryan, J. and Thomas, F. (1980) *The Politics of Mental Handicap*. Harmondsworth: Penguin.

Saint-Simon, H. (1825) *De L'Organisation Sociale*. For relevant material see: *Saint-Simon (1975) Selected Writings on Science, Industry and Social Organisation* (ed. K. Taylor) London: Croom Helm.

Salaman, G. (1986) *Working*. London: Tavistock.

Sarre, P. (1989) 'Race and the class structure'. In Hamnett, C., McDowell, L. and Sarre, P. (eds) *The Changing Social Structure*. London: Sage.

Saunders, P. (1990) *A Nation of Home Owners*. London: Unwin Hyman.

Saunders, P. (2000) *Unequal But Fair? A Study of Class Barriers in Britain*. London: Institute of Economic Affairs.

Savage, M. (1992) 'Women's expertise, men's authority: gendered organisation in the contemporary middle classes'. In Savage, M. and Witz, A. (eds) *Gender and Bureaucracy*. Oxford: Blackwell.

Savage, M. (2000) *Class Analysis and Social Transformation*. Buckingham: Open University Press.

Savage, M. and Miles, A. (1994) *The Remaking of the British Working Class, 1840–1940*. London: Routledge.

Savage, M., Barlow, J., Dickens, P. and Fielding, T. (1992) *Property, Bureaucracy and Culture: Middle Class Formation in Contemporary Britain*. London: Routledge.

Scambler, G. (ed.) (1997) *Sociology as Applied to Medicine* (4th edn). London: W.B. Saunders.

Scase, D. and Goffee, L. (1982) *The Entrepreneurial Middle Class*. London: Croom Helm.

Scheper-Hughes, N. (2001) *Saints, Scholars and Schizophrenics: Mental Illness In Rural Ireland*. Berkeley: University of California Press.

Schumpeter, J. (1942) *Capitalism, Socialism and Democracy*. New York: Harper Row.

Scott, J. (1991) *Who Rules Britain?* Cambridge: Polity Press.

Scott, J. (1994a) 'Class analysis: back to the future'. *Sociology*, 28(4), 933–42.

Scott, J. (1994b) *Poverty and Wealth: Citizenship, Deprivation and Privilege*. Harlow: Longman.

Scott, J. (1996) *Stratification and Power: Structures of Class, Status and Command*. Cambridge: Polity Press.

Scott, J. (1997) *Corporate Business and Capitalist Classes*. Oxford: Oxford University Press.

Scott, S. and Freeman, R. (1995) 'Prevention as a problem of modernity: the example of HIV and AIDS'. In Gabe, J. (ed.) *Medicine, Health and Risk*. Oxford: Blackwell.

Scott, S. and Watson-Brown, L. (1997) 'The beast, the family and the little children'. *Trouble and Strife*, 36: 17–28.

Scully, D. (1990) *Understanding Sexual Violence: A Study of Convicted Rapists*. London: Unwin & Hyman.

Seager, J. (1997) *The State of Women in the World Atlas* (Rev. edn). Harmondsworth, Penguin.

Seidman, S. (1996) *Queer Theory/Sociology*. Oxford: Blackwell.

Seidman, S. (1997) *Difference Troubles: Queering Social Theory and Sexual Politics*. Cambridge: Cambridge University Press.

Sen, A. (1983) 'Poor, relatively speaking'. *Oxford Economic Papers*, 35: 153–69.

Sen, A. (1985) 'A sociological approach to the measurement of poverty: a reply to Professor Peter Townsend'. *Oxford Economic Papers*, 37: 669–76.

Sen, A. (1987) *The Standard of Living: the Tanner Lectures*. Clare Hall, Cambridge, 1985 (ed. G. Hawthorn). Cambridge: Cambridge University Press.

Sen, K. (1994) *Ageing: Debates on Demographic Transition and Social Policy*. London: Zed Books.

Senior, M. and Viveash, B. (1998) *Health and Illness*. London: Macmillan – now Palgrave Macmillan.

Shahar, S. (1990) *Childhood in the Middle Ages*. London: Routledge.

Shakespeare, T., Gillespie-Sells, K. and Davies, D. (1996) *The Sexual Politics of Disability: Untold Desires*. London: Cassell.

Sharpe, S. (1995) *Just Like a Girl* (2nd edn). Harmondsworth: Penguin.

Shy, C. (1997) 'The failure of academic epidemiology'. *American Journal of Epidemiology*, **145**: 479–87.

Simon, W. (1996) *Postmodern Sexualities*. New York: Routledge.

Sinfield, A. (1994) *The Wilde Century*. London: Cassell.

Skelton, C. (1993) 'Women and education'. In Richardson, D. and Robinson, V. (eds) *Introducing Women's Studies: Feminist Theory and Practice*. London: MacMillan – now Palgrave Macmillan.

Skolnick, A. (1973) *The Intimate Environment: Exploring Marriage and the Family*. Boston: Little, Brown.

Skolnick, A. (1980) 'Children's rights, children's development'. In Empey, L. T. (ed.) *Children's Rights and Juvenile Justice*. Charlottesville: University of Virginia Press.

Smith, A. ([1776]1976) *An Inquiry into the Nature and Causes of the Wealth of Nations* (ed. E. Cannan). Chicago: University of Chicago Press.

Smith, D. (1979) 'A peculiar eclipse: women's exclusion from men's culture'. *Women's Studies International Quarterly*, **1**: 281–95.

Smith, D. J. (1974) *The Facts of Racial Disadvantage*. London: Political and Economic Planning.

Smith, D. J. (1981) *Unemployment and Racial Minorities*. London: Policy Studies Institute.

Smith, M. (1986) 'Pluralism, race and ethnicity in selected African countries'. In Rex, J. and Mason, D. (eds) *Theories of Race and Ethnic Relations*. Cambridge: Cambridge University Press.

Social and Community Planning Research (1999) *Geographical Variations in Health Indicators by Health Authority, 1994–1996*. London: Department of Health.

Solomos, J. and Back, L. (1996) *Racism in Society*. Basingstoke: Macmillan – now Palgrave Macmillan.

Song, M. (1996) '"Helping out": children's participation in Chinese take-away businesses in Britain'. In Brannen, J. and O'Brien, M. (eds) *Children in Families*. London: Falmer.

Spybey, T. (ed.) (1997) *Britain in Europe*. London: Routledge.

Stacey, M. (1960) *Tradition and Change: A Study of Banbury*. Oxford: Oxford University Press.

Stacey, M., Batstone, E., Bell, C. and Murcott, A. (1975) *Power, Persistence and Change*. London: Routledge & Kegan Paul.

Stanworth, M. (1984) 'Women and class analysis: a reply to Goldthorpe'. *Sociology*, **18**(2): 159–70.

Stepan, N. (1982) *The Idea of Race in Science*. London: Macmillan – now Palgrave Macmillan.

Stone, L. and Stone, J. (1984) *An Open Elite?* Oxford: Oxford University Press.

Strong, P. (1990) 'Black on class and mortality'. *Journal of Public Health Medicine*, **12**: 168–80.

Sydie, R. (1987) *Natural Women, Cultural Men.* Buckingham: Open University Press.

Syme, S. (1996) 'To prevent disease: the need for a new approach'. In Blane, D., Brunner, E. and Wilkinson, R. (eds) *Health and Social Organisation.* London: Routledge.

Synge, J. M. (1911) *The Playboy of the Western World.* Dublin: Maunsel.

Tam, M. (1997) *Part-time Employment: A Bridge or a Trap.* Aldershot: Avebury.

Tamir, Y. (1993) *Liberal Nationalism.* New Jersey: Princeton University Press.

Taunton Commission (1868) Commissioners School Inquiry Report, 23 volumes. London: Taunton Commission.

Taylor, I., Evans, K. and Fraser, P. (1996) *A Tale of Two Cities.* London: Routledge.

Taylor, M. (ed.) with Brice, J., Buck, N. and Prentice-Lane, E. (2003) *British Household Panel Survey User Manual,* vol. A: *Introduction, Technical Report and Appendices.* Colchester: University of Essex.

Taylor, S. and Field, D. (1997) *Sociology of Health and Health Care* (2nd edn). Oxford: Blackwell.

Theakston, K. and Fry, G. (1989) 'Britain's administrative elite: permanent secretaries 1900–1986'. *Public Administration,* **67**: 129–47.

Thompson, E. P. (1968) *The Making of the English Working Class.* Harmondsworth: Penguin.

Thompson, F. (1963) *English Landed Society in the Nineteenth Century.* London: Routledge & Kegan Paul.

Thomson, R. (1994) 'Moral rhetoric and public health pragmatism: the recent politics of sexual education'. *Feminist Review,* **48**: 40–60.

Thomson, R. and Scott, S. (1991) *Learning about Sex: Young Women and the Social Construction of Sexual Identity.* London: Tufnell Press.

Thorne, B. (1987) 'Re-visioning women and social change: where are the children?' *Gender and Society,* **1**(1): 85–109.

Thorne, B. (1993) *Gender Play: Girls and Boys in School.* Buckingham: Open University Press.

Thorogood, N. (1990) 'Caribbean home remedies and their importance for black women's health care in Britain'. In Abbott, P. and Payne, G. (eds) *New Directions in the Sociology of Health.* London: Falmer Press.

Tilly, C. (1992) *Coercion, Capital and European States, AD 990–1992.* Oxford: Blackwell.

Tinker, C. (forthcoming), 'Islamophobia and the state funding of Muslim schools'.

Tolman, D. (2002) *Dilemmas of Desire.* Cambridge, MA: Harvard University Press.

Tönnies, F. ([1887]1955) *Community and Association.* London: Routledge & Kegan Paul.

Topf, R., Mohler, P., and Heath, A. (1989) 'Pride in one's country: Britain and West Germany'. In Jowell, R., Witherspoon, S. and Brook, L. (eds) *British Social Attitudes: Special International Report.* Aldershot: Gower.

Townsend, P. (1957) *The Family Life of Old People: An Inquiry in East London.* London: Routledge & Kegan Paul.

Townsend, P. (1979) *Poverty in the United Kingdom, A Survey of Household Resources and Standards of Living*. Harmondsworth: Penguin.

Townsend, P. (1985) 'A sociological approach to the measurement of poverty: a rejoinder to Professor Amartya Sen'. *Oxford Economic Papers*, 37: 659–68.

Townsend, P. and Gordon, D. (2002) *World Poverty: New Policies to Defeat an Old Enemy*. Bristol: Policy Press.

Townsend, P., Davidson, N. and Whitehead, M. (1992) *Inequalities in Health: The Black Report and the Health Divide* (Rev. edn). Harmondsworth: Penguin.

Townsend, P., Phillimore, P. and Beattie, A. (1986) *Poverty and the London Labour Market: An Interim Report*. London: Low Pay Unit.

Trudell, B. N. (1993) *Doing Sex Education: Gender, Politics and Schooling*. New York: Routledge.

Turnball, C. (1984) *The Forest People*. London: Triad/Paladin.

Turnbull, C. (1966) *Wayward Servants: the Two Worlds of the African Pygmies*. London: Eyre & Spottiswoode.

Tyler, M. (1997) Women's Work as the Labour of Sexual Difference: Female Employment in the Airline Industry. PhD Thesis. Derby: University of Derby.

Union of Physically Impaired Against Segregation (1976) *Fundamental Principles of Disability*. London: Union of Physically Impaired Against Segregation.

United Nations (2002) *World Population Ageing: 1950–2050*. New York: Population Division, Department of Economic and Social Affairs, United Nations, http://www.un.org/esa/population/publications/worldageing19502050/index.htm.

Valentine, G. (1996) 'Angels and devils: moral landscapes of childhood'. *Society and Space*, 14: 581–99.

van den Berghe, P. (1967) *Race and Racism*. New York: Wiley.

van Every, J. (1996) 'Heterosexuality and domestic life'. In Richardson, D. (ed.) *Theorising Heterosexuality: Telling it Straight*. Buckingham: Open University Press.

Varo-Watson, D. (1998) 'Does it work?', *Disability NOW*. April: 13.

Veit-Wilson, J. (1986) 'Paradigms of poverty: a rehabilitation of B.S. Rowntree'. *Journal of Social Policy*, 15: 69–99.

Veit-Wilson, J. (1992) 'Muddle or mendacity? The Beveridge Committee and the poverty line'. *Journal of Social Policy*, 21: 269–301.

Veit-Wilson, J. (1994) 'Condemned to deprivation? Beveridge's responsibility for the invisibility of poverty'. In Hills, J., Ditch, J. and Glennerster, H. (eds) *Beveridge and Social Security*. Oxford: Clarendon Press.

Vernon, A. (1998) 'Multiple oppression and the disabled people's movement'. In Shakespeare, T. (ed.) *The Disability Reader: Social Science Perspectives*. London: Cassell.

Victor, C. (1991) *Health and Health Care in Later Life*. Milton Keynes: Open University Press.

Vincent, J. (1995) *Inequality and Old Age*. London: UCL Press.

Vincent, J. (1996) 'Who's afraid of an ageing population?' *Critical Social Policy*, 16(1): 3–26.

Vincent, J. (2001) *Politics and Old Age: Older Citizens and Political Processes in Britain*. Basingstoke: Ashgate.

Vincent, J. (2003) *Old Age*. London: Routledge.

von Zugbach, R. (1988) *Power and Prestige in the British Army*. Aldershot: Avebury.

von Zugbach, R. and Ishaq, M. (1999) 'The decline in social eliteness in the senior ranks of the British army'. In Strachan, H. (ed.) *British Army, Manpower and Society: Towards 2000*. Abingdon: Frank Cass.

Waites, M. (2005) *The Age of Consent: Young People, Sexuality and Citizenship*. London: Palgrave Macmillan.

Walby, S. (1986) *Patriarchy at Work*. Cambridge: Polity Press.

Walby, S. (1990) *Theorising Patriarchy*. Oxford: Blackwell.

Walker, A. (1993) 'Wither the social contract? Intergenerational solidarity in income and employment'. In Hobman, D. (ed.) *Uniting Generations: Studies in Conflict and Cooperation*. London: Age Concern England.

Walker, R. (1987) 'Consensual approaches to the definition of poverty: towards an alternative methodology'. *Journal of Social Policy*, **16**(2): 213–26.

Walker, R. (ed.) (1999) *Ending Child Poverty: Popular Welfare for the 21st Century*. Bristol: Policy Press.

Wallace, C., Mateeva, L. and Abbott, P. (2004) *Women and Enlargement*. Report to the European Parliament. Vienna: Institute for Advanced Studies.

Wallis, R. (1976) *The Road to Total Freedom: A Sociological Analysis of Scientology*. London: Heinemann.

Wallman, S. (1986) 'Ethnicity and the boundary process in context'. In Rex, J. and Mason, D. (eds) *Theories of Race and Ethnic Relations*. Cambridge: Cambridge University Press.

Walsh, J. (1999) 'Myths and counter-myths: an analysis of part-time female employees and their orientations to work and working hours'. *Work, Employment and Society*, **13**(2): 179–203.

Ware, J. (1993) 'Measuring patients' views: the optimum outcome measure'. *British Medical Journal*, **306**: 1429–30.

Warwick, D. and Littlejohn, G. (1992) *Coal, Capital and Culture*. London: Routledge.

Waskler, F. (ed.) (1991) *Studying the Social Worlds of Children*. London: Falmer.

Watney, S. (1987) *Policing Desire*. London: Routledge.

Weber, M. ([1914]1968) 'The distribution of power within the political community: class, status, party'. In Roth, G. and Wittich, C. (eds) *Economy and Society*. New York: Bedminster Press.

Weber, M. ([1920]1968) 'Status groups and classes'. In Roth, G. and Wittich, C. (eds) *Economy and Society*. New York: Bedminster Press.

Weeks, J. (1991) 'Pretended family relationships'. In Clark, D. (ed.) *Marriage, Domestic Life and Social Change*. London: Routledge.

Weeks, J. (1995) *Invented Moralities*. Cambridge: Polity Press.

Weiner, M. (1981) *English Culture and the Decline of the Entrepreneurial Spirit*. London: Heinemann.

Wellings, K., Field, J., Johnson, A. and Wadsworth, J. (1994) *Sexual Behaviour in Britain*. London: Penguin.

Wellman, B., Carrington, P. and Hall, A. (1988) 'Networks as personal communities'. In Wellman, B. and Berkowitz, S. (eds) *Social Structures*. Cambridge: Cambridge University Press.

Whelan, C., Layte, R., Maître, B. and Nolan, B. (2001) 'Income, deprivation and economic strain: an analysis of the European Community Household Panel'. *European Sociological Review*, 17(4): 357–72.

Whitley, R. (1974) 'The city and industry'. In Stanworth, M. and Giddens, A. (eds) *Elites and Power in British Society*. Cambridge: Cambridge University Press.

WHO (World Health Organization) (1999) http://www.who.init/aboutwho/en/definition. html.

Wight, D. (1993) *Workers not Wasters*. Edinburgh: Edinburgh University Press.

Wight, D., Abraham, C. and Scott, S. (1998) 'Towards a psychosocial theoretical framework for sexual health promotion'. *Health Education Research*, 13(3): 317–30.

Wilkinson, R. (1996) *Unhealthy Societies: The Afflictions of Inequality*. London: Routledge.

Williams, G. and Popay, J. (1994) 'Lay knowledge and the privilege of experience'. In Gabe, J., Kelleher, D. and Williams, G. (eds) *Challenging Medicine*. London: Routledge.

Williams, R. (1983) 'Concepts of health: an analysis of lay logic'. *Sociology*, 17(1): 185–204.

Willis, P. (1977) *Learning to Labour*. Farnborough: Saxon House.

Willmott, P. (1986) *Social Networks, Informal Care and Public Policy*. London: Policy Studies Institute.

Wilson, B. R. (1966) *Religion in Secular Society: A Sociological Comment*. London: Watts.

Wilson, B. R. (1970) *Religious Sects: A Sociological Study*. London: Weidenfeld & Nicolson.

Wilton, T. (1996) 'Which one's the man? The heterosexualisation of lesbian sex'. In Richardson, D. (ed.) *Theorising Heterosexuality: Telling it Straight*. Buckingham: Open University Press.

Winquist, K. (2002) *Women and Men Beyond Retirement*. Brussels: European Commission.

Wright, E. O. (1985) *Classes*. London: Verso.

Wright, E. O. (1989) *The Debate on Classes*. London: Verso.

Wright, E. O. (1993) *Interrogating Inequality: Essays on Class Analysis, Socialism and Marxism*. London: Verso.

Wright, E. O. (1997) *Class Counts*. Cambridge: Cambridge University Press.

Wright, P. (1985) *Living in an Old Country*. London: Verso.

Wyness, B. (2005) *The Sociology of Childhood*. London: Palgrave Macmillan.

Yeandle, S. (1984) *Women's Working Lives: Patterns and Strategies*. London: Tavistock.

Yinger, J. M. (1986) 'Intersecting strands in the theorisation of race and ethnic relations'. In Rex, J. and Mason, D. (eds) *Theories of Race and Ethnic Relations*. Cambridge: Cambridge University Press.

Yinger, J. M. (1994) *Ethnicity: Source of Strength? Source of Conflict?* Albany: State University of New York.

Young, I. (1986) 'The ideal of community and the politics of difference'. *Social Theory and Practice*, 12(1): 1–26.

Young, M. and Willmott, P. (1957) *Family and Kinship in East London*. London: Routledge & Kegan Paul.

Yuval-Davis, N. and Anthias, F. (eds) (1989) *Woman-Nation-State*. London: Macmillan – now Palgrave Macmillan.

Zweig, F. (1961) *The Worker in an Affluent Society*. London: Heinemann.

Index